Gender & Globalization

Patterns of Women's Resistance

Edited by

Erica G. Polakoff and
Ligaya Lindio-McGovern

GENDER & GLOBALIZATION
PATTERNS OF WOMEN'S RESISTANCE

Edited by Erica G. Polakoff and
Ligaya Lindio-McGovern

ISBN 978-1-897160-34-3

Copyright © 2011 de Sitter Publications

Articles from Journal of Developing Societies Vol 23 (1-2) reproduced by permission of SAGE Publications Copyright © 2007 SAGE Publications www.sagepublications.com (Los Angeles, London, New Delhi and Singapore).

All rights are reserved. No part of this publication may be reproduced, translated, stored in a retrieval system, or transmitted in any form or by any means, electronic, mechanical, photocopying, recording or otherwise, without prior written permission from the publisher.

Cover image: 'Cut' © Stefan Rajewski / www.fotolia.com
Cover and book design by de Sitter Publications

LIBRARY AND ARCHIVES CANADA CATALOGUING IN PUBLICATION DATA

A catalogue record for this book is available from the Library and Archives Canada.

de Sitter Publications
111 Bell Dr
Whitby, ON, L1N 2T1
CANADA

289-987-0656
www.desitterpublications.com
sales@desitterpublications.com

DEDICATION

From Erica:

To T.F.S., Jr., and souls that reverberate through time

From Ligaya:

*In memory of my good brother
Teofilo Lindio, Jr., 1944-2010*

Contents

Foreword by *Richard L. Harris* x

Preface xii

Acknowledgments xi

Introduction
    Women's Resistance to the Violence of Global
    Capitalist Penetration
    Erica G. Polakoff 1

Part 1: Neoliberal Policies, Migration and Women's Resistance ... 31

Chapter 1
    Neoliberal Globalization in the Philippines
    Its Impact on Filipino Women and Their Forms of Resistance
    Ligaya Lindio-McGovern 33

Chapter 2
    We're Better Off Outside Our Country: Diasporic
    Ecuadorian Women in Spain Since the 1990s
    estheR Cuesta 57

Part 2: Women's Resistance and Capitalist Production for Export ... 93

Chapter 3
    Push and Pull Factors in Female Labour Migration:
    Evidence from Sri Lanka's Garment Workers
    Judith Shaw 95

Chapter 4
    Historical Consciousness and Collective Action:
    Finding Women's Resistance Where North Meets South
    Mary E. Frederickson 121

Chapter 5
    Waves of Resistance in the Colombian Flower Industry
    Olga Sanmiguel-Valderrama 139

Part 3: Alternative Trade Associations and Women's Resistance .. 175

Chapter 6
Free Trade, Alternative Trade and Women in Peru: A First Look
Jane Henrici 177

Chapter 7
Women's Rights and Collective Resistance:
The Success Story of Marketplace India
Margaret A. McLaren 191

Part 4: Responses to Poverty: Women's and Children's Resistance 211

Chapter 8
Urban Poverty Reborn: A Gender and Generational Analysis
Jeanine Anderson 213

Chapter 9
Challenging Traditional Female Roles Through Social Participation: Tensions in Women's Experiences in Argentina's Picketing Movements
Ada Freytes Frey and Karina Crivelli 233

Chapter 10
The Feminization of Poverty in Post-Apartheid South Africa: A Story Told by the Women of Bayview, Chatsworth
Saranel Benjamin-Lebert 259

Chapter 11
Global Capitalist Penetration, Child Labor and Children's Collective Resistance in Defense of Their Rights
Erica G. Polakoff 291

Conclusion
Women and Neoliberal Globalization: Inequities, Resistance and Alternatives
Ligaya Lindio-McGovern 327

Contributors 345

Author Index 349

Subject Index 354

LIST OF TABLES

Table 3.1: Age Distribution 98

Table 3.2: Distribution of Respondents by Province of Origin 99

Table 3.3: Household Poverty Indicators: Respondent Households and Sri Lankan Population 100

Table 3.4: Respondent Households: Main Occupation of Household Head 101

Table 3.5: Rural Female Population Aged 15 and Over: Labour Force Status and Sectoral Distribution of Employment 104

Table 3.6: Female Wage Rates in Selected Occupations 105

Table 3.7: Economic Activities of Women from Respondents' Villages 108

Table 3.8: Main Reason for Moving to EPZ 108

Table 3.9: Principal Reason for Dissatisfaction with EPZ Employment 109

Table 3.10: Mean Components of Monthly Pay for December 2003 110

Table 3.11: Mean Composition of Monthly Expenditure 111

Foreword

The Evolution and Significance of this Volume of Essays

In 2006, I first began collaborating with the editors of this volume of essays, professors Polakoff and Lindio-McGovern, when they agreed to co-edit a special issue on women and globalization for the *Journal of Developing Societies* (JDS), which I direct as managing editor. They had both presented papers at an international symposium on women and globalization held at the Center for Global Justice in San Miguel de Allende, Mexico in 2005. They agreed to select and edit the best research papers presented at this conference and organize them into a special issue for the journal. We hoped at the time this special issue of the journal might be the *progenitora* of a subsequent state of the art book-length volume of essays on this subject. But the difficult task of organizing and editing the collection of papers which JDS published in two back-to-back issues in 2007, consumed all our attention and energy at the time. Nevertheless, we retained the hope this project would be followed by a book on this subject.

The special issue of the JDS–with the superior quality, critical substance and the international scope of its essays–was a highly welcomed contribution to a small but growing body of literature. It provided a broadly interdisciplinary and multidimensional focus on the local, national and global impacts of neoliberal capitalist globalization on women and their families, as well as on the societies in which they live. Due to the positive reception of the special issue, I was encouraged to seek out a publishing company that would republish the essays in an updated and more thematically integrated volume. Fortuitously, Shivu Ishwaran, the former editor and publisher of JDS, contacted me in September 2009 about revising and publishing some of the recent special issues of JDS as new books to be produced and distributed by his publishing company, de Sitter Publications of Canada.

As a result, I contacted Polakoff and Lindio-McGovern to see if they would be interested in working with Ishwaran to update, revise and republish the essays on women and globalization they had organized and co-edited for JDS, and they enthusiastically agreed to serve as the co-organizers and co-editors of this new book project. We then approached the current publisher of JDS, SAGE India, to give de Sitter Publications permission to republish the essays from the JDS special issue on women and globalization. Our friends in New Delhi gave their approval and Polakoff and Lindio-McGovern contacted the authors of the essays contained in the following pages of this volume to ask them to prepare their essays for publication in this new book.

As Polakoff and Lindio-McGovern state in their preface to this volume, they decided to re-conceptualize the focus of the original collection of essays in the JDS special issue. They informed the authors of the essays in the special issue that they would like them to update and revise their essays for this new book, which would give particular emphasis to women's resistance to neoliberal capitalist globalization. Under Polakoff's and Lindio-McGovern's adept leadership as the co-editors of this new publication, the international assemblage of authors in this volume aligned their essays with the new focus on the politics of women's resistance to neoliberal capitalist globalization. Polakoff and Lindio-McGovern also produced new introductory and concluding essays which deftly frame, contextualize and synthesize the contributions of the collection of authors in this volume.

Consequently, de Sitter Publications has now published this remarkable collection of essays which goes beyond the original groundbreaking nature of the JDS special issue by giving particular emphasis to the ways women have resisted the harmful, inequitable and unjust effects of the policies, practices and ideologies that have accompanied the neoliberal capitalist globalization of their societies. As recently as five years ago, it would have been almost impossible to produce this kind of world-class collection of essays on this topic. The body of research and knowledge on this subject was still at a premature stage of evolution. The book as a whole represents a cutting edge of the existing body of knowledge on this subject. Moreover, these essays on women's resistance to globalization are state of the art in quality. It is the crowning achievement of Polakoff's and Lindio-McGovern's visionary, skillful and arduous efforts to collect, integrate and synthesize the critical perspectives, research findings and analyses produced by an extraordinary international collection of scholars, researchers and social activists who share concerns about, and critically understand the ways in which women have resisted the negative impact of neoliberal policies and corporate globalization on their everyday lives and on their societies. As Polakoff states in the introduction, this book examines and reveals 'the diverse ways in which women challenge racism, sexism, classism and other forms of oppression and dehumanization, and their consequences'. And as Lindio-McGovern states in the concluding chapter, this book also reveals the various ways women's resistance to neoliberal capitalist globalization 'offers strategies, insights and practical ideas about how a better, more just world can be achieved'.

Richard L Harris, Ph.D
Managing Editor, *Journal of Developing Societies*
Waikoloa, Hawai'i

Preface

'Attentiveness only deepens what it regards'
— Jane Hirshfield, *Nine Gates* (Harper/Perennial, 1997)

We could say that this book began in the town of San Miguel de Allende in the state of Guanajuato, in Central Mexico during the summer of 2005. Nearly 200 scholars and activists from 13 countries gathered for a conference organized by the Center for Global Justice, to discuss the impact of 'globalization' on women and their families. In the spirit of mutual respect and collaboration across boundaries, borders and continents, we engaged in dialogue and critical questioning, seeking long-term strategies and solutions to global crises, inequalities and injustices. Over the course of nine or ten days, there were sixty presentations focusing on women's participation in neighborhood associations, community organizations, alternative trade organizations and labor unions, and on overcoming obstacles to building alliances throughout the world. At breakfast on one of those days, Ligaya Lindio-McGovern–who was to become my co-editor on this project–and I, remarked about the quality of the presentations and the research, wondering if there was a plan for publishing conference 'proceedings.' When we inquired, one of the conference organizers, Cliff Durand, simply said, why don't *you* do it? Cliff suggested that I write to Richard Harris, the Managing Editor of the *Journal of Developing Societies*. Cliff put in a good word for us and Richard said the Journal would publish some of the essays in a special issue on 'women and globalization,' provided that Ligaya and I were willing to act as guest editors and select and edit the articles. One and a half years later, in January 2007, the special issue was published.

Since then, we have found the special issue to be especially useful in teaching about global issues, feminisms and research methods. I teach advanced undergraduate courses in sociology (political economy), cultural anthropology and women's studies at a small, private liberal arts college in New Jersey. Most of my students are 'non-traditional students,' that is, they tend to be older than the typical college student. Many are women of color from low-income and 'working class' families; often they are single parents and have multiple significant others to care for including children of their own, elderly and infirm parents and younger siblings. Their families come from the south of the United States or from Newark, New Jersey and the surrounding towns; others have their roots in Peru or Ecuador, Haiti, the Dominican Republic, Puerto Rico, El Salvador, the Philippines, Korea or Nigeria. Many have endured a lot of hardship in their lives. Frequently, they have had less than the best educational preparation for college and/or speak English as a second or third language, and many work full-time to support their families. Somehow they find their way to Bloomfield College and settle in for a few years as Sociology majors with aspirations to pursue careers in teaching, nursing, urban planning, the law, or human services. Many are committed to returning to their communities to offer services and opportunities that were not available to them as youth.

Like the stories of the women included in the articles of the special issue, my students' stories of struggle and sacrifice shape the foundations of their identities, but many are not yet aware of that; nor are they generally aware of the relationship between their own struggles and those of women throughout the world. Instead, at the beginning of every semester in my Senior Research Seminar (my department's version of the Senior Thesis), my students look anxiously at the syllabus and the required reading list. Most are terrified about the prospect of writing a thesis. They all know they must pass this course in order to graduate. They are nervous that they do not know enough about what is happening in the world. Many are not convinced that global issues are even relevant to their lives. What does the IMF, World Bank or World Trade Organization, for example, have to do with them? How can deregulation in Peru, the privatization of water in South Africa, the dollarization of Ecuador's currency, violence against women and girls in India, the freezing of wages and undermining of labor unions in Colombia, child labor in Haiti, Mexico or China, labor export policies of the Philippines, or unemployment and domestic violence in Argentina, possibly affect their lives? However, once we begin reading the essays, watching key documentary films together and discussing these issues, they start to make the connections and their worlds slowly expand. They begin to see how macro-economic policies, structures and institutions affect the life choices and experiences that real people have. With encouragement, most choose to write their senior thesis on their own country of origin or their own heritage, researching the impact of 'global capitalist penetration' on their families and communities, or, for example, on the relationship between 'welfare reform,' poverty and domestic violence. They interview family members about their decisions. Why did they leave Peru or Ecuador? What were conditions like when their parents decided to leave Haiti and come to the United States? What were their experiences as children in Korea or the Philippines or Nigeria? How were their families affected by de-industrialization in Newark or Jersey City, and by cutbacks in the provision of social services? In seeking answers to these questions, students become teachers. They teach us all about their worlds, our world.

Hence, when Richard Harris suggested to us this past winter that de Sitter Publications, Canada was interested in a book version of the special issue, both Ligaya and I jumped at the opportunity. I tracked down and contacted the authors of the essays we had decided to include, and all of them enthusiastically agreed to revise and update their essays. And, at Ligaya's urging, we reconceptualized the work: instead of merely examining the impact on women and their families, of the neoliberal policies that accompany global capitalist penetration, why not concentrate on women's resistance to those policies? While many of the articles in the journal had touched upon women's resistance, not all of them had. So here was an opportunity for all of us to refocus our attention in a way that was consistent with what has been transpiring globally during the past five years. That is, there has been a shift in struggles for survival and petitions for social justice, a number of victories in the 'anti-globalization' movement, the continued development of local alternatives to capitalist exploitation, and an increase in transnational strategies to address global inequalities. This book is the result.

Needless to say, we have been truly inspired by our collaboration with all of our contributors–their graciousness in accepting our suggestions, their trust in our editorship, the sharing of their excitement about the work they are engaged in, and especially about providing spaces for women's voices to resonate and to teach us all. To quote poet and 'woman warrior,' Audre Lorde, "The transformation of silence into language and action is an act of self-revelation…because in this way alone we can survive, by taking part in a process of life that is creative and continuing, that is growth." It has been an incredible and humbling experience to communicate across continents, with scholars and activists living and working in South Africa, Argentina, Colombia, Ecuador, Peru, Spain, India, Australia, Sri Lanka, the Philippines and across the United States. We know that policymakers, NGOs, scholars, activists and our students will appreciate being able to reflect on the lives and experiences of women and their families globally; they will all be inspired by women's resistance to global capitalist penetration. For clearly, as we turn our attention outward, we also deepen our knowledge of ourselves. We can think of no greater gift than this and we are grateful to all who have made it possible.

Erica G Polakoff
July 2010

'Third World feminisms run the risk of marginalization or ghettoization both from mainstream (right and left) and Western feminist discourses'.
— Chandra Mohanty, *Feminisms Without Borders*

Before I came to the conference on Women and Globalization in San Miguel de Allende, to present a paper on the Filipino women's resistance to neoliberal globalization, I already had in mind to put together an edited book that would focus on globalization and Third World women and their collective struggles. This idea was part of my response to my discontent about the invisibility of Third World women's experiences in the mainstream literature on globalization that I reviewed both for my teaching and research. Such invisibility, I thought, perpetuates their marginalization, exploitation and oppression, and work that will bring visibility to their experience is not only an important dimension of scholarship, but also part of being engaged in social justice movements. I was especially moved as I listened to the testimonies of the grassroots women who participated in the conference, such as the Mexican woman who worked in the maquiladora industry about the exploitation and the company's control of her labor that degraded her human dignity, and her struggle with others for social justice and labor rights. I found affinity with her given my Third World origin and being a Filipina who also embodies the experience of neo-colonialism that capitalist globalization perpetuates in the Philippines. I recalled memories when I joined peasant women, workers, urban poor and other activists from various sectors, some even from other countries, protesting in the streets of Manila and carrying a huge streamer with the slogan, "Oppose Imperialist Globalization". I thought that her Mexican experience and that of other Third World womens must find a place in texts to raise scholarly awareness of our oppression. It was this quiet passion that sustained me in co-editing with Erica the special issue of the Journal of Developing Societies, titled *Women and Globalization*, and this book into which that journal has evolved. I suggested its new title, *Gender and Globalization: Patterns of Women's Resistance,* to capture and emphasize the agency and struggles of women that not only invite us to participate in seeking a more humane and just world, but also spark rays of hope to sustain us in the difficult struggle.

As neoliberal globalization fails to deliver its promise of greater progress for the impoverished, the production and dissemination of knowledge to understand better its dynamics–so we can be better informed to organize policy-oriented collective action to change the global inequalities it produces–becomes even more urgent. Such production/dissemination of knowledge would be better served through collaborative efforts so as to bring multiple voices of women, men and children experiencing the structural violence of neoliberalism in different social, cultural, historical, and political contexts. Sometimes putting together an edited volume like this can be an appropriate way to bring together these multiple voices. Such collaboration can be a way of creating intellectual communities that are engaged in the world that they write about, creating new ways of knowing the world where hierarchies of knowledge production and the culture of individualism that global capitalism promotes are deconstructed. After all, individualism that is antithetical to cultures of cooperation, collaboration and community necessary in combating the structural violence of global capitalism permeates academic circles and institutions and it becomes part of the hidden curriculum that some of our students may imbibe. However, as publishers turn more to single-authored books as a cost-saving measure, partly due to the economic crisis, collaboratively bringing together multiple voices of communities of struggle and resistance through edited volumes can be challenging. That is why I highly value and I am thankful for Richard Harris of the Journal of Developing Societies (who also graciously agreed to write the Foreword in this book), and Shivu Ishwaran of de Sitter Publications for creating the opportunity for us and our wonderful contributors to put women's experiences into texts that can be widely disseminated. I would like to heartily say, that this book is not only *about* the women we write about. This book is *their* book. They are co-editors, they are co-authors of the world we write about. Without their struggles where they put their flesh and blood on the line there is no resistance to write about. It is for this reason that I pledge a donation from the small royalty from this book to the women's movement in the Philippines I wrote about in this volume.

As well, I found the articles in the special journal issue from which this book evolved useful in my graduate course on Globalization, Development and Social Policy and in my upper level courses like Sociology of Development, and Collective Action and Social Movements. The journal issue complemented the more theoretical and sometimes polemical texts on globalization, or texts that minimally touch on women/gender and globalization. Students often need more concrete illustrations of alternatives to neoliberal policies and how people actually engage in bringing about change. This volume will be useful as well in disciplines other than sociology, such as political science, international studies, women's studies, area studies, political economy, and labor studies. It complements my other co-edited volume (with Isidor Wallimann), *Globalization and Third World Women: Exploitation, Coping and Resistance* (2009, Ashgate Publishing), that others and I have also used in teaching and research.

Ligaya Lindio-McGovern
July 2010

Acknowledgments

The evolution of this collection into a book has been made possible through the pooling together of the efforts of many people to whom we are sincerely thankful. We especially want to thank:

- Richard Harris, the Managing Editor of the *Journal of Developing Societies (JDS)*, who favorably and highly recommended to de Sitter Publications, the publication of a book based on 'Women and Globalization' (2007), the special double issue (1-2) of the *Journal of Developing Societies*, that we guest co-edited. Most of the chapters in this volume are articles selected from this special issue.
- Sage Publications, the publisher of the aforementioned *JDS* special issue, for agreeing without hesitation to de Sitter Publication's proposal to publish this volume.
- Shivu Ishwaran of de Sitter Publications who worked with us diligently to complete this project.
- our contributors who willingly and patiently updated and revised their articles into chapters for this volume.
- the Center for Global Justice in San Miguel de Allende, Guanajuato, Mexico, sponsor of the international conference, 'Women and Globalization' in 2005, that brought together 185 community activists and scholars from 13 different countries. Most of the chapters selected for this volume were originally revised versions of the contributors' presentations at this conference out of which the special journal issue was produced.
- the co-sponsoring organizations of the aforementioned conference–the Radical Philosophy Association, the Argentina *Autonomista* Project, the Global Studies Association-USA, the Feminist Aid to Central America, and the Union of Radical Political Economists, in collaboration with *El Recreo Centro Cultural* and *Mujeres Productoras* of San Miguel de Allende.
- the women and the various organizations discussed in this volume whose struggles inspired us to bring this project to completion. Their resistance teaches us many lessons about the struggle for global social justice amidst the structural violence of neoliberalism.
- our colleagues for their wisdom and critical questioning.
- our students who persist in their pursuit of knowledge despite the obstacles confronting them in their own lives.
- our friends and families who gave us moral support and inspiration to complete this project.

In our recognition of these collective efforts, we would like to convey the message that while resistance to neoliberal globalization requires the collaboration of diverse sectors and groups, the collective production and dissemination of knowledge about it can also be a form of resistance that needs to be waged on all fronts and at all levels.

Ligaya Lindio-McGovern and Erica G Polakoff

INTRODUCTION

Women's Resistance to the Violence of Global Capitalist Penetration

Erica G. Polakoff
Bloomfield College

This volume seeks to understand the impact of contemporary macro-level economic and political forces–ideologies, structures, institutions, policies and practices–associated with the expansion and penetration of capitalism globally, on the daily lives and livelihoods of women and their families. In particular, it seeks to examine the diverse ways in which women challenge racism, sexism, classism and other forms of oppression and dehumanization, and their consequences–impoverishment, exploitation, marginalization and exclusion. Our focus is on the collective strategies that women use to resist material inequalities, and the physical, psychological and spiritual violence of global capitalist penetration which values power and the accumulation of wealth above social reproduction, human dignity, and the security and well-being of the planet.

A number of social analysts have highlighted the impact of global forces on 'the material foundations of life, space and time' (Castells, 1997:1). In the words of Frances Fox Piven and Richard Cloward (1998:12), globalization has brought 'convulsive changes not only in the patterns of production and exchange, but (also) in patterns of culture and politics'. For Noam Chomsky (1998:19), one consequence of globalization has been 'the spread of the Third World social model, with islands of enormous privilege in a sea of misery and despair'. Leaving no one and nowhere untouched, global or 'turbo-capitalism' has reached, 'the remotest parts of individual countries and the most far-flung corners of the earth' (Wichterich, 1998). Driven by networks of power, capital and technology, global processes, according to Manuel Castells, 'are shaking institutions, transforming cultures, creating wealth and inducing poverty, spurring greed, innovation and hope, while simultaneously imposing hardship and instilling despair' (Castells, 1997:1-2).

The terminology used by researchers, scholars and activists (including the authors of the selections in this text), to describe these global forces and processes, includes variations of the term 'globalization', usually with a descriptor to indicate the type of globalization that is being discussed, as in 'economic globalization', 'corporate globalization' or 'neoliberal globalization'. In addition, there are variations of the term 'capitalism' as in 'corporate capitalism', 'turbo-capitalism', 'global capitalism', and 'global capitalist penetration', and other variations on the use of 'global' as in 'global apartheid'. While not a complete list, these demonstrate how multifarious the naming process is. Analysis and 'mapping' of the language used to describe these processes therefore, may be useful.

Admittedly, 'globalization' by itself, sounds broad and vague, deceptively innocuous, neutral or even 'positive'. It may call to mind a sort of give-and-take or equal exchange of products, cultural forms, media, arts, technologies and communications. 'Economic globalization' focuses our attention on the economies that are being acted upon or on the economic forces that are acting upon us all. 'Neoliberal globalization' compels us to consider the neoliberal ideologies, policies and practices of 'free trade' (or trade 'liberalization'), deregulation and privatization, for example. 'Corporate globalization' seems to refer to the bureaucratic entities of transnational corporations that are doing the 'globalizing', or becoming 'globalized'. We can conjure up images of McDonald's, Disney, Nike, Walmart, or BP, for example, which may have positive or negative associations, as Mark Achbar and Jennifer Abbott (2003), demonstrate in their documentary film, *The Corporation*. 'Turbo-capitalism' focuses our attention on technology as a force and implies an unstoppable, overpowering thrust of 'capitalism' into people's lives.

'Global apartheid' focuses on structure and consequences–the racist political, economic and cultural institutions and ideologies of apartheid–which had been legitimized and practiced in South Africa–applied to these same processes taking place throughout the world. South African apartheid created a hierarchy of worth and worthlessness, privileging and empowering a small group of individuals (descendants of White, European colonialists) at the expense of the majority (descendants of Black, indigenous and native peoples). Salih Booker and William Minter (2001) conceptualize 'global apartheid' as:

> an international system of minority rule (characterized by) differential access to human rights; wealth and power structured by race and place; structural racism embedded in global economic processes, political institutions, and cultural assumptions; and international practice of double standards that assume inferior rights to be appropriate for certain

'others' defined by location, origin, race or gender (in Rothenberg, 2006:517-18).

'Global apartheid' not only describes a system of 'haves' and 'have-nots' based on race, it is also used to represent the subordination, marginalization and exclusion of those defined as 'other' (or 'alien') as a result of where they live or their position in the global hierarchy (location); the communities they belong to or their cultural heritage (origin); and their gender. All of these, of course, are indivisible elements of collective identity and an individual's sense of 'being' in the world. Global apartheid is a powerful concept. For our purposes however, it has one drawback. Though Booker and Minter refer to 'global economic processes' in their definition of global apartheid, the force driving those processes is neither indicated nor implied.

'Global capitalist penetration' immediately brings to mind the method or means used to accumulate 'capital' or extract 'profit' on a global scale–that is, 'penetration' implies an act of violence that accompanies capitalism, the depth of its incursion into, and extraction out of, peoples and places worldwide. 'Penetration' also implies that there is 'resistance' or 'a force in opposition' to capitalism that must be overcome in order for capitalism to become 'triumphant'. Although the contributors to this volume adopt many different terms, because of the dual implications of 'global capitalist penetration', it is particularly useful for describing the processes discussed in the selections here.

Before we analyze the impact of these global forces and their consequences for nations, communities, families and especially women worldwide, it would be useful to understand what global capitalist penetration is. As Maria Mies noted (in Benholdt-Thomsen et al., 2001), in order to create a sustainable world, one community of people cannot be 'de-colonized' at the expense of other communities. Thus, building alliances, developing strategies of resistance and collectively organizing against the forces of oppression and 'colonization' that exploit and impoverish the majority of the world's people today, all require that we identify and understand those forces. Paolo Freire (1979) called the process of becoming aware, *'concientización'*, and noted that 'the oppressed are not marginals living outside' the structures that oppress them. They have always been 'inside'. In order for the oppressed to become liberated they must become conscious of those forces. The goal is not to have the oppressed become integrated into the structures of oppression but to change the structures so that the oppressed can become 'beings for themselves' instead of 'beings for others'. We need to undergo *'conscientizacion'* and learn about the structures and processes that are exacerbating existing inequalities–creating tremendous wealth on the one hand, while on the other, causing increased hardship, despair and misery for the overwhelming majority of peoples throughout the world. We need to understand how these processes are infiltrating the most 'far-flung corners of the earth' (Wichetrich, 1998).

Characteristics of 'Global Capitalist Penetration'

According to the International Forum on Globalization (IFG) the key characteristics of global capitalist penetration, or what the IFG refers to as 'economic globalization', are:

- Promotion of hypergrowth and unrestricted exploitation of environmental resources to fuel that growth.
- Privatization and commodification of public services and of the remaining aspects of the global and community commons.
- Global cultural and economic homogenization and the intense promotion of consumerism.
- Integration and conversion of national economies, including some that were largely self-reliant, to environmentally and socially harmful export production.
- Corporate deregulation and unrestricted movement of capital across borders.
- Dramatically increased corporate concentration.
- Dismantling of public health, social, and environmental programs already in place.
- Replacement of traditional powers of democratic nation-states and local communities by global corporate bureaucracies (IFG, 2002:19).

The corporation's accession to wealth and power and its dominance worldwide, have contributed to many of these crises. Corporations exist beyond national boundaries; they have no allegiance to nations, and no accountability to communities, workers, families, or individuals. The *raison d'être* of the corporation is the profit motive and the drive for expansion.

Corporations dominate societies and help create power structures that rule us, yet they remain paradoxically ephemeral entities. Although such names as Exxon/Mobil, McDonald's, Shell, Microsoft, Disney, Sony and Monsanto are emblazoned in our brains, as familiar to us as old friends, in fact these institutions have no real physical existence. They own buildings and stadiums, and wield stupendous powers, but corporations themselves have no concrete form. They have people who work in them, but corporations are themselves not alive, so they cannot embody the same range of values and emotions that we expect of responsible people: altruism, shame, community concern, loyalty to one another, and so on (IFG, 2002:126).

Corporate interests and values are protected by governments and the military, upheld by international financial and trade institutions, supported by academic and research institutions, rationalized by the 'demand' for technological 'progress' and consumer goods, and enshrined in trade agreements such as: the North American Free Trade Agreement (NAFTA) between the U.S., Mexico and Canada, the Dominican Republic-Central American Free Trade Agreement (CAFTA-DR) between the nations of Central America, the Dominican Republic and the U.S., *Plan Colombia* between the U.S. and Colombia, *Plan Dignidad* (Plan Dignity) between the U.S. and Bolivia, the Korean-U.S. Free Trade Agreement (KORUS), etc. Global corporate bureaucracies are involved in the creation of policy and are behind the development of trade agreements. For example, 'Monoliths such as Cargill and Monsanto were both actively involved in shaping international agreements, in particular, the Uruguay Round of the General Agreement on Tariffs and Trade, which led to the establishment of the WTO' (Shiva, 2000:9).

The World Trade Organization (WTO)'s Articles of Agreement are essentially a set of rules regarding the flow or 'free trade' of goods, services and intellectual property that the governments of 153 member nations have 'agreed' to follow.[1] Although four-fifths of the membership is made up of 'developing' nations, the distribution of power within the WTO clearly favors wealthy nations (Wade, 2003; Jawara and Kwa, 2004). In fact, 'strong-arm tactics'–political and economic pressure, intimidation and threats–are used by the major 'developed' countries and the international financial institutions that represent their interests to 'break the solidarity of the developing countries' (Jawara and Kwa, 2004:xxxix), and to secure 'corporate access to the markets and resources of the developing world' (Ibid:3). According to Michel Chossudovsky (2003:26) and the Center for Research on Globalization, 'Under WTO rules the banks and multinational corporations can legitimately manipulate the market forces to their advantage leading to the outright re-colonization of national economies'.

'Free trade' agreements have consistently provided corporations and international banks with the power to exert pressure on governments and subvert national laws. More specifically, transnational corporations, with or without the complicity of governments, have been able to ignore and violate minimum wage laws, child labor laws, environmental protections, occupational, health and safety regulations, and civil and human rights.[2] Moreover,

> the WTO almost neutralizes "with the stroke of a pen" the authority and activities of several agencies of the United Nations including the United Nations Conference on Trade and Development (UNCTAD) and the International Labor Organization (ILO). The articles of the WTO are not only in contradiction to pre-existing national and international laws, they are also at variance with the "Universal Declaration of Human Rights" (Ibid:24-25).

International financial institutions like the World Bank and the International Monetary Fund (IMF), established in Bretton Woods, New Hampshire at the end of World War II, also promote global capitalist penetration worldwide and support global corporate control. The neoliberal policies and practices of these institutions—referred to as 'structural adjustment programs' or 'austerity programs'—restructure the economies of indebted nations, to ensure repayment of their loans and accelerate their integration into the global capitalist market. The IMF and World Bank have pressured governments to open up their borders to foreign investment; to devalue their national currency; to enforce the privatization of national or State industries and natural resources (land, water, minerals, and national forests); to encourage the exploitation of human resources; to gear local economies toward export production; to deregulate the market, that is, to remove barriers (like import and export duties, or subsidies for domestically produced goods) to the influx of foreign goods onto the local market; to deregulate corporate operations (removing price controls, environmental protection standards, occupational health and safety standards, labor protections, etc.); to raise prices for basic goods to international levels; and to reduce the State sector and drastically cut government-sponsored social programs (e.g., public health, education, social welfare, food programs, public transportation, pensions, social security, etc.).

These institutions frequently work together and with national and international military forces:

> The IMF, World Bank and WTO–which police country level economic reforms–also collaborate with NATO in its various "peacekeeping" endeavors, not to mention the financing of "post-conflict" reconstruction under the auspices of the Bretton Woods institutions (Chossudovsky, 2003:10).

In sum, the confluence of transnational corporations, bi-lateral and multi-lateral trade agreements between governments, international financial and trade institutions and neoliberal policies characteristic of (but not limited to) structural adjustment programs, contribute to the global expansion and penetration of capitalism into people's lives. Contrary to what most policymakers would have us believe, these policies, practices and ideologies are not neutral (Galeano, 1991). As suggested earlier, they cause misery, despair, hardship, suffering, desperation and inhumanity for the majority of peoples worldwide. In other words, they inflict violence and destruction on women and men, families and communities, and the environment. The violence they inflict is a kind of insidious violence that is structured into social, political and economic institutions by the dynamics of historical relations between 'colonizers' and 'colonized'–that is, by the legacies of colonialism (which include, for example, slavery, exploitation, racism, sexism, hierarchies of class, and economic dependency between the former colonies and their colonizer nations)[3]–combined with the complex contemporary forces (outlined above) that are controlled and promulgated by wealthy and powerful elites and the neoliberal governments that represent their interests.

Colonialism and its Legacies of Violence

In order to subdue and conquer a people, colonizing and imperialist patriarchal forces–the predecessors to, and building blocks of, contemporary global capitalism–used physical violence (e.g., torture, slavery and annihilation), the threat of violence, and mechanisms of psychological, spiritual and 'symbolic' violence (e.g., exacerbating existing, or creating new, divisions of clans, peoples, and territories, separating families, imposing hierarchies based on modes of production, language, culture, religion, race and sex, and so on). According to Mies (in Benholdt-Thomsen et al., 2001:5), 'Capitalism would not have emerged without the destruction of the self-sufficient and self-sustaining subsistence systems' of indigenous peoples. Colonial territories were used to extract and accumulate resources for the colonial centers, which led to increased dependency on the colonizers, and made the colonized more vulnerable to exploitation (Wolf, 1997). Destruction of the subsistence economies of indigenous peoples was accomplished through 'trade' and Europe's insatiable demands for agricultural products and land, furs, minerals and labor. Disruption of indigenous patterns of subsistence resulted from the dispossession and displacement of indigenous peoples from the land through forced migration and relocation, forced labor and slavery, and the privatization of the land.[4] Hierarchies of 'religion' were used by colonizers as adjuncts to domination, and served to undermine the cosmic stability of indigenous peoples worldwide. Hierarchies of 'race' undermined the collective identity of the colonized and created additional divisions among them, while also providing the colonizers with justifications for enslaving and brutalizing them (Memmi, 1968). The imposition of hierarchies based on gender further divided the colonized, leading to the domination and exploitation of women by men, from both outside and inside (Étienne and Leacock, 1980). Together, these hierarchies, which were based on 'differences'–whether 'real' or 'imagined' (Memmi, 1968)–created a system of oppression in which beliefs about the 'natural' existence of inferior and superior beings would become internalized.[5]

The internalization of oppression serves to numb the oppressed and, for the most part, quell opposition and resistance. As Johan Galtung (1990:291) noted, 'Symbolic violence built into a culture does not kill or maim like direct violence or the violence built into the structure. However, it is used to legitimize either or both'. Those who manage to resist the impact of these oppressions–of racism, sexism, class privilege, divisions based on ethnicity, family, clan and community, for example, and of the system constructed to maintain them–threaten the power of the oppressors and of those who benefit from the system of oppression. Resistors lay bare the myth of inferiority and superiority, and serve as role models for the resistance of others. Historically, responses by the powerful to those who had the audacity to think they were 'equal' in worth, often included severe, public demonstrations of the colonizers' power through the use of torture, brutality and execution, and more intensive repression of the communities of the colonized. Thus, violence and cruelty were used to enforce obedience among the colonized to the colonizers' values, to 'ensure' acquiescence to the latter's demands for land, resources, and labor in the quest for greater wealth and more power, to terrorize and instill fear, and to undermine resistance. However, public demonstrations of violence reveal the identity of the perpetrators to the people they victimize. This is potentially problematic for the perpetrators, since once the 'victimized' can identify their 'victimizers', presumably they are able to fight back and resist oppression.[6] Thus, there is an inherent contradiction–the means that are used to repress opposition and resistance, may actually give rise to them.

Today, however, the perpetrators of global capitalist penetration are 'shielded' or 'cloaked' behind transnational institutions, trade agreements and treaties, and corporate bureaucracies; and the violence they perpetrate is embedded in the racist, sexist and dehumanizing ideologies of an economic and cultural system that 'terrorizes' people (Galeano, 1991), and then blames them for being victims. This does not mean that physical violence, brutality and cruelty are excluded; nor does it exclude the implementation of mechanisms that serve to create and maintain false consciousness leading to the internalization of oppression and containment of resistance. Rather, these violences are integrated into a larger system of violence. In other words, the violence that best characterizes contemporary global capitalism is *structural violence.*

The Structural Violence of Global Capitalist Penetration

> We live in a time in which violence is right before our very eyes. The word is applied in extremely varied contexts, but each is marked by open violence–by violent acts, fury, hatred, massacres, cruelty, collective atrocities–but also by the cloaked violences of economic domination, of capital-labor relations, of the great North-South divide, to say nothing of all of the "everyday" violences perpetrated against the weak: women, children, all those excluded by the social system.
>
> – Françoise Héritier, *De la Violence* (in Farmer, 2003: 7-8).

Structural violence is violence that limits options and creates vulnerabilities to the violations of human rights and the indignities of poverty and its consequences, including hunger, ill health, homelessness, illiteracy, extreme suffering *and* physical violence. Structural violence, according to Johan Galtung,[7] is the 'avoidable impairment of fundamental human needs...or the impairment of human life' (in Farmer et al., 2006). It is *structural* because it refers to the economic, political, legal, cultural and religious structures that prevent people from meeting their basic needs and thereby violate their human rights. Rights violations are intertwined; they are difficult to disentangle or determine cause and effect, or as Ho (2007: 9) explains, using poverty as a starting point:

> Poverty consists of a systematic or structural denial of basic freedoms... resulting in agency constrained to the extent that individuals are unable or lack the 'capability' to meet their basic needs. The denial of one freedom amplifies or multiplies the denial of other freedoms, rendering the poor disproportionately vulnerable to a whole array of violations.

In other words, poverty is not accidental; it is multi-layered and compounded by intersection and convergence with other forms of oppression like racism and sexism, which may prevent access to education, training, employment, housing, land, water, food and health care. Medical anthropologist, Paul Farmer (2003) calls the system that creates and perpetuates violations of human rights and extreme suffering, 'the political economy of brutality', and describes the ideologies of those who construct that system, as 'pathologies of power'.

> Human rights violations are not accidents; they are not random in distribution or effect. Rights violations are, rather, symptoms of deeper pathologies of power and are linked intimately to the social conditions that so often determine who will suffer abuse and who will be shielded from harm (2003: 7).

Structural violence, therefore, is systematic or structured into social institutions and bureaucratic organizations. As discussed earlier, it is promoted through trade agreements between governments that take place behind closed doors. It includes pressures on 'developing' countries by core countries in WTO negotiations. It is integrated into neoliberal policies–like privatization of public institutions and services, deregulation of industries, and trade 'liberalization' promulgated by neoliberal states or imposed on governments by the IMF and World Bank. And, it is in the practices of transnational corporations that create unsustainable conditions of work that exploit and dehumanize workers, undermine communities and families and destroy the environment.

Vulnerabilities to structural violence are influenced by constellations of socially constructed 'axes' such as 'race', 'culture', ethnicity, socio-economic status or 'class', geography, 'refugee' or immigrant status, *and* 'gender' (Farmer, 2003); that is, by location, origin, race and gender to recall Booker and Minter's (2001) concept of 'global apartheid'. These social constructions intersect with each other differently, at different points in history and in different places, and contribute to the oppression of individuals, groups and communities. Because of the complexity of these factors, and the fact that social injustices are mediated by an individual's or group's social location or 'positionality', and by people's 'lived' experiences (Crenshaw, 1994), we need to place at the center of our analysis of resistance to global capitalist penetration, the actual experiences of real people.

As a result of the adoption of neoliberal policies associated with bilateral and multi-lateral trade agreements like NAFTA, international trade institutions like the WTO, and structural adjustment programs of the IMF and World Bank, the lives and livelihoods of women and their children, and indeed, the future of the planet, have become increasingly precarious. Because women tend to carry the burden of the responsibility for the care and nurturance of their families, women have been particularly vulnerable to, and also targeted by, the structural violence of global capitalism. Furthermore, as noted by Héritier (ibid), women are vulnerable to dual structures of violence: in addition to being subjected to the inhumanity of global capitalist penetration which exacerbates poverty, unemployment, homelessness, and ill health, many women also confront the 'everyday' violence of patriarchy.

The Violence of Patriarchy

Patriarchy is the system of male dominance that subordinates women and privileges men at women's expense. Patriarchy appears to be a widespread, though not universal, phenomenon.[8] While patriarchy preceded the development of capitalism, 'Patriarchy has not vanished with progress. On the contrary, it is developing with progress' (Von Werlhof, 2001:15). Patriarchy has endured for at least four interconnected reasons. First, it has been institutionalized into the belief systems that shape women's (and men's) conceptions of themselves and the reality they inhabit, permeating virtually all of the structures of society (the economy, politics, religion, health care, the family, the medical establishment, education, the legal system and the laws). Second, women have been 'complicit' in the maintenance and perpetuation of patriarchy. Indeed, as Gerda Lerner (1986) noted, women's cooperation is absolutely essential:

> The system of patriarchy can function only with the cooperation of women. This cooperation is secured by a variety of means: gender indoctrination; educational deprivation; the denial to women of knowledge of their history; the dividing of women, one from the other, by defining "respectability" and "deviance" according to women's sexual activities; by restraints and coercion; by discrimination in access to economic resources and political power; and by awarding class privileges to conforming women (Lerner in Rothenberg, 2006:254).

Third, capitalism, as an economic and cultural system, and particularly, though not exclusively, in capital-labor dynamics, perpetuates and exploits already existing divisions like those present in patriarchal systems, to prevent solidarity among those it seeks to exploit, and thereby accumulate more capital (see: Mies, 1986).

Finally, like the mechanisms of violence perpetrated during colonialism, violence against women has been used to force compliance, obedience and control, and 'maintain and reinforce women's subordination' (WHO, 1997). According to the United Nations Declaration on the Elimination of Violence against Women, violence against women is 'any act of gender-based violence that results in, or is likely to result in, physical, sexual, or psychological harm or suffering to women, including threats of such acts, coercion or arbitrary deprivation of liberty, whether occurring in public or private life' (Ibid, 1997). And, although the violence of patriarchy manifests itself differently in accordance with specific cultural norms and practices, gender-based violence is a fact of life for the majority of women worldwide affecting them throughout their life cycle–beginning before they are born, that is, when they are *in utero* (as in sex-selective abortion especially in cultures where boys are preferred), in infancy, girlhood, adolescence, adulthood and when they are elderly (Ibid, 1997).

In 'Losing Faith in Progress', Claudia Von Werlhof (2001: 20) theorizes that violence is inherent to patriarchy: '(A) form of 'violent thinking' which is formative for the reality (that patriarchy) constructs... is permanently connected to a politics of brute force that will ruthlessly remake anything in its way which does not fit its theory'. Furthermore, Von Werlhof notes that this 'violent thinking' lays claim to the myth of male superiority or that the better, more divine world is the one inhabited by the...birth-giving...and thus legitimately ruling Father-God, or his Father-Law instead of the 'natural right' of the mother' (Ibid). Religion, a major institution for shaping people's world view, embraces and promotes male dominance in the name of protecting 'traditional' (i.e., patriarchal) society and culture, and thus has been a powerful anti-feminist force.[9]

Women of the global South today are subjected to the intertwined oppressions of patriarchy, racism and the infiltration of capitalism. That is, the forces of global capitalism have exploited the legacies of the oppressions that preceded them and integrated them into a larger structure of exploitation and marginalization. As noted earlier, global capitalist penetration represents a different kind of challenge for women worldwide. To identify contemporary global structures of power, to confront governments that are complicit with international forces or are pressured to comply with their demands, and to address and redress policies that not infrequently descend suddenly upon communities, and are written behind closed doors or by 'absentee' bureaucrats, new kinds of organizational strategies are required. These strategies often traverse geographical, cultural, national, color, class, language, and/or religious borders and boundaries. From local grassroots and community-based organizations to national and transnational feminist networks, women's groups and communities of women are challenging and resisting the threats to their dignity and their very survival posed by the global expansion and penetration of capitalism. How do we then understand the 'myriad ways women are organizing against the gendered, racialized and regionalized processes of global capitalist expansion' (Naples and Desai, 2002:12), that is, how do we understand the significance of women's resistance to the violence of global capitalist penetration?

Women's Resistance to the Violence of Global Capitalist Penetration

> Women's resistance...is shaped by the dailiness of women's lives (and has) a profound impact on the fabric of social life. It is central to the making of history...and is the *bedrock of social change.*
>
> – Bettina Aptheker, *Tapestries of Life* (1989:173-4, emphasis mine)

Individually and collectively, women resist the 'expansion' or penetration of global capitalism into their lives. Since women are ultimately responsible for the care and well being of their families, resistance is a survival strategy. That is, when faced with the prospect of hunger and homelessness, of watching their children die of starvation or disease, of laboring in super-exploitative conditions, or of forfeiting their education and their futures, many women are compelled to take a stand and defend their families. Women resist as mothers, daughters, breadwinners, members of communities and activists intent on creating a better world for themselves and their families. Women resist by refusing to give in and refusing to surrender. Even if forces of oppression have subdued them in the past, a different kind of resistance can emerge, re-emerge, or rise up. Believing they have nothing to fear and nothing more to lose, resistance by withstanding the effect of those forces, can transform into resistance by 'exerting force in opposition', in order to 'counteract or defeat' the forces of oppression and exploitation. Thus, past, present and future attempts by oppressive forces to vanquish, subdue, dominate or control can be overcome.[10] For this reason, women's resistance threatens to destabilize the oppressive institutions of patriarchy, the equally oppressive forces of global capitalist penetration (Franco, 1998:287), and the policies that intertwine them.

The forms of organization and methods of resistance that women adopt are fluid and changeable, 'continually evolving in response to economic and social change' (Rosa, 1994:75). Increasingly, women are recognizing the global nature of their 'personal problems' and the local issues with which they are confronted. This is especially true in the global South where 'women organizing for survival–for food, water and health–have learnt to see their individual suffering as the symptom of a wider structure of injustice' (Wichterich, 1998:145-6). In the fight for 'dignity and daily bread' (Rowbotham and Mitter, 1994), collective consciousness (or *concientización*), increasingly, is taking shape as women's collective resistance.

In *There is an Alternative: Subsistence and Worldwide Resistance to Corporate Globalization,* Veronika Benholdt-Thomsen, Nicholas Faraclas and Claudia Von Werlhof (2001:x) emphasize that successful resistance to 'corporate globalization' is possible by re-integrating all the facets of our being, that is, by cultivating

> ...a renewed sense of the indivisible whole to which our bodies, minds, souls, spirits, and means of production and

reproduction belong, despite centuries of patriarchal scientific and religious programming that has attempted to atomize these fundamental aspects of our existence in order to construct false dichotomies, such as body vs. mind or subjectivity vs. objectivity. Beyond the rejection of these illusory binarisms...a necessary condition for effective resistance to corporate globalization is the re-establishment of our sense of individual and collective power over our bodies, beliefs, communities, land, food, markets, and so on, in order to redirect our labour towards the creation of use value, abundance, fertility and life and away from production of exchange value, scarcity, violence and death.

This volume centers on women's resistance to global capitalist penetration and its racist, sexist and classist ideologies, structures, processes and consequences, highlighting the ways in which women fight to overcome the violence associated with labor exploitation and labor export, unemployment and underemployment, poverty, homelessness, illness, migration, discrimination, the derogation of their rights and freedoms, assaults on their identities and domestic abuse. Women are struggling against the conditions of work and life imposed upon their families and their communities as a result of the integration of their local economies into the world market. And, as the chapters in this volume suggest, women are resisting by creating trade union alliances in an environment that is hostile to unionization and workers' rights. They are organizing migrant workers, the unemployed, neighborhoods, the landless, and the homeless. They are creating alternative trade associations, educating themselves and each other about the laws of their countries and the conditions of international agreements. They are standing up to and fighting against the privatization of the public domain and 'the commons'. They are confronting the perpetrators of structural violence–transnational corporations, international financial institutions, 'free trade' agreements, neoliberal policies and the complicity and corruption of their governments, all of which seek to dominate their lives and control their livelihoods. Women are creating their own networks of support and are resisting by forming transnational alliances and meshing these with local, regional and national organizations–labor unions and associations, human rights organizations, trade associations, neighborhood associations, etc. In other words, they are collectively organizing against the inhumanity, violence and non-sustainability of patriarchal capitalist exploitation and cultural hegemony.

As the work of the scholars and activists included here demonstrates, women collectively resist with their bodies, minds and spirits. In the process, they are empowering themselves, forging new identities and creating constructive alternatives for the future that all of our children will inherit; that is, for a future that would be characterized by compassion, social justice, responsibility and accountability, rather than by greed and immorality. In each case, the authors highlight the diversity in women's activism and their strategies of collective resistance in the context of different intersections of gender, race, ethnicity, culture, socio-economic class, geography, language and immigration status. The chapters are organized in four sections as follows. In the first section, 'Neoliberal Policies, Migration and Women's Resistance', we are introduced to the differential impact of global capitalist penetration on women in the Philippines and Ecuador and among Ecuadorian migrants to Spain, and Philippine emigrants, generally. Section two, 'Women's Resistance and Capitalist Production for Export', focuses on women's labor struggles and collective resistance in the textile and garment industries in Mexico, the United States and Sri Lanka, and in the production of flowers for export in Colombia. Section three, 'Alternative Trade Organizations and Women's Resistance' includes selections on women's trade organizations in Peru and India. Finally, in 'Responses to Poverty: Women's and Children's Resistance', responses to poverty are examined at the neighborhood and community level in Peru, Argentina and South Africa, and among children worldwide.

Neoliberal Policies, Migration and Women's Resistance

In 'Neoliberal Globalization in the Philippines', Ligaya Lindio-McGovern provides an overview of neoliberal policies and their impact on families, especially women, in the Philippines. She explains the ways in which the processes of trade liberalization, deregulation, privatization, finance capitalism, labor flexibilization and labor export are mutually reinforcing and how they all contribute to increased poverty, unemployment, and insecurity. For example, labor flexibilization policies serve to decrease wages and worker benefits and contribute to greater financial and food insecurity; the privatization of health care services and water causes tremendous hardship and illness, and threatens the very survival of low-income women and their families; the Philippine government's official policy of 'labor export' is a misguided attempt to 'solve' the problem of high unemployment. It not only creates great physical, psychological and emotional trauma for families, it also contributes to a tremendous loss of human capital. Many women who leave their families to find employment abroad have advanced professional or semi-professional training but due to discrimination and labor import policies tied to immigration policies in receiving countries, they end up in jobs requiring little formal education or training.

Lindio-McGovern also draws our attention to two key associations–GABRIELA and Migrante International–which have been organizing resistance to these policies both within the Philippines and internationally. GABRIELA has played an important role in popular education and consciousness-raising in the Philippines as well as challenging government policies that place global capital interests above the well-being and sovereignty of the people. Migrante International promotes the rights of Philippine (and other) migrants worldwide by challenging both the Philippine government on its labor export policies and the governments of labor-receiving nations on their labor policies and conditions of work.

In 'We're Better Off Outside Our Country: Diasporic Ecuadorian Women in Spain Since the Mid-1990s', estheR Cuesta's interviews with Ecuadorian women migrants to Spain reveal experiences of exploitative labor conditions, discrimination (and violence) in the workplace and society, and painful separation from family and community. In addition, like women migrants in the Philippines (as discussed by Lindio-McGovern), many Ecuadorian women migrants, regardless of whether they are documented or undocumented, professional or semi-professional workers, experience downward mobility in terms of the status of the jobs they are able to obtain abroad, especially given the relatively high level of their skills and educational backgrounds.

In order to understand the significance of their migration, Cuesta provides us with an analysis of Ecuador's political economy–the dollarization of the national currency, cutbacks in social programs, trade liberalization, and the integration of the economy into the global market. These neoliberal and neocolonial policies have resulted in very high unemployment rates, extremely low wages (even for professional workers), and a high cost of living, all of which have contributed to increased poverty, erosion of the value of human development and rapid destruction of the environment. In other words, Ecuadorian women face the prospect of their lives being unsustainable in Ecuador. Thus, in spite of having to endure prolonged separation from their families and a climate of discrimination, racism and exploitation in Spain, many Ecuadorian women believe that by migrating to Spain, they have a chance at a better life and a better chance of supporting their families. Finally, Cuesta highlights the importance of representation in resistance to discrimination and racism and in the formation of collective identity. She notes that Ecuadorians are creating their own images and representations of themselves in Spain by producing their own radio programs and online versions of Ecuadorian newspapers, and broadcasting Ecuadorian television programs. These not only provide information and a sense of collective identity for migrants in Spain but also challenge the stereotypes of Ecuadorians in the Spanish media.

Women's Resistance and Capitalist Production for Export

Neoliberal policies are responsible for increasing unemployment, underemployment, and landlessness–thus contributing to and exacerbating poverty. In previously agrarian societies, both small farmers and indigenous communities alike are finding it increasingly difficult to make a living from the land, because they do not have access to (or 'own')–individually or collectively–enough arable land to grow the crops they need to survive. In a number of instances, the government, the military or private corporations have displaced them from their land, often as a result of structural adjustment mandates, in order to produce export crops (which depends on and exploits the labor of the now landless, migrant farmers and their families), build 'free trade' (i.e. export-processing) zones, construct dams or airports, or extract natural resources. In addition, greater vulnerability to world market prices, and natural disasters like floods and droughts, have contributed to increasing indebtedness and have pushed people off their lands. Consequently, masses of people have been migrating across national borders in search of paid labor (as we have already seen in the cases of women from the Philippines and Ecuador), from rural to urban areas, and to export-processing or 'free trade' zones (EPZs or FTZs). In many countries of the global South, young women and girls are recruited to work in foreign-owned, agricultural or industrial EPZs in both rural and urban areas, often replacing their fathers as the primary or sole wage earners.

Two chapters examine the struggles of women workers in the manufacturing industries especially in EPZs and FTZs. In 'Push and Pull Factors in Female Labour Migration: Evidence from Sri Lanka's Garment Workers', Judith Shaw analyzes the employment decisions of women garment workers in Sri Lanka's EPZs. The majority of women in her study have been pushed into working in the EPZs due to poverty. Over 90 percent are young women from rural areas who work reluctantly in factories characterized by unsafe conditions, and the suppression of trade unionism. As unmarried migrant women, they also experience a high degree of social stigma. Not infrequently, they are the sole wage earners in their families. Despite being somewhat older and having more formal education than the average *maquila* worker of Mexico or Central America (see Frederickson, below), Shaw finds that these young Sri Lankan women have few other options to earn a living.

In 'Historical Consciousness and Collective Action: Finding Women's Resistance Where North Meets South', Mary E. Frederickson compares the exploitation of women workers in the textile industries of the southern states of the United States during the late 19th and early 20th centuries, with 21st century struggles of women workers in the *maquiladoras* south of the U.S.-Mexico border, and other regions of the Global South, including Haiti and China. She compares conditions of work and strategies of resistance, emphasizing the 'human costs of industrialization and globalization' for low-income workers. In all instances, 'across place and time', and especially during periods of economic crisis, she finds that women and children have been subjected to exploitative conditions both at home and in the workplace. Capital mobility and the dispersal of production in the era of globalization have necessitated new forms of resistance that cross national boundaries. Just as earlier generations of women workers in the U.S. South collaborated with feminist activists and labor organizations, transnational feminist organizations, NGOs and human and labor rights' organizations play key roles in contemporary struggles against women's oppression.

Collective resistance to exploitative practices in agribusiness—that is, in capitalist agricultural production for export and profit—is the subject of 'Waves of Resistance in the Colombian Flower Industry'. Here, Olga Sanmiguel-Valderrama analyzes the collective resistance of women workers in the lowest ranks of the Colombian fresh-cut flower industry (CFI), who face precarious conditions of work, and the lack of enforcement of their legal rights to health insurance, pensions, family subsidies and unionization. They confront an industry that is increasingly self-regulated and thus has negligible official, independent oversight to protect workers. Moreover, the industry undermines workers' efforts to unionize in defense of their rights and gain international support, by creating company-managed 'codes of conduct' and associations and by promulgating globally, a false image of its practices through non-independent certification. In spite of having to struggle against legal and political forces in order to defend their rights to dignified work, women workers in the CFI have recently succeeded in creating independent unions that are supported by, and integrated into, national and transnational associations of workers, communities, and NGOs.

The resistance processes in the CFI are representative of the developing convergence of New Social Movements (NSMs) and the labor struggle. Sanmiguel-Valderrama finds that the plight of women workers and local labor struggles in the CFI have become globalized as the result of two main factors: the nature of the resistance strategies themselves, which are necessarily transnational and diverse in response to the industry's use of diverse tactics to undermine workers; and the globally dispersed nature of the support networks. Sanmiguel-Valderrama emphasizes that transformation of the 'dynamics of racialized and feminized labour practices in the CFI' will require deployment of diverse, 'interlocking and interconnected strategies' that not only challenge the class-based discrimination and exploitation of capital-labour relations, but also challenge racism and patriarchy in intersectional terms.

Alternative Trade Associations and Women's Resistance

Alternative trade organizations, which have arisen in a number of countries throughout the global South, have been organized by nongovernmental organizations (NGOs) and sometimes by neighborhoods associations, as a means to create a livelihood for those who no longer work the land, and have virtually no other means of earning a living. Two chapters focus on the trade organizations that women have created to survive. In 'Free Trade, Alternative Trade and Women in Peru: A First Look', Jane Henrici examines relationships between gender and trade, the role of NGOs in the creation of alternative trade organizations (ATOs), and the impact of trade regulations and 'free trade' agreements on the lives and livelihoods of women working in ATOs, especially in the production of handicrafts, in Lima and the southern highlands of Peru. Henrici emphasizes the importance of taking into account the diversity in women's identities and the ways in which transnational processes like trade often fail to challenge existing and longstanding inequalities based on gender, 'race' and ethnicity. Furthermore, although ATOs may provide a limited source of income for poor women, many of these organizations and the processes associated with them, also serve to reinforce and maintain inequalities, and therefore may be only a bandaid solution to poverty.

In contrast, Margaret A. McLaren's chapter, 'Women's Rights and Collective Resistance: The Success Story of Marketplace India', uses the example of an umbrella organization, Marketplace/SHARE, which is made up of 13 cooperatives with its origins in Mumbai, India, to highlight the importance of economic empowerment. As a framework for her study, McLaren analyzes debates regarding women's rights, and maintains that all too often, economic rights are ignored in the struggle to obtain political and legal rights. Through the use of feminist methodologies that give voice to women's experiences, she demonstrates that meaningful employment and social and educational programs provided by the mechanism of a cooperative movement, offer rural women a degree of real economic independence. The programs include the production and marketing of traditional artisan goods, job training, and social action. The social action program in particular, encourages solidarity and leadership among the members of each coop as they tackle local issues and problems. McLaren demonstrates that Marketplace/SHARE not only provides women with an opportunity to expand their options and support themselves, each other and their communities through the collective efforts of their membership, but also the cooperatives engender confidence to challenge the policies and practices of local and national governments and bring about social change that improves the quality of life.

Responses to Poverty: Women's and Children's Resistance

All of the neoliberal policies that characterize economic globalization have served to produce high unemployment and underemployment, heightening the vulnerability of low-income families to poverty, food insecurity, violence and ill health. The impact of these pressures on families and communities has been tremendous. As families increasingly find themselves without any source of livelihood or are drawn into super-exploitative labor conditions, they are compelled to resist. The chapters in this final section explain how poverty is exacerbated and perpetuated, in particular, by the privatization of vital services on women and their families, and how women and children are collectively responding to poverty.

We begin this section with Jeanine Anderson's chapter, 'Urban Poverty Reborn: A Gender and Generational Analysis'. Anderson sets the stage with her longitudinal study of a poor neighborhood in Lima, Peru, by challenging theories regarding the intergenerational transmission of poverty. In particular, she debunks the 'blaming the victim' ideology implied in many theories of poverty, and delineates the social and economic mechanisms that help explain the persistence of poverty and inequality in Latin American cities. She identifies critical points in young people's transition to adulthood and notes that the absence of opportunities to create a life different from the one their parents experienced, condemns youth in Peruvian shantytowns, especially young women, to a life of poverty. She emphasizes the structural and historical components of poverty. These include institutional arrangements and social and economic policies in a 'new economy' that is characterized by privatization of services, trade liberalization, flexible labor, the demise of trade unions, insecure employment, and extremely low wages.

Privatization of the state sector and of publicly owned resources and services like water, electricity, education, and health care has occurred at a rapid pace throughout the global South. In addition to causing almost immediate, widespread unemployment, privatization also has the effect of impoverishing and marginalizing whole sectors of a society, as already demonstrated in previous chapters. Argentina is no exception. In spite of the fact that Argentina had, at one time, a strong national private industrial sector, competition with foreign industries under the new terms of trade enforced by the WTO and trade agreements, and by IMF structural adjustment policies promoting foreign investment, has prompted many Argentine industrialists to declare bankruptcy and has led to what appear to be 'permanent' lay-offs of thousands of workers. As a result, and in the absence of social policies or a 'safety net' for the unemployed, whole communities have plunged into poverty.

In 'Challenging Traditional Female Roles through Social Participation: Tensions in Women's Experiences in Argentina's Picketing Movements', Ada Freytes Frey and Karina Crivelli investigate the role of women in four of Argentina's picketing movements which were organized throughout the country and especially in the neighborhoods surrounding Buenos Aires in order to contest the neoliberal social and labor policies of the government and international institutions. The authors track the changes in the movements over time, focusing on the ways in which attitudes about appropriate gender roles had begun to unravel especially at the local and neighborhood levels as a result of women's involvement in these movements. They note that while women constituted the majority of participants in the movements, few were in leadership roles at regional or national levels.

As the movements started to demobilize and downsize in 2004, women increasingly turned to micro-enterprises, including the production of artisan goods, and participated in 'micro-projects' like housing and sanitation. These initiatives constituted important sources of income for women, and this often led to conflicts between men and women regarding 'appropriate' gender roles. Freytes Frey and Crivelli note that while many women (and men) left the movements, some women continued to participate. As a result, domestic conflicts–especially the problem of domestic violence–have been drawn out of the 'private' sphere of the home, into the sphere of 'public' exchange in the 'women's spaces' of neighborhood meetings and workshops. In this way, women collectively 'de-naturalize' gender roles and the violence they experience in their relationships. They also provide medical, legal and emotional support for other women who have been abused, and they confront and sanction their abusers. The authors thus highlight the importance of 'women's spaces' for providing women with a sense of collective identity and solidarity to resist the structural violence of political economic policies, on the one hand, and the 'everyday' violence of patriarchy with which they are confronted at home, on the other.

In 'The Feminization of Poverty in Post-Apartheid South Africa: A Story Told by the Women of Bayview, Chatsworth', Saranel Benjamin-Lebert examines the impact of neoliberalism on women in post-apartheid South Africa, where the privatization of water, electricity and health care, has further impoverished many already poor families. She demonstrates how the burden of poverty is borne by women. She discusses the impact of the structural violence of the State's neoliberal policies on the everyday lives and livelihoods of women and their families, coupled with domestic violence or the violence of patriarchal domination, that women confront within their homes. Together, these two levels of violence–from the 'public sphere' and the 'private sphere'–represent violence not only to the physical bodies of women, but also to their psyches and spirits. Using ethnographic and feminist methodologies, Benjamin-Lebert works alongside the poor women in one township where they have organized a residents' association to provide each other with physical and emotional support. Through their struggle, the women of Bayview, Chatsworth have, to some extent, been able to resist the privatization of basic services and resources, and collectively organize against being evicted from their homes. Their struggle has been supported by, and has provided inspiration to, other communities and organizations throughout the country, to stand up and resist the forces of global capitalist penetration. And, in the process of collectively fighting for survival, they have also transformed their sense of themselves from victims of abuse to agents of social change.

As many of the contributors to this volume have demonstrated, the most vulnerable in society are those generally targeted for exploitation–women, low-income families, immigrants, racialized communities, and as the last chapter documents, children. In 'Global Capitalist Penetration, Child Labor and Children's Collective Resistance in Defense of Their Rights', Erica G. Polakoff analyzes the relationship between global capitalist penetration, poverty, and the exploitation of child labor in the global North and South. In spite of international covenants and domestic laws that have been written to protect the rights of children, she demonstrates that global (and local) economic forces have made it necessary for many families to rely on the labor contributions of their children for survival. Children work everywhere–in agriculture, manufacturing, construction, domestic service, on the streets and in the commercial sex trade. Girls and young women are particularly exploited. Not unlike the child laborers exploited during the industrial revolution in Europe and the United States (see: Frederickson in this volume), children of the 'fourth world'–the marginalized and impoverished communities throughout the world today–labor in unsafe, unhealthy and dehumanizing environments that not only provide very little in terms of wages or benefits but also diminish their future opportunities for education and development.

Thus, contemporary capitalism has expanded not only through space, but also through time 'penetrating' the futures of families, communities and nations globally. But at least since the late 1970s and early 1980s, children have been mobilizing to fight against the forces that seek to subdue and exploit them. Polakoff provides contemporary examples of children organizing children, of children educating children, of children challenging the dominant stereotypes, ideologies and images of children as defenseless or naïve, by creating their own images of themselves. Children are also collectively petitioning their governments and the international community in defense of their rights as citizens and in support of a different kind of 'globalization' or global economy–one characterized by social justice, humanitarian values and peace.

While the themes addressed in this volume are neither exhaustive of the problems, nor representative of the range of solutions to global capitalist penetration, the authors of the chapters featured here seem to share a vision of a better world where people are not forced merely to subsist in misery, but to live with dignity and respect. In the words of Salih Booker and William Minter (in Rothenberg, 2006:522), '(G)enuine globalization requires that global democracy replace global apartheid'. Or, as feminist scholars and activists, Gita Sen and Caren Grown (1987:80-81) wrote over twenty years ago,

> We want a world where inequality based on class, gender, and race is absent from every country, and from the relationships among countries. We want a world where basic needs become basic rights and where poverty and all forms of violence are eliminated. Each person will have the opportunity to develop her or his full potential and creativity, and women's values of nurturance and solidarity will characterize human relationships...What is lacking is not resources, but political will. But in a world and in countries riven with differences of economic interest and political power, we cannot expect political will for systemic change to emerge voluntarily among those in power. It must be fostered by mass movements that give central focus to the 'basic rights' of the poor, and demand a reorientation of policies, programmes and projects toward that end.

We hope that the chapters in this book provide a forum for discussion and debate, and an opportunity to learn from the experiences of those who are collectively resisting exploitation and dehumanization, in their efforts to create a sustainable life for themselves and their families, and a just and peaceful world for all.

REFERENCES

Alexander, M.J. and Mohanty, C.T. (eds.) (1997) *Feminist Geneologies, Colonial Legacies and Democratic Futures.* NY: Routledge.

Aptheker, B. (1989) *Tapestries of Life: Women's Work, Women's Consciousness and the Meaning of Daily Experience.* Amherst: The University of Massachusetts Press.

Bass, N. (2002) 'Implications of the TRIPS Agreement for Developing Countries: Pharmaceutical Patent Laws in Brazil and South Africa in the 21st Century'. *George Washington International Law Review* 34: 191.

Benholdt-Thomsen, V., Faraclas, N. and Von Werlhof, C. (eds.) (2001) *There is an Alternative: Subsistence and Worldwide Resistance to Corporate Globalization.* London/New York: Zed Books.

Booker, S. and Minter, W. (2001) 'Global Apartheid: AIDS and Murder by Patent'. *The Nation*, 1 July 2001.

Castells, M. (1997) *The Power of Identity (The Information Age: Economy, Society and Culture*, Volume II*)*. Oxford: Blackwell Publishers.

Chomsky, N. (1998) 'Notes on NAFTA: The Masters of Mankind', in C. Bowden, *Juarez: The Laboratory of Our Future*. New York: Aperture.

Chossudovsky, M. (2003) *The Globalization of Poverty and the New World Order.* 2nd ed. Ontario, Canada: Global Outlook.

Crenshaw, K.W. (1994) 'Mapping the Margins: Intersectionality, Identity Politics and Violence Against Women of Color', pp. 93-118, in M.A. Fineman and R. Mykitiuk, *The Public Nature of Private Violence: The Discovery of Domestic Abuse.* NY: Routledge.

Étienne, M. and Leacock, E.B. (eds.) (1980) *Women and Colonization: Anthropological Perspectives.* NY: Praeger.

Farmer, P.E., Nizeye, B., Stulac, S. and Keshavjee, S. (2006) 'Structural Violence and Clinical Medicine'. *PLoS Medicine* 3(10): e449. Accessed 4 July 2010 from www.ncbi.nlm.nih.gov/pmc/articles/PMC1621099.

Farmer, P.E. (2003) *Pathologies of Power: Health, Human Rights and the New War on the Poor.* Berkeley: University of California Press.

Franco, J. (1998) 'Defrocking the Vatican: Feminism's Secular Project', in S.E Alvarez, E. Dagnino, and A. Escobar (eds) *Cultures of Politics, Politics of Cultures: Re-visioning Latin American Social Movements,* pp. 278-289. Boulder, CO: Westview Press.

Galeano, E. (1991) *The Book of Embraces.* New York: Norton.

Galeano, E. (1997) *Open Veins of Latin America.* NY: Monthly Review Press.

Ho, K. (2007) 'Structural Violence as a Human Rights Violation'. *Essex Human Rights Review* 4(2): 1-17. Accessed 25 June 2010 from http://projects. essex.ac.uk/ehrr/v4n2/ho.pdf.

Galtung, J. (1990). 'Cultural Violence'. *Journal of Peace Research* 27(3):291-305.

Greene, F. (1971) 'How It Began', excerpted from *The Enemy.* NY: Random House. Reprinted in P.S. Rothenberg (2006) *Beyond Borders: Thinking Critically About Global Issues,* pp. 88-97. NY: Worth Publishers.

International Forum on Globalization (IFG) (2002) *Alternatives to Economic Globalization.* San Francisco: Berrett-Koehler.

Jawara, F. and Kwa, A. (2004) *Behind the Scenes at the WTO: The Real World of International Trade Negotiations/The Lessons of*

Cancun. London: Zed Books.
Joseph, S. (2003) 'Pharmaceutical Corporations and Access to Drugs: The "Fourth Wave" of Corporate Rights Scrutiny'. *Human Rights Quarterly* 25:425-452.
Kloby, J. (2004) 'The Legacy of Colonialism' excerpted from *Inequality, Power and Development*. Amherst, NY: Humanity Books. Reprinted in P.S. Rothenberg (2006) *Beyond Borders: Thinking Critically About Global Issues,* pp. 99-106. NY: Worth Publishers.
Lavie, S. and Swedenburg, T. (eds.) (1996) *Displacement, Diaspora and Geographies of Identity*. NC: Duke University Press.
Lerner, G. (1986) *The Creation of Patriarchy.* Oxford: The University of Oxford Press. Reprinted in P.S. Rothenberg (2005) *Beyond Borders: Thinking Critically About Global Issues*, pp. 253-255. New York: Worth Publishers.
Memmi, A. (1968) 'Attempt at a Definition', from *Dominated Man.* NY: Penguin. Reproduced in P.S. Rothenberg (2006) *Beyond Borders: Thinking Critically About Global Issues*, pp. 173-179. NY: Worth Publishers.
Mies, M. (1987) 'Woman, Nature and the International Division of Labour': Maria Mies interviewed by Ariel Salleh in V. Benholdt-Thomsen, N. Faraclas, and C. Von Werlhof. *There is an Alternative: Subsistence and Worldwide Resistance to Corporate Globalization*, pp. 3-14. London: Zed Books.
Mies, M. (1986) *Patriarchy and Accumulation on a World Scale: Women in the International Divison of Labour.* London: Zed Books.
Mintz, S.W. (1989) *Caribbean Transformations.* NY: Columbia University Press.
Naples, N.A. (2002) 'Changing the Terms: Community Activism, Globalization, and the Dilemmas of Transnational Feminist Praxis', in N.A. Naples and M. Desai (eds) *Women's Activism and Globalization: Linking Local Struggles and Transnational Politics.* London: Routledge.
Navarro, S.A. (2002) 'Las Mujeres Invisibles/The Invisible Women', in N.A. Naples and M. Desai (eds) *Women's Activism and Globalization: Linking Local Struggles and Transnational Politics.* London: Routledge.
Piven, F.F. and Coward, R. (1998) 'Eras of Power'. *Monthly Review,* January.
Rosa, K. (1994) 'The Conditions and Organizational Activities of Women in Free Trade Zones: Malaysia, Philippines and Sri

Lanka, 1970-1990', in S. Rowbotham and S. Mitter (eds.) *Dignity and Daily Bread: New Forms of Economic Organizing Among Poor Women in the Third World and the First.* London: Routledge.

Rothenberg, P.S. (2006) *Beyond Borders: Thinking Critically About Global Issues.* New York: Worth Publishers.

Rowbotham, S. and Mitter, S. (eds.) (1994) *Dignity and Daily Bread: New Forms of Economic Organizing Among Poor Women in the Third World and the First.* London: Routledge.

Sen, G. and Grown, C. (1987) *Development, Crises and Alternative Visions: Third World Women's Perspectives.* NY: Monthly Review Press.

Shiva, V. (2000) *Stolen Harvest: The Hijacking of the Global Food Supply.* Cambridge: South End Press.

Wade, R. (2003) 'What Strategies Are Viable for Developing Countries Today? The World Trade Organization and the Shrinking of "Development Space".' *Review of International Political Economy* 10(4):621-644.

Wichterich, C. (1998) *The Globalized Woman.* London: Zed Books.

Wolf, E.R. (1997) *Europe and the People Without History.* Berkeley, CA: The University of California Press.

World Health Organization (WHO). (1997) 'Violence Against Women'. Reproduced in P.S. Rothenberg (2006) *Beyond Borders: Thinking Critically About Global Issues*, pp. 278-287. NY: Worth Publishers.

NOTES

[1] According to the WTO's website, as of July 2008, there are 153 member nations. Accessed 27 June 2010 from www.wto.org/english/thewto_e/whatis_e/tif_e/org6_e.htm.

[2] See for example, the pharmaceutical industry's ('Big Pharma's) use of the WTO to file suit against the governments of South Africa and Brazil for violating patent laws by purchasing generic drugs for the treatment of HIV/AIDS (Bass, 2002; Booker and Minter, 2001; Joseph, 2003).

[3] For examples of the enduring impacts of colonialism that is, the legacies of colonialism in specific regions of the world, see: Wolf (1997); Greene (in Rothenberg, 2006); Kloby (in Rothenberg, 2006).

[4] See Eric Wolf (1997)'s *Europe and the People Without History,* for examples of how Europe's increasing demand for furs served

to undermine the subsistence economy of the 'original' peoples of North America; see Galeano's *Open Veins of Latin America*, for examples of how the European demand for silver produced great wealth for the Spanish but destroyed indigenous systems of land use in Peru and Bolivia; see Wolf (Ibid) and Sidney W. Mintz's (1989) *Caribbean Transformations*, about how the slave trade and the establishment of plantation agriculture undermined indigenous communities and effectively destroyed their patterns of subsistence; see Jaimes Guerrero (in Alexander and Mohanty, 1997) for the devastating impact of displacement on Native peoples in the United States, through policies of privatization and relocation.

5   And, while the 'colonized' or 'marginalized' have resisted and decentered the Center and transformed themselves, the 'Empire often strikes back', as Lavie and Swedenburg point out:

> Although racialized and gendered subjects may act out a multiplicity of fractal identities, the dominant forces still police the boundaries of binary opposition (between margin and center; self and other...). Because the Eurocenter constantly consolidates itself against the margins' assaults, it continually redeploys these binaries in an effort to contain the margins by reasserting their identity in terms of the Other. (Lavie and Swedenburg, 1996:5)

6   Unfortunately, since most of history has been told by the conquerors and colonizers, resistance by the 'vanquished' has not generally been part of the 'official story' (See Wolf, 1997).

7   Johan Galtung coined the term in the 1960s during the emergence of liberation theology and its 'preferential option for the poor'.

8   In reports written by clergy accompanying the colonial voyages to North America, the greater equality of native women, the complementarity of gender roles, and systems of matrilineal descent and matrilocality, were viewed as indications of the inferiority and primitive natures of indigenous peoples (Étienne and Leacock, 1980). Women of many of the nations or 'tribes' of North America were valued especially for their roles as negotiators between communities; they also made decisions about who should be chief and about cycles of planting and the production and distribution of food. Oral histories regarding traditions and practices among those who managed to survive the conquest and

colonization provide additional evidence for women's greater equality in pre-colonial North America. Étienne and Leacock also note that the ideology of male dominance was imposed upon many indigenous peoples by Europeans and resulted in the greater subordination of women. Thus, patriarchy existed before capitalism in Europe and was transferred to and superimposed upon the colonial territories, evolving into one of the legacies of colonialism.

[9] Fundamentalist and conservative religions in particular, are virulently anti-woman. It should come as no surprise then, that an alliance of sorts has been forged between the anti-feminist ideologies of neoliberalism and the sexist and misogynist, heterosexist and homophobic ideologies of fundamentalist and conservative religions (Franco, 1998).

[10] 'Resist', according to Merriam-Webster's Dictionary (2006) is derived from the Latin 'to take a stand'. To resist is 'to exert force in opposition; to exert oneself to counteract or defeat; to withstand the force or effect of' (Merriam Webster Dictionary, 2006). Accessed 17 June 2010 from www.merriam-webster.com/dictionary/resist. 'Resistance' is 'the power or capacity to resist; the inherent ability of an organism to resist harmful influences (as disease, toxic agents, or infection); the capacity of a species…to survive exposure to a toxic agent…formerly effective against it' (Merriam-Webster Dictionary, 2006). Accessed 17 June 2010) from www. merriam-webster.com/dictionary/resistance.

PART I

Neoliberal Policies, Migration
and Women's Resistance

CHAPTER 1

Neoliberal Globalization in the Philippines
Its Impact on Filipino Women and Their Forms of Resistance

Ligaya Lindio-McGovern
Indiana University Kokomo

ABSTRACT

In this chapter I argue that neoliberal globalization is not a neutral process. It is gendered and has exacerbated pre-existing inequalities. This has made globalization therefore a contentious process. An examination of the Philippine experience shows that neoliberal policies have exacerbated poverty especially within already marginalized communities, and especially among women, while benefiting transnational capital and wealthier nations. Consequently, neoliberal globalization has engendered conflict and resistance both on the home front and across national borders. The politics of GABRIELA, the militant women's movement organization in the Philippines, and Migrante International, a coalition of Filipino migrant organizations overseas, are examined. Both organizations challenge neoliberal globalization in the Philippines. The nation-state is implicated in the implementation of neoliberal policies and in the politics of resistance. In the former, the state plays an instrumentalist role; in the latter, the state is a target for transformation and is called upon to take the side of those who are harmed by globalization.

Keywords: Filipino women, globalization, resistance, neoliberal policies, Philippines, Philippine women's movement, Filipino overseas migration.

Introduction

Globalization is not a neutral process: it is gendered and classed, exacerbating inequalities in the global political economy (Lindio-McGovern and Wallimann, 2009). It hurts the poor, especially poor women in the Third World. Mary John Mananzan (1999:2), a Filipina feminist scholar, defines globalization as: 'the integration of the economies of the whole world into the liberal capitalist market economy controlled by the Group of Seven'. This definition recognizes the controlling power of advanced capitalist countries comprising the

G-7 (Japan, the USA, France, Germany, Great Britain, Canada, Italy) in the creation of policies that ensure the survival of monopoly capitalism. The process requires maintaining the 'transnational elite' (Robinson, 1996:33) which is also referred to as the 'transnational capitalist class' (Sklair, 2001);[1] it requires an abundant source of cheap labor, thus creating a highly stratified global political economy, with Third World women largely at the bottom of the hierarchy. The World Trade Organization (WTO), the International Monetary Fund (IMF), and transnational corporations–whose policies and practices serve the interests of monopoly capital–are the major propellers of neoliberal globalization.

The Philippines provides a good case to examine the contentious process of neoliberal globalization. Neoliberal globalization in the Philippines is characterized by interlocking features, each having a detrimental impact on women. These include policies that promote: (a) economic liberalization, (b) deregulation, (c) privatization, (d) finance capital investment, (e) labor flexibilization, and (f) labor export. Based on my ongoing research on globalization and resistance in the Philippines, I first analyze the negative impact of key features of globalization on women in the Philippines. Then I examine the strategies that GABRIELA (the above-ground Philippine militant women's movement organization) and Migrante International (the militant international alliance of Filipino migrant organizations in different parts of the world) use to resist neoliberal policies.

Main Features of Globalization in the Philippines

Economic Liberalization

Economic liberalization attempts to create a relatively borderless economy through the dismantling of controls on the flow of goods, services and capital, allowing less restricted entry of foreign investments. Although seemingly neutral, this process has a devastating impact on Third World countries' economies as 'powerful countries [push] for 'free trade' while engaging in extreme protectionism' (IBON Facts & Figures, 2004a:3). The General Agreement on Tariffs and Trade (GATT) under the WTO enshrined the fundamental principle that export goods should freely enter into the importing country based on the premise that free trade would benefit equally all WTO member countries. To the contrary, what has happened can be best described as 'unfair trade'. For instance, while annual global trade had reached US$7 trillion in 1999, the total exports of developing countries represented only 28 percent, while the share of the least developed countries was 0.5 percent; North America and EU had the largest share of world trade in goods and commercial services (del Rosario-Malonzo, 2001:2).

In the Philippine case, economic liberalization has reduced protective tariffs and trade restrictions, giving free-play to the market. For example, the average tariff was reduced from 43 percent in 1980 to 28 percent in 1986, and restrictions on more than 900 items between 1981 and 1985 were lifted (Bello, 2004:16). Importation of goods from other countries has been less restricted, so that the percentage of goods under import restrictions has been progressively reduced from 34 percent in 1985 to 17 percent in 1986 and 8 percent in 1989 (Yoshihara, 1994). This progressive loosening of import restrictions has led to an inundation of the market with imported goods, contributing to export stagnation and a widening of the trade deficit by 307 percent as of 2003 (Guzman, 2004:12), and as of 2008, net exports "have been chronically negative as 90% of components depend largely on imported materials" (Balangue, 2008:9). In 2007, there was a negative trade balance of US$5 billion (US$50.2 billion in exports; $55.3 billion in imports).

Import liberalization is justified by the notion that this is good because consumers will have multiple choices and the ensuing competition will reduce prices. But flooding the market with imported goods destroys local industries and livelihoods, resulting in increased poverty and unemployment.[2] The reduced rate of protection for manufacturing (from 44 percent to 20 percent within a period of two decades) has resulted in bankruptcies of local industries as locally produced goods suffer from unfair competition by cheap imports. Among the industries severely affected were 'paper products, textiles, ceramics, rubber products, furniture and fixtures, petrochemicals, beverage, wood, shoes, petroleum oils, clothing accessories, and leather goods' (Bello, 2004:25). Of these, the textile industry suffered the biggest blow: it 'shrank from 200 firms in the 1970s to less than 10' (Bello, 2004:25). It can be argued that the shrinking of local industries contributes to the massive displacement of workers (IBON, 2006a). Rosario Bella Guzman (2004:14) says: 'Every day for the past four years, eight establishments retrench their workers or close down due to economic liberalization: 196 workers are being displaced every day as a result'. The Philippine Department of Labor and Employment reported that a total of 287, 556 workers were displaced within a period of four years (2000-2003).[3] In January 2006, the number of Filipinos unable to find work increased by 15 percent from the previous year, bringing the number to 2.8 million from 2.5 million in 2005 (IBON, 2006b). Sony Africa (2010:1) writes:

> The period 2001-2009 is the longest period of high unemployment in the country's history with the true unemployment rate averaging 11.2% (correcting for the government's not counting millions of jobless Filipinos as unemployed since 2005). The number of jobless and underemployed Filipinos grew to 11.4 million in January 2010 which is 3.1 million more than in January 2001, when Pres. Arroyo came to power. The 4.3 million jobless Filipinos as of last January [2010] is an increase of 730,000 from nine years ago...

Philippine agriculture also suffered from the implementation of the WTO's Agreement of Agriculture (AoA). Although world trade increased by 25 percent, Philippine products' access to the world market was restricted, resulting in accumulated trade deficits of $5.2 billion since 1995. Since the WTO regime, the agricultural share of the Philippine GDP (gross domestic product) has been declining: down to 18 percent in 2002, to 18.1% in 2009 from 28 percent in the pre-WTO regime. This decline in agricultural productivity coupled with unrestricted imports has contributed to the decline in agricultural jobs (since 1994 when the Philippine government signed the WTO), devastating farmers' livelihoods. In 2000 alone, approximately two million jobs were lost (del Rosario-Malonzo, 2004a:9).

The less restricted entry of agricultural products creates import dependency for basic needs and ultimately results in food insecurity. Under the WTO's AoA, the Philippines is required to allow the progressive importation of rice (1 percent of domestic consumption in 1995, 2 percent in 2000, and 4 percent by 2004) and the tariffication of rice was required to start in July 2005 (del Rosario-Malonzo, 2004b:4). This has partly, if not significantly, contributed to the Philippines becoming a net importer of rice from formerly being the largest rice exporter in Asia. For example, data from the Bureau of Agricultural Statistics show that from 1995-2001, rice imports were greater than rice exports (del Rosario-Malonzo, 2004b: 4). And in 2002 alone, rice importation reached roughly 1.25 million metric tons, which was higher than the previous year's total of 808,250 metric tons (del Rosario-Malonzo, 2004b:4). From 2003-2006, there was no exportation of rice, only importation with a total trade imbalance of 5,425,000 metric tons (Bureau of Agricultural Statistics, cited in Balangue, 2008:4). The unrestricted importation of cheaper rice did not result in lowering the price of rice since rice traders continued to sell it at higher prices in order to maximize their profit (del Rosario-Malonzo, 2004b:5). The result was food insecurity that threatened the majority of Filipinos' access to their staple food, and increased the vulnerability of those with special nutritional needs such as low-income pregnant women and children. This is another manifestation of how an unregulated market serves the interests of capital, that is, of transnational corporations and richer foreign nations that are able to control the local market, forcing local production and local entrepreneurs, especially those engaged in small-scale industries, out of the market. Thus, economic liberalization has entrenched foreign control of the Philippine economy–a process that was initiated during colonialism and that has continued in the neocolonial or post-colonial period.[4]

Deregulation

Deregulation goes hand in hand with liberalization and limits the state's role in regulating the economy in the interest of its people and national sovereignty. It gives free reign to market forces in the organization of economic activities placing the highest value on profit, sacrificing consumer and labor rights, as well as social and political rights. In the Philippine context, however, the nation-state becomes what William Robinson (1996:36) calls the 'neoliberal state', which, in this case, I would call the peripheral neoliberal state since it becomes instrumental to neoliberal policies largely controlled by core countries.

Deregulation lifts price control systems and thereby most intensely hurts the poor, especially women. For instance, in June 2001, the prices of basic commodities in the Philippines had increased by 6.7 percent from 2.6 percent in the early part of the previous year (Guzman, 2001:10). The same pattern is seen in December 2007 to June 2008, with a 17.4 % food inflation and prices of all major food types steeply increasing, with the price of rice and corn showing the most dramatic increase (Balangue, 2008, citing Philippine National Statistics Office). Deregulation has also led to the overpricing of oil resulting in the increase, not only of transportation services and electricity, but also of the price of many other commodities. During the year 2000, for example, oil companies in the Philippines increased their prices six times, with a PhP 2.58 per liter overprice (Guzman, 2001:11). Pilipinas Shell, Caltex Philippines, and Petron Corporation, known as the Big Three of the local oil industry, have garnered profits in billions of pesos, a sum of PhP 6.8 billion for the three companies in 2002 (Padilla, 2004:6). During the year 2008, from January to July, gasoline and petroleum prices increased more steeply than in any other period since the domestic oil industry was deregulated in 1996; the price of unleaded gasoline, diesel and kerosene increased by as much as P16 per liter. At the same time, we find that poor Filipino women, who generally are the ones to attend to the daily needs of the family, are the first to suffer the social psychological impact of the price escalation of food and of other basic daily needs for their families (Lindio-McGovern, 1997).

Privatization

Privatization is at the core of IMF/World Bank structural adjustment policies. Consistent with, and reinforced by, trade liberalization and market deregulation, privatization puts all productive activities, including social services, into the private sector or private capital. It eliminates public subsidies on social services and public sector corporations as they get sold off to the private sector.

In the Philippines, privatization facilitates the penetration of foreign capital into sectors of the economy that might have been under state control or under the control of local entrepreneurs and communities (Bello, 2004:192-193). This process entrenches foreign control of the local political economy, especially by transnational corporations. Thus, privatization opens new frontiers for the expansion of capital and profit-making on a global scale, while further minimizing poor people's access to basic social services.

In the Philippines, the privatization of health care, which has been carried out in compliance with the dictates of the IMF's structural adjustment program, is slowly but surely killing the poor, especially women and children. The current government's Health Sector Reform Agenda and Executive Order 102 have diminished the role of the state in the provision of health care services (HEAD, 2001:2). Consequently, 38 public hospitals intend to privatize by 2010 (HEAD:9). The privatization of health care will deny affordable and accessible basic health services to the poor, estimated by IBON Databank Foundation to comprise 88 percent of the Philippine population (Roque, 2005). Increasingly, the government has decreased its budget allocation for government hospitals where the poor go. For example, from 1999–2001 there has been an accumulated decrease in the hospital budget for 10 government hospitals in Metro-Manila amounting to more than PhP 307 million (HEAD, 2001:21). From 2001-2009 the government, under the Macapagal-Arroyo administration, budgeted only 1.8% to health, lower than in the previous administrations (Africa, 2010). The Philippine Constitution requires that 5 percent of the GNP be allocated for health care services, but in a span of 15 years, the GNP allocation averaged less than 1 percent (0.6 percent). Ultimately, the main beneficiaries of health care privatization will be the transnational pharmaceutical corporations,[5] while poor women and children–who have special health care needs due to changes in their life cycles–will be most detrimentally affected. Furthermore, the privatization of health care reinforces the IMF's structural adjustment policies on Philippine political economy as it opens new areas for capitalist penetration. The IMF also benefits from interest paid on its loans that comes, in part, from cuts in government spending on social services, thus making those services less accessible to poor women, men and children.

Another sector that increasingly is being privatized is water. The privatization of water has serious consequences for the poor, especially since it is vital for survival. As the price of water increases, poor families' access to water could be limited, risking their survival. The privatization of state-owned water utilities was one of the loan conditionalities in the 1995–1997 structural adjustment policies of the IMF (Bello, 2004:197). This led to the much-contested privatization of the Metropolitan Waterworks and Sewerage System (MWSS), the oldest state-owned utility in the Philippines. Foreign companies, such as Bechtel, Northwest Water, Lyonnaise des Eaux (a French transnational giant) also got a share in the water privatization scheme along with the local business concessionaires (Bello 2004:200). Instead of water being a communal/public commodity accessible to every citizen, the privatization of water makes profit the central concern. Thus, contrary to the government's promise that privatization would lower the cost of water, the opposite occurred. For example, between 1997-2004, on average, water rates in Metro-Manila and the surrounding areas drastically increased 226 percent per cubic meter for Maynilad and 350 percent per cubic meter for Manila Water (IBON, 2004b:6). This increase added a significant financial burden to low-income families who were already struggling to meet their basic needs. Women, especially poor women, who still perform most of the reproductive labor, have felt the brunt of water privatization. Meanwhile, private business and transnational corporations are making a profit from a basic service that should be under community control and equitably accessible to everyone. Thus, privatization, the prime engine of capital accumulation on a global scale that continually seeks new spheres for profit, is reinforced.

Finance Capitalism

According to Tony Porter (2005:4), finance can be defined as 'the process by which savings are transferred from one entity to another for a period of time in exchange for a payment'. In this process of exchange, money is viewed more in terms of 'its use in facilitating payments and measuring value'. Finance capitalism is making profit out of this financial exchange.

Some analysts argue that one of the crises of monopoly capitalism is manifested in 'the crisis of over-production' (Sison, 2005), which means that transnational corporations have to seek other spheres from which to make a profit besides investing in the production of commodities deemed no longer profitable. The crisis of over-production is partly created by the depression of wages that consequently contracts the market. While advances in technology have allowed transnational corporations to increase production of goods, they are producing more than the world's consumers can buy (Villegas, 2000:72). Finance capitalism, making profit out of money, then becomes central to neoliberal globalization to deal with the crisis of over-production, which is its own creation. As a result, finance capitalism gives priority to financial speculation over human needs, increasing speculative investment more than productive investments that can generate employment. Thus, while in 1976, 80 percent of all international transactions involved the buying and selling of goods and services, by 1997, only 2.5 percent of international transactions involved such transactions; 97.5 percent were for speculative investments (EILER, 2000:7-8). In the Philippines, finance capitalism is partly reflected in the progressive increase of portfolio investment. For example, portfolio investment has increased from 66 percent in 1993 to 70 percent in 1994, to 75 percent in 1995, to 86 percent in 1996. By the first quarter of 1997, portfolio investment reached 70 percent of total investment flow. Overall, 85 percent of portfolio investment is foreign–with the US taking the lead (33 percent), but having the least share of direct (productive) investment at only 6 percent (Villegas, 2000:47).

Finance capitalism also involves opening the Philippine financial and banking systems to greater foreign control. This has resulted in mergers and consolidations that have displaced thousands of male and female workers (approximately 7,000 bank workers), while the small local corporate elite and foreign investors increased their profits (Villegas, 2000:43, 46). The increased unemployment that is produced by finance capitalism further heightens the rate of poverty in the Philippines. The problem of unemployment worsens when we look at labor flexibilization.

Labor Flexibilization

Labor flexibilization can be viewed as 'the micro-economic or firm-level aspect of the ongoing economic restructuring of the world economy' (EILER, 2000:3) that goes hand in hand with macro-level liberalization, deregulation and privatization. Labor flexibilization involves work organization and employment schemes designed to maximize profit extraction (EILER, 2000:1). These schemes to maximize profit include labor-only-contracting, subcontracting, hiring of casuals and contractuals, and the hiring of apprentices. As mentioned earlier, neoliberal globalization requires an abundant and cheap labor force. Labor flexibilization partly serves that goal.

In the Philippines, labor flexibilization is used synonymously with *contractualization* or *casualization of labor*. While labor flexibilization may garner super profits for the big capitalists, it increases the exploitation of workers, poses obstacles to their militant unionization, and raises the rate of unemployment and underemployment. Due to contractualization, 60,000 regular workers lost their jobs in 1996, another 62,736 in 1997, and yet another 129,965 in 1998; an average of 4,000 workers lost their jobs daily since 1997 (Villegas, 2000:54, citing Department of Labor and Unemployment estimates). Almost 10 million Filipinos, approximately 1/3 of the entire labor force, are unemployed and actively seeking jobs (Beltran, 2001:6). The unemployment rate in the Philippines was 11 percent in 1997 (Villegas, 2000:54), 11.2% in 2009 (Africa, 2010, using National Statistics data).

With increasing unemployment, poverty also continues to rise. Even when measured by the low official poverty line (based on P42 per person per day), the number of poor families increased by 530, 642, or 13% since 2000, climbing to 4.7 million in 2006 (Africa, 2010). Between 2000 and 2006 there was a 2.1 million increase in the number of poor Filipinos, bringing it to 27.6 million in 2006 (Ibid). When measured with a higher threshold of P86 per person per day the number of Filipinos classified as poor doubles (Ibid). While the numbers of poor peole are growing, the 20 richest Filipinos continue to amass wealth; their net worth of P801 billion (US$15.6 billion) in 2006, for example, was equivalent to the combined income of the poorest 10.4 million Filipino families in the same year.

Even greater trends of labor contractualization are likely to be found in foreign-owned or affiliated firms and those that are export-oriented. For instance, LAWS Textile, which exports shirts mainly to the US with JC Penny as one of its major clients, has 1,700 contractuals who are contracted for just three months at a time, but only 390 regular workers. In Export Processing Zones (EPZs) or Special Economic Zones (SEZs), subcontracting and contractualization are mechanisms that transnational corporations use to maximize profits. For example, major international brands like Reebok, Adidas, Timex, Calvin Klein, Fujitsu, and Intel, have a large share of their workforce subcontracted as contractuals, the majority of whom are women and youth, forced to work overtime hours, six to seven days a week, for a period of three to four months at a time (EILER, 2000:25-26).

Contractualization also happens in the service sector where the majority of the labor force is women. In the retail trade, a notorious example is ShoeMart, the biggest department store chain in the Philippines. Of its estimated 20,000 employees, 85 percent of whom are women, only 1,731 (or 8.7 percent) are regular workers, while the rest are subcontracted through recruitment agencies as temporary workers for less than five months at a time (EILER, 2000:26).

Labor flexibilization could partly explain why the minimum daily wage (P367 for agriculture, P404 for non-agriculture in the capital region), even with the recent increase of P22.00 a day, remain way below the cost of the minimum daily needs of PhP 620 for an average family of six (Roque, 2005; Department of Labor and Employment). Moreover, labor flexibilization potentially undermines the collective bargaining power of workers as many casual workers without a long-term base of support are created and reproduced, that is, there is a continual turnover of workers in any one plant. Thus, neoliberal globalization increasingly uses labor flexibilization as a weapon to control workers. This supports Janet Bruin's (1999:10) argument that globalization weakens the 'bargaining position of workers everywhere'.

The economic crisis created by the interlocking consequences of the neoliberal policies of deregulation, liberalization, privatization, finance capitalism, and labor flexibilization certainly hurt most of the ordinary Filipino men and women, and thus contribute to the creation of the preconditions for economic migration on which labor export feeds.

Labor Export

Labor export is when the state facilitates overseas labor migration for temporary or contractual work. In the Philippines, labor export has become a key feature of neoliberal globalization, making the country the top labor-exporter in the world (IBON, 1998; Oishi, 2005). During the Macapagal-Arroyo government, a public statement urged that the annual deployment of overseas workers be raised to one million annually (Roque, 2005) from an average of approximately 800,000 workers (747,696 to different countries as of 1997) (IBON, 1998). This call resulted in 1.42 million deployed in 2009, with now close to 4,000 (3,898 to be exact) Filipinos emigrating for work every day (Africa, 2010, citing POEA). The period 2001-2009 has seen the most labor migration in the country's history (Africa, 2010).

Labor export is the government's strategy of dealing with its increasing foreign debt which is now P4.36 trillion (Africa, 2010, citing Bureau of Treasury) and the growing unemployment–both created to a large degree by the structural adjustment policies of the IMF and the other key features of globalization discussed above. Labor export is the leading industry in the Philippines and has become the biggest source of foreign exchange for the government's debt servicing of an annual average of more than $5 billion (Capulong, 2001: 30; Tujan, 2001:3), accounting for more than 30 percent of the government budget (Guzman, 2004:9). Labor export has led to an economic diaspora of now more than 9 million (Africa, 2010, citing Department of Foreign Affairs-Commission on Filipinos Overseas) in over 180 countries (Roque, 2005), making them most vulnerable to abuse, human rights violations, labor exploitation and control.

Labor export has produced the following patterns: (a) commodification of Filipino migrant labor as it has become a source of profit-making for the Philippine government and private employment agencies in the Philippines and in the receiving countries; (b) trafficking of women in domestic service and in the entertainment and sex trade in the richer countries; (c) creation of an exploitable and expendable cheap labor force in the receiving countries; and (d) feminization of migrant labor since increasingly it is Filipino women who comprise the majority of export labor (61 percent in 1998; 70 percent in 2000). Ultimately, women are the ones carrying the brunt of foreign debt; they are more commoditized, more trafficked, and suffer the triple oppression of gender, race/ethnicity/ nationality and class as overseas migrants.

Women in domestic service work comprise the bulk of Philippine labor export. Many of these women have college degrees and a good proportion have professional work experience as teachers and nurses. Thus, they experience downward occupational mobility in the labor-receiving countries. In a country where there is a simple literacy of 93.4% and functional literacy of 84.1% (National Statistics Office, QUICKSTAT, April 2010), this results in the brain drain from the Philippines and a waste of human capital. In other words, even though the Philippine society has invested in the human capital development of these women, their educational training is wasted or underutilized in the labor-receiving countries. In effect, these women and the Philippine nation are made to subsidize the privatization of social reproductive labor or domestic care work in the richer labor-receiving countries. To make the privatization of social reproductive labor beneficial to the labor-receiving country requires the creation of a cheap, flexible labor force. It is migrant women from poor countries who are made into the source of cheap reproductive labor.

Further, the concentration of Filipino female export labor in domestic service work reinforces labor segmentation in the host countries based on gender, race/ethnicity, and class. This consequently entrenches a transnational division of female labor where low-wage, low-prestige domestic work is generally assigned to migrant women from poorer countries while their female and male employers engage in formal labor with more prestige, better pay and better working conditions. Undocumented migrant domestic workers are in a worse situation since they are more vulnerable to severe exploitation. This reinforces the unequal transnational division of female labor. Thus, the globalization of domestic service work perpetuates the subordinate status of Filipino women in the global political economy.

In the health sector, for many years now, the Philippines has been training health workers, especially nurses, for export. Professional nurses and caregivers constituted 6.8 percent of the overseas Filipino workers deployed in 2008. Seventy percent of nursing graduates migrate for overseas work; and some big hospitals have been losing an average of 10-12 nurses a month since 2001 (Barcelona, 2010). Recently 200 hospitals have closed and 800 more are partially shut-down because of lack of health personnel (Ibid). The Philippines has become the largest supplier of nurses in the global healthcare labor market; in the USA for example, Filipino nurses constitute 76% of foreign nurse graduates (Ibid). Quoting the World Health Organization, Noel Barcelona says: "[W]hen large numbers of doctors and nurses leave, the countries that financed their education lose a return on their investment and end up unwillingly providing the wealthy countries to which their health personnel have migrated with a kind of "perverse subsidy" (Ibid:2)

Women who are sexually trafficked are the most exploited since their whole being is totally controlled as their bodies are commodified for profit in the sex industry in richer countries, like in Japan, Germany, and the Netherlands. Several actors participate in the commodification of their bodies: the state, the male consumers, the recruitment agencies, and the capitalists of the sex industry.

Labor export has tremendous social costs that affect women more adversely than men. Since the majority of export labor is women in domestic work, they are the ones who suffer more the loneliness of working in foreign households, the difficulties of adjustment in a foreign culture, gender-race-class discrimination in the labor-receiving country, and the pain of separation from family and children whom they leave behind with their spouses and/or other relatives.

Ironically, labor export has not mitigated unemployment in the Philippines since foreign exchange earnings through remittances is not invested in employment-generating projects; most of it goes to debt servicing: about 87 percent (about US$5.9 billion) of the US$6.79 billion remittances in 1999 went to debt servicing (Episcopal Commission for the Pastoral Care of Migrants and Itinerant People, 2000:4). From 2001-2009, the Philippine government paid P5.1 trillion in debt service, tripling the P1.8 billion of debt payments made over fifteen years (Africa, 2010, citing Bureau of Treasury). While deployment of export labor has consistently increased from 660,122 in 1996 to 747, 696 in 1997, to 755,684 in 1999, to 841,628 in 2000 (Bultron, 2001:2) to now over a million, the unemployment rate has also increased from 9.8 percent in 1999, 11.2 percent in 2000, and 12.2 percent in 2001 (Dizon, 2001:5) and an average increase of 11.2 percent in the unemployment rate from 2001-2009 (Africa, 2010, using IBON Foundation estimates correcting for the government's not counting of millions of jobless Filipinos as unemployed since 2005). Meanwhile, the Philippine government garners millions of revenues per day through the pre-departure fees alone (McGovern, 2001).

Following a regional trend among poor countries in Asia (like Pakistan, India, Sri Lanka, Bangladesh), Philippine labor export has become a major source of foreign exchange revenue (Bultron, 2001). For example, as of 2004, remittances from migrant Filipinos amounted to US$8.5 billion or PhP 467.5 billion–which was greater than the value of the top five Philippine export products (semi-conductors, finished electricals, garments, crude coconut oil, and copper bars and rods). This amounted to almost a hundred times the 2003 foreign direct investments in the Philippines, and more than half of the 2005 Philippine national budget of PhP 907 billion (Roque, 2005). In 2008, the amount of remittances doubled to $16.4 billion (Herrera, 2009, quoting Bango Sentral ng Pilipinas), $17.3 billion in 2009, and as of January 2010, it grew by 8.5 %–registering a year-on-year growth of $1.4 billion (Allingod, 2010, citing Bangko Sentral ng Pilipinas).

Overall, these characteristics of neoliberal globalization in the Philippine nation-state interlock with the macro-structures of globalization that are embodied in the IMF's structural adjustment policies, the WTO, and practices and circuits of capital promoted by transnational corporations.[6] Although the interlocking of these features plays a role in the social construction of neoliberal hegemony, it also creates the context for global resistance to and the struggle against that hegemony. The Philippine resistance movement is a major participant in that struggle.

Women's Resistance to Globalization

The negative impact of neoliberal policies has been contested by Filipino women on the home front and overseas. At home, women's resistance to globalization is being led by GABRIELA, a militant, national coalition of women's organizations. GABRIELA has facilitated the organization of grassroots women. It has conducted study sessions to raise a critical political consciousness among its members and the larger public on the impact of neoliberal globalization on Filipino women. One of its major political campaigns over the past two decades is the Purple Rose Campaign, an international campaign against the sex-trafficking of Filipino women and children. One of the major accomplishments of the campaign has been the passing of legislation that criminalizes sex trafficking in the Philippines. This is a historical milestone because with the passage of this law, the movement against sex-trafficking now has a legal frame that can be invoked, in order to put an end to the practice.

GABRIELA works in alliance with other organizations to combat and campaign against some of the tenets of globalization, like the privatization of water in the Philippines. GABRIELA was one of the more than 400 participants in the First National People's Convention on Water held on 10-11 August 2004, at University of the Philippines, sponsored by IBON Foundation (a progressive think-tank NGO) and BAYAN, a national coalition of progressive organizations in the Philippines. This convention formulated a Filipino People's Water Code that called for the reversal of the policy of water privatization based on the basic principles that access to potable and sanitary water is a right, that water is a national and a people's resource that should be under public domain and state responsibility, and that equality in access to water means 'preferential treatment and positive action for the poor and marginalized sectors' (that could include the unemployed poor, children and women). GABRIELA formulated and disseminated a press release that reiterated the basic principles in the People's Water Code, and criticized the government for being subservient to the profiteers of globalization that privatize public utilities, guaranteeing benefits to foreign and local capitalists at the expense of the 'already poverty-stricken people'. The press statement also gave voice to women in Metro-Manila who claimed that even though they pay increased water rates, the water that comes out of their faucets smells and looks dirty. They complained that the poor quality of water posed difficulties for all women, but particularly for poor women whose work–as food peddlers, laundresses, and operators of small street restaurants, for example–relies mainly on water. The statement concluded constructively with a call for a government takeover of water service and the regulation of water rates.

GABRIELA has a research arm, the Women's Resource Center, which has conducted grassroots-oriented research on issues related to globalization. For example, it has conducted a study on the social cost of the migration of women and has a pamphlet about it for popular education and consciousness-raising. The social cost of labor export, such as family dislocation, break-up and separation, is something that the government hardly talks about when it dubs the overseas workers 'modern day heroes', and continues to promote labor export as a long-term development policy.

Defying the 'hyperglobalist' notion that globalization withers away the state (Held et al., 1999:3), GABRIELA targets the state in its politics of resistance.[7] This action recognizes the argument of the "skeptical" view that the state plays an active role in ensuring continued economic liberalization and in the regulation of cross-border activities that have not narrowed down the North-South inequality and the marginalization of Third World nations (Ibid:5-6). GABRIELA, therefore, has denounced and participated in the nationwide campaigns against the growing militarization in the Philippines that suppresses progressive and radical groups that oppose the current pattern of globalization in the Philippines. One significant contribution that GABRIELA has made in the long-term process of changing the Philippine state is the formation of a Women's Party, which has been able to elect GABRIELA's candidates into Congress, such as Representative Liza Largosa Masa. The Women's Party, through Representative Masa, has been instrumental in legislating against the sex-trafficking of Filipino women and children in the sex trade and around US military bases. In the 2010 elections, the GABRIELA Women's Party List, has also been able to garner votes, indicating its growing political power in the parliamentary politics.

Overseas, another organization–Migrante International–plays a significant role in facilitating organized resistance to globalization among migrants. It has established chapters in various countries. In the areas where I conducted my fieldwork (Hong Kong, Taiwan, Rome, and Vancouver in British Columbia) domestic workers have formed organizations that are linked to Migrante International. These organizations participate in Migrante International's international Congress, its highest policy-making body that meets every three years, where they discuss issues, share their experiences of resistance, plan a program of action, and elect the next set of officers.

A major concept in the discourses of Migrante International is the concept of commodification of migrant/export labor. This was, for example, a central theme in the International Migrants' Conference held in Manila in 2001 that Migrante International convened with other NGOs concerned about migrants' rights. The concept also runs through the discourses of the United Filipinos in Hong Kong (UNIFIL), a chapter of Migrante International, composed mostly of Filipino domestic workers.

Migrante International targets the state, both the Philippine government and the labor-receiving governments, in its politics and strategies of resistance. Since its actions are policy-oriented it confronts the state in its demands to change the policies of neoliberal globalization. Such action resists deregulation that diminishes the role of the state in protecting migrants' rights and welfare.

Both Migrante International and GABRIELA believe in economic self-determination, genuine land reform that will redistribute land to the tiller, and national industrialization that will create jobs in the Philippines. This agenda for change is consistently subverted by neoliberal globalization. However, the broad resistance movement in the Philippines to which Migrante International and GABRIELA are linked, also has persistently sustained its resistance both at the national and international levels.

As resistance intensifies, militarization also intensifies, making the Philippine state a violent enforcer of the neoliberal globalization agenda. The mass organizations have viewed the increased militarization of the state as 'state terrorism' aimed at suppressing militant people's actions. In their view, the United States has participated in 'state terrorism' by sending American troops to the Philippines, which violates the Philippine Constitution. The government of the United States has labeled the Philippine liberation movement and its leaders 'terrorists', which the movement views as an infringement of the Filipino people's right to self-determination. The Philippine liberation movement consists of a broad alliance of progressive and militant groups, including the underground National Democratic Front and the revolutionary New People's Army, that carry on the completion of the decolonization process to end the poverty of many Filipinos. Hence, they reject the US government's labeling of them as 'terrorists'; in their view it is American imperialism that has terrorized the Filipino people.

Therefore, it has become important for the anti-globalization movement in the Philippines, of which the women's movement is a part, to address imperialism and militarism in the Philippines, and to militantly push for a new Philippine state that will assert Philippine economic and political sovereignty already enshrined in the Philippine Constitution. It is this new Philippine state, born out of the people's struggle, that will legitimize the agenda of the progressive movement and the women's movement in their efforts to create alternatives to the neoliberal agenda.

In the final analysis, therefore, what is required to support the politics of resistance and to create alternatives to neoliberalism, is a new state–one that does not wither away under pressure from global neo-colonial and capitalist forces. What is called for is a transformative, liberating state that will align itself with and support those who are injured by neoliberal globalization. Feminist politics and social movements in the Philippines and overseas, play an important role in the process of shaping this new state.

Conclusion

Neoliberal globalization is not a neutral process: it is gendered and classed. It has brought more misery to the poor, especially women in the Third World. The Philippines is a microcosm in which we can examine the contentious process and consequences of neoliberal globalization. Neoliberal policies such as trade liberalization, deregulation, privatization, finance capitalism, labor flexibilization, and labor export as a response to the debt crisis have negatively affected the economic well-being of the majority of Filipinos, especially poor Filipino women. These policies have destroyed the local economy resulting in higher unemployment, increased poverty, and people's inadequate access to basic resources and services. The consequences have been especially severe for women and children. The Philippine government plays an active role in implementing these neoliberal policies within the nation-state, negating the hyperglobalist view that diminishes the state's role in the globalization process. These nation-state-based neoliberal policies are linked to macro-structures/policies of neoliberal globalization promoted by the IMF/World Bank, the WTO and transnational corporations, complicating its dynamics and resistance to it. The power of micro-structures of neoliberal globalization lies in its subtleties to penetrate micro-structures within the nation-state, in some instances entangling with colonial legacies.

However, resistance to neoliberal globalization in the Philippines has been sustained despite attempts to suppress it. Both on the home front and overseas, Filipino women participate in this process. The existence of activist formations, such as GABRIELA and Migrante International that resist the policies of neoliberal globalization, attest to the contentious nature of neoliberal globalization imposed on the peoples of developing societies. The nation-state is implicated in these conflicts, and activists are demanding that the state adopt a more transformative, liberating role in protecting the people's rights and patrimony of the nation from the onslaught of imperialist and capitalist globalization that reinforce gender, ethnic and class inequalities.

Thus, viewing neoliberal globalization as a contentious rather than as a neutral process becomes an important premise in the analysis of globalization. Not only does it allow us to see who gets hurt and who benefits in the complex power dynamics of neoliberal globalization, but it also leads us to recognize the contending forces and makes us see with whom to align ourselves as scholar-activists and as feminists.

ACKNOWLEDGEMENTS

I am grateful to the following that provided financial support for the broader research project and longer work on Philippine labor export that required fieldwork in different sites from which this chapter is drawn: (1) the American Sociological Association for awarding me the Small Grant for the Advancement of the Discipline, (2) Indiana University International Program, (3) Indiana University Faculty Grants-in-Aid, (4) Indiana University Summer Fellowships. I would like also to thank Indiana University for funding my attendance at the Mexico conference to present the earlier version of this chapter.

NOTES

[1] William Robinson argues that the transnational elite–where concentration of capital and economic power resides–is based in core countries and they have counterparts in peripheral countries (conceived as the technocratic elites) who oversee rapid processes of social and economic restructuring. He refers to the transnational elite as that class drawn around the world that are 'integrated into fully transnationalized circuits of production' and whose ideology and practices are oriented to global rather than local accumulation. The transnational elite's economic project is neoliberalism (a model which seeks total mobility of capital), and a political counterpart to that economic project is the elimination of state intervention in the economy and the individual nation-states' regulation of capital's activities in their territories.

Leslie Sklair thinks of the transnational capitalist class within his global system theory that proposes that the three most important transnational forces are (a) the transnational corporations, (b) the transnational capitalist class, and (c) the culture-ideology of consumerism. He conceives of the transnational capitalist class as consisting of four fractions. The first and dominant group composed of those who own and control the major corporations (the corporate fraction). The other three are considered supporting members of the transnational capitalist class: globalizing bureaucrats and politicians (the state fraction), the globalizing professionals (the technical fraction), the merchants and media (the consumerist fraction) that promote the consumerist culture on which capitalism thrive. By pointing out the presence of the transnational elite and the transnational capitalist class Robinson and Sklair make visible some main actors who propel neoliberal globalization.

[2] James Petras and Robin Eastman-Abaya, in their article 'US-Backed Repression Soars Under President Gloria Macapagal: Philippines the Killing Fields of Asia', say that in the 1960s the Philippines was considered the most economically progressive country in Southeast Asia by most economists, but because of economic liberalization it has become one of the poorest countries in Asia and one of the most unequal societies in the world, with 20 percent unemployment and 30 percent underemployment rates in a population of over 85 million (see Petras and Eastman-Abaya, 2006).

3   Based on my computation of workers displaced yearly in 2001–2004 as reported in a table of 'Establishments Resorting to Permanent Closure/Retrenchment Due to Economic Reasons and Workers Displaced', cited in Guzman (2004:15).
4   It can be argued that capitalist globalization was initiated in the Philippines during the Spanish colonization and continued during the American colonial regime since it transformed the communal mode of production and displaced local industries, such as the textile industry, then largely controlled by women. Contemporary neoliberal globalization follows the same pattern. See for example, Eviota (1992) and Lindio-McGovern (1997).
5   Medicines in the Philippines are 18 times more expensive than in India and Canada, so transnational pharmaceuticals benefit (HEAD, 2001:5).
6   In her talk, as a featured speaker at the Midwest Sociological Society conference in Chicago in 2003, Saskia Sassen argued that macro-structures of globalization enmesh with micro-structures of the nation-state.
7   The hyperglobalist notion of the state argues that globalization withers away the state in order to give market forces free rein. But the nation-state, if it follows the dominant ideology of neoliberalism, actually plays an active role in locally implementing neoliberal policies–thus creating a neoliberal state. Even in the colonial stage of neoliberalism, a colonial state is constructed in order for the colonizer to establish its colonial rule. See, for example, Go and Foster (2003). In the social construction of this colonial state, an elite class was created whose existence and maintenance were ensured by collaborating with the colonial power in establishing its rule. This colonial elite would persist in the neo-colonial stage. The main features of neoliberal globalization build on and entrench these neo-colonial structures in the nation state. But there are also forces within the nation-state, as in the Philippine case, that challenge this neo-colonial state, attempting to transform it, or even dismantle it and radically replace it with a revolutionary state that can complete the process of national liberation.

REFERENCES

Africa, Sony (2010) 'Dark Legacies: The Economy Under Arroyo'. IBON Foundation. Accessed 12 June 2010 from www.ibon.org/ibon_features.php.

Alingod, Kris (2010) 'Remittances From Filipino Overseas Workers

Rise 8.5 Percent in January'. *All Headline News.* Accessed 14 June 2010 from www.allheadlinenews.com/articles/7001810958 3?Remittances%20Filipino.

Balangue, G.C. (2008) 'The Economy in Midyear 2008: Anatomy of a Crisis'. *IBON Facts and Figures* 31(13), 15 July 2008.

Barcelona, N. (2010) 'Philippine health sector dying, says doctors' alliance', March 15, 2010. Accessed 21 June 2010 from http://pilipinasreporter.wordpress.com/2010/03/15/philippine-healthcare-system-dying%e2.

Bello, W. (2004) *The Anti-Development State:The Political Economy of Permanent Crisis in the Philippines.* Diliman, Quezon City: University of the Philippines; Bangkok: Focus on the Global South.

Beltran, C. (2001) 'Message to the International Migrant Conference'. Paper presented at the International Migrant Conference on Labor-Export and Forced Migration Amidst Globalization, 4-8 November 2001, Manila, Philippines, organized by Migrante International in cooperation with GABRIELA-Philippines, CONTAK-Philippines, and Asia Pacific Mission for Migrants-Hong Kong.

Bruin, J. (1999) *Global Crisis at the End of the Twentieth Century.* Manila: Institute of Political Economy.

Bultron, R. (2001) 'Recruitment Costs, State Exaction and Government Fees'. Paper presented at the International Migrant Conference on Labor-Export and Forced Migration Amidst Globalization, Organized by Migrante International in cooperation with the GABRIELA-Philippines, CONTAK-Philippines, and Asia Pacific Mission for Migrants, 4-8 November 2001, Manila, Philippines.

Bureau of Agricultural Statistics, cited in "The Economy in Midyear 2008: Anatomy of a Crisis". IBON Facts and Figures, 31(13), 15 July 2008.

Capulong, R.T. (2001) 'A Human Rights Perspective on the International Instruments, Laws and Institutions on Migrant Workers' Rights', Paper presented at the International Migrant Conference on Labor-Export and Forced Migration Amidst Globalization, 4-8 November 2001, Manila, Philippines, organized by Migrante International in cooperation with GABRIELA-Philippines, CONTAK-Philippines, and Asia Pacific Mission for Migrants-Hong Kong.

del Rosario-Malonzo, J. (2001) 'WTO Fourth Ministerial Conference: The Bid for a New Round'. *IBON Facts and Figures, Special Release* 24(11), 15 June 2001.

del Rosario-Malonzo, J. (2004a) 'WTO Agriculture Agreement Review Negotiations: Entrenching Unjust Trade, Undermining Food Sovereignty'. *IBON Facts and Figures, Special Release* 27(10), 15 May 2004.

del Rosario-Malonzo, J. (2004b) 'Globalizing the Philippine Rice Sector'. *IBON Facts and Figures, Special Release* 27(2), 31 January 2004.

Department of Labor and Employment (2010). Accessed 6/13/2010 from www.nwpc.dole.gov.ph/pages/statistics/stat_current_regional.html.

Dizon, A. (2001) 'Philippine Overseas Employment Program', Paper presented at the International Migrant Conference on Labor-Export and Forced Migration Amidst Globalization, organized by Migrante International in cooperation with GABRIELA-Philippines, CONTAK-Philippines, and Asia Pacific Mission for Migrants, 4-8 November 2001, Manila, Philippines.

EILER Inc. (2000) *Labor Flexibilization and Imperialist Crisis: Intensifying Exploitation, Dismantling Job Security, Liquidating Unions.* Manila: Institute of Political Economy.

Episcopal Commission for the Pastoral Care of Migrants and Itinerant People (2000) *Migration: Situationer and Impact, Biblical Inspiration, Pastoral Challenges.* Catholic Bishops Conference of the Philippines.

Eviota, E.U. (1992) *The Political Economy of Gender: Women and the Sexual Division of Labour in the Philippines.* London and New Jersey: Zed Books.

Go, J. and Foster, A. (2003) *The American Colonial State in the Philippines: Global Perspectives.* Durham and London: Duke University Press.

Guzman, R.B. (2001) 'The Economy Under Arroyo: Crisis and Bitter Pills'. *Bird Talk, IBON Economic and Political Briefing*, 11 July 2001, pp. 3-18.

Guzman, R.B. (2004) 'The Philippine Crisis:Will A New Presidency Still Make A Difference?' *IBON Economic and Political Briefing*, 15 July 2004, pp. 3-22.

HEAD (Health Alliance for Democracy) (2001) *Privatization of Health Care: A Cause for National Concern.* Manila: HEAD.

Held, D., McGrew, A., Goldblatt, D. and Perraton, J. (1999) *Global Transformations: Politics, Economics and Culture.* Stanford: Stanford University Press.

Herrera, E.F. (2009) 'Policy Peek: Scared for their jobs, OFWs cut remittances, spending'. *The Manila Times*, Tuesday, April 14, 2009. Accessed 13 July 2009 from www.manilatimes.net/national

/2009/April14/yehey/ opinion/200941op2.html.
IBON (1998) 'The Philippine Labor Export'. *Facts and Figures* 21 (17-18).
IBON (2004a) *Facts and Figures, Special Release* 27(10), 15 May 2004.
IBON (2004b) 'Maynilad Bailout: Exposing the Flaws of Water Privatization'. *Facts and Figures, Special Release* 27(7).
IBON (2006a) 'Removing Economic Sovereignty Provisions in Charter Won't Bring Dev't'. Media Release, 21 March 2006, media@ibon.org.
IBON (2006b) 'Rising Job Scarcity Refutes Gov't Claim of 'Improving the Economy'. Media Release, 17 March 2006.
Lindio-McGovern, L. (1997) *Filipino Peasant Women: Exploitation and Resistance.* Philadelphia: University of Pennsylvania Press.
Lindio-McGovern, Ligaya and Wallimann, Isidor (2009) *Globalization and Third World Women: Exploitation, Coping and Resistance.* Surrey, England: Ashgate Publishing Company.
Mananzan, M.J., OSB (1999) 'Building Women's Unity and Solidarity Against Globalization', in GABRIELA (ed.) *Women Against Globalization: Issue, Challenges and Strategies*, pp. 1-8. Quezon City, Philippines: Steadfast Publications and Allied Services.
McGovern, L.L. (2001) 'The Export of Labor and the Politics of Foreign Debt: The Case of Overseas Filipino Domestic Workers'. Paper presented at the International Migrant Conference on Labor-Export and Forced Migration Amidst Globalization, organized by Migrante International in cooperation with GABRIELA-Philippines, CONTAK-Philippines, and Asia Pacific Mission for Migrants-Hong Kong, 4-8 November 2001, Manila, Philippines.
National Statistics Office, cited in Glenis C.Balangue, 'The Economy in Midyear 2008: Anatomy of A Crisis'. *IBON Facts and Figures*, 31(13), 15 July 2008.
National Statistics Office, QUICKSTAT (A Monthly Update of Philippine Statistics), April 2010. Accessed 12 June 2010 from www.census.Gov.ph/.
Oishi, N. (2005) *Women in Motion: Globalization, State Politics, and Labor Migration in Asia.* Stanford. California: Stanford University Press.
Padilla, A. (2004) 'The Truth About Oil Prices and the Myth of an OPEC Cartel'. *IBON Facts and Figures, Special Release* 27(8), 30 April 2004.
Petras, J. and Eastman-Abaya, R. (2006) 'US-Backed Repression Soars Under President Gloria Macapagal: Philippines The Killing Fields of Asia'. *CounterPunch*, 17 March. Accessed 17 March

2006 from www.counterpunch.org/petras 03172006.html.
Porter, T. (2005) *Globalization and Finance.* Cambridge Polity Press.
POEA (Philippine Overseas Employment Agency).
Ramirez, M.M. and Desa, A.B. (1997) *When Labor Does Not Pay: The Case of Filipino Outmigration,* Occasional Monograph 9. Manila, Philippines: Asian Social Institute.
Robinson, W.I. (1996) *Promoting Polyarchy: Globalization, US Intervention, and Hegemony.* New York: Cambridge University Press.
Roque, L. (2005) 'On the Losing End: The Migration of Filipino Health Professionals and the Decline of Health Care in the Philippines'. Paper presented at the 10th International Metropolis Conference, Toronto, Canada, 17-19 October 2005.
Sison, J.M. (2005) 'Junk the WTO! Resist Imperialist Plunder and War!' Unpublished paper for the Forum on Globalization and Trade during the People's Action Week in Hong Kong in protest against the WTO 6th Ministerial Conference, 14-16 December 2005.
Sklair, L. (2001) *The Transnational Capitalist Class.* Oxford: Blackwell.
Tujan, A., Jr. (2001) 'Labor Export and Forced Migration Under Globalization'. Paper presented at the International Migrant Conference on Labor-Export and Forced Migration Amidst Globalization, organized by Migrante International in cooperation with GABRIELA-Philippines, CONTAK-Philippines, and Asia Pacific Mission for Migrants, 4-8 November 2001, Manila, Philippines.
Villegas, E.M. (2000) *Global Finance Capital and the Philippine Financial System.* Manila: Institute of Political Economy.
Yoshihara, K. (1994) *The Nation and Economic Growth.* Kuala Lumpur: Oxford University Press. Cited in Bello, W. (2004) *The Anti-Development State: The Political Economy of Permanent Crisis in the Philippines,* p. 17.

CHAPTER 2

'We're Better off Outside Our Country:' Diasporic Ecuadorian Women in Spain Since the Mid-1990s[1]

estheR Cuesta
University of Massachussetts Amherst

ABSTRACT

Increasing sociopolitical and economic instability–stemming, in part, from the adoption of neoliberal policies–compelled more than two million Ecuadorians (approximately 16 percent of the total population) to migrate to the United States and member states of the European Union, in search of jobs and a means to survive. It is estimated that more than half a million Ecuadorians live in Spain, and constitute one of the largest immigrant national groups in this country, after Rumanians and Moroccans. Women, who initially migrated without their families, make up more than half of this diaspora. This transdisciplinary study is based on interviews with Ecuadorian women in Spain and Ecuador, and informed by feminist methodologies. It situates the epistemological standpoints of women from (lower) middle and professional classes within recent Ecuadorian migrations. It also analyzes the impact of Ecuadorian women's migration to Spain on the sociocultural life of Ecuador and Spain. Despite the discrimination, racism, and xenophobia that Ecuadorian women experience abroad, most agree that for now they are 'better off outside' of their country.

Keywords: Ecuadorians, migrants, diaspora, women, Spain

Introduction

Ecuadorian women migrants are seldom viewed by mainstream Southern/Mediterranean European societies as narrators and inscribers of their own experiences and subjectivities, or as agents of their own self-representation. Ecuadorian migrants in Spain appear in European media, usually in reports of murder, rape, or violent attacks related to racist or xenophobic situations, or crimes of passion. For instance, the Spanish and Ecuadorian media followed the case of 21-year-old Sergi Xavier Martín, who attacked a 15-year-old Ecuadorian young woman in Barcelona's metropolitan train the night of October 7, 2007 with racist and xenophobic slurs and physical violence. Soon after, the video recordings from the Ferrocarrils de la Generalitat de Catalunya's security cameras travelled the world through cyberscapes, via YouTube, electronic mail, and Facebook. While Spanish authorities continuously labeled Martín's behavior as racist and viewed it as an isolated case, the Ecuadorian government manifested its solidarity and supported the minor and her mother with legal, diplomatic, economic, and emotional assistance. In March 2009, Sergi Xavier Martín was condemned to eight months in prison, with a €360 fine and a three-year prohibition against going within 1,000 meters of her, in addition to the €6,000 indemnity to the young woman.

This xenophobic event in Barcelona is evidence of an attitude, ideology and violence that may not always surface in public spaces or become public information, but all too often occurs in private. It is only in the last few years that an increasing number of diasporic Ecuadorians have felt empowered to denounce unjust treatment and discriminatory and racist violence, which in some cases, has included murder by white supremacist groups.[2]

Within European unification discourses of the racialized, cultural, and religious 'other,' however, the Ecuadorian diaspora in Spain, has remained in the fictive shadows of the *unwanted* compared to other racialized groups, such as Muslims, North Africans, Western Asians, and Roma people. The discrimination and social exclusion of North Africans in Spain points to historically grounded anti-Muslim politics and Islamophobia in Spain and other parts of Europe, and the supposedly already large numbers of North Africans in Spain. As a Catalan man told me in an informal conversation, 'the problem is not that there are immigrants, the problem is that there are too many, and the *moros* do not assimilate. At least the Ibero-Americans speak our language, we share some culture, they integrate themselves to our society–but not the *moros*.'[3] Often perceived as the 'good humble/noble migrants,' Ecuadorian women in Spain, as domestic workers and more *domesticatable* Christian migrants, have been almost invisible in anti-immigrant discourses in the media.

This chapter seeks to create a bridge between Ecuadorian women's life histories and testimonies, and academic approaches to migration studies. My goal is to better understand some of the complexities and intricacies of Ecuadorian women's migrations to Spain by examining the specific socioeconomic, cultural, and political forces, as well as some of the migratory policies that have shaped the gendering of this migration. This work is part of a larger project on diasporic Ecuadorian women consisting of a critical feminist study of the interstices of race, ethnicity, class, gender, and sexuality in (failed) Ecuadorian migrations, which locates indigenous, Afro-descendant, and mestiza women's subjectivities at the forefront of migratory processes in global capitalism.

It is estimated that more than a million Ecuadorians, out of an approximate population of 13 million, migrated primarily to the United States, Spain, Italy, Germany, France, and the Netherlands between 1993 and 2005.[4] Today, the Ecuadorian diaspora numbers more than two million. Of these, more than 500,000 migrated to Spain, turning it into the second migratory destination of Ecuadorians, after the US. Ecuadorian women make up more than half of this diaspora. In fact, Ecuadorians are the largest Latin American immigrant group in Spain, and are one of the largest immigrant national groups in the country, after Rumanians and Moroccans. Compared to France, Germany, and the United Kingdom, Spain is a country of relatively recent immigration. Only in the last two decades, has Spain shifted from a country of emigration to one of immigration. Although in absolute numbers Spain may have fewer foreigners from non-EU countries (3,149,000), they represent a higher percentage of the total population in Spain (7 percent) than they do, for instance, in Germany (5.8 percent), France (3.8 percent), and the UK (3.9 percent).[5] These figures reflect the relatively short time migrants have resided in Spain, as most have not yet obtained citizenship status.

With the aging of the Spanish population, Spain's astonishing low birth rate (one of the lowest in the EU), Spanish women's increasing access to higher education and wage labor outside the household, and limited social services for caretaking, there has been an incremental need for cheap (migrant) female workers to do the jobs traditionally performed by Spanish women (Arango, 2000; Solé and Parella, 2003). In the last 10 years or so, Ecuadorian women migrated to Spain by themselves and were later joined by their families, often their children. Most have found temporary jobs as domestic servants and hostel workers, baby-sitters, and caretakers of the elderly, the ill, and the disabled, in urban centers such as Madrid, Barcelona, and Bilbao. Domestic service, 'characterized by its invisibility, vulnerability and insecurity, has become practically their [women migrants' from the global South] only opportunity to work, regardless of their level of education and previous work experience' (Solé and Parella, 2003:62). Many women migrants live in the houses where they work. This labor situation allows them to accumulate more savings than those accumulated by men (Solé and Parella,

2003:71). In fact, it is in a foreign country such as Spain where domestic workers can earn and save more than dentists and lawyers in their country of origin, despite not always having the legal documentation to work.

While scholarship on Latin American migrations to the US and the EU has increasingly focused on transnational issues–including transnational families, where the parents are usually the migrants and the children and grandparents remain in the country of origin– women's heterogeneous subjectivities, epistemological standpoints, and realities have often been obviated from analyses and understated in theorizations on Ecuadorian diasporas, especially in studies conducted by US and EU academicians. The conceptualization of the nuclear family has been somewhat applied to family relations among Ecuadorians, who may understand 'family' as a larger and more complex and flexible structure. Most important, Ecuadorian women's fairly recent ability to migrate by themselves in large numbers, and be joined by their children and their extended family, needs to be especially considered in light of stringent US and European border patrols, growing surveillance cultures, anti-immigrant backlash, as well as recent immigration and 'security' policies that seek to criminalize, incarcerate, and deport undocumented migrants, as well as those who may help them to get a place to live, to work, and to move from one place to another.

Ecuadorians in Spain, as in Ecuador, are a heterogeneous group–including indigenous people, Afro-descendants, mestizos, impoverished people from urban and rural areas (though most had already migrated to urban settings at the time of transnational migration), professionals of (lower) middle-class, and women and men of all ages, from the 24 provinces of the Coastal, Andean, Amazon, and Galapagos regions. This study focuses on lower middle-class, skilled, and semiskilled migrations of Ecuadorian women. Little attention has been paid to Latin American skilled women's migrations, and the role of bi-national marriages, not only as a 'survival strategy' used by impoverished women from the southern hemisphere to improve their standard of living and to obtain residence permits, but also as a result of local tensions between the sexes, the exoticization and idealization of foreign women, and love (Riaño, 2003). Similarly, these aspects of the migratory experiences of Ecuadorian women have not been adequately studied.

Considering the heterogeneity of the people living in Ecuador, in terms of ethnicity, race, culture, access to capital, and identification with the nation-state, as well as multiple life experiences in Ecuador and Spain, this chapter addresses the following questions: 1) Why have Ecuadorian women increasingly migrated by themselves since the mid-1990s? 2) What does this migration represent/signify to them and their families? and 3) How are Ecuadorian women's migrations altering the Ecuadorian and Spanish societal and cultural paradigms?

Research Methods and Methodologies

There are, of course, many parallels between Ecuadorian transnational migrants and those from other nation-states of the global South migrating to the North. At the same time, migratory experiences are very specific to each individual, town and country of origin, social class, gender, sexuality, and point of destination. Keeping in mind these specificities, this chapter is informed both by archival research and ethnographic research consisting of in-depth interviews with eight Ecuadorian women, conducted in Spanish during the summer of 2005 (and in some cases, followed by additional interviews in November 2005). Two of the women were skilled, undocumented workers from the lower middle classes, who had lived in Spain (Madrid and Barcelona) since 2001. Four of the women were living in Guayaquil (Ecuador's largest city and main port, with a population of approximately three million) and had relatives in Mallorca, Madrid, and Barcelona. Two women were living in Ecuador and wished to migrate in the next few years.[6]

As an Ecuadorian woman who migrated to the United States and lived there for nearly 15 years, transnational migration is not merely an academic interest or a subject of study. It is an everyday reality, a painful family issue, as well as part of intimate conversations and strategizing with friends (Cuesta, 2007). In my analysis of Ecuadorian women in Spain, I draw my arguments from the epistemological standpoints and 'situated knowledges' of the Ecuadorian women interviewed, while being cognizant of the power differentials in the relationships between the interviewees and me.[7] While I concur with Harding (1993:56, 66) that feminist knowledge involves 'starting thought from the lives of marginalized groups' and 'from multiple lives that are in many ways in conflict with each other, each of which has multiple and contradictory commitments,' my interactions with these women migrants have made me view them more reflexively and critically. While Ecuadorian women migrants and those who have remained in Ecuador may be perceived as relatively marginal groups of study from a North American or European academic perspective, in fact, they do not perceive themselves as marginal, but rather as active transformative agents of their own realities. In a sense, my role here as researcher involves also joining their voices to make *our* voices more internationally audible, more academically readable. In this study, I aim to develop a diasporic Ecuadorian epistemology that exposes some of the particularities of the multiple subjectivities and experiences of Ecuadorian women, which, I hope, will contribute to the emerging Ecuadorian diasporas' collective concerns about Ecuadorian women migrants.[8]

In addition, I build on Mohanty's (2003) critique of dominant Western feminist discourses and Collins' (2000:47) analysis of African-Americans as objects of knowledge prior to the 1970s, as a part of the absence of Black people in the US academy, especially in positions of authority.[9] In the same vein, a large majority of Ecuadorian migrants has not *yet* attained higher education in the countries in which they reside, nor are they in positions of authority.[10] As an Ecuadorian migrant/researcher affiliated to a US university and studying Ecuadorian women migrants in Spain, while I conducted this research and wrote on it, I often felt both as an insider and an outsider. While these positionalities are ever fluid and shifting (Naples, 2003:49), I perceived myself as an insider because of my Ecuadorian-ness, my experiences as a migrant in the North, my gender, and my 'professional-working' class.[11] I also felt as an outsider in terms of my specific experiences in the US and in Ecuador. I know that many of the migrants with whom I talked, even within a community of migrants, may have regarded me as an 'other' based on my phenotype, my appearance, my education, among other categories that 'other' me from them. Despite this 'othering,' I seek to build knowledge *with* them and bring their subjectivities and realities to other worlds, beyond their intimate circles.[12]

Brief Overview of Ecuadorian Political Economy: Neoliberalism and Neocolonial Globalization: Why a Transatlantic Migration Now?

Although, since 1963, Ecuadorians did not need a visa to enter Spain as tourists for a maximum stay of 90 days, it was not until the mid-1990s that Ecuadorians started migrating to Spain in large numbers.[13] The Ecuadorian migration to its former colonizing empire, Spain, reminds us of the global mechanisms that transcend colonialism and bind migrants' receiving and sending countries, which are linked to colonial histories and current neo- or quasi-colonial relationships (Sassen, 1999:9). The latter includes processes of economic globalization that increase a country's dependency on foreign investment and the presence of multinational corporations in the consumer markets of migrant-sending countries. In the case of Ecuador, its colonial and postcolonial histories with Spain, its neocolonial relationship with the US and with the international financial institutions controlling the global markets, as well as the almost total hopelessness that most Ecuadorians experienced in Ecuador, while envisioning 'better lives' in the so-called 'first world', all have had an impact on recent Ecuadorian migrations to Spain and the US. Dialectically, the negative ways in which recent Ecuadorian migrants have been perceived in Spain and the US (invading, disrupting the national identity, taking citizens' jobs, etc.) have to do with the historic amnesia in the dominant national discourses of these three countries.[14]

Between the period of 1984-2006, Ecuador's neoliberal policies attempted to attract multinational corporations and foreign investment, while reducing fiscal spending, especially on human development, ecological sustainability, and social programs, in order to ensure the repayment of loans to international lending institutions. Historically, Ecuador has imported more products than it has exported; and the demand for imported products steadily grows. In fact, until recently, neoliberalism–which has been the dominant paradigm of development in Latin America–framed Ecuador's economic policies (Correa, 2005:77). Neoliberalism in Ecuador was based on the notion that trade liberalization and the integration of national and international markets would solve all economic and social problems; meanwhile corruption, and economic and cultural subordination deepened, and the ecological debt was ignored (Correa, 2005:77).[15]

In recent years, millions of Ecuadorian women and men found it impossible to function in the Ecuadorian capitalist system that had kept them stagnant in their living conditions. Living in Ecuador meant having the inescapable desire to access capital and acquire commodities, but for the majority, those dreams were impossible to realize. Many women found that migrating transnationally would allow them to achieve a better and more dignified life for them and their children. Upon arrival in Spain, however, many had to share a tiny apartment with 20 or 39 people: a living condition that prompted conflicts and all sorts of abuses. In Spain, Ecuadorians may be discriminated against, work hard, even under appalling conditions, or may be currently unemployed, and not infrequently be extorted by their own compatriots, and still help their families in Ecuador by regularly sending remittances.

The effects of the formal dollarization of the currency in 2000, the lack of accountability and credibility of government institutions, inefficient economic policies, widespread poverty in rural and urban sectors, and lack of job opportunities drove Ecuadorian women to migrate in the last decade. Other factors–including high unemployment and underemployment rates, a cost of living much higher than the average salary, inflation reaching 52 percent in 1999 and 96 percent in 2000, with convertibility problems that came after the country's formal 'dollarization', the 'freezing' of bank accounts, and the closing of 16 banking institutions between 1999 and 2000– prompted thousands of Ecuadorians to migrate to Spain in search of jobs and higher salaries. The current capitalist crisis, particularly experienced in Spain, with a 19.1 unemployment rate in 2010, and more than 4 million unemployed, in turn, prompted 26,357 Ecuadorians to leave Spain (out of more than half a million). In spite of all this, most Ecuadorians still see prospects of a better life in Spain than in Ecuador.[16]

In the period 1994-2005, Ecuador's social, economic and political instability intensified, as evidenced by having eight presidents in less than 10 years. In addition, the Ecuadorian state neither worked toward active democratic participation of its social agents, nor toward its citizens' social welfare. Instead, it obediently complied with the demands of the international financial institutions (IMF, World Bank, IDB, etc.). It should be noted that since 2007, when Rafael Correa officially became President of Ecuador, there have been radical changes in Ecuador's political economy that are beyond the scope of this chapter. What is important here is that since 2007 for the Ecuadorian state, the demands of international financial institutions and hegemonic theories of development no longer take precedence over a less dominant understanding of human and social development and sustainability.

Despite macro-social and economic factors, what ultimately shape the subjects' decisions to emigrate are their respective levels of exposure and degrees of connectedness to migratory networks in their places of origin and destination (Ramírez Gallegos and Ramírez, 2005:142), and their specific subjectivities and socioeconomic realities, as the women interviewed indicated. In 2002, 45 percent of the Ecuadorian population wanted to 'get out' of the country (*Vistazo*, 2002), and this percentage has probably increased since then, especially in the upper-middle class and the middle class. In conversations with Ecuadorians living in Ecuador, and also noted in the detailed study by Camacho Zambrano and Hernández Basante

(2005), most Ecuadorians expressed a desire to leave or, at least, help their children to study, work, and build a life outside of Ecuador.

Migratory Policies, Migratory Shifts

Diversity in class, race, and point of origin and destination has not always been the case in Ecuadorian migrations. From the 1960s to the first half of the 1990s, Ecuadorians migrated primarily to the US. Most were young men from impoverished rural areas in the southern Andean provinces of Cañar and Azuay, who relocated in the New York metropolitan area (Borrero Vega and Vega Ugalde, 1995; Carpio Benalcázar, 1992; Miles, 2004). Many of these migrants were light and dark-skinned mestizos with low levels of formal education–and some had been laborers and entrepreneurs in the 'Panama' hat business (Jokisch and Pribilsky, 2002; Kyle, 2000; Kyle and Liang, 2001).

In contrast, since the mid-1990s, migratory movements have arisen also from urban (lower) middle-classes (Herrera, 2003; Herrera et al., 2005; Pedone, 2002; Ramírez Gallegos and Ramírez, 2005). Many are professionals or with some higher education, from the 24 Ecuadorian provinces, but mainly from Ecuador's largest cities and its surrounding areas: Quito, Guayaquil, and Cuenca. Their choice of destination is not only the US, but a variety of countries, particularly Spain. In 1995, there were 1,963 Ecuadorians with residence permits in Spain. In 1998, 7,046; in 1999, 12,933; in 2000, 50,000, and in 2004 there were 390,297 Ecuadorians with residence permits in Spain (Alou Forner and Instituto Nacional de Estadística [INE], quoted in *El Universo*, 16 June 2004). According to the INE, by January 1, 2010, there were 421,426 Ecuadorians in Spain, constituting 7.5 percent of Spain's total foreigners; and it is estimated that there are more than 500,000 Ecuadorians ('*regulares*' and '*irregulares*' [documented and undocumented]) in Spain.

The growing uneven distribution of capital (including natural resources and means of production) has prevented the impoverished from migrating while enabling middle-class migrations–as the former does not often have the capital and networks necessary to migrate (passport, visa, plane ticket, a relative or friend who can lend them money for travel and contact a potential or 'fake' employer), and is likewise under greater risk of being 'swindled, jailed, deported, robbed, or violently abused, including rape and murder' (Kyle and Liang, 2001: 9). For instance, from January to April 2006, about 568 Ecuadorians were repatriated in their attempt to migrate to the US (*El Universo*, 25 April 2006). In 2004, the figure was 3,500.

In 2002, at least 2,321 Ecuadorians failed in their attempts to migrate; 1,139 were deported, 924 were detained and 258 were 'excluded,' and were forced to return immediately upon arrival at the intended country of destination for not presenting proper documentation (Ramírez Gallegos and Ramírez, 2005).

The migratory shifts since the mid-1990s can be explained, in part, by the fact that for the first time, not only impoverished peasants (and former 'Panama' hat makers and traders), but all non-elites were directly and profoundly affected by changes in the global markets, the region's neoliberal structural adjustment programs, Ecuador's weakening unstable economy, and its ungovernability. At the same time, migration to the US became more dangerous and costly, and finding jobs without a work permit and a social security number became more difficult, with less remuneration, and more exploitative conditions.

Similar to other EU countries, Spain's increasing demand for female migrant labor, its marked decline of birth rate, its aging population, and a scarcity of workers who are willing to take care of the elderly, the sick, the disabled, and children for low wages, made this former empire an attractive and possible migratory destination. In most cases, immigrants take low-waged jobs that are unstable and unappealing to Spaniards, with less social protection, such as jobs in agriculture, construction, hotel and restaurant businesses, and domestic work (Arango, 2000:263-5).

Although migrants have entered the Spanish labor force, most are not yet being hired in jobs sought by Spaniards.[17] Most Ecuadorian immigrants do not yet compete with Spaniards for higher paying jobs due to the formers' presumed lack of formal education and skills. However, it may be more accurate to state that many immigrants are forced to take unskilled and semiskilled jobs because they have not been able to validate their professional degrees, in part because of lack of money and information about the possibility of taking and having time to study for certification exams [*homologación*], residence permits, in addition to having a sense of insecurity and inferiority. Riaño (2003:2) notes that 'although studies on female migrants have contributed much to our understanding of migration, at the same time, they have focused too much on unskilled workers.' This is also the case of most studies on Ecuadorian women migrants, which have not included the particularities of middle class, skilled women, who are more eager to take the certification exams in order to be able to practice their professions. Before passing the exams, many women try to work in their professional fields, even as assistants or non-certified staff, getting paid much less for their professional services.

The working permits that Spain has issued are short term, often for seasonal work. Unlike the Moroccan government, which has been a relatively 'cooperative' diplomatic partner in regulating Moroccan emigration (Huntoon 1998:430), the Ecuadorian government made insufficient efforts to control the unchecked emigration of its citizens and to eliminate *coyotaje*.[18] The Ecuadorian government, however, is increasingly making substantial efforts to prevent further unchecked emigrations and human trafficking. For instance, Ecuador's Secretaría Nacional del Migrante (SENAMI) sponsors campaigns to disseminate information in Ecuador about transnational migration. It also organizes seminars and cultural events, while offering legal and economic assistance to Ecuadorian migrants and their families in Ecuador through its offices in Madrid, Barcelona, Milan, New York, and Caracas. Working in collaboration with Ecuadorian Consulates and Embassies around the world, SENAMI's efforts abide by the 2008 Ecuadorian Constitution, which recognizes the right to migrate. It also establishes that no human being is identified as or considered illegal based on her or his migratory situation. Therefore, for the Ecuadorian state, migration is a right, not an illegal action for which to feel guilty.

Because massive migration to Spain is a relatively new phenomenon, Spaniards are gradually marrying more foreigners. Bi-national marriages take place, partly, because Spanish men believe that Latin American women will make better housewives and be more dedicated to childrearing. An added factor to bi-national marriages, which also happen elsewhere in Europe, is the exoticization of Latin American women (Riaño, 2003). Bi-national marriages, however, also work to the advantage of Latin American women migrants, as they are able to obtain Spanish residence permits in a relatively short period of time. Despite the fact that some women marry European and Spanish men only to secure legal stay in Spain, both parties generally benefit from this agreement. He may get money, sex, companionship, and affection; she gets the needed documents, better labor conditions, and a more stable economic situation for herself and her family. Sometimes, it is an agreement of friendship; and if problems arise, migrant women have more to lose.

In 2005, with Spain's Ley de Extranjería (Immigration Law), close to 700,000 migrants were able to get work permits and start the process of legal residence. After a year, family reunification was possible for these migrants. Two of the requisites were to have a job contract and to have resided in Spain continuously for at least two years. Another way was through *arraigo* (having already strong ties in Spain), for which migrants were required to prove that they had lived in Spain for at least three years, had familial relationships with Spaniards or foreigners with residence permits, and a job contract. Thanks to this law, about 135,783 Ecuadorians were able to 'regularize' their migratory status, and 52 percent of these were women (*El Comercio*, 4 August 2005).[19] Nevertheless, it was estimated that after the 2005 Ley de Extranjería, 300,000 migrants remained 'irregulars', i.e., without residence permits. The two women I interviewed in Spain were within this group. They were unable to apply because they did not have a permanent employer to sign a job contract with them, nor were they able to get one from a new employer. One married in 2005 and was in the process of obtaining her residence permit, while the other was undocumented without prospects of obtaining a residence permit. They also mentioned that they knew other women who had been unable to 'fix' their status under this law.[20]

The Feminization of the Ecuadorian Diaspora since the 1990s

> You cannot save money here [in Ecuador]; everything you earn is for daily expenses, to pay debts, for today, not for tomorrow or the day after tomorrow. Even potable water is so expensive now. I have no hope here. I'm in total debt. Salaries are miserable. One cannot live like this.

These are the words of Graciela, a Guayaquileñean woman eager to migrate within the next three years. At the time of the interview, she was 31. She added that she had to plan her migration because she was married and had a child. She worried about migrating and leaving her elderly parents in Guayaquil. Whether she will actually be able to migrate is unpredictable, but she was certain that she could no longer live in Ecuador. Countless Ecuadorian women have found transnational migration to be the only way to obtain a relatively stable job, a dignified wage, social security with real security once they retire, a place to live with less violence and fewer crimes, and a sense of working toward a better life for themselves and their families (García, 2004:2-3).

Sandra, a light-skinned woman from Guayaquil, recounted that she had to pay more than $2,000 for a business-class ticket to Madrid shortly before 3 August 2003, when a visa to enter a Schengen space became a requirement to enter Spain as a tourist.[21] Sandra added that according to the travel agency she visited, first-class tickets were also available, and these were the only 2 types of tickets on sale at the time. She said:

> I asked my godmother to lend me the money. My mother didn't want me to go, but I was fed up with Ecuador. I couldn't take it anymore! I'm a dentist, a professional! And couldn't get a decent job, and was tired of the corruption. During an internship at the City Hall of Guayaquil, travelling in a van to the poorest neighborhoods in the City, and basically removing molars, I didn't get paid one cent, not even for a soda. The people in the communities many times gave us lunch when they got to know us. Imagine, these people who barely had money for themselves were more generous than the people working in the City Hall or the dentists in high positions of the Regional Dentists' Association! Then, I managed to get hired for 6 months and had to pay $100 a month to the person who got me the job, out of the $250 I earned monthly. Then, I didn't get a permanent contract. I didn't have the right connections in the City Hall.[22]

At the time of the interview, Sandra was 34. She was married and had no children. Before migrating, she lived with her mother and grandmother in a middle-class neighborhood in the north of Guayaquil. She added that she had thought about migrating to Argentina before the economic collapse in 2001, but she did not want to migrate before getting her professional degree. She graduated; soon after, the economic crisis in Argentina became evident. In Spain, Sandra has worked as a dentist in several offices. But because she did not have a work permit at the time, Spain-certified dentists easily exploited her. The 'employment' agreements included that Sandra received no salary, saw patients in the morning (when there were fewer) and she had to pay half of what patients were charged to the dentist who owned the office. She has also worked as a babysitter and caretaker of several elderly women.

The gendered and ethnic stratification of labor already in place in Spain has restricted Ecuadorian migrant women to the private sphere as domestic workers (Solé and Parella, 2003:65). While agricultural and construction labor is geared toward male laborers, female migration is funneled toward domestic labor. It may be considered 'easier' for women to obtain work permits as domestic workers, as opposed to working in other sectors (hotels, retail) and many

Spanish families have signed employment contracts with women migrants. The women interviewed, however, stated that many Spanish families tell domestic migrant workers that they will help them to get work permits, with the condition of paying them even lower wages and under more exploitative conditions, and then fail to sponsor them. Other Spanish families show a willingness to help migrants, but are unable to do so because they do not meet the minimum income requirements to sponsor and legally hire a migrant worker as a domestic. It was also suggested that many Spanish families have developed love relationships, and have 'world-travelled'–to borrow Lugones' concept of loving perception in seeing oneself in the eyes of others to understand others, and understand oneself from the position of others–in their interactions with migrant workers and have helped them to obtain work permits. On the other hand, even though many immigrants have been 'regularized', often, it is only for a short period of time. Many are not able to renew their job contracts because their employers do not want to re-hire them for several reasons, including having to provide them with more social benefits.

In the case of Catalonia, the Basque Country, and other regions where Catalan, Euskera, and other languages besides Castilian are officially spoken, linguistic and cultural differences become more evident. The Ecuadorian immigrant in these regions must have some fluency in these languages in order to obtain better paying jobs and thus to be less socially marginalized. Sandra, who lives in Barcelona, has paid for and taken free Catalan language lessons, but she is still not fluent, although she understands most of it. She stated:

> If you don't speak Catalan, they [Catalans] think you're uneducated, which is what they think most immigrants are. I have to learn it to function here; my husband doesn't speak Catalan, and has no intention to learn; he came to Barcelona because the jobs are here.

A native of a small rural town in Andalusia, her husband is a semiskilled worker in a glass factory. Sandra acknowledges that he loves her more than she loves him, and a key aspect in deciding to get married was the fact that she did not have a residence permit in Spain and she was already in her thirties. I argue that if Sandra had stayed in Ecuador, it would have been unlikely that she would have married a semiskilled factory worker, given her professional class/status in Guayaquil. However, the fact that her husband is a white European already places him in a 'high' category in the Ecuadorian social hierarchy. While she is marrying 'down' in the sense that her husband does not have a university degree and is from a rural town, she is marrying 'up' by marrying a white European. In other words, intranational linguistic, cultural and socioeconomic differences in Spain, make migration to Spain a complex transnational and transcultural process.

Negotiating Structures, Shifting Positionalities

Patricia, a woman from Tulcán (a northern Andean city), who currently lives in Guayaquil and has no college education recounted the following:

> You feel you're going nowhere. You work, work, and see no progress, but the country is getting into more poverty and corruption. Men don't want to get married anymore. At work people want you to look nice, but with what money?...There are no jobs for women older than 35, especially if you don't have a career. If you aren't young, you're screwed.

A key aspect to a better understanding of why Ecuadorian women have been migrating in large numbers since the mid-1990s, is the negotiation of their subjectivities in the machista and heteropatriarchal organization of Ecuadorian society, depending on their age at the time of migration. In urban centers, most Ecuadorian women, generally with less formal education than men, work in the service sector. Women older than 35 have extremely limited job opportunities since they are no longer considered 'attractive', according to white supremacist aesthetics (hooks, 1996). Young women, especially those who wear miniskirts and present themselves as 'physically attractive' are given priority over older women. Unlike previous migrations, since the mid-1990s, a large number of women over 35 have migrated to Spain. To be hired to clean a house, to take care of the elderly or disabled, one must not look 'attractive'. What matters is the reliability, affection, and intimacy developed between the parties, coupled with the amount agreed upon to perform the job.

The very rigid social hierarchies make it almost impossible for impoverished, working class, lower-middle class, indigenous-looking people, and Afro-descendants to move up in the Occidentalist capitalist social ladder; and the experiences of Ecuadorian women in Spain reflect this. The domestic worker, 'works the whole day, they don't let you breathe, it enslaves you, they humiliate you, they call you dumb, retrograde, and if you're darker, it's worse', as Mariela notes. Mariela is an Ecuadorian medical doctor who lives in Spain and sporadically takes care of an elderly woman.[23] As this testimony suggests, darker women who are phenotypically indigenous and/or of African ancestry encounter more discrimination in the workplace and other spaces in Spain and Ecuador alike. The discrimination and socioeconomic exclusion that African diasporas have had in the Americas continue in the former colonizer's nation-state, as these Eurocentric ideologies were developed by Europeans to perpetuate uneven hierarchical power relations. That is, subjection to modern colonial regimes of racial classification and stratification (Quijano, 2000), the products of a world system based on racial capitalism and Western racisms–the legacies of colonial domination–are everyday experiences of Afro-descendants and indigenous Ecuadorian women, whether they identify themselves as such or not.

Despite the historic and current structures of power, in the last two decades, indigenous and Afro-descendant communities have become active agents in Ecuador's political life, but more visibly in the case of the indigenous movement. Ecuadorian society, however, is still plagued by Eurocentric racist notions about ethnicity, class, and race. For instance, it is well known in Guayaquileñean upper- and middle-class circles that *empleadas* or *niñeras* (domestics or babysitters), whether or not they live on the employers' premises, are usually dark-skinned Ecuadorians (recently, also Peruvians). Domestic workers in Ecuador are usually from towns and *favelas* surrounding large cities. If the worker is from the Andes, she may be derogatorily called *longa*. If she is a dark mestiza from the Coast, she may be called *chola*. If she is Afro-descendant from diverse parts of the country, particularly from the province of Esmeraldas or the Chota Valley, she may be called *negra*.[24] From my conversations with women migrants, I noted that darker-skinned women worked longer as domestics and caretakers in Spanish homes than did lighter-skinned women; and light-skinned Ecuadorians tried to 'pass' for Spaniards by adopting Spanish accents in public spaces as a strategy to avoid ID-verification by the police.[25] While most of the time police do not stop women to ask for residence permits, Mariela, an undocumented migrant at the time of the interview, mentioned that she always consciously kept a low profile, not becoming visible, when police were around.

There is no doubt that migration has offered a series of advantages denied at home. By migrating, many Ecuadorian women have had access to more capital and to cosmopolitan experiences. They have been able to leave their parents' house without having to get married. In Ecuador, most women leave the family house once they marry or move in with a male partner. Single mothers, women separated or divorced, with children or not, often live with their parents because they cannot afford to live by themselves. If a woman has not married by the age of 30, the social pressure to do so increases, and she may feel as if she has not accomplished what is expected of her. In Spain, Ecuadorian women enjoy some independence that they did not and would not have in Ecuador. They have reached an unprecedented level of socio-economic and emotional autonomy. They are less controlled by male figures (fathers, brothers, or husbands) or female ones (mothers, grandmothers). What seems to be in place is a network of care and solidarity among women who live together or share a friendship, although it is sometimes accompanied by envy and selfishness.

Diasporic Ecuadorian women have altered their social experiences and their status within the Western logic of social stratification developed in modern capitalism. Most, however, are still in subalternized social strata. Those who have professional degrees and become domestics and caretakers for the first time, 'lower' their social status, which causes them to experience a sense of inferiority and alienation. In Spain, Ecuadorian women may sometimes reside with strangers, relatives, friends, or acquaintances. They may feel isolated, discriminated against, or marginalized by Spanish society. Simultaneously, the anonymity of Spanish cities allows Ecuadorian women to enjoy a sense of freedom not experienced in the country of origin. Another aspect to consider is the impact of men's physical, emotional, and psychological violence against women. In Spain, Ecuadorian women feel more protected by the law. At the same time, men may be more careful and hesitant to be violent toward women because they fear that Ecuadorian women may use the law to protect themselves. In Ecuador, it had been relatively easy for abusive men to bribe authorities, including the police, judges, and lawyers, to get away with physical and psychological abuse of women. It should be noted, however, that Ecuadorian women continue to be physically and emotionally abused by men, in part because, historically, they have not been socialized to denounce abusive male partners and husbands, but to accept 'men as they are' for the sake of the 'family union'.

Queerness continues to be a hypocritical taboo in Ecuador in the sense that everyone knows or 'suspects' who may be queer, but most people do not discuss it openly. Although gays, lesbians, bisexuals and transgender people are increasingly gaining cultural visibility, queer people in Ecuador still lack important civil rights as couples and have reached few political allies at the national level. Now that gay marriage is possible in Spain (although there are pressures to have it revoked), Spain offers alternatives to many Ecuadorian queer women and men.

Transnational Families: Long-Distance Relations with Remittances

Many of the women who migrated to Spain by themselves had children, and did not have a steady partner at the time of migration. Many of these children had not been acknowledged by their fathers; and even when they were, their mothers still had almost full responsibility for their care. At migration, women often left their children with relatives. If children were over 18, they would remain in the household by themselves. In the case of Verónica, who was in her early twenties when her mother migrated to Spain in 2001, it was very difficult to adjust to a daily life without her mother. She indicated the following:

> It was a change of 360 degrees when my mom left because I had depended so much on her. I had to learn to depend on myself to emotionally support my younger brother, to be a sister and a mother to him. We knew that my mom sacrificed for our own sake. I couldn't disappoint her. I continued studying and working. Before my mom left, I almost never got sick. When she left, I developed allergies, got the flu; it was rather something psychological. But even after she left, she has been with us for everything. She calls me every Saturday. I yearn for the moment I'll see her. I have valued her much more now that she's far away. I thank God for protecting her.

In Ecuador, Carla, Verónica's mother, was the head of the household. There was no father figure around. In 1999, she 'retired' from the position of attaché of the wife of a prominent political leader, for whom she had worked for decades and had dedicated herself, even neglecting her own children. As compensation for retirement, Carla was offered a house in a lower middle-class neighborhood in Guayaquil. Soon after, Carla moved to this house with her children. A few months later, however, Carla found out that the house had never been put under her name, and only the down payment had been paid. After a series of arguments with the politician's wife, Carla obtained the title deed under her name and those of her children. Being very disappointed at the woman for whom she had worked and unable to pay the mortgage of the house, Carla migrated to Spain.

After Carla left, Verónica and her brother–who was still in high school–took turns cooking and cleaning the house, and learned to take care of each other. When asked why Verónica's mother, then 47, left instead of her, Verónica responded that her mother did not want her to make the sacrifice of working as an immigrant, and thus have to 'lower her head' to Spaniards by feeling inferior in an unknown society. In Guayaquil, Verónica did not see her mother Carla for more than 4 years. In 2004, she finished her studies in journalism. In 2005, she received a non-livable wage ($220 per month) while working full-time for a multinational financial corporation as a customer representative. Simultaneously, Carla made about $800 per month taking care of an elderly person in Mallorca, with whom she lived; and sent between $200 and $300 per month to her children through bank wires. Because Carla had not yet obtained a residence permit in Spain, she was unable to be at Verónica's wedding in 2004. During the entire ceremony, however, Carla was connected with her family by cellular telephone. Undoubtedly, technology has helped families to keep in touch and to help each other financially, while also coping with the absence of loved ones.

While some Ecuadorians have been able to maintain contact with family members who live abroad, others have not had such luck. For instance, Mariela, who, at the time of the interview, was unemployed and without a residence permit, stated the following:

> I couldn't go to Ecuador when my mother was very sick. First, my siblings didn't tell me that she was sick until a week before she died, once she was already in the hospital. In Ecuador, I lived with my mother and stepfather, who raised me like a daughter, and my two brothers. The other siblings lived nearby. Soon after I came to Spain, my stepfather died, then my mother. No one was really there for my mother when she was sick. And I couldn't be there to take care of her; my sisters had their own families, my brothers were of not much help. I have nothing in Ecuador. No house, no mother, no real family. Even if I still don't have papers, I get temporary jobs, and I'm often times unemployed, I'd rather stay here. In Ecuador, what I always got was part-time jobs. What could I do there now? The same?

As suggested above, daughters are expected to take care of the sick and the elderly. Although Mariela's two single brothers were living with their mother when she was extremely sick, they were somehow 'excused' on the basis that they were male. The irony of this migratory experience is that Mariela has taken care of elderly people in Spain, but was unable to lovingly attend to her own mother when she was sick.

Before migrating to Spain, and with a three-month visa, Mariela had stayed six months in the Netherlands to take care of her female cousin's newborn and toddler. She barely got out of the house and felt exploited by her cousin and her husband, getting paid about $400, in addition to the plane ticket and food for the six months she worked as a baby-sitter. She stated:

> She [her cousin] made me feel afraid of the police after my visa expired. She didn't want me to go out, not even in the evenings or the weekends, when she and her husband were home with the children. When I went out, it was always with her and her family. But later on, I got in contact with my brothers [Jehovah's Witnesses] and they helped me and were my support there. They told me about my rights and that I should not be afraid if I were stopped by the police. I don't know Dutch or English, so it was easier for my cousin to take advantage of me. She didn't want me to take evening language classes, always coming up with an excuse.

In terms of language, Mariela felt more at ease in Spain. Although she did not practice her profession, she occasionally participated in *Añoranzas: El corazón de los ecuatorianos* (Yearnings: The Heart of Ecuadorians), a radio program in Barcelona, initiated by a female Ecuadorian friend–while sporadically taking care of elderly women, covering the shifts of friends and acquaintances.

While a significant number of transnational families are being formed, the fact that many diasporic Ecuadorians do not have residence permits keeps relationships long distance for years and often, for decades. During this time, however, migrants send remittances to their families and relatives, which are used to cover daily expenses, support their children and parents, pay debts, medical costs, school fees, house remodeling costs, or to invest in real estate. In recent years, the proliferation of malls and stores that attract immigrants' families and receivers of remittances is quite remarkable in Ecuador's largest cities. For instance, in Guayaquil, Mall de California is located in a popular neighborhood of irregular settlements in the western hills of the city. Here one can find home appliances, construction materials, clothes, shoes, etc. No credit cards are required since stores often have their own credit lines, with higher interest rates than popular credit cards. The creation of this mall in this particular neighborhood points to the relevance of the consuming capacity of families that are receiving remittances from relatives abroad, as well as the business investments transnational families make.

Since 2000, remittances sent by Ecuadorian women and men are Ecuador's second largest revenue, only after petroleum. In 2002, $1,450 million officially entered Ecuador in the form of remittances, a figure larger than the total value of Ecuador's traditional exports of banana, shrimp, coffee, cocoa, and tuna (*Vistazo*, 7 February 2002; Ramírez Gallegos et al., 2005:75). In 2004, this amount rose to $1,600 million. From Spain, Ecuadorians received 31 percent of total remittances to Ecuador (*El Universo*, 7 May 2005), the second largest percentage of remittances, after the US. According to the Banco Central del Ecuador, in 2009, almost $3,000 million were received in Ecuador as remittances. While Ecuadorians in the US are the main senders of remittances (sending per capita $43.9 a month), Ecuadorians in Spain (sending per capita 34.5 a month) send 48 percent of the total influx of remittances (Aguiar Lozano 2008:102). This means that Ecuadorians in Spain are sending more in proportion to their numbers (approximately 500,000 people sending Euros), which reflect the proximity and sense of responsibility the latter group of migrants feels toward their families back in Ecuador. In part, this sense of closeness can be attributed to the relatively recent migration to Spain and the family ties migrants still have in Ecuador–especially if we consider that half of this diaspora is composed of women.

The Spanish and Ecuadorian Media

As stated earlier, Ecuadorians have concentrated in Spanish urban sectors where they were able to find jobs and knew someone who provided some guidance at the beginning. By living in Spain's largest cities, playing music in the most important plazas or working as street vendors, Ecuadorians acquired a relative degree of visibility in everyday Spanish life. Simultaneously, a kind of xenophobia and racism developed, linked to colonial histories and Eurocentric notions of race, ethnicity and culture. While Spaniards have insisted on lumping South Americans together by using the derogatory term *sudacas*, in fact, Ecuadorians are the most noted foreign national group for being the largest Latin American immigrant group.

During the highest point of the Ecuadorian migration to Spain, the Spanish international, national, and local media often practiced a kind of 'cultural fundamentalism' in their diffusion of news, manifesting xenophobic attitudes and using exclusionary rhetoric (Pedone, 2002). Concentration of workers from non-EU countries residing in several neighborhoods and cities rendered immigrants 'visible' in a negative way, worsening their social, economic, cultural status and accentuating their spatial segregation (Pedone, 2001:2-4). Other times, immigrants have become 'visible' temporarily as a result of a tragedy. For instance, in January 2001, 12 Ecuadorians died in an accident in Lorca, Murcia–where there is a large Ecuadorian community, working primarily in agriculture. As a result of the accident, Ecuadorian immigrants, as well as their exploitation by Spaniard employers, became 'visible' to Spaniards, and semi-slavery working conditions were denounced. However, after a month, Ecuadorians returned to invisibility in the media (Pedone, 2001).

Throughout Spain, Ecuadorians are creating their own radio shows that aim to connect Ecuadorian communities in Spain and Ecuador, while disseminating information about migration laws, social services, and legal assistance. Today, Ecuadorian networks such as TC Televisión, Ecuavisa, Ecuaplus, and TV4 broadcast a daily version of their programming for Ecuadorians living in Spain, while publicizing a range of services for migrants, as well as Ecuadorian products, services, and real estate. With this programming, Ecuadorians are not only being informed about Ecuador from Ecuadorian perspectives, but Spaniards are also confronted with 'Ecuadorian-ness' on cable TV.

Through globalized media, Ecuadorians are learning more about what happens outside Ecuador's borders. Until about 10 years ago, the visual images that arrived in Ecuador were mainly from the US in the forms of feature films, music videos, cartoons, and TV series. Now, visual images often come from Spain, Germany, Japan, Chile, Brazil, Colombia, among other countries. Simultaneously, the Ecuadorian diaspora has changed the way Ecuadorian newspapers present news regarding migration. For instance, *El Universo*, a major newspaper based in Guayaquil, has a permanent section called 'Migración' in the printed and online versions, which has included passport requirements, a list of countries that require visas for Ecuadorians, the 2001 Spain-Ecuador bilateral migratory agreement, and the latest news on what happens to Ecuadorians residing abroad. The subsection, 'Voces de Emigrantes' (Emigrants' Voices) showed about 500 brief messages from Ecuadorians living in an array of cities in Chile, Germany, Italy, Spain, United Kindgdom, Switzerland, Belgium, Australia, the US, and Canada, greeting their families who live throughout Ecuador, while also attaching pictures. Today, *El Universo* has a subsection called "El Mapa de los Ecuatorianos" (The Map of Ecuadorians), where one can locate oneself on a world map and write a short public message.

The online version of *El Comercio*, another major national newspaper based in Quito, has a section called 'Ecuatorianos en el mundo' (Ecuadorians in the World). A few years ago, it had a subsection 'Album Familiar', where immigrants were able to attach pictures to their messages, and a similar (and smaller) subsection was later included in the newspaper's printed version. The section: 'What are we doing outside?' encouraged letters from immigrants in the form of testimonials about their experiences, struggles, goals, and achievements in the country in which they resided. The new subsections of fora, surveys and blogs are attracting many young diasporic Ecuadorians. On Fridays, *El Comercio* publishes a weekly version in Madrid, and seeks to expand its market in Spain. In addition, there is a growing number of websites and blogs created by and for Ecuadorian associations, activists, and individuals in Spain, which keep the larger Ecuadorian diaspora connected and socially active, and sometimes nostalgic for their country.

The fact that Ecuadorians have concentrated in Spanish metropolitan areas, especially in its capital city, has offered Ecuadorians multiple advantages to be active producers of culture, to organize themselves, and to become dynamic social agents. Thus, larger cities that have institutional infrastructures and national political and socio-economic relevance, have rendered diasporic Ecuadorians more 'visible' and politically important both in Spain and Ecuador.

Some Preliminary Conclusions

Ecuadorian women have rendered the lives of Spanish families, especially Spanish women, more comfortable and relaxed, by taking care of their loved ones in exchange for a low salary and performing a socially unrecognized job. After long hours of work, often times, six days a week, Ecuadorian women have very little time, energy, and affection left to devote to their own families in Spain, in particular their children. This situation relates to the social difficulties that a significant number of Ecuadorian youth experiences in Spain. The formation of transnational gangs and belonging groups, youth violence and crime, drug use and sale, teenage pregnancy, and school dropout and failure rates, are some of the issues that many Ecuadorian women confront after having chosen to bring their children with them to Spain.

In the case of Ecuadorian women's histories and testimonies, language becomes an everyday tool with transformative qualities, which enables women to forge local, national, and transnational communities and networks of solidarity that seek to ease the migratory processes from Ecuador to Spain. It is through this language of greetings, pictures, online histories, testimonies and the formation of networks–which provide support for women when they leave their families, friends, jobs, and social milieu–that diasporic Ecuadorian women disrupt some of the historically-embedded Ecuadorian societal norms. Such translocations challenge and subvert the conventional male/heteropatriarchally-dominated patterns of migration and representation.

On the other hand, Ecuadorians in Spain have organized themselves much more effectively and promptly than those living in the US. They have created numerous associations, while working in conjunction with the civil society and religious groups in Ecuador, Spain and other EU countries, as well as with the state. The Asociación Hispano-Ecuatoriana Rumiñahui is perhaps the largest and most important diasporic Ecuadorian Association. [26] As Victoria Lawson (2000:262) points out, transnational migrants explicitly call into question dominant narratives of citizenship, the nation, and development. The Rumiñahui Association has been an effective and forceful vehicle in organizing the Ecuadorian diaspora in Spain and assisting diasporic Ecuadorians, while also prompting the Ecuadorian government to pay attention to the needs of Ecuadorian migrants in Spain and Italy. In fact, for the 2006 Ecuadorian presidential elections, there was a higher rate of registered voters in Spain than in the US. The timing, the availability of technology, the geopolitical location, the educational attainment of migrants, and their percentage in relation to the Spanish migrant population, have made this diaspora a collective of active agents both in Ecuador and Spain.

As expected, there was a decrease in Ecuadorian migration to Spain since 3 August 2003, when Ecuadorians were required to obtain a Schengen visa to enter Spain as tourists (and all Schengen 'spaces' since June 2003). Despite discrimination, xenophobia, racism, job instability, family fragmentation and restructuring, most Ecuadorians agree that they 'are better off' living outside of Ecuador. In fact, discrimination and racism are not foreign experiences to most Ecuadorians. Unlike most countries in the north, the Ecuadorian 'common sense' is to welcome foreigners as long as they are from Europe or North America, as they have been historically constructed as 'better' than most Ecuadorians, in that they are thought to be better trained, more educated, and of 'better races' (Anglo/European). It seems ironic that while thousands of Colombians, Peruvians, Iraqis, and Afghanis continue migrating to Ecuador as a way to escape violence, displacement, and poverty in their homelands, they are not necessarily being welcomed by most Ecuadorian citizens. In other words, Ecuadorians often act the same way they (or their relatives) have been treated abroad by other nationals who considered them weaker, poorer, ignorant, and more vulnerable.

Due to the economic and political impact of these relatively new migratory waves, Ecuadorian diasporas have become a constant subject of study and debate of intellectuals and academics. There have been numerous symposia, conferences, roundtables, and transnational and interdisciplinary research teams on the subject held and based in Latin America, Italy, Spain, and other EU countries.

There are currently 13 Ecuadorian consulates in Spain, which, in conjunction with SENAMI, serve the second largest number of Ecuadorian immigrants, after the U.S. From the onset of the massive Ecuadorian migration to Spain, there have been regular dialogues between both governments regarding migratory policies. In fact, for the VI EU-Latin American and the Caribbean Summit, to be held 16-19 May 2010 in Madrid, Ecuador's government, supported by other Latin American and Caribbean states, will appeal to EU-member states to ratify the 'International Convention on the Protection of the Rights of All Migrant Workers and Their Families,' which was adopted by the UN General Assembly on 18 December 1990, and entered into force in March 2003.

While Ecuadorians constantly know about the risks, exploitation, abuses, deaths, and deportations that people experience in their attempt to migrate to the US and the EU, and efforts have been made by non-profit organizations, NGOs, the civil society, and the state, to assist and inform migrants and those who plan to migrate, it seems that the Ecuadorian media and family conversations mainly stress the 'positive' aspects about transnational migration. Detailed information about deportations, abuses by authorities, and human trafficking, usually of women and children are presented as isolated cases, without offering a clear picture of the gruesome and entangled nature of human trafficking and the harsh living conditions of many migrants. In addition, the extortion of Ecuadorian citizens who entered the US or EU countries with the 'aid' of unscrupulous intermediaries, for sums ranging from $6,000 to $12,000 per person, has brutally disrupted a sense of self and family life.

Assuming that people know about these risks, they still take the chance. This indicates their (our) level of desperation. While we may live in a world of cultural and economic flows across formally entrenched national boundaries, 'the world continues to be divided, in stark terms, between its 'developed' and 'underdeveloped' sectors, and goods continue to travel with more ease than most human beings. The 'unsatisfaction,' desperation, and determination of Ecuadorian women in migrating and *staying* in Spain–with the aim to prosper within the logic of Enlightenment–against all odds, epitomize the signs that they 'have been left out of the global dream of prosperity' (Gikandi, 2000: 628-29), deployed in what Appadurai (1996) calls global mediascapes and ideoscapes. Nevertheless, it is fair to state that after a few years living and working in Spain, most Ecuadorian immigrants see themselves as 'better off,' in the sense that they have earned higher salaries that have allowed them to support themselves, and provide for their families both in Ecuador and Spain.

'It has become impossible to live in Ecuador,' I was told by Graciela. Ecuadorian women, more than ever, ventured to foreign lands without Schengen visas, or any visas in most cases, paying thousands of dollars, and getting into debt. Many had someone to contact in the place of final destination: a relative, a friend, or acquaintance who may help them at the beginning. Thus, people have been the most reliable resources on which Ecuadorian women count.

The unfinished project of the Ecuadorian nation-state failed them. From the standpoint of human development and sustainability, neoliberalism has failed in Ecuador, as it has elsewhere throughout the global South (Acosta and Falconí, 2005b:17). As in previous migrations, Ecuadorian women translocated themselves because they had lost hope that the conditions in their country would change. It seems to me that the perspective that 'we're better off outside our country' has permeated the consciousness of Ecuadorians living both in Ecuador and abroad, an idea (and fact) that must not be severed from historical capitalist processes and Eurocentric discourses of linear history and development, which located Latin America as a world region–especially Andean countries–at the peripheries of global economic, cultural and political processes, while knowledges and achievements of indigenous, Afro-descendant and mestizo people, especially women, living in Ecuador have been obscured and considered non-existent.

NOTES

[1] I wrote this paper between 2005 and 2006. It was originally published by the *Journal of Developing Societies* Vol. 23.1-2 (2007): 113-143. Between 2006 and 2010, many things have changed in Ecuadorian transnational migration, EU migration policy, as well as global and local political scenarios. While the main arguments presented here were based on research I conducted more than 6 years ago, in revising this essay, I have tried to incorporate some of the major changes of these ever-fluid processes of transnational migration, and how these affected Ecuadorian women migrants. In a telephone conversation with Sandra, an Ecuadorian woman living in Barcelona, while we were sharing our respective experiences outside of Ecuador, she playfully and reflexively interjected that '*la verdad es que estamos mejor fuera del país*' ('the truth is that we're better off outside our country'). This inherently situated truth, this translated, incomplete, *partial* truth (Clifford, 1986:7) can be understood as an allegory with multiple meanings for different Ecuadorian women with regard to their experiences outside of Ecuador. Throughout this chapter, due to space limitations, I have included only my English translations of the Spanish language narratives of Ecuadorian women. In all instances, I have translated to the best of my knowledge. I thank Miliann Kang, my fellow graduate students in the Spring 2006 seminar 'Issues on Feminist Research' at the University of Massachusetts Amherst, Erica Polakoff, and Ligaya Lindio-McGovern for their helpful comments and ongoing dialogue. All mistakes are mine.

[2] For instance, on November 8, 2008, Ecuadorian immigrant Marcelo Lucero, 37, was stabbed to death by Anglo-American teenager Jeffrey Conroy–accompanied by six of his school classmates–in a parking lot of Patchogue train station, Long Island, NY, as part of the 'Mexican-hopping' they practiced. Latino and migrant activist organizations have been vigilant of every step of this legal process. *The New York Times* and major Ecuadorian newspapers, including *El Universo* and *El Comercio* have often reported on this and other similar cases of murder of Ecuadorian migrants.

[3] I conversed with this Catalan man one evening, after using the internet services he provided in his cybercafé/*locutorio* (mostly used by non-European migrants). The derogatory term *moro* refers to the exclusion of Muslims in Spain during *la Recon-*

quista [The Reconquest] and thereafter, which involved, among other things, the expulsion of Jewish and Muslim peoples from Iberian territories.

4   According to the Dirección Nacional de Migración [Ecuadorian National Migration Office], between 1993 and 2004, 957,158 Ecuadorians migrated (cited in Ramírez Gallegos and Ramírez, 2005:44, 235). This figure, of course, is only an estimate since many Ecuadorians migrate without obtaining a passport, a departure permit, a plane ticket, etc. Besides EU countries and the US, Ecuadorians have also migrated to Canada, Russia, Chile, Venezuela, Brazil, and other Latin American nation-states.

5   For instance, by 2008 there were 2,391,000 foreigners from non-EU countries living in France. In Germany, this figure was 4,740,000. In the UK, this figure was 2,406,000 (Eurostat).

6   By interviewing Ecuadorian women in Spain and Ecuador, I sought to 'start off thought' from the lives of Ecuadorian women, their situated knowledges, and social locations in order to generate critical questions about Ecuadorian women's migration (Harding, 1993). The different geopolitical locations of these women represent different standpoints and can thus contribute different knowledges about the Ecuadorian diaspora. For instance, the interviews with Ecuadorian women in Spain helped me to understand the complexities in the migratory process to Spain and their familial relationships. The interviews with Ecuadorian women living in Ecuador, who had relatives in Spain, were intended to enable a contextualization of the migration from the perspectives of those relatives left behind by the migrants, while also aiming to understand how migration shapes the dynamics and relationships of the 'transnational' family. The women in Ecuador provided a detailed perspective on the difficulties in carrying out the wish and need to migrate. Throughout this essay, the names of the women interviewed have been altered in order to protect their privacy, as they themselves suggested. The sample of the women was selected on the basis of preexisting personal contacts of the author, and those later contacted through the first few women interviewed.

7   Here I am in dialogue with Haraway (1988:585) who calls for an 'objectivity that privileges contestation, deconstruction, passionate construction, webbed connections, and hope for transformation of systems of knowledge and ways of seeing'.

8   As Hesse-Bibber and Yaisser (2004) have noted, feminist standpoint begins with research questions rooted in women's everyday

existence, which reflect the multiplicity, multidimensionality, and fluidity of women's subjectivities and structural differences within a society. Following Smith (1974, 2004:35), in this essay I have attempted not to 'rewrite the other's world or impose upon it a conceptual framework which extracts from it what it fits with ours [mine]'. I have tried to explicate and analyze their experienced world rather than administering it, and framing it within current theories that may 'fit' their experienced world.

[9] Here I refer particularly to Mohanty's insightful essay 'Under Western Eyes: Feminist Scholarship and Colonial Discourses' (2003:17-22), in which she addresses much of Western feminisms' rendering of the 'Third World woman' as a singular, monolithic subject, representing 'Third World' women and producing an image of an 'average Third World woman', who lives an essentially truncated existence based on her feminine gender (sexually constrained) and her being 'Third World' (ignorant, poor, uneducated, tradition-bound, domestic, family-oriented, victimized, etc.). While I contend that the term 'Third World' is an imposed and inadequate category to refer to women living in or originally from nation-states located mostly in the Southern hemisphere and formerly colonized by European empires since 1492, I believe Mohanty offers a valuable critique for understanding women in subalternized positionalities from non-Occidentalist perspectives.

[10] Needless to say, there are clear distinctions between the historic and current situations of Ecuadorian migrants in Spain and other countries in the northern hemisphere and African Americans in the US. Addressing the specificities of these differences is beyond the scope of this chapter. While there is a growing number of Ecuadorian migrants and first generation US children born to Ecuadorian migrants who graduate from US colleges and universities, most do not seem to stay in the academy and to work from there–for financial reasons, personal and professional choices. Ecuadorians from the upper-middle classes, however, increasingly enroll in US and EU universities as international students. Facilitated by the use of Castilian in most universities, the relatively low cost of higher education, as well as prior socialization and class, Ecuadorians are increasingly enrolling in Spanish universities at a much faster rate than Ecuadorians in the US and Italy (the third country of Ecuadorian migratory destination). It is still too soon to speculate on first generation youth born (or raised) in Spain to Ecuadorian migrants. In 10 years, we will have a clearer understanding and more detailed statistics.

[11] Because traditional Marxist definitions of social class do not necessarily apply to all people in the early twenty-first century, I understand members of 'professional-working' class as the households of wage earners who may have a university degree or some higher education. Their salaries, access to capital, alienation, and exploitation, however, may not be too different from the working class (the proletariat) lacking a professional or university degree.

[12] As Narayan (1989, 2004:218) states, 'important strands in feminist epistemology hold the view that our concrete embodiments as members of a specific class, race, and gender, as well as our concrete historical situations necessarily play significant roles in our perspective on the world; moreover, no point of view is "neutral" because no one exists unembedded in the world'. Narayan adds that 'Knowledge is gained not by solitary individuals but by socially constituted members of groups that emerge and change through history'. For further discussion about feminist epistemological standpoints and situated knowledges as employed in this chapter, see Alcoff and Potter (1993), Harding (1993), and Hesse-Biber and Yaisser (2004).

[13] In October 1963, Spain and Ecuador signed an agreement in which a tourist visa for a stay in either country shorter than 90 days was not required. In 4 March 1964 both countries signed another agreement, which allowed *doble nacionalidad* [Double Nationality], and it was modified on 25 August 1995. As a way to regulate the massive Ecuadorian migration to Spain, on 31 January 2001, Ecuador and Spain signed a kind of 'Bracero/Guest-Worker Program'–a Spanish government's guest-worker program, which prompted the migration of temporary Ecuadorian workers, regulating entry and encouraging return migration. This program was geared primarily to attract workers to rural and agricultural areas, based on specific Spanish job offers. After the job contract expired, Ecuadorians would be forced to return to Ecuador, unless they found another employment, an extended job offer, and thus an extension of their residence permits in Spain.

[14] I understand historic amnesia as the erasure of the collective history of invasion of the Americas by Spaniards (and other Europeans) since 1492, the colonization and genocide of indigenous populations, as well as the accumulation of wealth in Western Europe through the exploitation of human labor and natural resources of the Americas. Moreover, I am alluding to the declin-

ing US economic and cultural hegemony, multinationals located in Ecuador, including those extracting petroleum from the Amazon, and the US military base in Manta (Ecuador's second most important port) during the period of 1999-2009, which are other factors not considered in the analyses of current forces that shape Ecuadorian migrations. A full discussion of these elements of historic amnesia is beyond the scope of this chapter. The inter-relationships of these historical events and Ecuador's current realities are not sufficiently analyzed in the context of recent Latin American (and other nations from the global South) migrations to Spain (and other EU member states). Gloria Camacho (2004) is one of the few intellectuals historicizing Ecuadorian female migrations, especially in context of the Spanish imperial conquest and colonization.

[15] Since the 1970s, Ecuador's public debt had been signed under dubious circumstances, its repayment represented more than 40 percent of the GDP, and was not used for the purposes for which it was acquired. On 9 July 2007 President Rafael Correa created the Comisión para la Auditoría Integral del Crédito Público [Integral Audit of Public Debt Commission], in charge of analyzing the negotiating processes of Ecuador's public debt. By ecological debt, I refer to Acosta's (2005a), Acosta and Falconí's (2005b) and Correa's (2005) respective analyses of the relationship between Ecuador's *sobre-endeudamiento* [overdebt] and the global ecological importance of the Amazon region–in particular its forests and humid tropical jungles, which represent one third of all tropical forests in the planet, and has one of the world's richest and most diverse fauna and flora. Although the Amazon region is considered 'the lungs of humanity' and its ecological importance is acknowledged in international fora, as Acosta (2005a) points out, the extraction of petroleum in the region by transnational corporations–including Texaco and Oxy–has put life under serious risk, in order to serve the purposes of capital accumulation. While Ecuador is the eighth-largest supplier of oil to the US and its productivity and revenue in the last few years have made Oxy earn the No. 6 spot on the BusinessWeek 50 list of top corporate performers (*BusinessWeek Online*, 2006), and international financial institutions coerce Amazonian nation-states to pay for *their* debt, the Amazon region does not receive compensation for the service it provides to the entire planet (as its lungs) because the air is free. For a detailed analysis and serious reflection of this subject, see Acosta (2005a).

[16] The figure of 26,357 Ecuadorians who left Spain in 2009, according to the INE could also be interpreted as the result of other factors including: unemployment, mortgage payment crisis, Spanish citizenship laws denying Spanish citizenship to children born in Spain to foreign parents whose national laws allow their children to keep their citizenship (as in the case of the 2008 Ecuadorian Constitution), and which in turn prevent immigrants from obtaining residence permits, as well as Ecuador's government programs to promote the return of migrants, through the Secretaría Nacional del Migrante (SENAMI) [National Secretariat of Migrants]. All of these factors may have contributed to the significant decrease in the numbers of Ecuadorians in Spain. It should be considered, in addition, that many of these Ecuadorians, through migratory networks of family and friends, may have migrated to other European countries, including Germany and Italy.

[17] This, of course, does not apply to prior migrations of citizens of the Southern Cone–most being exiles and descendants of European migrants–during the military dictatorships in the 1970s and 1980s, nor to other (upper) middle-class and formally educated migrants, émigrés, and exiles.

[18] *Coyotaje* can be loosely defined as the transnational/translocal business of the unchecked transportation of people who wish to migrate and are unable to do so through legal means. The *coyote* usually charges large amounts of money and may take advantage of the vulnerability of people desperate to migrate at all costs.

[19] Throughout this chapter, I use the term 'regularize' in reference to the dominant usage in Spain of the verb 'regularizar', which points to the process of changing one's migratory status from being 'undocumented' [*sin papeles*] to being 'documented' or 'legal'.

[20] I use the term 'fix' and 'regularize' interchangeably, as a way to convey the meaning of the Spanish word *arreglar*, which Ecuadorian migrants use to refer to the process mentioned in the note above.

[21] The Schengen zone, a region without border controls, has its origins in the Schengen Agreement of 1985, signed by Belgium, Netherlands, Luxembourg, Germany and France. By the Schengen Convention of 1990, Spain and Portugal had joined. The Schengen area currently consists of 25 countries: Austria, Belgium, Denmark, France, Finland, Germany, Greece, Italy, Luxembourg, Netherlands, Portugal, Spain, Sweden, the Czech Republic,

Estonia, Hungary, Latvia, Lithuania, Malta, Poland, Slovakia, Slovenia, as well as the two non-EU countries, Norway and Iceland and, as of 12 December 2008, Switzerland. (Gateway to the European Union). While the Schengen area abolished checks at internal borders, created common requirements for short-stay visas for persons from non-Schengen countries, and developed the Schengen Information System, it restricted its external borders and further marked the distinction between who is allowed to be inside and outside of Europe.

[22] Sandra, who currently lives in Barcelona, stated that the Regional Dentists' Association had the connections that made it possible for dentists to work for the City Hall.

[23] Mariela, 56, is a dark-skinned Ecuadorian who first migrated to Madrid in 2001. After being unable to find a stable job and a place to live, she and a female friend–who had also recently arrived–moved to Barcelona. Besides being a medical doctor, Mariela has a degree in journalism and studied diplomacy for two years.

[24] All these terms that have been constructed within Occidentalist notions of race and ethnicity as derogatory, have been appropriated by Ecuadorian and transnational social movements as terms of self-identity and self-consciousness toward participatory democracy, the construction of pluricultural societies, and the claim of rights and reparations.

[25] I should add that many women and men with whom I talked in Spain had acquired Spanish accents and idiomatic expressions in their everyday communication, in part because of their socialization with Spanish citizens and their watching of Spanish television.

[26] Interestingly, Rumiñahui refers to the symbolic last warrior of the Tawantinsuyo, who, until his death, resisted the Spanish conquistadores.

REFERENCES

Acosta, A. (2005a) *Desarrollo glocal: Con la Amazonía en la mira*. Quito: Corporación Editora Nacional.

Acosta, A. and Falconí, F. (2005b) 'Otra política económica, deseable y posible', in A. Acosta and F. Fander (eds.) *Asedios a lo imposible: Propuestas económicas en construcción*. Quito: FLACSO-Ecuador and ILDIS-FES.

Aguiar Lozano, V.H. (2008) 'Las remesas y la oferta de trabajo en Ecuador', *Cuestiones Económicas* 24(2):93-112. Accessed May 2010 from www.bce.fin.ec/frame.php?CNT=ARB0000006.

Alcoff, L. and Potter, E. (eds.) (1993) *Feminist Epistemologies.* New York and London: Routledge.
Appadurai, A. (1996) *Modernity at Large: Cultural Dimensions of Globalization.* Minneapolis: University of Minnesota Press.
Arango, J. (2000) 'Becoming a Country of Immigration at the End of the Twentieth Century: The Case of Spain', in King, Russell, Lazaridis, Gabriella and Tsardanidis, Charalambos (eds.) *Eldorado or Fortress?: Migration in Southern Europe.* New York: St. Martin's.
Banco Central del Ecuador (www.bce.fin.ec).
Borrero Vega, A. and Vega Ugalde, S. (1995) *Mujer y migración: Alcance de un fenómeno nacional y regional.* Quito: Abya-Yala.
BusinessWeek Online (2006) 'The Heat on Oxy in Ecuador', 24 April 2006. Accessed May 2006 from www.businessweek.com /magazine/content/06_17/b3981061.htm.
Camacho Zambrano, G. (2004) 'Feminización de las migraciones en Ecuador' in F. Hidalgo et al. (eds) *Migraciones: Un juego con cartas marcadas.* Quito: Abya-Yala.
Camacho Zambrano, G and Hernández Basante, K. (2005) *Cambió mi vida: migración femenina, percepciones e impactos.* Quito: UNIFEM and CEPLAES (Centro de Planificación y Estudios Sociales).
Carpio Benalcázar, P. (1992) *Entre Pueblos y metrópolis: la migración internacional en comunidades austroandinas del Ecuador.* Cuenca: Abya-Yala.
Clifford, James (1986) 'Partial Truths', in J. Clifford and G. E. Marcus (eds.) *Writing Culture:The Poetics and Politics of Ethnography.* Berkeley: University of California Press.
Collins, P. Hill (2000) 'What's Going? Black Feminist Thought and the Politics of Postmodernism', in E. St. Pierre and W.S. Pillow (eds.) *Working the Ruins: Feminist Poststructural Theory and Methods in Education.* London and New York: Routledge.
Correa, R. (2005) 'Otra economía es posible', in A. Acosta and F. Falconí (eds.) *Asedios a lo imposible: Propuestas económicas en construcción.* Quito: FLACSO-Ecuador & ILDIS-FES.
Cuesta, e. (2007) 'Guayaquileña (In)Documentada: One-Way Ticket to My Diaspora(s): A Testimonio', in N. R. Mirabal and A. Laó-Montes (eds.)*Techno-Futuros: Critical Interventions in Latina/o Studies.* Lanham: Rowman and Littlefield.
García, P. (2004) 'La migración de argentinos y ecuatorianos a España: representaciones sociales que condicionaron la migración', *Amérique Latine: Histoire et Mémorie.* Migrations en Argentina II (9). Accessed June 2005 from http://alhim.revues.org/document399.html.

Gateway to the European Union. 'Commission adopts revised mechanism for verifying the application of Schengen rules in the Member States'. Reference: IP/09/359. 5 March 2009. Accessed May 2010 from http://europa.eu/rapid/pressReleasesAction.do?reference=IP/09/359&format=HTML&aged=0&language=EN&guiLanguage=en.

Gikandi, Simon (2000) 'Globalization and the Claims of Postcoloniality', *South Atlantic Quarterly* 100(3): 627-58.

El Universo. Guayaquil, Ecuador. Available at http://www.eluniverso.com.

Eurostat. News Release 184/2009 16 December 2009. Available at [http://epp.eurostat.ec.europa.eu/cache/ITY_PUBLIC/3-16122009-BP/EN/3-16122009-BP-EN.PDF], accessed 20 March 2010.

Harding, S. (1993) 'Rethinking Standpoint Epistemology: What is "Strong Objectivity"?', in L. Alcoff and E. Porter (eds.) *Feminist Epistemologies.* New York and London: Routledge.

Haraway, D. (1988) 'Situated Knowledges: The Science Question in Feminism and the Privilege of Partial Perspective', *Feminist Studies* 14(3): 575-99.

Herrera, G. (2003) 'La migración vista desde el lugar de origen. Comentarios al dossier 'Los claroscuros de la migración', *Iconos* 15: 86-94.

Herrera, G., Castillo, M. and Torres, A. (eds.) (2005) *La migración ecuatoriana: transnacionalismo, redes e identidades.* Quito: FLACSO-Plan Migración, Comunicación y Desarrollo.

Hesse-Biber, S. and Yaisser, M. (eds.) (2004) *Feminist Perspectives on Social Research.* New York and Oxford: Oxford University Press.

hooks, b. (1996) *Reel to Real: Race, Sex, and Class at the Movies.* New York and London: Routledge.

Huntoon, Laura (1998) 'Immigration to Spain: Implications for a Unified European Union Immigration Policy', *International Migration Review* 32(2): 423-50.

Jokisch, B. and Pribilsky, J. (2002) 'The Panic to Leave: Economic Crisis and the "New Emigration" from Ecuador', *International Migration.* 40(4): 75-101.

Kyle, David (2000) *Transnational Peasants: Migrations, Networks, and Ethnicity in Andean Ecuador.* Baltimore: John Hopkins University.

Kyle, D. and Liang, Z. (2001) 'Migration Merchants: Human Smuggling from Ecuador and China', Working Paper 43, October 2001. *The Center for Comparative Immigration Studies.* University of California, San Diego.

Lawson, V.A. (2000) 'Questions of Migration and Belonging: undertandings of migration under neoliberalism in Ecuador'. *International Journal of Population Geography* 5: 261-76.

Miles, A. (2004) *From Cuenca to Queens: An Anthropological Story of Transnational Migration.* Austin: University of Texas.
Mohanty, C.T. (2003) *Feminism Without Borders: Decolonizing Theory, Practicing Solidarity.* Durham: Duke University Press.
Naples, N. (2003) *Feminism and Method: Ethnography, Discourse Analysis, and Activist Research.* New York and London: Routledge.
Narayan, U. (1989, 2004) 'The Project of Feminist Epistemology: Perspectives from Nonwestern Feminist', in S. Harding (ed.) *The Feminist Standpoint Theory Reader: Intellectual and Political Controversies.* New York and London: Routledge.
Pedone, C. (2001) 'Los medios de comunicación y la inmigración: la inmigración ecuatoriana en la prensa española', *Scripta Nova. Revista Electrónica de Geografía y Ciencias Sociales*, 94: 43. Accessed 21 June 2005 from http://www.ub.es/geocrit/sn94-43.htm.
Pedone, C. (2002) 'Las representaciones sociales en torno a la inmigración ecuatoriana a España'. *Iconos* 14: 56–66.
Quijano, A. (2000) 'Colonialidad del Poder y Clasificación Social'. *Journal of World-Systems Research* VI(2):342-86.
Ramírez Gallegos, F. and Ramírez, J.P. (2005) *La estampida migratoria ecuatoriana: crisis, redes transnacionales y repertorios de acción migratoria.* Quito: Abya-Yala.
Riaño, Y. (2003) 'Migration of Skilled Latin American Women to Switzerland and Their Struggle for Integration', in Y. Mutsuo (ed.) *Emigración Latinoamericana: Comparación Interregional entre América del Norte, Europa y Japón.* Population Movement in the Modern World VII. JCAS. Symposium Series 19. Osaka: The Japan Centre for Area Studies, National Museum of Ethnology.
Sassen, S. (1999) 'Transnational Economies and National Migration Policies', in M.J. Castro (ed.) *Free Markets, Open Societies, Closed Borders?: Trends in International Migration and Immigration Policy in the Americas.* Coral Gables: North-South Center Press at the University of Miami.
Smith, D. (1974, 2004) 'Women's Perspective as a Radical Critique of Sociology', in S. Hesse-Biber and M. Yaisser (eds.) *Feminist Perspectives on Social Research.* New York and Oxford: Oxford University.
Solé, C. and Parella, S. (2003) 'Migrant Women in Spain: Class, Gender and Ethnicity', in J. Andall (ed.) *Gender and Ethnicity in Contemporary Europe.* Oxford and New York: Berg.
Vistazo (7 February 2002) Guayaquil, Ecuador.

PART 2

Women's Resistance and
Capitalist Production for Export

CHAPTER 3

The Employment Decisions of Female Garment Workers in Sri Lanka's Export Processing Zones

Judith Shaw, Monash University, Australia

ABSTRACT

This study used a sample survey methodology to investigate the factors underlying the employment decisions of female garment workers in Sri Lanka's Export Processing Zones (EPZs). It found that most were pushed rather than pulled into EPZ employment by poverty and a weak labour market. Workers came from poorer than average households. Their remittances made a vital contribution to family welfare, and were often the sole source of regular household income. Generally low levels of job satisfaction and workers' employment preferences indicated that most would have preferred to be elsewhere, but their employment choices were constrained by a limited and unattractive range of alternative livelihoods. The impact of the changing global competitive environment on job quantity and quality in the EPZs is briefly discussed.

Keywords: Asia, Sri Lanka, export processing zones, women, employment

Introduction

Over the last two decades there has been a phenomenal expansion in garment manufacturing in South and East Asia. This rapid growth is attributable to a variety of factors including competitive regional labour costs, the widespread adoption of export-oriented growth policies and, until very recently, guaranteed access to Western markets under the terms of the Multi-Fibre Agreement (MFA). In Sri Lanka, the export-oriented garment industry had become a key sector of the economy by the turn of the century, contributing 17 percent of the gross domestic product (GDP), 4 percent of jobs and 47 percent of export earnings (CBSL, 2003). About two-thirds of investment in the sector was foreign-sourced, mainly from South Korea, Taiwan and Hong Kong. Production and employment were concentrated in the metropolitan Western Province, where around three quarters of garment factories were located, particularly in the Katunayake and Biyagama Export Processing Zones (EPZs). Nearly 90 percent of garment workers were young women who migrated from rural areas to live in the dormitory precincts surrounding the Zones.

In a weak labour market, where unemployment and marginal, intermittent informal sector jobs were the norm for unskilled workers, the Zones were virtually the only source of regular, secure work available to young rural women. Nevertheless, persistently high turnover and vacancy rates indicated that EPZ factories had difficulty attracting and retaining staff.[1] There is a substantial literature on labour standards and living conditions in the Sri Lankan garment industry, most of it highly critical. Unsafe working conditions, under-payment of wages, excessive hours, harsh discipline, poor career development prospects, suppression of trade union rights, substandard accommodation arrangements and the social stigmatization of garment workers have been extensively documented (ACFFTU, 1995; CENWOR, 2001; Gunatilaka, 1999; Hettiarachchi, 1992; Heward, 1997; Kelegama and Epaarachchi, 2002).

This article investigates the factors underlying the employment decisions of Sri Lankan EPZ workers. The assumption that most garment workers are poor is supported by anecdotal evidence, but there has been little attempt to test it empirically. The section 'The Workers and Their Families' compares the socioeconomic status of EPZ workers' households with that of the wider population. The section 'Young Rural Women and the Labour Market' reviews the labour market for rural women, and examines the EPZ employment decision in the context of the accessibility and attractiveness of alternative livelihoods.[2] Few studies have sought to gauge the perceptions and motivations of the workers themselves (for an exception see CENWOR, 2001). The section 'Life in the Zone' examines workers' views on their lives as 'factory girls'. The concluding section discusses recent labour market developments affecting rural Sri Lankans and their consequences for the future of work in the EPZs.

Methodology

The principal survey instrument was a structured questionnaire administered in January 2004 to garment workers in Sri Lanka's oldest and largest EPZ, the Katunayake EPZ, located 30 kilometres from the national capital, Colombo. One hundred workers were interviewed over a three-week period. The questionnaire contained a mix of open-ended and limited choice questions covering respondents' demographic and socioeconomic backgrounds; their reasons for seeking EPZ employment and perceptions of alternative labour market opportunities; pay, conditions, accommodation and travel arrangements in the EPZs; and general levels of satisfaction with their working and living conditions. The questionnaire was supplemented by focus group interviews with 20 randomly selected respondents.

The questionnaires were administered by staff from the Katunayake Working Women's Centre, an NGO providing advocacy and health services to garment workers. As former garment workers themselves, the interviewers were familiar with the issues covered in the questionnaire, and were able to empathise with the respondents' concerns and gain their confidence. As interviewers were unable to enter the Zones due to the controversial 'gate pass' requirement which denied entry to unauthorized personnel,[3] interviews were conducted in the residential areas outside the Zone precincts. Interviewers identified respondents by visiting randomly selected accommodation facilities within the residential areas after the main day shift, and requesting women who were present to participate in the survey. When workers declined to be interviewed, interviewers were instructed to approach others until they had completed their allocated interviews. Response rates were high: nine women declined to participate when initially approached, but most displayed interest in the survey process and were keen to take part.

The Workers and Their Families: Socioeconomic Characteristics

The garment industry workforce profile was overwhelmingly young, single and female: women accounted for 87 percent of garment factory workers, although men predominated in management positions.[4] Over 90 percent of the 100 respondents were under 30 (Table 3.1), and 89 percent were unmarried. Nearly three quarters had completed at least 10 years of schooling, and 13 percent had completed their high school 'A-levels', a rate of attainment consistent with the national profile and reflecting Sri Lanka's commendable performance in public education in comparison with other developing countries.

With urban and rural poverty rates of 8 and 26 percent respectively, poverty in Sri Lanka is predominantly a rural phenomenon (DCS, 2003). The rural sector, which accounts for about three quarters of the population, contains 88 percent of the country's poor. Poverty incidence is highest in remote, largely subsistence-based agrarian regions, somewhat lower among the semi-urban populations of regional towns and along the country's arterial transport routes, and lowest of all in the metropolitan Western Province. The EPZ workforce profile was overwhelmingly rural agrarian: 79 percent of the sample came from farming villages and a further 15 per-

Table 3.1
Age Distribution

Age group	Frequency
Under 20	15
20-24	52
25-29	24
30 and above	9
Total	**100**

cent from very remote locations more than a kilometer from a village, while only 6 percent were from cities or regional towns. Only one respondent came from the prosperous Western Province.

Over 80 percent of the respondents came from the Northwestern, North-central and Central provinces (Table 3.2), a finding consistent with evidence elsewhere that the propensity for rural-to-urban labour migration was highest in the rural regions surrounding industrial centres, and declined with distance (Dunham and Edwards, 1997). In comparison with more centrally-located districts, the remote northern and south-eastern regions are poorly integrated into the cash economy, insulated from the cultural pressures of globalization, and are likely to have stronger social prohibitions on the migration of unmarried women. Other factors which help to explain the low contributions of the Southern, Uva and Northeastern provinces to the Katunayake workforce are the absorption of labour from the southern districts by the Koggala EPZ, located in the Southern Province; and linguistic and ethnic differences between the majority Sinhalese population and the Tamil population which is concentrated in the Northern and Eastern provinces.

Respondent households were poorer than average. As Table 3.3 shows, they compared unfavourably with the wider population on a variety of indicators–location, household access to electrical power, and occupation of the household head–which are strongly associated with household poverty (Aturupane, 1999; World Bank, 2002). In addition, they were more than twice as likely as the general population to be female-headed. Sri Lankan census data indicates, somewhat counter-intuitively, that female-headed households are not significantly poorer than the general population (DCS, 2003; World

Table 3.2
Distribution of Respondents by Province of Origin

Province	Percent distribution (respondents)	Percent distribution (general population)	Poverty incidence*
North Western	52	11	34
North Central	17	6	31
Central	16	13	28
Southern	7	13	27
Sabaragamuwa	4	9	32
Northern and Eastern	2	14	n.a.
Uva	1	6	37
Western	1	28	14
Total	**100**	**100**	**100**

Source: World Bank 2002.

Bank, 2002).This finding was not supported by the EPZ sample, in which female-headed households scored below the sample average on a variety of poverty indicators, including housing quality, asset ownership and land ownership.

Household heads from respondent households were clustered in low-value activities. Only 11 percent were employed in the relatively high-income non-local and formal sectors. The non-farm informal sector, in which 13 percent were employed, is dominated by microenterprises, which are associated with a high poverty incidence, although some skilled artisans earn poverty clearing incomes (Shaw, 2004). Nearly a fifth of respondent household heads were 'economically inactive' due to age, illness or unemployment. Female household heads were overrepresented in the 'economically inactive' category, accounting for nearly 60 percent, reflecting both a scarcity of local economic opportunities for rural women and the relatively high proportion of elderly widows in this group.

Around 60 percent of household heads were employed in agriculture, another sector characterized by very high rates of poverty (World Bank, 2002). Despite substantial and long-term downward

Table 3.3
Household Poverty Indicators: Respondent Households and Sri Lankan Population

Poverty indicator	Respondents	Sri Lanka	z	p
Rural location	94	72	4.90	< .0001
Household access to mains electricity	43	60	-3.47	.0003
Household head educated to post-primary level	54	59	-1.02	.15
Household head employed in agriculture	59	36	5.22	< .0001
Female-headed households	26	10	5.33	< .0001

Sources: World Bank 2002, DCS 2003, Aturupane 1999, UNDP 1998.

Note: z scores and p values relate to difference between the respondents' proportions and the corresponding proportions from Sri Lankan census data. The differences between the percentage figures of the respondents and those derived from Sri Lankan census data were represented as z-scores in order to establish whether the respondents' percentages were significantly different from the Sri Lankan population as a whole. In all but one instance, the differences were significant. There was no significant difference between the two figures on the percentage of household heads educated to post-primary level.

pressures on farm incomes exerted by rising production costs and falling producer prices (Dunham and Edwards, 1997), farmers on holdings of 2 acres or more are usually able to meet household food requirements and produce a marketable surplus. On holdings of less than 2 acres, however, agriculture is a subsistence activity which earns little or no cash income, while landless and near-landless households, which lack access to the means for food security, are among the poorest of the rural poor (Shaw, 2004). Most respondent households were unable to earn a poverty-clearing income from farming as they occupied plots below the 2-acre threshold (52 percent) or were landless (32 percent).

Most respondents were junior household members in terms of their relationship to the household head: 90 percent were daughters, while only 8 percent were wives, sisters or sisters-in-law, and 2 percent were household heads themselves. Nevertheless, they made a substantial contribution to household income. As regular local employment is scarce, rural households tend to rely on a shifting portfolio of low-earning seasonal activities, supplementing farming with non-farm microenterprises during the lean season, and it was not unusual for EPZ earnings to constitute the household's only regular income source. Nearly 60 percent of households had two sources of cash income, 18 percent had three and 11 percent had four or more. In many households with multiple income sources, the additional income came from non-local employment: a female family member working in the Middle East, a son in the military or a second daughter in a garment factory.

Table 3.4
Respondent Households: Main Occupation of Household Head

Occupation	Percent
Self-employed farming	44
Farm labour	15
Local non-farm employment (informal sector)	13
Local non-farm wage employment (formal sector)	5
Non-local employment	6
Economically inactive	17
Total	**100**

These findings provide further evidence of the increasing role of remittances in rural households. Sri Lanka has not undergone the massive rural-to-urban drifts which have occurred in other developing countries in recent years, but the stability of the rural population disguises the importance of non-local income sources in the rural economy. There is little evidence of significant relocation of whole families from the countryside to the cities, but it is common for individuals to migrate to the Western Province for work, remitting part of their wages and returning to their homes weekly or monthly.

With the failure of the slow-growing, rural nonfarm sector to offset deteriorating farm incomes, non-local income sources (notably government welfare transfers and remittances from family members employed in the military, the Western Province and overseas) have become increasingly important in the rural economy. Estimates of the contribution of transfers and remittances to rural household income vary between 40 percent (World Bank, 1998) and 70 percent (Dunham and Jayasuriya, 1998).

Young Rural Women and the Labour Market

Sri Lankans classify the labour market into 'good jobs' in the public and white-collar sectors, and 'bad jobs' in farming, the non-farm informal sector, overseas domestic service and the Zones (Lakshman, 2002; Rama, 1998; World Bank, 2002). The paradox of simultaneous high female unemployment and high EPZ vacancy rates persists because the greatest labour market expansion in recent years has been in 'bad' jobs, notably in the Zones and overseas, while the supply of 'good' jobs has contracted. Young women whose families are willing and able to support them prefer to remain under-employed or unemployed at home, and only the poorest are compelled to seek EPZ employment. Thus, rather than being 'pulled' to the Zones by the prospect of regular work, young women are 'pushed' by poverty and a lack of alternatives into jobs which they would not otherwise take.

In the last two decades, neoliberal policy reforms have had a profound impact on household livelihoods. Significant among the reforms was the promotion of export-oriented manufacturing, reduction of the public sector through privatization and the curtailment of social sector expenditure, and the progressive withdrawal of subsidies and price protection in the smallholder farm sector. As a result, there was a general shift of resources and employment out of the rural, agrarian and public sectors into the urban, non-farm and private sectors (Dunham and Edwards, 1997; Shaw, 2001).

Over the same period there was a substantial influx of women into the labour market, due to a combination of demand and supply side factors including strong public investment in girls' education, declining fertility rates and a rise in the average age at which women marry, the post-1977 policy reforms which provided new opportunities for women's employment in manufacturing, and the declining ability of traditional livelihood practices to support rural households. Women's employment grew at a greater rate than men's, albeit from a lower base. Between 1993 and 2002 the number of in-country jobs for men increased by about 850,000 (23 percent), while women's employment has increased by about 630,000 (39 percent) (DCS, 2002). In 2002, women held about a third of jobs in Sri Lanka. Stable participation rates and falling unemployment among men indicate that the growth in women's employment is coming from job creation rather than the displacement of male labour.

High gender equality in access to education has not translated into employment equality. The influx of women into the labour force has outpaced the growth of acceptable job opportunities, and women's unemployment rates are double those of men, particularly in the 15-29 age group, in which 27 percent of women were unemployed in 2002 (DCS, 2002). Women remain clustered in a narrow range of sectors, notably agriculture, manufacturing and overseas employment, while men are spread more evenly across the occupational spectrum. Within occupational sectors the pattern of gender segregation persists: in manufacturing, women are concentrated in garments and textiles production, and in the professions, they are concentrated in teaching and nursing.

Table 3.5 describes the structure of the labour market for rural women. Due to the limitations of the various official data sources, which are difficult to reconcile with each other and do not rigorously disaggregate employment by gender, location or sector, the data presented here are indicative rather than definitive. Just over half of rural women were employed in the local informal sector. Agriculture remained the largest employer, accounting for a third of employment, although its share fell during the 1990s. A fifth of rural women were employed in trade, personal services and other informal sector non-farm occupations, in which the share of employment has remained relatively stable. Most of the increase in rural women's employment since the early 1990s has been in non-local sectors, which pay significantly more than most of the local alternatives (Table 6.5).

'Good jobs' in the public sector or white-collar private sector were scarce. The latter accounted for less than 3 percent of the country's jobs, and had a miniscule impact on rural employment, as most jobs were held by members of the English-speaking Colombo elite. The state remains a significant employer, but its share of the labour market is shrinking, having fallen from 23 percent in 1991 to 13 percent in 2003 (CBSL, 2003). While public sector pay fell in real terms in the 1990s, and compared poorly with the private sector at senior management and professional levels, lower grade public sector jobs easily outranked the available alternatives in terms of pay and conditions, job security, pension entitlements and social status,[5] and a

Table 3.5
Rural Female Population Aged 15 and Over: Labour Force Status and Sectoral Distribution of Employment[a][b]

	'000	Composition of labour force (%)	*Labour force participation*
Local employment: formal sector	212	8.6	
Public sector	152	6.2	
Two hundred garment factory program	60	2.4	
Local employment: informal sector	1295	52.8	
Agriculture, fishing and forestry	818	33.3	
Non-farm sector[c]	477	19.4	
Non-local employment	758	30.9	
EPZ garment factories	158	6.4	
Overseas domestic service	600	24.4	
Unemployed	189	7.7	
Total labour force	2454	100	52.6
Not in labour force	2211		47.4
Total	4665		100

Sources: DCS 2000, DCS 2002, Ministry of Women's Affairs 2003.

(a) In this table women employed overseas are included as employed labour force participants, whereas they are classified as non-participants in official DCS statistics. As a result, the labour force participation rates presented here are higher than those indicated by the official statistics, and unemployment rates are lower.
(b) Includes rural migrant workers resident in the Western Province.
(c) Trade, manufacturing, animal husbandry, personal services, construction, miscellaneous non-farm work n.e.s.

government job remained the first preference of young labour market entrants, consistently outranking other occupations in surveys of employment preferences (Lakshman, 2002; World Bank, 1999). In practice, however, job opportunities for women in the public sector were mostly confined to middle-class, post-secondary educated women in the nursing, teaching and clerical occupations. For young women from poor rural households, the prospects of finding a public sector job were remote, as few possessed the required educational qualifications and political connections.

Table 3.6
Female Wage Rates in Selected Occupations

Occupation	Pay range (Sri Lankan rupees per month)*
Local	
Public sector (entry level for non-graduates)	6,000
THGPF garment factory	2,300-3,100
Agricultural labour	1,000-2,000*
Non-farm microenterprise	Usually below 2,500
Non-local	
EPZ garment factory	4,500-8,000
Overseas employment	11,000-13,000

Source: CBSL 2002, TieAsia 2003
* The SLR:$US exchange rate at the beginning of 2004 was approximately 100.
** Averaged over twelve months.

An additional source of rural wage employment was the Two Hundred Garment Factory Program (THGFP), a government initiative aimed at promoting rural industrialization, which employed about 60,000 women in rural factories. The THGFP compared poorly with the EPZs in terms of wages and job security. Many THGFP factories laid off staff during quiet periods and factory closures were common (CENWOR, 2001; Shaw, 2001). Nevertheless, while valued less highly than public sector jobs, THGFP jobs were highly sought after as they provided scarce regular employment without the personal costs associated with migration to the EPZs or overseas. THGFP workers were free from the pervasive social stigma attached to unmarried women who leave the parental home, and from the personal security risks faced by EPZ workers (Heward, 1997). As one THGFP worker explained, 'Everyone knows me, from my home to the factory gate, this gives me a certain amount of protection. Women who work in the FTZ don't have this protection' (Dent, 2000:10).

As with the public sector, the access of poorer rural households to the THGFP was limited, with evidence that THGFP jobs flowed disproportionately to non-poor families. The poorest households were over-represented in remote areas with limited transport facilities, while factories were located in regional towns and on major roads. Furthermore, as with public sector jobs, the allocation of jobs in the state-subsidised factories was influenced by political patronage. A study of rural livelihoods in Hambantota district found that THGFP workers were exclusively from non-poor families which had been able to obtain the 'letter from a politician' necessary to secure employment in a local factory (Shaw, 2001).

The rural labour market was dominated by the informal sector, which accounted for more than half of rural women's employment, and was characterized by poor working conditions and low and intermittent earnings. It included seasonal farm labour, local non-farm wage employment and microenterprises, in which women worked as owner-operators or unpaid household employees. Daily rates for farm labour compared well with those in the non-farm informal sector (CBSL, 2002), but employment was intermittent, confined to the peak paddy planting and harvesting seasons. Some wage employment was available in rural manufacturing workshops, where conditions compared unfavourably with those in larger, urban factories: low labour replacement costs and inadequate policing by the under-resourced Ministry of Labour allowed employers to ignore basic labour standards (Institute of Policy Studies, 1998), and average wage levels in small factories were less than half of those in larger firms (DCS, 2001). Women's microenterprises were typically part-time, seasonal, semi-subsistence activities with earnings well below the poverty line. As the returns from wage labour were usually higher than those from self-employment, many women worked principally as farm labourers, resorting to their microenterprises during the agricultural off-season.

A major sector of expansion in women's employment has been in overseas work. Most labour migrants are unskilled women, predominantly from poor rural households, who work as domestic servants in the Middle East. Between 1986 and 2002 the proportion of women among Sri Lankans departing for overseas employment rose from one- to two-thirds. In 2002, there were 133,000 female departures, an increase of 26 percent from 1998 (Ministry of Women's Affairs, 2003). With the relaxation in 1996 of the requirement for migrating workers to register with the Bureau of Foreign Employment, the precise number of overseas workers is unknown, but was estimated at around a million (Government of Sri Lanka, 2002). A conservative estimate is that around 750,000 Sri Lankan women were employed overseas in 2003, and that around 600,000 were from poor rural households.

While overseas employment was the most remunerative occupation available to rural women, it was not widely viewed as a viable option for the young unmarried cohort from which EPZ workers are drawn. It was regarded as a hazardous occupation: excessive workloads, isolation, physical and sexual abuse and the withholding of pay by unscrupulous employers or agents were widely reported in the local media (CENWOR, 2001; Gamburd, 2000). Households preferred to send married women, due to fear of moral corruption and damage to the marriage prospects of single women. In addition, some recipient countries imposed age restrictions: Saudi Arabia, for instance, only admits domestic servants aged between 30 and 43. As a consequence, overseas migrants are older on average than EPZ workers: fewer than a third of women departing in 2002 were in the 20-29 age range, and fewer than 1 percent were under 20 (Ministry of Women's Affairs, 2003).

In their assessments of the attractiveness and availability of alternative jobs, the respondents confirmed the general picture described above. When asked to describe the main income-generating activities of women from their home villages, overseas employment and agriculture were by far the most commonly reported occupations, followed by non-farm microenterprises in occupations such as petty trade, fish-drying, brick-making, tailoring and animal husbandry (Table 3.7). Ten percent reported wage employment in the informal non-farm sector. Employment in the THGFP was confined to villages close to a factory, and was reported as a significant local income source by 7 percent of the respondents.

Table 3.7
Economic Activities of Women from Respondents' Villages

Occupation	Percent of respondents reporting activity
Overseas employment	71
Farming and farm labour	93
Non-farm microenterprise	38
Local non-farm wage employment	17

When asked why they took EPZ jobs rather than one of the alternatives, the women responded overwhelmingly that they were unable to earn poverty-clearing incomes from local activities. Most added that parental pressure and the perceived hazards of overseas employment had dissuaded them from taking an offshore job. As Table 3.8 indicates, 'push factors', in the form of acute economic pressure to contribute to family income or to relieve the economic burden of a non-contributing individual, were the main motivation for moving to the EPZs in more than two thirds of cases. For the remaining third, most of whom were motivated by less acute, longer-term aims (e.g., the accumulation of a dowry), rather than by immediate survival imperatives, the decision to take an EPZ job had a larger voluntary component. Nevertheless, for the vast majority the EPZs were not the preferred employment avenue: 69 percent nominated a public sector job as their first employment preference, indicating what seems to be an unrealistic assessment of their labour market options; 20 percent wanted 'a good job' in the private sector; and only 5 percent nominated the EPZs as their first preference.

Table 3.8
Main Reason for Moving to EPZ

Reason	Percent
To contribute to household income	62
To reduce burden on relatives	8
To save for marriage	23
Other*	7

*   Desire to leave home, desire to save for non-marriage purposes.

Life in the Zone

Respondents were asked to rate their levels of satisfaction on a range of variables relating to their work and non-workplace environment. On the positive side, 85 percent reported that they had made new friends, and 59 percent believed that their jobs were equipping them with useful skills and experience. Nearly all valued the opportunity to contribute to family income, and more than 70 percent reported that their contributions had led to improvements in their status within their families. A minority felt that their marital prospects had been harmed by EPZ work, but respondents were more likely to report that the opportunity to save for a dowry had improved their chances of making a good marriage. Nevertheless, levels of satisfaction were generally low: only 20 percent reported that in general they were satisfied with their lives as garment workers, 70 percent were dissatisfied, and an overwhelming 86 percent reported that they would return to their villages if a regular job became available. Typical among the responses was 'If I could find decent work in my village, I would quit today'.

Table 3.9
Principal Reason for Dissatisfaction with EPZ Employment

Reason	Principal reason for dissatisfaction (percent)
Pay	16
Working conditions	15
The non-work environment	59
Separation from family	10
Total	**100**

Wages

Monthly take-home pay in the EPZs was well above the statutory minimum of Rs 3,900 (Table 3.10), a finding consistent with recent research (CENWOR, 2001) and which was probably attributable to slackness in the labour market. There was no evidence of avoidance of statutory payment obligations by employers. Take-home pay varied widely, with medians of Rs 4,300 and Rs 7,980 respectively in the lowest and highest deciles. Discretionary pay, in the form of allowances and overtime, accounted for almost a third of take-home pay. Commonplace allowances included an 'attendance bonus', which was reduced or forfeited for lateness or absence, and 'recruitment bonuses' for the introduction of new employees. In addition, most factories set two or three production targets per month, with attached bonuses. The setting of onerous production targets was a commonly reported source of dissatisfaction, with claims that supervisors deliberately set targets at unachievable levels to avoid payment of bonuses.

Table 3.10
Mean Components of Monthly Pay for December 2003

Item	Amount
Basic wage	4565
Attendance allowances, other allowances and production bonuses	503
Overtime	1103
Total	**6171**

Overtime payments, which ranged up to Rs 4,000, were the major source of variation in take-home pay. Just under a quarter of workers (23 percent) did no overtime work over and above the statutory 48-hour working week, 36 percent worked 10-20 hours overtime, and 6 percent worked more than 20 hours overtime. Respondents' views on their working hours were mixed: while 28 percent complained that their long working week left them little time for sleep and non-work activities, some 20 percent complained of limited opportunities to work overtime and stated that they would increase their working hours if they could.

The respondents overwhelmingly felt that their pay was insufficient: only 15 percent were satisfied with their salaries, while 54 percent reported dissatisfaction. They were more inclined to cite the high costs of living in the EPZs than the undervaluation of their work. As Table 3.11 shows, margins for discretionary expenditure were limited, with food, housing, transport and remittances accounting for two-thirds of take-home pay. At Rs 1,454, mean food expenditure was above the threshold of Rs 1,338 deemed necessary to meet basic nutrition requirements (DCS, 2002); but given the inflation of prices by shopkeepers in the Katunayake area (Gunesekara, 1998), the poor quality of cooking facilities and lack of time to prepare meals, it is likely that a substantial proportion of garment workers have inadequate dietary intakes. The main items in the 'other expenditure' category were medical expenses, clothing and other personal items, contributions to weddings and other village festivals, and interest on loans (a significant expense, as workers commonly borrowed from moneylenders to cover unexpected outlays, at rates in excess of 10 percent per month).

Table 3.11
Mean Composition of Monthly Expenditure

Item	Percent of take-home pay
Accommodation	13.6
Food	23.6
Transport	6.3
Outings and entertainment	6.5
Savings deposits	11.0
Remittances	22.8
Other expenditure n.e.s.	16.2
Total	**100**

Working Conditions and Industrial Relations

In principle, EPZ enterprises are bound by national laws covering pay, conditions and trade union rights, but in practice they are effectively exempt from labour law enforcement, through administrative measures which restrict the interventionary powers of the Ministry of Labour (MoL) and the operation of trade unions. The MoL, constrained by chronic budgetary and staff shortages, has delegated some of its regulatory functions in the EPZs to the Board of Investment (BoI), the autonomous statutory body which oversees export-oriented manufacturing. Thus, responsibility for enforcement of standards and investigation of breaches falls on the BoI rather than the national legal and regulatory system. Observers have pointed to the conflict of interest inherent in the assigning of responsibility for labour standards to an agency mandated to attract foreign investment (Gunatilaka, 1999).

The survey revealed widespread breaches of national legislation on health and safety. Requirements to provide protective clothing and first-aid facilities with trained attendants were widely ignored, with 28 percent of respondents reporting that masks and hair-nets were not provided, 20 percent that first-aid supplies were not available, and 10 percent that their factories did not have a first-aid attendant. Several reported breaches of the statutory requirement for one latrine per 25 workers, with one report of a factory providing 26 latrines for 2,500 workers, a ratio of 1:96. Workers were required to obtain permission from their supervisors to use the latrines, which they were reluctant to do due to fear of public humiliation and scolding, and in some cases were prohibited from visiting the latrines outside their rest periods.

Thirty-seven percent reported having experienced at least one work-related illness or injury, a finding consistent with those of other studies which report occupational health problems in up to half of EPZ workers (ACFFTU, 1995; Gunatilaka, 1999). Among the conditions reported were soreness from being kept standing for long periods (30 percent), minor injuries such as needle pricks (14 percent), and potentially more serious problems such as the catching of hair in machinery (5 percent) and chronic respiratory conditions resulting from the inhalation of fibres (10 percent).

Employee relations were generally poor: over two thirds complained that they were regularly subjected to verbal abuse from their supervisors, and 14 percent complained of physical abuse. The findings are consistent with those of previous studies which report authoritarian management practices which emphasise control of performance and attendance and avoidance of dialogue with workers, with low priority accorded to the maintenance of morale or resolution of employee grievances (Gunatilaka, 1999; Hettiarachchi, 1992). Relations between employees and their immediate supervisors were particularly poor, with evidence that the majority of industrial disputes were prompted by calls for the dismissal of individual supervisors (Kelegama, 1998).

One third of the respondents reported that unions were prohibited in their workplaces. Surveys indicate that around two thirds of EPZ garment workers are interested in joining a union (ACFFTU, 1995), although actual union membership falls well short of this figure. Barriers to increasing a union presence in the EPZs include difficulties for outside organizers in gaining access to factories; shift work and long working hours, which give workers little time to organize; as well as high labour turnover and the fact that few workers have a long-term interest in their jobs. Moreover, young women from rural backgrounds have little understanding of labour movement traditions and practices, come from a cultural tradition which discourages women from drawing attention to themselves, and tend to be inarticulate and lacking in self-confidence.

Employers sought to work through in-house unions or 'Employees' Councils' (ECs) rather than externally-based unions. Evidence on the effectiveness of ECs is scant, but what there is reflects common criticisms of enterprise-level unions elsewhere: that they are management creatures, with little genuine worker participation or bargaining power, and that in the event of disputes, they leave workers more vulnerable to management reprisals (ACFFTU, 1995; Gunatilaka, 1999; Hettiarachchi, 1992). Among the 85 respondents reporting that their factories had an EC, only 29 believed that it was effective in addressing their grievances. Fifty-eight percent reported at least one instance of having received unfair treatment from their employers. Commonly reported grievances included the setting of onerous production targets and non-payment of production bonuses, denial of leave and non-payment of attendance allowances. In most cases, respondents chose not to pursue the matter, as they were afraid of being punished or losing their jobs.

The Non-work Environment

The quality of life outside the workplace was a key determinant of women's satisfaction with their jobs and lives as garment workers. The three most commonly cited problems related to the poor quality of accommodation, threats to their personal security and the social marginalization of EPZ workers.

Most workers lived in the densely populated dormitory region around the EPZ, in boarding houses which have been widely criticized for providing substandard accommodation (see for example: CENWOR, 2001; Hettiarachchi, 1992). Many boarding houses were hastily constructed in response to the influx of migrant workers to Katunayake in the 1980s, without approval from the local regulatory authorities, and failing to meet basic ventilation, lighting and sanitary standards. Most buildings lack furniture, running water and indoor kitchen facilities. Boarding house residents typically share a room with three or four others, and share kitchen and latrine facilities with 30 to 40 other occupants.[6]

Inadequate security arrangements were a major source of concern for the respondents. Within the boarding houses residents had no safe place to store their valuables, and theft was a widely reported problem. More important, they had little protection from intruders, as most boarding house owners lived off-site, visiting twice monthly to collect rents, and did not employ watchmen or housekeepers. Several respondents reported harassment by gangs of men, mostly off-duty personnel from a nearby military base, who roam the residential precincts and sometimes enter the boarding houses. Two thirds reported having experienced sexual harassment while travelling to work, and nearly 80 percent believed it was not safe to travel to work alone. Respondents complained that: 'We have to stay indoors because it is not safe to go out', and 'We cannot walk on the road alone without being waylaid'.

The phenomenon of women's labour migration has placed considerable pressure on traditional expectations that women should remain in their fathers', and later in their husbands' homes throughout their lives. Nevertheless, those who leave home face strong societal disapproval, fueled by sensationalized media reports of immoral behaviour among 'unsupervised' young women in the Zones. The presence of men in the residential precincts reinforces the attitudes of hostility and contempt towards garment workers which are prevalent among boarding house owners and the wider community. Matrimonial advertisements in the daily newspapers commonly specify that 'factory girls' need not apply. Respondents complained that they were treated with contempt by boarding house owners, jeered at in public places and singled out for over-charging by shopkeepers; and three quarters felt that their lives were made more difficult by the negative images attached to garment workers.

Conclusion

Several global developments since 2004 are of significance for the Sri Lankan garment industry. With the phasing-out of apparel quotas following the expiry of the Multi-Fibre Agreement in 2005, the limited but guaranteed access to Western markets enjoyed by developing country garment producers was replaced by a hybrid of free trade and regional and bilateral agreements. Of greater significance was the accession of China to the WTO in 2001 and subsequent emergence as the world's largest garment exporter, with increasing dominance over key markets in the US and EU. While fears that the Sri Lankan garment industry would collapse without the protection of quotas proved unfounded, with an increase of one third in the value of garment exports between 2004 and 2008, its global market share declined from 1.2 per cent to just under 1 per cent over the same period, due largely to Chinese export growth (WTO 2009, CBSL 2008, 2009).

More recently, the global economic downturn has impacted the garment sector, although the evidence suggests that the impacts have been concentrated in small and medium enterprises rather than in the EPZs. Although garment export earnings grew more slowly in 2008 and 2009 than in previous years, they continued to increase in absolute terms, suggesting that in the EPZs, which account for more than 80 per cent of garment exports, the downturn had little impact on output (CBSL 2009). The crisis has nevertheless had a significant impact on garment factory employment, with the loss of an estimated 26,000 jobs between September 2008 and March 2009. These job losses were concentrated in small and medium enterprises: fewer than 3,000 jobs were lost in EPZ factories over the same period, the majority resulting from the closure of a single factory which laid off 2,538 workers in January 2009 (Gunatilaka, 2009). Thus, limited effects on employment and output, together with evidence of a recovery in export growth in the second half of 2009 (CBSL, 2009), suggest that the EPZs have emerged relatively unscathed from the downturn.

The decision whether to take the 'low road' of price competitiveness based on low labour costs, or the 'high road' of quality-based competitiveness has important implications for job quality. Whereas a focus on price competition typically depresses labour standards, the improved skills and labour productivity associated with value addition exert upward pressure on wages and conditions. Observers were optimistic that a combination of consumer pressure and market re-positioning would improve job quality in the Zones, pointing out that the post-MFA market would be increasingly sensitive to consumer demands for adherence to internationally acceptable labour standards (CBSL, 2002). It was further argued that the post-MFA environment presented an opportunity for Sri Lanka to strengthen its market position by emphasising quality and value addition rather than price competition, given its potentially significant competitive advantages of relatively low costs, a well-educated workforce, and well-developed urban transport and communications infrastructure (Kelegama and Epaarachchi, 2002).

The global market developments described above have altered the composition of the Sri Lanka garment industry. Whereas there has been a decline in employment among small and medium producers, the largest EPZ employers have improved their competitiveness by focusing on high value added products, upgrading human capital and responding to demands from buyers for increased attention to working conditions. As a result of the success of the Clean Clothes Campaign, the Ethical Trading Initiative and similar campaigns in the West, many large buyers now insist on producer codes of conduct and carry out workplace inspections in factories to which they subcontract work. Since the conditions of Sri Lankan garment workers are generally superior to those in other low-income producing countries, the Sri Lankan industry has by and large benefited from such initiatives, with some large manufacturers having established global reputations as 'fair trade' employers. There is evidence that the growth of 'social audits' has contributed to a general improvement in labour standards and rights within the EPZs (Sivananthiran 2008). At the same time, however, it appears that these benefits have been at least partially offset by the loss of some jobs and extensive wage cuts in the wake of the global economic downturn (Gunatilaka 2009).

In a further ominous development, the EU in March 2010 announced its intention to cancel the Generalised System of Preferences ('GSP-plus') for Sri Lankan imports due to concerns regarding the government's human rights record with respect to the treatment of the country's Tamil minority. The withdrawal of the GSP-plus will increase tariffs on Sri Lankan garment imports from zero to 9.6 per cent, making it difficult to compete with other Asian countries such as Bangladesh which continue to have tariff-free access to the EU, and is likely to result in further job losses.

Thus, grounds for optimism regarding improvements in job quality in the EPZs are at best tentative. Moreover, there is little prospect of relief from the overarching problem of women's unemployment, which is likely to worsen as Sri Lanka struggles to hold its own in an increasingly competitive global environment. The closure of uncompetitive factories, mostly in the small to medium sector, has cut garment jobs by an estimated 25 percent since 2000. As in other developing countries, employment opportunities have not kept pace with labour force growth, and the Sri Lankan economy faces a formidable task finding remunerative jobs for new labour force entrants (about 100,000 annually) and the existing unemployed, whose numbers have been swelled by the recent global downturn. With an anticipated further contraction of employment resulting from the cancellation of the GSP-plus and the failure of successive governments to develop convincing workforce strategies, it is likely that offshore labour markets and marginal informal sector jobs will continue to absorb the bulk of young, poor, rural women in the foreseeable future.

NOTES

1. Estimates of vacancy rates in the garment sector vary from 6 percent (Kelegama and Epaarachchi, 2002) to 11 percent (World Bank, 1999).
2. This section is intended to provide a context for survey data collected in 2004, and therefore focuses on labour market conditions that prevailed at that time. While developments since 2004 are beyond the scope of this chapter, they are likely to have had implications for the attractiveness and accessibility of EPZ jobs relative to other economic options, and hence on the employment decisions of young rural women. Among the most notable of these developments are recent wage increases for Sri Lankan women working as housemaids in most Arab Gulf states, and a substantial recent increase in male labour migration (SLBFE 2007). The additional household income provided by remittances from male migrants may reduce pressure on young women to leave home to work in the EPZs.
3. Anyone wishing to enter the EPZs must obtain a 'gate pass'. The issue of gate passes is at the discretion of the Board of Investment (BoI), the autonomous statutory body responsible for foreign investment in Sri Lanka. Even Ministry of Labour officials can only enter the Zones by prior appointment, an arrangement which compromises effective monitoring and enforcement and reportedly on occasion have been denied entry (Heward, 1997).The gate pass provision is routinely used to deny entry to trade union officials and nonaligned observers, as well as to troublesome workers, whose employment can be terminated by the BoI's withdrawal of their identity cards (Gunatilaka, 1999; Kelegama, 1998).
4. Women were employed mainly in low-level positions. While men predominated in upper management, women occupied 72 percent of supervisory positions and more than 90 percent of the production workforce (Kelegama and Epaarachchi, 2002).

[5] Low-level public sector workers earn 60 to 100 percent more than workers in similar private sector jobs but at senior management and professional levels, compression of pay schedules has reduced the public sector's competitiveness with the corporate private sector, and is argued to be contributing to weaknesses in public sector management capacity (Rama, 1998; World Bank, 1999).

[6] About a quarter of the respondents opted for better-quality accommodations with local families, who usually provide tenants with a room of their own, a cupboard to store their belongings, adequate kitchen facilities and physical security. The average cost of accommodation with a family is between Rs 1,000 and Rs 1,500, in comparison with around Rs 500 for boarding house accommodation. Not surprisingly, respondents living with a family were considerably more likely to report satisfaction with their accommodation arrangements (37 percent) than boarding house residents (7 percent).

REFERENCES

ACFFTU (1995) *Rights at Risk: A Study on Sri Lanka's Free Trade Zones*, unpublished mimeo. All Ceylon Federation of Free Trade Unions, Asian-American Free Labour Institute.

Aturupane, H. (1999) 'Poverty in Sri Lanka: Achievements, Issues and Challenges'. Unpublished mimeo, Ministry of Finance and Planning, Colombo.

Board of Investment Sri Lanka (2003) *Overview: The Textile Industry*. Colombo: Board of Investment.

Central Bank of Sri Lanka (CBSL) (various years) *Annual Report*. Colombo: Central Bank.

CENWOR (2001) *Impact of Macroeconomic Reforms on Women in Sri Lanka: The Garment and Textile Industries*. Colombo: Centre for Women's Research.

Dent, K. (2000) 'Trials and Tribulations of Women FTZ Workers'. *Social Justice* 155, March 2000.

DCS (2000) *Sri Lanka Labour Force Survey 2000 (With Province-level Data)*. Colombo: Department of Census and Statistics.

DCS (2001) *Annual Survey of Industries 2001*. Colombo: Department of Census and Statistics.

DCS (2002) *Quarterly Report of the Sri Lanka Labour Force Survey, Fourth Quarter 2002*. Colombo: Department of Census and Statistics.

DCS (2003) *Household Income and Expenditure Survey 2002: Preliminary Report.* Colombo: Department of Census and Statistics.
Dunham, D. and Edwards, C. (1997) *Rural Poverty and the Agrarian Crisis in Sri Lanka, 1985-95: Making Sense of the Picture.* Colombo: Institute of Policy Studies.
Dunham, D. and Jayasuriya, S. (1998) 'Is All So Well with the Economy and with the Rural Poor?' *Pravada* 5(10-11): 22-27.
Gamburd, M.R. (2000) *The Kitchen Spoon's Handle: Transnationalism and Sri Lanka's Migrant Households.* Ithaca: Cornell University Press.
Government of Sri Lanka (2002) *Regaining Sri Lanka: Vision and Strategy for Accelerated Development.* Colombo: Government Printing Office.
Gunesekara, S. (1998) 'Working Conditions in the FTZ'. Paper prepared for Workshop on Workers in the Free Trade Zone, August 1998, Renuka Hotel, Colombo.
Gunatilaka, R. (1999) *Labour Legislation and Female Employment in Sri Lanka's Manufacturing Sector.* Colombo: Institute of Policy Studies.
Gunatilaka, R. (2009) *Rapid Assessment of the Impact of the Global Economic Crisis on Employment and Industrial Relations in Sri Lanka.* Colombo: ILO.
Hettiarachchi, T. (1992) *Working in the Zone.* Hong Kong: Asian Human Rights Commission.
Heward, S. (1997) *Garment Workers and the Two Hundred Garment Factory Program.* Colombo: Centre for the Welfare of Garment Workers.
Institute of Policy Studies (1998) *Sri Lanka: State of the Economy 1998.* Colombo: Institute of Policy Studies.
Kelegama, S. (1998) 'Globalization and Industrial Relations in Sri Lanka'. Paper prepared for ILO Japan's Regional Programme on Globalization and Industrial Relations: National Tripartite Seminar on Effects of Globalization on Industrial Relations, 21-24 May 1998, Trans-Asia Hotel, Colombo.
Kelegama, S. and Epaarachchi, R. (2002) 'Garment Industry in Sri Lanka', in J. Gopal (ed.) *Garment Industry in South Asia: Rags or Riches?*, pp. 197-240. New Delhi: International Labour Organisation.
Lakshman, W.D. (2002) 'A Holistic View of Youth Unemployment in Sri Lanka: An Exploratory Study', in S.T. Hettige and M. Mayer (eds.) *Sri Lankan Youth: Challenges and Responses.* Colombo: Friedrich Ebert Stiftung.

Ministry of Women's Affairs (2003) *Handbook on Sex-Disaggregated Data, Sri Lanka 2003*. Colombo: Ministry of Women's Affairs.

Rama, M. (1998) *The Sri Lankan Unemployment Problem Revisited*. Poverty Reduction and Economic Management Unit, World Bank, Washington D.C.: World Bank.

Shaw, J. (2001) 'No Magic Bullet: Microenterprise Credit and Income Poverty in Rural Sri Lanka'. PhD thesis, Monash University.

Shaw, J. (2004) 'Microenterprise Occupation and Poverty Reduction in Micro-finance Programs: Evidence from Sri Lanka'. *World Development* 32(7): 1247-64.

Sivananthiran, A. (2008): Promoting Decent Work in Export Processing Zones (EPZs) in Sri Lanka, ILO, Geneva

Sri Lanka Bureau of Foreign Employment (SLBFE) (2007): Annual Statistical Report on Foreign Employment 2007, SLBFE, Colombo

UNDP (1998) *National Human Development Report: Sri Lanka*. Colombo: United Nations Development Program.

World Bank (1998) *Sri Lanka: Recent Economic Developments and Prospects*. World Bank, Washington D.C.

World Bank. (1999) *Sri Lanka:A Fresh Look at Unemployment*. Poverty Reduction and Economic Management Unit, World Bank, Washington D.C.:

World Bank. (2002) *Sri Lanka Poverty Assessment*. Washington D.C.: World Bank.

World Trade Organisation (2009): *International Trade Statistics 2009*. Available at www.wto.org/english/res_e/statis_e/its2009_e/its09_ toc_e.htm.

CHAPTER 4

Historical Consciousness and Collective Action:
Finding Women's Resistance Where North Meets South[1]

Mary E. Frederickson
Miami University, Ohio

ABSTRACT

In the early 20th century, a sizable cohort of activists, scholars and labor organizers argued that the future of the North American labor movement depended on the successful organization of women workers in the U.S. South. Today, activists, scholars and labor organizers make markedly similar arguments about the important role being played by young women entering factories throughout the Global South. Divided by time and place, these two groups of workers share the legacy of paying the human costs of industrialization and globalization. In both groups, a significant minority of women responded to the economic and social changes confronting them by turning to activism and fighting back. Collective organization, workers' education and feminist cooperation are the hallmarks of women's activism for social and economic justice today, just as they had been in the previous century. The success of these efforts among maquiladora workers, like their predecessors, depends on women locating places where they can develop historical consciousness, find their voices and openly speak their minds.

Keywords: labor, women, workers, *maquiladoras*, south, global, resistance

Introduction

The U.S. labor movement began to pay close attention to the 'New South' as early as 1880, when scores of hastily constructed factories began to dot the landscape like 'beads on a necklace', in an arc that eventually stretched from southern Maryland to eastern Texas. Labor organizers sent into the region in the early 20th century struggled to establish unions in an avowedly anti-union region heavily dependent on child labor. From Texas in 1911, one organizer wrote, 'Unionism is a signal failure...about one-third or more of the hands are children, most of them too small to take into a union' (Frederickson, 1985: 158). World War I speed-ups made child labor less practical and shifted the focus to young women who entered the mills between ages 14 and 16. Gradually, a plethora of activists, scholars and writers, along with representatives from women's organizations, workers' education alliances and political organizations focused their attention on the South, arguing that the future of the US labor movement depended on the successful organization of the thousands of young women filing into mills and factories across the region. Southern industrialization was rapid, investments made huge returns, and state and local incentives attracted manufacturers like magnets.

In the early 21st century, activists, scholars, and labor organizers make markedly similar arguments about the important role being played by women entering *maquiladora* factories, U.S.-owned multinational corporations, and sweatshops in the Global South (Arriola, 2000; Cravey, 1998; Haberland, 2001). Beginning in the mid-1960s, not coincidentally as southern industry racially integrated its workforce, numerous companies crossed the border into Mexico to chase even lower wage rates, escape from U.S. unions, locate a malleable workforce, and take advantage of economic enticements being offered by the Mexican state and local officials. Just as the move a century earlier from New England to the U.S. South had resulted in increased profits and a sharper competitive edge, so did forays into the Global South, a massive region that faces a myriad of serious challenges, including poverty, human and civil rights abuses, and ethnic conflicts, yield enormous benefits for the corporate bottom line. At the same time, Global South nations comprise enormous emerging markets for economic growth, natural resources, and workers, just as the American South did in the last century. In 2005, business journals advised industrialists to keep looking south to find the 'fastest path to increased profits with minimum expenditures and responsibilities.' Few of these articles openly discussed the specific advantages of a majority female workforce. The place of women in ads about *maquiladoras* was in the subtext, hidden in the 'immense pool of labor...available at extremely competitive wages' Similar advertisements attract the attention of companies looking for low wage workers in China. (Maquiladora Management Services, 2005).

The experiences of women workers in the 1920s, 1930s, and 1940s, provide historical models for contemporary workers in the Global South. Despite enormous obstacles to organizing, a significant minority of women responded to the economic and social changes confronting them by turning to activism and specific forms of gendered resistance. Collective organization, workers' education, and feminist cooperation were the hallmarks of women's activism for social and economic justice in the U.S. South. Most important, the success of efforts in each of these areas depended on women workers locating places where they could see themselves as part of history, find their voices, and openly speak their minds.

Parallel Lives

The life stories of women in the American South in the first half of the 20th century and women workers in the *maquiladoras* on the Mexican-U.S. border and in garment assembly plants throughout the Global South in the early 21st century follow strikingly parallel narratives. In each region women migrated to factories from rural areas; in both places women were often the first members of their families to work in a factory, and often the first to earn cash wages. All of the women involved, across time and place, have worked for wages so low that they could not support themselves or their children above poverty levels; in both cases these wages provided more cash than any other available job, except prostitution (Hall, 1986; Janiewski, 1985; La Botz, 1999).

In the U.S. South, white women entered racially segregated factories from families whose economic situation was in decline; just as in today's Global South decreasing standards of living and downward mobility across generations delineate the lives of factory workers from Mexico to Guatemala, from China to Vietnam. In both the U.S. South and the Global South, young women came of age in communities where religion reinforced traditional ideas of male authority and female submission. In the U.S. South, many of these young women came from families where harsh child-rearing practices socialized both girls and boys to emotional and physical violation. In the Global South, *machismo* and domestic abuse have also restricted the lives of both women and men. In both locations, incidents of exploitation within the family increased exponentially during frequent periods of economic crisis.

The colonial nature of industrialization in the American South, with a majority of manufacturers based outside of the region, meant that workplace conditions in southern mills and factories operated at a 1:4 wage differential when compared to northern factories. In the Global South, that differential is often even greater, with some workers being paid as little as 10 percent of the wages earned by their northern counterparts. In both areas, women have been pulled into factories by the promise of jobs and cash wages, as well as by hopes for a better life and an increased measure of personal autonomy. In the U.S. South, a system of racial occupational segregation set aside industrial jobs for white workers. But industrialists hired black workers as strikebreakers and took full advantage of the reserve labor force that waited on the other side of the color line. In the 1920s and 1930s those white southern workers who held coveted industrial jobs were pitted against both higher paid workers in the North and even lower paid workers across the region as industrialization spread from the states of Maryland to Virginia, to the Carolinas, then further south to Georgia, Alabama and Mississippi, and West to Tennessee, Arkansas and Texas. This pattern is being repeated now as Mexican workers compete against northern workers in the U.S. and workers even further south, as *maquiladoras* open across Central America and the search for cheap labor continues in countries across Asia–from India and Bangladesh, to China, Vietnam, Laos, and Cambodia (Delfino and Gillespie, 2005).

In the U.S. South, industrialists practiced a form of paternalism that although severe and harsh, appears relatively benevolent when compared to 21st-century management styles in a global market economy that emphasizes worker 'self-actualization', and absolves manufacturers of responsibility. In the early 20th century, most factory owners had names and faces; 21st-century corporate structures encourage industrial anonymity. Twentieth-century mill owners often constructed entire villages for their workers. Some had hastily constructed tiny wooden houses without running water or sewers, but others had well-constructed company housing, schools, a newly-built infrastructure, water systems, sewage treatment, parks, and churches. These amenities drew workers to mill towns and also helped regulate the workforce, policing behavior, and controlling individual choice within a closed community that 'outsiders', especially labor organizers, could not easily penetrate (Hall et al., 2000). In creating and nurturing isolated industrial communities throughout the South, southern state and local governments provided multifaceted assistance to manufacturers. Company towns often provided workers with double-edged benefits: housing that was tightly regulated; a close community that kept outsiders at bay and limited personal independence. Desirable amenities came with a price, as can be seen in 2010 throughout the Global South.

Both the New South and the Global South have been touted as havens from organized labor, and state and local governments throughout the region strived to maintain both the image and reality of union-free states. Company benefits, from pomegranates to swimming pools, have proved to be powerful antidotes to unionization around the world. Edith Kowski, a New York City garment worker and Amalgamated Clothing Workers of America (ACWA) member, visited one of these towns in 1928. The mill in West Durham, North Carolina, employed 1,100 workers and provided housing, a community center complete with gym, bowling alleys, library, movies, night high school classes, and clubs for everyone from baby to grandmother. Kowski found the workers' lives so absolutely entrenched in the village life that 'there is no leaving it and Mr. Erwin, the owner reigns as "God Almighty".'[2] Many decades later in 2004, a reporter visiting the Guangdong Chigo factory in Nanhai, China described August 3 as a 'red-letter day for dozens of workers who stood in line for (pomegranates, a) rare treat in this dusty industrial town' (Fong, 2004).

From the beginning of the twentieth century in the American 'New South,' southern states provided manufacturers with military assistance in strikes. Local government authorities routinely routed union organizers from their communities, often at gunpoint. Governor Eugene Talmadge of Georgia dramatically demonstrated this in 1934 when he declared martial law and had national guard troops bring striking textile workers to a detention facility at Ft. McPherson, just south of Atlanta, that had been used for German prisoners during World War I (Salmond, 2002). After 1947, 'right-to-work' laws outlawing closed union shops were passed in many southern states, and, fearing the competition of union labor, manufacturers in non-union strongholds within the region used their political influence to prevent unionized firms from moving into the area. In the twenty-first century Global South, thousands of worker protests against low wages, withheld pay, and abusive working conditions have been labeled 'illegal demonstrations.' As a consequence, workers from Mexico to China, from Uzbekistan to Vietnam, have been arrested, detained and sentenced to prison terms for protesting working conditions and organizing collectively.

How then, within this historical southern landscape of low wages, virulent anti-unionism and massive state support for industry, did women workers mobilize to resist oppression and shape the world in which they lived? First, unions gradually came to understand the key roles that women workers would play in southern organizing. Second, women workers from a broad range of industries: cotton textiles, hosiery, garments, rayon, tobacco and canneries, were recruited to participate in independent workers' education programs organized by activists from both outside and inside the region. And third, national and regional women's organizations, now called non-governmental agencies or NGOs, committed to cooperation across class and racial lines worked to improve the working and living conditions of southern women workers.

Collective Organization

Unions organizing in the U.S. South initially denied the importance of women workers. As early as 1900, however, in strikes and lockouts in three dozen North Carolina cotton factories, women played key leadership roles. The walkouts of the pre-World War I era, the wave of strikes in southern textiles from 1927 through 1934, labor battles in the post-World War II period, and later union struggles in the Civil Rights decades of the 1960s and 1970s, all involved thousands of women workers. Women played multiple roles in these fights, at times leading hundreds of male and female workers out of factories; or walking in the front ranks of strike parades, or filling conspicuous posts on picket lines. Without question, the actions of women workers were crucial to labor's struggles in the South throughout the 20th century. A number of southern union drives specifically targeted women workers. In 1946, for example, the Congress of Industrial Organizations' (CIO) 'Operation Dixie' focused on union benefits for women workers in southern textiles. This was at a time when 75 percent of *unionized* textile workers in the U.S. were in the North, while almost three-quarters of all textile workers were employed in the South where only 15-20 percent of the industry was unionized. Specific efforts to attract southern women into unions were quite successful, although most of these campaigns were rife with bitter intra-union conflicts, anti-union police and National Guard forces, and employers who met worker resistance with armed violence and blacklists.[3]

Women organizers worked closely with activist workers across the South. Heroic leaders, like the 'Hellraising' Mother Jones, martyr Ella Mae Wiggins, and grandmotherly Lucy Randolph Mason, a stalwart CIO organizer, drew attention to women's issues in the workplace, the home, and the community. But it was on the shop floor and in working-class neighborhoods that women forged the connections they needed in order to commit themselves to collective action. Gendered resistance had a powerful multiplier effect in workplaces and communities where women transformed their autonomy as workers into acts of confrontation. Southern women workers, as their predecessors in the North, gradually changed the terms of their employment by speaking their minds, whether quietly to each other, or loudly, in walk-outs or strikes (Frederickson, 1991).

Today, in communities across the Global South, new leaders, like 'Hellraising' Martha Ojeda, supporters of the martyrs of Ciudad Juarez, like Mireille Rocatti and Lourdes Portillo, and Alma Mejia and Yesenia Bonilla of Honduras, are once again stepping forward and putting themselves on the line for economic justice, working through independent organizations or in trade union federations, such as the Frente Auténtico del Trabajo (FAT).[4] In China Pun Ngai and Chan Wai Ling head the Chinese Working Women's Network (CWWN) a Hong Kong-based NGO committed to community-based labor organizing in the Special Economic Zone of Shenzhen (Ngai and Ling, 2004:10-11).

Workers' Education

Southern industrial women increased the effectiveness of their actions at the local level by connecting with workers' education programs established in the region after World War I. The National Women's Trade Union League (NWTUL), Brookwood Labor College, and the Bryn Mawr Summer School were national programs that sponsored southern organizing initiatives as the region became increasingly industrialized. The Southern Summer School for Women Workers in Industry was established in 1927, as a residential program to train grass-roots leaders in union organizing, labor history, economics, and public speaking. In 1932, Highlander Folk School established a workers' education program in Tennessee that served both men and women as it brought together labor leaders and activists from throughout the region. Both the Southern Summer School (SSS) and Highlander ran educational programs in numerous local communities and provided direct assistance to striking southern workers.[5]

Throughout the late 1920s and 1930s, the SSS was a place where women workers and activists from across the South came together each summer. Students shared their individual life stories and came to see themselves as part of a long history of labor activism and struggle. Knowing about the past empowered them to act in the present, in the belief that they could shape a different future for their children. The school was founded by a group of educators and activists from various class and regional backgrounds. Breaking the boundaries of class and region, and eventually racial barriers as well, these women assumed what Edward Said defined as an 'affiliative' social position, one that moved away from individual identity (or filiative legacy) toward a genuinely humane commitment to economic justice (Zandy, 2000).Workers who attended the school were often leaders in their unions and local community organizations. Working together gave them a broader vision of what was possible: from connecting with regional and national organizations, to obtaining essential legal information, honing organizing skills, and taking control of their own lives.

Groups that evolved from the Southern Summer School and the Highlander Folk School of the 1920s and 1930s, the Southern School for Union Women and the Highlander Research and Education Center, as well as STITCH-Women Organizing for Social Justice in Central America and US/LEAP-Labor Education in the Americas Project, the United Electrical Workers Union (UE)-FAT Labor Workshop and Studies Center, and the AFL-CIO Solidarity Centers in Guatemala and El Salvador, are working to end discrimination against women on the job and to help women workers become strong union leaders. Each of these groups affirms the experiences of individual women workers and the power of the collective; they run leadership training, research and education programs with a transnational focus in communities throughout the Americas.[6] Like workers' education activists in the New South, the CWWN operates outside the traditional trade union model to establish a platform from which organizing can begin. Programming focuses on educational programs that teach labor rights, protection against sexual discrimination, legal training, and health education. Pun Ngai encourages 'cultural projects to facilitate the migrant workers as a collective to fight for their labor and feminist rights and strengthen workers' solidarity' (Ngai and Ling, 2004:10-11).

Feminist Cooperation

Gender-specific education and organization was crucial for women workers who had to negotiate a male-controlled labor movement and mobilize against a male-dominated industrial power structure. Cross-class alliances proved particularly useful as women workers practiced navigating unfamiliar terrain. Working women were particularly adept at garnering the support of cross-class women's organizations for educational resources and information about strategy and tactics. Groups like the National Consumer League (NCL) provided information about how to organize boycotts and label campaigns; the League of Women Voters (LWV) supplied information about legislation and government procedure; the Young Women's Christian Association (YWCA) organized dozens of 'industrial clubs' across the South, many of them in communities where union organizing was difficult, if not impossible. Frequently these 'clubs' raised questions about wages, hours, and health and safety issues in local industries by brokering support from progressive middle- and upper-class women in the community (Goodman, 2004; Scott, 1992).

While feminist cooperation across class lines in the South was never a substitute for unity among men and women in factories and unions, such alliances became the resources women workers could tap as they sought more education and expertise. At the same time, these alliances transformed activist women from different class backgrounds, helped them forge affiliative social positions, develop critical engagement, and commit themselves to social and economic justice. For the women who participated, these women-centered organizations offered a vital social space in which they could articulate opinions, stake-out positions, argue, compromise and grow.

Throughout the Global South a sense of rights, individual and collective, has been slow to develop as industrialization has spread. Nevertheless, as in the New South a century ago, the work of international labor organizations and non-governmental organizations (NGO's) has fostered labor dissent and kept workers' rights front and center. Groups including Oxfam, Human Rights Watch, China Labor Watch, the National Labor Committee, the Clean Clothes Campaign, Anti-Slavery International and Free the Children play the role that organizations like the YWCA Industrial Department, the Women's Trade Union League, the National Child Labor Committee and the International Labour Organization, founded in 1919, did in an earlier era. Regularly monitoring wages, working conditions, and human rights violations, these groups, by focusing attention on the human costs of international capitalist development, work to shape and reshape the global economy that has emerged since the 1980s.

In 2010, transnational feminist organizations include a broad range of organizations that work around the world. In the Americas, the Coalition for Justice in the Maquiladoras, Women on the Border, the Colectiva Feminista Binacional, the Comité Fronterizo de Obreros (CFO)-Committee of Women Workers, and La Mujer Obrera focus on organizing in Mexico and Central America. The Coalition of Labor Union Women (CLUW), and the Association for Women's Rights in Development (AWID) work across the globe. A number of groups that can trace their roots back to organizing efforts in the U.S. South of the 1930s–the YWCA, the League of Women Voters, and Highlander Research and Education Center, now have global initiatives that target women and build leadership skills through education and exchange programs.[7]

The Global South

In China between 2002 and 2009, there has been increasing evidence that labor unrest is on the rise. Some reports suggest that the number of workers involved in strike actions doubled in the first half of the 1990s; others that there were 30,000 workers' protests of significant size in 2000, averaging more than eighty per day. As China has become the workshop of the world, or as some say, the sweatshop of the world, workers facing ten- to twelve-hour days, rigid production quotas, abysmally low hourly wages or piece rates, have begun to use tactics pioneered by industrial unions in the 1930s in the United States. For example, in late 2001, 2,000 workers occupied the Shuangfeng Textile Factory, protesting pay cuts and missing pension funds. Workers refused to leave the factory and went back to work only after the company promised to return lost savings and pensions worth US$14 million (Mitra, 2003).

In 2002, workers at the Nanxuan Wool Textile Factory in the much touted Pearl River Delta region in southern China, participated in a three-day riot. By 2004 as China sold off more than 190,000 state companies to private investors, such strikes and protests increased dramatically: 6,800 workers went out for seven weeks at China Resources, a Hong Kong-listed retailer in northern China; in Shaanxi province, another 7000 workers, the majority of them women, struck at the Tianwang Textile Factory. According to China Labor Watch, a US labor-rights group, '[a]bout 1,000 police appeared at the factory gates with water cannons four days into the strike....They were met by thousands of works who surrounded them, forcing them to back down' (Cheng, 2004).

By January 2008, with labor shortages in south China, higher wages, and inflationary pressure, one labor activist reported that [at] least one strike involving more than 1,000 workers occurs every day in China's manufacturing hub in the Pearl River Delta area, underscoring rising labor unrest in the country. By June 2008 the *China Labour Bulletin* reported that a continuous wave of industrial action has forced the government to reassess workers' needs in light of a constitutional amendment (1982) that made the word 'strike'(*bagong*) taboo. China has trade unions tightly organized and with the world's largest membership rosters, but they are widely considered 'an embarrassing joke,' and Chinese workers do not have the constitutional right to strike. But like their counterparts in the New South in the 1920s and 1930s, they are walking out anyway and the accumulated effect of thousands and thousands of shutdowns, slowdowns, and sit-downs is becoming difficult to ignore. Factories in Vietnam, one of the fastest growing economies in the Global South, have been hit by waves of strikes for the last three years (China Labour Bulletin, 2008).

Historical Consciousness and Women's Activism in Haiti

When the earth cracked and buckled beneath Haiti on January 12, 2010 killing more than 200,000 people, hundreds of women workers died at their sewing machines when the three story Palm Apparel T-shirt factory in the Carrefour neighborhood, collapsed. The factory sustained one of the largest losses of life in any place in Haiti. The women of Carrefour and their employers had been part of an international plan–where North met South–to encourage economic development in the struggling country by promoting garment manufacturing. The United Nations, the International Monetary Fund, and the United States joined forces to forge favorable trade agreements and provide low interest loans to encourage investors; low wages and long workdays by Haitian workers sustain profits. In Haiti, historical consciousness had infused the work of a small but strong group of activists who worked steadily to support women's rights in the workplace and protect women and girls from violence and domestic abuse in a country with a chronically unstable economy and government.[8]

The earthquake took the lives of three of the nation's most dedicated feminists, Myriam Merlet, Anne Maria Coriolan, and Magalie Marclin, who had spent their careers raising awareness of human rights issues in Haiti, from rape to sex trafficking and enslavement to economic exploitation. The earthquake killed scores of NGO staff, destroyed the offices of EnfoFam, Kay Fanm and the Ministry for the Status of Women and the Rights of Women and buried the historical records of their work. The rebuilding began two weeks after the earthquake when Latin American and Caribbean feminists, working with the AWID and MADRE established the International Feminist Solidarity Camp named for Merlet, Coriolan and Marclin to provide ongoing assistance to Haitian women's organizations and monitor the work of international aid agencies to ensure attention is paid to the specific needs of women and girls. The International Textile, Garment and Leather Workers Federation coordinated relief efforts by the international trade union movement. Two weeks after the earthquake those workers who managed to escape alive from the Palm Apparel factory went back to work in a factory by the Port-au-Prince airport owned by the same employer. A month later, international business leaders dusted off their 'pre-quake plan' to expand the low-wage garment assembly industry as the 'linchpin of recovery' in Haiti.[9]

Conclusion

Divided by time and place, these groups of 'southern' women workers share the legacy of paying the human costs of industrialization and globalization. Both groups of women migrated to factories to earn cash wages, frequently in order to support families left in rural areas. But low wages, long hours, and the rising cost of living made it difficult, if not impossible, to get ahead. Often illegally hired as young girls, workers have faced a plethora of wage violations (not being paid on time, no wage statements, no overtime rates, broken time clocks and pressure to take work home). Safety violations abound: fire hazards, the absence of safety guards, exposed belts and pulleys. Women industrial workers have paid a high price in terms of health risks from poor ventilation, heavy dust, exposure to toxic materials, poor lighting, and inadequate rest rooms.

The New South template of industrial development, that veritable dream of progress and profit, has both a history and a future, it goes backward and forward in time: from England to New England; from New England to the U.S. South; from the U.S. South to Mexico and then on to Central and South America, and simultaneously around the globe. Africa remains the only untapped continent left for massive industrial expansion, and Chinese companies are actively investing there and hiring the next generation of 'nimble fingers.' The point where North meets South, a metaphor for development/undeveloped nations, is constantly shifting. But the signification of women's activism does not change. Workers' efforts to organize themselves and negotiate collectively for fair wages and safe working conditions offer the best possibility of realizing basic human rights and social and economic justice, locally, nationally, and internationally. In 1958 when Eleanor Roosevelt asserted, 'where, after all, do universal human rights begin? In small places, close to home so close and so small that they cannot be seen on any maps of the world', she affirmed the world of the individual person within the collective milieu of the community and workplace. These are the places, she argued, that people seek 'equal justice, equal opportunity, equal dignity without discrimination.' She concluded that 'Unless these rights have meaning there, they have little meaning anywhere. Without concerted citizen action to uphold them close to home, we shall look in vain for progress in the larger world' (Roosevelt, 1953).

What can be learned from 200 years of industrial history in terms of women's resistance to economic oppression? At the first Southern Summer School, in 1927, Virginia textile worker Elbe Robertson questioned, 'Should we spend our lives making others richer, while our own wants are deferred?' (Frederickson,1991). Eighty years later, Honduran worker Alma Mejia argued that 'the transnational companies have always wanted to exploit and pay women less. Recently, we had two or three *compañeros*...speaking out about women's needs'. In the Global South today, women's cross-border cooperation involves traversing different boundaries, and requires new forms of organization, but as a UE member, Lynda Leech wrote recently about the UE's 'Hands Across the Border' organizing of women workers: 'Let history repeat itself, as oppression is overcome'. Today's activists need access to the contested and suppressed labor history of 'other souths', for while each generation creates its own future, the historical consciousness of workers, activists, and trade unionists can move the struggle forward toward economic justice.[10]

NOTES

[1] Originally presented at the Women and Globalization Conference, 27 July–3 August 2005, at the Center for Global Justice, San Miguel De Allende, Mexico, this essay is dedicated to Susan Porter Benson, beloved friend, labor historian and teacher, who worked tirelessly to understand the past and shape new worlds for women workers. Her death on 20 June 2005 has left a great void. Many thanks to the Editors, Erica Polakoff and Ligaya Lindio-McGovern, for their comments, and to my colleagues Brigid O'Farrell and Dan La Botz for their careful critiques.

[2] Edith Kowski to A.J. Muste, 8 September 1928, Box 70, Brookwood Labor College Record, Walter P. Reuther Library, Wayne State University, Detroit, MI.

[3] For an overview of southern organizing see: Daniel (2001); Fink (2003); Honey (1993); Irons (2000); Korstad (2003). On Operation Dixie, see Griffith (1988) and quote from Frederickson (1991: 173): 'I know which side I'm on'.

[4] See Hollander (1999); Urquidi (2005); Excerpts from 'Women Behind the Labels' Worker Testimonies from Central America, STITCH and the Maquila Solidarity Network, Toronto, Ontario, Canada, 2000. See also Hathaway (2000); La Botz (2005) and Fleeson (2003).

[5] For the women's summer schools see Kornbluh and Frederickson (1984). On the Southern Summer School, see Frederickson,

"Recognizing Regional Difference: The Southern Summer School for Women Workers," in Kornbluh and Frederickson. On Highlander's history see Glenn (1996). For information on the Highlander Research and Education Center's current transnational work 'Across Races and Nations' see: [http://www.highlandercenter.org/r-arn.asp], accessed 6 March 2010.

6   See STITCH Women Organizing for Worker Justice at [www.stitchon line.org], accessed 6 March 2010 and US/LEAP:About us/Join Us in the Fight for Worker Rights Worldwide; for information about the UE-FAT see UE and Mexican FAT federation organize mutual support and Alexander and Gilmore (n.d.); for the AFL-CIO Solidarity Centers, see [http://www. solidaritycenter.org/], accessed 6 March 2010.

7   Information about the Coalition for Justice in the Maquiladoras is available at [http://coalitionforjustice.info/cjm_website/index.html], accessed 6 March 2010; regarding Women on the Border, see: [http://www.womenontheborder.org/], accessed 6 March 2010; for the Association for Women's Rights in Development see: [http://www.awid.org], accessed 6 March 2010; and for material on the work done by the Comité Fronterizo de Obreros (CFO)-Committee of Women Workers see: [http://www.cfo-maquiladoras.org], accessed 6 March 2010. The Binational Feminist Collective is an independent group organized to promote the human rights of female workers in the *maquiladora* industry with regard to gender issues. The Binational is associated with the non-governmental organization CITTAC (Centro de Información para Trabajadoras y Trabajadores A.C) in Baja California.

8   Deborah Sontag, 'Defiant Vow to Rebuild Amid Ruins and Bodies,' *New York Times*, January 18, 2010; Associated Press, 'Can Low-Paying Garment Industry Save Haiti?' *New York Times*, February 21, 2010; Bernice Robertson, 'Haiti's Women Rise from the Rubble,' *International Crisis Group,* February 22, 2010.

9   Maria Suarez Toro, 'Guardians of History,' *Feminist Peace Network*, February 4, 2010; ITGLWF, 'Working to Shape a Response to Support Haitian Garment Workers, *International Textile, Garment and Leather Workers Federation,* January 25, 2010; Associated Press, 'Can Low-Paying Garment Industry Save Haiti,' *New York Times*, February 21, 2010.

10 See STITCH 'Women Behind the Labels: Worker Testimonies from Central America' and Leech, 'Hands Across the Border.'

REFERENCES

Alexander, R. and Gilmore, P. (n.d.) 'An International Approach to Economic Justice: The UE-FAT Strategic Organizing Alliance'. Accessed 3 April 2010 from www.docstoc.com/docs/14822425/An-International-Approach-to-Economic-Justice.

Arriola, E. (2000) 'Voices from the Barbed Wires of Despair: Women in the Maquiladoras Latina Critical Legal Theory and Gender at the US-Mexico Border'. *De Paul Law Review* 49: 729-815.

Associated Press (2010) 'Can Low-Paying Garment Industry Save Haiti?' *New York Times*, February 21.

Cheng, A. (2004) 'Labor Unrest is Growing in China'. *Bloomberg News*, 27 October.

China Labour Bulletin (2008) 'Trade Union Official Says China Is Just One Step Away from the Right to Strike'. 17 June.

Cravey, A.J. (1998) *Women and Work in Mexico's Maquiladoras.* Rowman and Littlefield.

Daniel, C. (2001) *Culture of Misfortune.* Ithaca: ILR Press.

Delfino, S. and Gillespie, M. (eds.) (2005) *Global Perspectives on Industrial Transformation in the American South.* Columbia: University of Missouri Press.

Fleeson, L. (2003) 'Leaving Loredo'. *Mother Jones*, September/October.

Fong, M. (2004) 'A Chinese Puzzle: Surprising Shortage of Workers Forces Factories to Add Perks'. *Wall Street Journal*, 16 August.

Frederickson, M. (1985) '"I know which side I'm on": Southern Women in the Labor Movement in the Twentieth Century', in R. Milkman (ed.) *Women, Work and Protest: A Century of U.S. Women's Labor History*, p. 158. New York: Routledge.

Frederickson, M. (1991) 'Heroines and Girl Strikers: Gender and Organized Labor in the Twentieth Century South', in R. Zieger (ed.) *Labor in the South.* Knoxville: University of Tennessee Press.

Fink, L. (2003) *The Maya of Morgantown: Work and Community in the Nuevo New South.* Chapel Hill: University of North Carolina Press.

Glenn, J. (1996) *Highlander: No Ordinary School.* Knoxville: University of Tennessee Press.

Goodman, R. (2004) *World, Class, Women.* Abington: Routledge-Falmer Press.

Griffith, B. (1988) *The Crisis of American Labor: Operation Dixie and the Defeat of the CIO.* Philadelphia: Temple University Press.

Haberland, M. (2001) 'Women's Work: The Apparel Industry in the United States South, 1937-1980'. Diss. Tulane University, 2001.

Hall, J.D. (1986) 'Disorderly Women: Gender and Labor Militancy in the Appalachian South'. *Journal of American History*, September, 73: 354–82.

Hall, J.D., et al. (2000 [1987]) *Like a Family: The Making of a Southern Cotton Mill World*. Chapel Hill: University of North Carolina Press.

Hathaway, D. (2000) *Allies Across the Border: Mexico's 'Authentic Labor Front' and Global Solidarity*. Cambridge: South End Press.

Hollander, E. (1999) 'Outlook: "Hellraiser Martha Ojeda"'. *Mother Jones*, November/December.

Honey, M. (1993) *Southern Labor and Civil Rights*. Urbana: University of Illinois Press.

International Textile, Garment and Leather Workers Federation (2010), 'Working to Shape a Response to Support Haitian Garment Workers'. January 25.

Irons, J. (2000) *Testing the New Deal: The General Textile Strike of 1934 in the American South*. Urbana: University of Illinois Press.

Janiewski, J. (1985) *Sisterhood Denied: Race, Gender, and Class in a New South Community*. Philadelphia: Temple University Press.

Kornbluh, J. and Frederickson, M. (1984) *Sisterhood and Solidarity: Workers Education for Women, 1914-1984*. Philadelphia: Temple University Press.

Korstad, R. (2003) *Civil Rights Unionism: Tobacco Workers and the Struggle for Democracy in the Mid-Twentieth Century South*. Chapel Hill: University of North Carolina Press.

La Botz, D. (1999) 'Women Maquiladora Workers', *Mexican Labor News and Analysis*, Special Issue on Women Workers, May 16, 4(9). Accessed 3 April 2010 from www.ueinternational.org/vol4no9.html.

La Botz, D. (2005) 'Mexico's Labor Movement in Transition'. *Monthly Review* 57(2): 62–72.

Leech, L. (2001) 'Hands Across the Border' *UE International Solidarity*. Accessed 3 April 2010 from www.ueinternational.org/SolidarityWork/murals.html.

Maquiladora Management Services (2005) 'Discover the Cost-Saving Benefits of Mexico Manufacturing with Maquiladoras'.

Mitra, S. (2003) 'Chinese Textile Workers Face a Lose-Lose Situation As China Joins the WTO'. *China Report* 39:1 (2003):81-86.

Ngai, P. and Chan, W.L. (2004) 'Community Based Labour Organizing'. *International Union Rights* 11:4.

Robertson, B. (2010) 'Haiti's Women Rise from the Rubble'. *International Crisis Group*, February 22.

Roosevelt, E. (1999) 'Remarks at the United Nations, March 27, 1953,' in *Courage in a Dangerous World: The Political Writings of Eleanor Roosevelt*. Columbia University Press.

Salmond, J.A. (2002) *The General strike of 1934: from Maine to Alabama*, Columbia: University of Missouri Press.

Scott, A.F. (1992) *Natural Allies: Women's Associations in American History*. Urbana: University of Illinois Press.

Sontag, D. (2010) 'Defiant Vow to Rebuild Amid Ruins and Bodies'. *New York Times*, January 18.

Toro, M.S. (2010) 'Guardians of History'. *Feminist Peace Network*, February 4.

Urquidi, A. (2005) 'The Women of Ciudad Juárez'. Paper No. 3, May, Center for Latin American Studies, UC Berkeley.

Zandy, J. (2000) 'An Essay about Triangle Fire Poetry'. Modern American Poetry Online Companion to *Anthology of Modern American Poetry*, C. Nelson (ed.). Oxford: Oxford University Press.

CHAPTER 5

Waves of Resistance in the Colombian Flower Industry

Olga Sanmiguel-Valderrama
University of Cincinnati

ABSTRACT

This chapter focuses on collective resistance to precarious forms of labour in the context of the Colombian fresh-cut flower industry (CFI). For decades, groups of workers led by women in many different plantations of the CFI have engaged in unionization efforts, with partially successful results. Unionization has been undertaken with the support of diverse national and transnational NGOs and community organizations, representative of 'new social movements'. The latter have also used new local and transnational strategies besides unionization to alter precarious forms of labour in the CFI. The author examines those diverse strategies and argues that the resistance movement in the CFI is a manifestation of networking and the convergence between new social movements and organized labour. Additionally, the resistance movement and the plight and struggle of CFI workers have been globalized through the actions of diverse transnational actors and the deployment of transnational strategies. In spite of these important and welcomed developments, combinations of interlocking and interconnected strategies to contest the power relations of patriarchy and racism, in intersectional terms, and those based on waged-labour struggles, are necessary to fundamentally transform the dynamics of racialized and feminized labour practices in the CFI.

Keywords: feminization of labour, racialization of labour, Colombian flower industry

Introduction

On 7 September 2009, in the changing room of the Colombian flower plantation La Belinda, workers took longer than usual to put on their worn out overalls imprinted with the slogan written in English 'We Grow Beautiful Flowers' (Untraflores, 2010:3). After changing into their overalls, the workers walked to a point of confluence, rather than entering the greenhouses where daily they grew carnations, roses and chrysanthemums. The workers from the greenhouses of La Belinda had started a strike and with it, the latest strike in the Colombia flower industry was set into motion (Untraflores, 2010:3-9). The terrains of La Belinda plantation are situated in the municipality of Facatativá, about half an hour drive west of Bogotá, Colombia. La Belinda's management had defaulted on many workers' rights: (a) not paying its monthly installments to private health insurance corporations to insure workers, so workers no longer had health insurance, (b) not paying obligatory disbursements to workers' pension funds (as mandated by Colombian law) even after the company made deductions from their wages, (c) not paying the legal family subsidy, (d) not providing overalls, boots and other gear for more than two years–even though they had the legal obligation to provide one set periodically, and (e) eliminating extra-legal benefits previously won by the union (Untraflores, 2010:3-9). Thirty Belinda workers had faced fierce political and legal struggles before successfully establishing a plantation-based union in 2001, *Sintrabelinda* (Untraflores, 2006:6).

This plantation, like many other industrial mono-crop export-led agribusinesses in Latin America, has been characterized by the precarious labour standards that mark production for the global market (Trupp, 1995). A number of publications in Spanish and English have examined the labour and living conditions of the mostly racialized female labour force of the Colombian fresh-cut flower export-led industry (*hereinafter* CFI).[1] In a 2007 article published in the *Journal for Developing Societies (JDS)*, I discussed and documented the problematic realities in the CFI for those who work in the lower ranks of the industry and experience precarious, feminized *and* racialized forms of labour. I argued that these jobs are not only 'feminized', but also 'racialized'. Scholars have used the term 'feminized labour' to capture the convergence of the increased participation of women in the global economy on the one hand, and the rise of flexible and deregulated employment for most workers on the other hand.[2] In other words, the term 'feminized labour' refers to first, the fact that women represent a large proportion of workers in industries producing for the global economy (such as the CFI); second, this work is characterized by the traditional informality and flexibility of labour relations and precarious labour standards that historically have characterized jobs for low-income women; and third, under neoliberal globalization, precariousness and flexibility have spread to all sorts of jobs for low- and middle- skilled workers–regardless of whether they are held by women, men, or children.

However, in the *JDS* article I argued that in the case of Colombia, not only women, but also racialized peoples have historically worked under precarious and informal conditions. Moreover, people of colour are generally overrepresented in precarious forms of labour throughout the global economy (Moody, 1997; Aguilar and Lacsamana, 2004; Bowe, 2007). Indeed, low remuneration, instability, informality, absence of benefits, lack of labour contracts, and non-unionization have characterized the types of jobs historically experienced by low-income racialized men, women and children. Besides gender and class, ethnicity, race and immigration status (documented versus undocumented workers) are also social regulatory relations that disadvantage people, as they locate and negotiate ways to earn an income. As a result, I suggested that the term 'feminized labour' be expanded to 'racialized and feminized labour', to acknowledge in our analyses and writings, the poor labour standards that racialized low-income people have historically endured, as well as the increasing number of racialized people in the global South and racialized immigrants in the global North who are working in precarious and contingent conditions at the bottom of the global division of labour. Thus, I emphasized the importance of considering the intersections of socio-economic status and race, together with gender and other oppressive social regulatory relations, when determining who benefits and who loses from production for the global market.

With regards to precarious jobs in the CFI, those that are feminized and racialized, have been created in the thousands, in fact, over 110,000 by 2010 (Asocolflores, 2010). The *JDS* article was dedicated to examining in detail those conditions which include: minimum wage; few or no benefits; short-term, flexible or no labour contracts; low rates of unionization or non-unionization; job insecurity; few or no possibilities for advancement; increasingly intensified requirements for output; longer working hours (especially during the high seasons just before St. Valentine's Mothers' Day and Christmas celebrations in the global North); and a labour environment that places workers' health at risk and is non accommodating to workers' social reproduction responsibilities (Sanmiguel-Valderrama, 2007:80; forthcoming, 2011).

The story of the low-rank workers of the CFI, however, wouldn't be complete without referring to processes of resistance by workers, community organizations and different initiatives and strategies undertaken by local and international solidarity movements to alter precarious feminized and racialized forms of labour in the industry. These include: (1) unionization processes created by workers themselves, with solidarity and support by international and local community organizations; (2) an umbrella organization to support workers; (3) solidarity activities and international campaigns organized by European and USA based non-governmental organizations (NGOs) to create awareness among consumers of the working conditions in the industry and to demand that the CFI adhere to international codes of conduct and follow international labor and environmental standard practices; (4) the yearly celebration of 'Flower Workers' Day' created in 2001 by the Colombian-based NGO 'Corporación Cactus', to take place on the same day that St. Valentine's Day is celebrated in USA and Europe–when the largest numbers of flowers are consumed.

These important initiatives represent resistance to hegemonic feminized and racialized labour conditions under neoliberal globalization. Based on my own ethnographic research, this chapter concentrates on examining the multidimensional resistance process and the lessons that can be learned from these struggles and mobilizations.[3] However, before I develop this chapter's objective, I would like to clarify the contradictory reports regarding the conditions of labour in the CFI. Asocolflores, the Colombian Association of Flower Growers, claims to be in complete compliance with the law. However, independent unions, NGOs, and the great majority of independent research show otherwise. It can be safely argued that standards are uneven *among* plantations *and within* plantations. Various interviewees emphasized this characteristic of the CFI. For instance, a worker who has been working for the CFI for more than two decades in different plantations commented:

> They [owners] have their biggest plantation well organized, with its [employer-controlled] unions, with all of it to show, with its cafeteria, its services: Floramerica, Flores Funza, Florex, Jardines de Colombia, Jardines de Los Andes. I do not know if Las Conchitas. But these are the ones to show during visits, during appearances [inspections] of the Minister of Labour. All of that is in these plantations, but they [main plantations] establish their satellite plantations, which is where the greatest violations of human rights take place. Therefore, Funza Flowers, for instance, presents itself very well…but it is the others [satellites] that have problems…where people get fired, where there is no labour stability and where any type of violations of human rights can happen, of labour [rights], of political [rights]; these rights are really violated.

Other testimonies emphasized that both formality and informality can take place simultaneously in the same site and together become a formula to create division and competition among workers. The following testimony illustrates this competition and how different types of contracts within a plantation make a difference in terms of status and payment of benefits. When asked about differences in the treatment of workers hired directly versus those hired through an independent contractor, one social activist stated:

> Ultimately I think that it is an invented discrimination because, at the end, the work is the same, either [if hired] by a plantation or by a contractor. However, among workers themselves, there is discrimination. They look with bad eyes on contractors' people because these ones are in the worst position. It is the people that work in exchange for anything; the people who are the poorest...Competition, which is invented, rises between them [workers] on very fragile bases, which are that one receives benefits and the other does not. ...Plantations, and this is a sure thing, take no notice of people brought by contractors. It is as if they didn't exist. If there is need for drinking water, it is brought for people on payroll, for the contractor's people no. Sometimes even the service of the washroom is denied...In other words, they are like pariahs within the plantations, and they do exactly the same work. Furthermore, they do more work...because they work for what they do. They do not have a schedule. It is piecework labour...

Through the CFI case study, I refer to the challenges that unionization and social movements based on identity politics such as gender, race, and nationality, face in confronting global patriarchal, racist capitalism. This chapter is organized as follows. Sections one to four focus on the resistance initiatives in the CFI: section one reviews the history and development of unionization in the CFI; section two discusses NGOs and other community-based organizations that resist feminized and racialized forms of labor relations in the CFI; section three looks at international campaigns and codes of conduct; and section four, examines the celebration of Flower Workers' Day. In order to discern theoretically the implications of the resistance processes in the CFI, section five engages with recent literature, feminist and otherwise, that argues for collisions and networking between the labour movement and what has come to be known as New Social Movements (*hereinafter* NSMs), that is, movements seeking to achieve social justice on the basis of the identity politics of gender, sexuality, ethnicity, community/nation, environment, anti-war, etc. This literature argues for networking among diverse movements, as well as for the deployment of multiple strategies to effectively confront global neoliberal capitalism and its consequences.

Organized labour in the CFI is not alone in confronting global capitalist social relations. It has been joined by multifaceted and diverse collisions of local, national and international organizations and individuals. Through diverse strategies, these organizations and individuals support struggles at the local level. Resistance in the CFI has been innovative in various ways: First, it represents the convergence of networking of organizations and individuals representative of NSMs and labour, located not only locally, but in different countries. Through networking they have joined efforts to collaboratively challenge feminized and racialized forms of labour in the CFI. Second, the plight of women workers in the CFI has been globalized through this networking and international solidarity processes, a strategy that has become important in making the local labour struggle more effective. Third, rather than relying only on unions, strikes and negotiations at the bargaining table, this transnational networking has diversified the strategies deployed to challenge feminized and racialized labour relations. Among these strategies are: (1) deploying an international campaign to denounce the labour and environmental problems in the CFI, thus gaining support from transnational consumers and other constituencies for demands for healthy and dignified work conditions; (2)the demand...; and (3) creating and transnationalizing Flower Workers' Day, celebrated the same day as St. Valentine's on February 14th. This day was chosen to value and validate the workers whose hard and poorly remunerated work is embedded in the flowers enjoyed during celebrations in the global North. Each of these strategies or initiatives, including unionization, is examined separately in the sections that follow this introduction.

Those committed to the resistance movement have deployed these transnational and diversified initiatives with a clear and strategic understanding of the connections between the local and global aspects of CFI production. While deploying these strategies, simultaneously, these loose coalitions have centred the agency of organized labour as essential to alter feminized and racialized forms of labour. Moreover, the labour struggle and the agency of labour have been privileged because without dignified wages and working conditions, the oppression of women as workers cannot be overcome. Although, the labour movement and the networking organizations have privileged labour struggles, not all issues of discrimination have been confronted (racism, heterosexism, and the unequal burden of the unpaid labour of social reproduction). Despite this shortcoming, the resistance processes in the CFI are manifestations of a developing convergence of NSMs and the labor struggle (and the feminist movements within both). This convergence of diverse transnational actors, combined with the deployment of diverse tactics and transnational strategies, have globalized the resistance movement in the CFI.

The History of Unionization Processes in the CFI Background

The right to workers' association and unionization have been, since the 19th century, the main mechanisms used by organized labour to increase solidarity among its members and improve its bargaining power vis-a-vis capital. Jim Murray points out that the improvement of labour conditions worldwide in general, including the right to unionize, was deemed necessary to preserve social cohesion at the end of World War I. That is, granting better labour standards and allowing unionization was capital's response to the perceived threat of social rebellion in Europe following the Bolshevik revolution of October 1917 in Russia, and social rebellion in other European countries–including the increased number of trade unionists, the spread of Marxist and socialist ideas among workers, and the growth of socialist and communist parties (Murray, 2001:37).

Similar concerns by the political elite and capital were present in Colombia. The relations between the Colombian state and unionization have been erratic, characterized by different stages of confrontations, corporativism, and periods of collaboration. However, in general, it could be argued that the Colombian socio-political and economic elite's fear of a strong unionized workers' movement has been reflected in the successive laws enacted since the beginning of the 20th century, oriented to mediate social relations between capital and labour. Although workers could legally associate, negotiate and have individual and collective rights and entitlements, they could only do so under close surveillance by the state. In other words, collective and individual rights that mirrored ILO principles were granted to labour, but were closely monitored and policed by the state through the Minister of Labour and other state agencies.[4]

This arrangement has drastically changed under current global neoliberal capitalism and since the collapse of the Soviet Union. Under current neoliberal reforms, the main problems that compromise unionization rights in Colombia are reforms at the level of the individual employment relationship and the direct violent actions against organized labour, both of which have contributed to the weakening of organizing efforts. Global governance institutions such as the World Bank and the International Monetary Fund have promoted flexibilization of labour relations. In particular in Colombia, with the compliance of the elites, there has been a series of legal reforms in labour regulations that have aimed to 'de-labourize' the employment relationship between workers and capital. In other words, law and policy have created or condoned mechanisms through which workers continue to work for industries, but they are not legally considered 'labour' or employees; rather, they are now considered independent contractors governed by civil and commercial law, rather than labour law. Alternatively, workers are hired through temporary work agencies or 'cooperativas de trabajo asociado' (cooperatives of associated workers), which provide subcontracted workers to employers. However, the regular rights entitled to workers hired directly by plantations are denied to associated/sub-contracted workers (including equal pay, benefits, vacations, and the right to unionize). Through these de-labouring and sub-contracting practices, employers have no direct labour obligations to their labour force, and workers now have to bear all the risks associated with their work, including the fact that they are no longer entitled to a minimum wage, and they pay individually for health insurance, equipment, transportation, etc.

The neoliberal labour reforms undertaken in Colombia during the 1990s and the first decade of the 21st century have contributed to weakening workers' organizing possibilities. Precarious forms of labour (temporary and contingent) not only undermine workers' employment security, compensation and benefits, but also undermine unionization since workers do not hold jobs long enough to start a union, and temporary contracts make them more vulnerable to dismissals. As well, sub-contracting practices through temporary employment agencies make workers change workplace sites more frequently, driving them into isolation. If workers do not have stability in employment, organizing or maintaining a union is very difficult. Unionization is even more uncertain when plantations hire workers through civil or commercial law de-labouring practices, such as cooperatives of associated workers. The rise of neoliberalism in Colombia since the end of the 1980s has resulted in a decrease of trade unionism in Colombia, from 20% in the 1980s to less than 5% during the first decade of the 21st century (International Trade Union Confederation, 2009, Colombia).

Unionization seems a nearly impossible endeavor under the conditions created by the state's promotion of non-standard forms of labour. However, in addition to the legal mechanisms used to undermine working conditions and weaken workers' organizations and collective action, non-legal mechanisms must be considered. That is, the prevailing violence against Colombian workers' collective action and demands. Colombia has been labeled the most dangerous place for labour activism in the world, since it has the highest rates of murder of labour leaders. Direct violence, including extrajudicial assassinations, arrests, threats by paramilitary forces to the lives of union leaders, union members or their families and relatives, have been common occurrences in Colombia for the past decades. Worldwide in 2008, at least 76 labour activists were killed as a result of their actions for workers' rights, 49 of whom were Colombian trade unionists–including 16 union leaders (4 of whom were women), a 25% increase over 2007 (International Trade Union Confederation, 2009, foreword).[5]

Constructing a Dual System of Unions: Independent Unions versus Management Controlled Unions in the CFI

In spite of the violence imposed by right-wing forces and the challenges to unionization posed by laws in Colombia throughout the decades, the CFI's racialized women workers have made multiple efforts to unionize. For instance, during the 1980s various independent unions (promoted, controlled, led and created by women workers themselves) were formed at a plantation level, many times with the support of male-dominated organized workers, such as the union of agricultural workers Sintrainagro, and the federation of agricultural workers and unions Fensuagro. Both were involved in the struggles of male-dominated export-led industries like the banana and African palm plantations. Various attempts to create independent unions in the CFI have been successful, and the government has formally recognized their existence (under Colombian law, unions need to be recognized by the government before they become legal institutions that represent workers). Among these during the 1990s, were unions in plantations such as Flores Bogotá, Ananichi, Flores La Vereda, Agrodex, Ucrania, Tuchani, and others. More recently, in the decade of the 2000s, plantation-based unions include Sintrabelinda, Sintrasplendor, Sintracondor, Sintrapacna, and Sintrafragancia. These unions are federated through *Untraflores* (Colombian Union of Flower Workers, 'Union Nacional de Trabajadores de las Flores'), which was founded simultaneously with Sintrabelinda in 2001.

However, the Ministry of Labour has also recognized the existence of management-formed and controlled unions in the CFI, such as the employer created, Federation Ultracun, or the plantation-based company union Sintraflor in Sintrasplendor—a plantation owned by DOLE. In 1999, an activist, referring to the case of the flower plantation 'La Vereda', explained how Ultracun has become a barrier to successfully bargaining by its independent union:

> The union of Flores la Vereda is affiliated with Ultracun, which is an employer dominated federation. However, this is a very singular case because the workers slowly appropriated the direction of the [plantation's] union. This is the reason why they are in this [confrontational] point because they succeeded in taking control of the organization. However, the great barrier is not even the plantation's management, but the federation [Ultracun] itself...At this moment [in 1999] a union that had more or less 100 members, after one year and a half of conflict, only 4 workers are left...apparently due to lack of appropriate advice and support by the federation... They [the remaining workers] are constantly pressured either to quit or to sign a [management unilaterally decided] collective pact.

Another interviewee, a 'unionized' worker in an owner-controlled union, stated the following when asked if she had a copy of the collective pact:

> No. Nobody has it. We do not even know it... For example, before, in the plantation where I used to work we had a collective pact where there was parity: 3 workers and 3 representatives of management. Here [current workplace] no. Here they simply told us: 'the collective pact is this one, with these and these [points]'. We asked the social worker: 'well, Doña Omaira, and the representatives of the workers, who are they?' She said: 'No, there aren't any'. So we told her: 'This is not a collective pact; this is a directive pact'...We do not get a copy of it...but we have to sign it...I know that is not a collective

pact, but we cannot say anything...We have to sign that pact, even if it is not a pact, because what can we do?

The devices used by the CFI to confront independent unionization have been as tenacious as the struggles to unionize, and through the decades have successfully destroyed many independent unions on plantations. Rather than sitting down and negotiating with independent unionized workers, plantations have used the following practices: creating or bringing in management-controlled unions (i.e., Ultracun and Sintraflor), firing independent union leaders, challenging the union's legal registration with the Colombian government, labeling union members as members of armed left-wing guerillas (FARC), refusing to reinstate fired union leaders despite court orders to do so, refusing to sit at the table to bargain with unions,[6] locking-out unionized workers and hiring scabs,[7] offering better contracts to non-unionized workers than to independent unionized workers, and even abandoning and declaring the bankruptcy of plantations and moving to another county to avoid collective bargaining and fair labour relations[8] (Cifuentes-Rueda, 2004; LAC, 2006).

Even when the judicial system fines CFI plantations for their illegal practices, plantations continue to use these tactics, as they have for decades. Of particular importance is the creation of owner-controlled so-called unions, which have created the image that the freedom of workers to associate is common in the CFI.[9] Additionally, and perhaps the most perverse tactic to undermine independent unionization has been the closing of plantations to lay-off unionized workers. To illustrate this point, I will highlight the recent case of Sintrabelinda, which I introduced at the beginning of the chapter.

Using Bankruptcy and Plantation Closings to Eliminate Independent Unionization: The Sintrabelinda Strike

Referring to processes of unionization in the 1990s, one social activist discussed bankruptcy as one way that independent unionization has been discouraged in the CFI, leaving the image among workers that plantations close when independent unionization is undertaken. She explained:

> One way is the closing of the plantations themselves. A bankruptcy is declared and a massive layoff of workers is undertaken. This always has left an image for workers: where there is a [an independent] union, the plantation closes. That has

always been the lesson...I could name some of the most salient and strongest experiences, for instance, Flores Bogotá, Plantation Ananichi, where there was a strong union and the plantation was closed and the union finished. In Agrodex, in Ucrania...where the union had been operating for approximately eighteen years, the plantation was closed and everything was liquidated...In Tuchani, one of the last unions in the flower sector of the CGTD [Confederation of Democratic Workers of Colombia].

More recently, in the case of La Belinda, at the beginning of 2009, its owners, one of the approximately 300 Colombian flower firms, divided the plantation into two different legal entities with different owners: 'Belinda' and 'Copa Flowers'. It assigned workers hired through temporary work agencies and contracted out workers to 'Copa Flowers'. Approximately 500 workers who held direct long-term labour contracts with full legal benefits, some of whom had worked for the plantation for more than 12 years, remained in La Belinda.[10] In addition to the labour rights' violations mentioned in the introduction, La Belinda's greenhouse plants were, by mid-2009, infected with fungi and other diseases and pests. At the end of August, management ceased to pay salaries to Belinda workers and asked them to take an obligatory unpaid leave for 120 days arguing the non-viability of production, at the end of which, management offered to hire them under new temporary contracts in Copa Flowers and without affiliation to the union. Alternatively, management asked them to quit their jobs voluntarily and to agree that their final compensation be cut in half and paid at the end of 2012 (Interview with Aidé Silva, president of Untraflores; Video 'Situación Belinda', Corporación Cactus, 2009).

About 70 workers accepted work as temporary employees in Copa flowers, automatically renouncing the benefits they had received as permanent workers. They started to work under temporary contacts with lower wages. The remaining workers started a strike that lasted 60 days and demanded that the employer's legal labour obligations be paid in full. Although affiliation to Sintrabelinda remained low through its 8 years of existence, the desperate circumstances that workers were facing compelled them to affiliate to the union en masse, opt to strike, and pressure management to pay their salaries and health insurance. Sintrabelinda offered management to end the strike and return to work if Belinda paid their salaries and health insurance (Untraflores:3-9).

But La Belinda was not interested in complying with its labour obligations. As a result, the government declared La Belinda bankrupt, so that by selling off its assets, it could pay the workers and other creditors. The owners of Belinda lost prime land and other assets and workers are arguably guaranteed full compensation to which they are legally entitled, even if they lost their permanent jobs– which they were going to lose anyway. Currently, the great majority of striking workers are working in temporary positions in other flower plantations or industries, except for the union leaders, whose names are now on a blacklist created by owners of plantations to exclude activists from employment at their plantations.[11]

Since the 1980s, processes similar to those experienced at La Belinda have been common in various plantations where independent unions have been formed: independent unions successfully form, but management erodes workers' movements by dispersing and reorganizing the company, financing satellite companies that only use workers from labor cooperatives to avoid paying full labour entitlements to workers. Another recent case was the closing in 2007 of one of the subsidiary farms called 'Splendor' owned by DOLE, where the largest independent union in the industry operated. The difference between the processes of the 1990s and those at Splendor in 2007 and at La Belinda in 2009, is that workers will get full compensation for the termination of their employment, which under Colombian Law is generous (one month's salary per year worked in the same firm), and owners lose some of their assets.

The La Belinda strike was considered a victory for the workers in the context of the CFI, and it would have not been possible if it were not for the solidarity among workers, and the experience of the now 9-year old industry-based Colombian Union of Flower Workers, *Untraflores*. So, although the union Sintrabelinda disappeared along with part of the plantation (Copa Flowers survived), the industry-wide union Untraflores continues its work with workers and unions from other plantations. The movement can build upon the experiences of La Belinda and of previous strikes, by identifying obstacles and becoming more strategic in the future. For workers, the lessons of solidarity and resistance are empowering. Workers themselves state that through the process of resistance, they have been able to preserve their dignity as humans, and that these experiences help to prepare them for greater struggles (Untraflores, idem).

The significance of *Untraflores* cannot be overstated. *Untraflores* has basically provided the stability to unionization processes in the industry that the legal subcontracting practices undermine. The key to *Untraflores* is that it is industry-wide, as opposed to opposed to plantation-by-plantation organizing that characterized unionization experiences in the CFI during the 1980s and 1990s. So even if management manages to destroy a union in a plantation, the workers' movement survives through *Untraflores*. Despite the hardships and sacrifices, the experience of resistance in the CFI is instructive. After many processes of trial and error, unionization has now found a way to become stable. Persistence and learning from past experiences have been the key.

The obstacles confronting unions in the CFI and in Colombia in general from the 1980s until fairly recently, hindered not only the capacity of workers to organize, but also to obtain leverage to negotiate better conditions in the industry. Before *Untraflores*, none of the unions had successfully negotiated a collective agreement. In addition to the success of *Untraflores* there is another reason for hope. The unions affiliated with *Untraflores* and that operated in DOLE's plantations 'Splendor-El Rosal' and 'Fragancia Flores' after years of struggle, now have collective agreements–the first granted by arbitration, the second negotiated directly by the union (International Labor Rights Fund, 2008). Additionally, in plantations owned by Colombian capital, 'Flores el Condor' and 'Pardo, Carrizosa and Navas', from the firm 'Grupo Chia', collective agreements were signed in 2009, the first by arbitration, the second directly negotiated by the union (Untraflores:2).

I would like to emphasize that unionization is a central mechanism for empowering workers, not only to improve their labour conditions, but also for empowering themselves as people and as a class under capitalist social relations. The independence of unionization from both CFI capital and the acquiescent Colombian state is paramount for workers' dignity, autonomy and successful organizing. As has been pointed out elsewhere, capital has successfully 'unionized' internationally with the acquiescence of nation-states, creating powerful liaisons with international financial institutions[12] and international trade and intellectual property rights agreements to protect their interests. This is also true for the case of the CFI, which is well organized under Asocolflores, with much leverage and lobbying power at local, national and international levels. This is so even while labour unionization and working conditions have been undermined with the complicit role of the state. Hence, the significance of an industrial-based independent union in the Colombian Flower industry is that it has provided more leverage and stability to the workers' organizations.

The processes of unionization and workers' plights have been supported by diverse loose coalitions with NSMs at local and transnational levels, and the deployment of diverse strategies as examined in the sections that follow. One of the most important strategies has been the networking with diverse constituencies that demand healthier and dignified work conditions and have created solidarity with the CFI's workers. I focus on this strategy in the next section.

Community Organizations and Social Movements in the Context of the CFI

For more than two decades now, local community organizations with the solidarity of international NGO movements, have undertaken different strategies complementary to trade unionism to address the problematic situation in the CFI. Local organizations did not want to rely solely on unionization to confront the unsustainable social and environmental conditions of the CFI, due in part to numerous failures to maintain a widespread labour movement within the CFI during the 1980s and 1990s. Moreover, workers and their surrounding communities understood the consequences of the merging of interests between the CFI producers and successive Colombian governments. One consequences was major deregulation of labour standards across the country, as the means to secure high profitability in export-led industries such as the CFI. In the 1990s and the first decade of the 21st century, the fact that successive neoliberal governments continued to pass legislation that further deregulated labour relations, suggests the failure of the state to address substantially widespread violations of environmental, labour and economic rights (such as freedom of association, a living wage, and democratic participation in the economic development model). As a result, communities began organizing a number of other initiatives besides unionization.

The first of such initiatives was 'The Inter-institutional Flower Commission' (La Comisión Inter-institutional de Flores, *hereinafter* the Commission), which operated at a local level from 1990 to 1994. Several interviewees referred to an initiative undertaken at the beginning of the 1990s by different local community organizations to organize and coordinate the popular sectors that had been working to improve the labour and environmental conditions in the CFI. These included: CFI workers; a national federation of agricultural workers, Fensuagro, and the union Sintrainagro; the National Union Institute; Censat, an environmental institute; the institute Colsalud, which works for alternative and indigenous forms of medicine; the Flower Workers'

Association 'Flowers of Work', whose main purpose was to advance popular education programs for workers; researchers from the National University of Colombia, such as the late Maria Cristina Salazar;[13] non-governmental human-rights organizations; some representatives of the Christian militancy from the lower levels of the Catholic Church (priests and nuns serving at a parish level; workers in plantations members of the Christian workers' youth or, in Spanish, Juventudes Obrero-Cristianas (JOC), and 'La Pastoral Obrera de Facatativá' or Pastoral for Working People from Facatativá), some members of the communities where workers live; and some professionals and independent social workers and activists.

The main task of the Commission was to coordinate and strengthen the work that each group had undertaken and to help a greater number of workers and communities to engage in these processes. The Commission repudiated a possible boycott of production or consumption of flowers, and did not attempt to alter the basic structure of capital-labour relations in plantations (e.g., adopting a more radical position like lobbying for instance for the re-distribution of land and other means and techniques of production, and creating self-sustainable communities, as the Brazilian landless movement did, for example). Rather, their goals included the creation of a strong unionization movement, strengthening workers' organizations such as the Association 'Flowers of Work' and creating community houses to provide services for workers and their families (i.e., health, legal advice and representation, childcare). Another goal was sharing information and knowledge to systematize the working and environmental practices of the industry, in order to have the 'scientific' basis for denouncing, nationally and internationally, those practices that violated environmental, human and community rights, and dignity.

The Commission officially emerged after the First Forum on the Impact of the CFI on the communities of the Bogotá Savannah held in 1991.[14] Before its disintegration in 1994, the Commission developed various tasks: flower workers traveled to Europe and North America providing testimony about the conditions of flower production in Colombia and showing the documentary film 'Love, Women, and Flowers' (produced in 1988 by Colombians Martha Rodríguez and Jorge Silva). The film documents labour conditions, the use of pesticides in greenhouses, and workers' struggles and obstacles to organizing. Colombian scholars undertook research and documentation,[15] and the unionization movement continued its campaign to unionize workers at different plantation sites.

However, by 1994, the Commission was severely weakened and divided for two reasons. The first was one of the bloodiest episodes of repression and systematic killings of members of the agricultural workers' union movement at the end of the 1980s and beginning of the 1990s, in which hundreds of banana workers and residents of their communities in the Urabá region in Colombia were murdered. The assassination of some members of the national directives of Sintrainagro and threats to other members of the Bogotá office, including representatives of Sintrainagro and Fensuagro within the Commission, created an environment of intimation, fear and distrust. There was justifiable fear of a military raid of their Bogotá office, where the files of the Commission were stored.[16] The violence weakened one of the most important actions of the Commission, which was to strengthen the union movement among flower workers. The secretary general of Fensuagro, who worked at the Commission went into to exile, while others members of the Commission who suffered attempts on their lives, continued their work at a lower profile.

A second reason for the ending of the Commission was a bias that favored workers as a privileged constituency and the authentic victims of oppression, disregarding the value of other representatives of the communities and other forms of oppression, such as gender, and race. International funds were provided only to the workers' organization 'Flowers of Work', whose main purpose had been to strengthen the educational levels of flower workers, rather than funding the Commission as a whole. Likewise, the union movement underestimated the value of the services provided by NGOs (legal, health, housing, and 'women's issues' such as day-care and sexual harassment) and grassroots organizations (environmental and health issues for the communities), the professional social workers and academic research. The divisions among different constituencies of grassroots organizations, unions, NGOs and academia, together with the problems resulting from the repression of agricultural sector unions, prompted them to continue working separately and at a distance, although collaboratively.

In other words, the centralized organization failed due to the violent political context in Colombia and the disregard for the importance of social movements besides labour. However, the ending of the Commission prompted a horizontal, non-hierarchical local and trans-national network of organizations that have continued to work with issues related to CFI up to today.

In spite of numerous failures in the 1990s, the tough work of organizing labour unions continued. Only after the creation of *Untraflores in* 2001 has labour been strengthened. Other projects of the Commission however were truncated, in particular the establishment and maintenance of centers to provide legal, health and community (e.g., daycare, and counseling) services to workers, and research endeavors. In fact, after the international campaign that denounced labour and environmental conditions in the industry, Asocolflores and flower plantations have become increasingly protective and suspicious of independent social scientists and researchers, resulting in plantations closing their doors to research.

The NGO Corporación Cactus was born out of the Commission's experience and has since pursued research and documentation of the labour and environmental conditions of the flower plantations through their '*Boletín Cactus*' (among other publications), provided legal advice and representation to individual workers, promoted international work with similar organizations in other South and Central American countries, Europe and North America (i.e., Labour Fund, which has contributed to publicize in the main market of Colombian flowers, the USA, the conditions of work in the CFI), and promoted national and international campaigns in solidarity with workers, such as the 'Flower Workers' Day' among other endeavors.

Other initiatives were also strengthened by this experience, particularly the solidarity work of the German based NGO, FIAN (Food First Information and Action Network), with whom the ex-secretary general of Fensuagro in exile had continued to work in international solidarity with unionized flower workers or those struggling to unionize. FIAN has also promoted the 'Flower Campaign' and the International Code of Conduct for the Production of cut-flowers, with the solidarity of various European Unions and local NGOs including Cactus[17] (Mantilla, 2008). In the next section, I discuss these international campaigns and codes of conduct. They are representative of the diversification and transnationalization of strategies to address feminized and racialized forms of labour in the CFI. They have effectively globalized the plight and resistance of CFI workers.

International Campaigns, Codes of Conduct and Reflexive Law in the Context of the CFI

The failure of successive Colombian governments to address the widespread violation of workers' rights in the country, has prompted what in legal studies is known as *reflexive law processes*. The term

Reflexive Law, first introduced by the German jurist Gunther Teubner, refers to 'a civil society regulating itself, supported, ...by the State. That is to say *regulated self-regulation...*' (Calliess, Gralf-Peter, 2002, emphasis in original). The term is associated with Tony Blair and Gerhard Schroder's 'third way', between the market and the state.

In the context of the CFI, reflexive law processes or alternative non-state self-regulations are those associated with corporate responsibility, and the current International Code of Conduct promoted by the International Campaign on Fair Trade in flowers advanced by national and international NGO communities. In the mid 1990s, ex-members of the Commission and Cactus initiated this campaign with the support of pressure by consumers and communities in Europe, as well as Dutch flower producers. This Campaign promoted 'El Sello de Calidad de Flores' or 'Certification of Flower Quality'. The campaign promoted a certification of quality in production in terms of labour standards and environmental management.

The 'Certification of Flower Quality' was proposed in 1995 by multiple national and international NGOs and was presented to Asocolflores in a forum in Bogotá that denounced the violations of labour and environmental rights (Defensoria, Cactus, and Fescol, 1996). The purpose of local community organizations, backed by pressure from Europe, was to work in conjunction with Asocolflores to improve the labour and environmental conditions in plantations.

However, Asocolflores responded independently. In 1996, facing increasing international pressure and a bad image in international circles, Asocolflores promulgated a self-regulating program known as 'Green Flower'–which Asocolflores labeled a 'code of conduct'. Green Flower, however, focuses mainly on improving environmental and human management practices, rather than improving labour conditions. Thus, Green Flower has to be understood as a re-engineering tool instead of a Code of Conduct, as the preamble of the Code itself states:

> It [Green Flower] is an integral strategy oriented towards the optimization of the use of resources with a long-term projection and a permanent dynamic *to improve the profitability* of the Colombian floricultural sector within a concept of sustainable development. (Asocolflores, 1998: 010-3) [emphasis added]

Besides promoting lower pesticide consumption and more efficient management of chemicals and water to lower costs and at the same time promote cleaner environmental production, Green Flower was a means to re-engineer human management systems, by deepening Taylorist principles, that is, segmenting workers' duties within plantations in order to increase workers' production levels. The program includes standardization of selection and recruitment practices, systematizing and filing information about workers, disciplinary measures, job description and analysis of duties, induction and training programs for new employees, absenteeism analysis, hygienic facilities, safe drinking water and programs such as 'Cultivating Peace in the Family', literacy campaigns, some recreation activities, supporting school reinforcement, childcare, training, and Asocolflores' involvement with community and municipality policies and programs.

At the same time, the program promotes some basic labour entitlements as mandated by Colombian law, such as on time payment of wages and bonuses for workers' output or performance, obligatory health insurance benefits and social security. Independent unionization continues to be restricted and there is no participation by workers or communities in the processes that created the program, its development, monitoring or certification. Monitoring and certification are done by a European firm named Société Générale de Surveillance, which by 2007 had certified 86 firms; another 53 are in the process of certification (Mantilla, 2008:75).

What is significant about Green Flower is that it secures the control by plantation owners over the parameters used to evaluate plantations and the certification process. In this way Asocolflores secured total control over labour processes and productivity. Moreover, besides recognizing some entitlements of labour, the program deepens the power relations between capital and labour and actually further alienates workers in the Marxist sense: (1) workers have no agency under Green Flower and the certification process; (2) labour has no control over the production process, nor its intensity or the fruit (flowers) of their labour; and (3) labour increasingly sees the plantation influencing the private sphere and public policy at municipal and national levels. The privatization of labor regulations–reflexive law–when assumed by corporations is very problematic because it has become a way for capital to further control labor without the mediation of the state. Corporate codes of conduct, therefore, are a facet of privatization under neoliberal globalism: privatization of the legal system and regulatory functions of the state.

Asocolflores has promoted Green Flower as *the* Colombian flower certification label and in this way excluded and undermined the initiatives of the international and national NGO community. Thus, Asocolflores co-opted a wide-based initiative (in much the same fashion that it co-opted unionization in the industry by creating owner-controlled unions) and used it to its advantage to claim corporate responsibility in the production of flowers, and in this way, cleaned up its image internationally (Madrid Berroterán, 2003; Madrid and Wright, 2007).

For its part, the International Flower Campaign altered its initiative of the 'Certification of Flower Quality', to the 'International Code of Conduct' (ICC), a proposal initiated in 1998 directed towards all producers of flowers in the world to encourage following minimum labour and environmental standards in the production of flowers (Brassel and Rangel 2001:26). The emblematic rights recognized in the ICC are freedom of association, collective bargaining, and a living wage. It promotes the ample participation of workers and communities in the monitoring and certification processes and equally important, continuing solidarity among workers not only at a South-South level, but also at a South-North level. The development of this initiative and its monitoring and certification processes are still in the planning stage. It is up to this community to exercise its power to expose Green Flower as a corporate-dominated scheme that hinders workers' agency and unionization. Certification under Green Flower has confused consumers and obscures the realities of anti-union tactics in the industry. Consumer power cannot be exercised if such obfuscation persists.

To summarize, the failure of the State's legal system to enforce human rights for CFI workers has started a transnational- and locally-based movement of appropriation of law through non-state reflexive law processes such as the ICC. Although the international movement around the ICC and fair trade is precarious, and not unexpectedly without problems, its ideals have encouraged appropriating regulatory regimes through the participation and empowerment of local communities in alliances with foreign-based communities, organizations and independent unions. Thereby, these coalitions and their initiative have contributed to the trans-nationalization of the resistance and struggle. Perhaps it may become a way to alleviate, although moderately, the difficult situation faced by women in the CFI.

In addition to the ICC, another initiative to confront feminized and racialized forms of labour in the CFI is the creation and celebration of Flower Workers' Day. It started as a local celebration in the municipalities around Bogotá. Today, however, it is celebrated in various sites of the global South. The transnational celebration of Flower Workers Day is also representative of the diversification of strategies of the resistance movement in the CFI, which has contributed towards its globalization. I turn to this initiative in the next section.

Colombian Flower Workers' Day

February 14th is known today in the global South as International Flower Workers' Day. This celebration highlights the dynamic under global patriarchal-racist capitalism, between racialized women workers as producers in the global South and women as receivers of flowers in the global North. Its celebration originated in the municipalities surrounding Bogotá in 2001 and it was conceived and organized by Corporación Cactus. Today this celebration is international: Mexico, Ecuador, Zimbabwe, Peru, India, Bolivia, Colombia, Kenya, Tanzania and Holland participate in it. All these countries produce flowers for export and local communities celebrate the contribution that workers make to national and international economies. This celebration has many purposes: (1) to promote workers' rights and demand compliance; (2) to motivate workers to share their experiences with other workers and motivate them to organize and strengthen existing organizations; (3) to generate awareness among local, national authorities, the media and the public at large of the social and labor practices in the CFI; and (4) to create international solidarity among organizations and workers in the diverse sites where production takes place (Corporación Cactus, 2010).

Celebrations generally involve a repertoire of activities that includes: cultural events, such as music and dancing; public speakers, including some coming from overseas to share their experiences as workers in other flower plantations across the globe or in other struggles; researchers deploying surveys that seek to document the experiences, opinions and voices of workers; creating spaces for workers to debate, reflect and share their experiences; sending greetings to sister organizations throughout the world; and in the North, sending letters and post-cards to public officials and Northern flower companies, denouncing labor conditions.

International Flower Workers' Day has become an important vehicle to generate solidarity for workers and awareness of their plight at local and global levels. However, not surprisingly, Asocolflores has its own 'festival of flowers' aimed at publicizing the contributions of flower production to the economy, as generators of employment, foreign exchange and, according to them, development. The festival of flowers is part of the recreational activities endorsed under Green Flower.

To Join or not to Join: Overcoming Fragmentation and Single Actions to Strategically Confront Global Capital

Historically there has been a divide between NSM and working-class women and men. The former do not see the traditional responses of labour as a means to resolve their concerns and causes, and the latter do not see NSM as a means to resolve class oppression (Novelli and Ferus-Comelo:37-38). But, these assumptions are currently being evaluated as awareness that 'single-issue activism is a dead end' increases among activists. On the one hand, the labour movement is assuming a broader understanding of class—one that does not equate class with waged labour, but is more inclusive to embrace waged and non-waged workers from diverse backgrounds, and paid and non-paid activities that sustain social reproduction (Colgan and Ledwing 2002; Frank 2005; Bieler, Lindberg, and Pillay 2008). On the other hand, there is increasing interest by NSM to work in intersectional terms and consider class central to the understanding of oppression. Theorists and activists in the labour movements and NSMs have recognized that the fragmentation of analyses and struggles have obstructed the possibilities for effectively confronting neoliberal global capitalism and concomitant exploitative social regulatory relations. The intersections of union movements and NSMs have become the centre of analyses by academics and activists alike. For instance, feminist Hester Eisenstein, criticizing mainstream feminism, warns us of the dangers of focusing only on gender to advance the fight against discrimination. Eisenstein uses the term 'Feminism Seduced' to signify the use of mainstream feminist ideals by capitalism:

> In the process of selling globalization, corporate leaders and other elites systematically have been trying to seduce women into embracing the expansion of capitalism. We have seen how the IFIs (International Financial Institutions) have embraced the idea of gender as central to economic development and how the corporate media publicize the achievements of women in high places. All of this has seemed to me to be an overall effort to smoothly fold feminism and feminist ideas into the corporate embrace. (Eisenstein, 2010:202)

Eisenstein argues that 'the feminist divorce from the Left leaves feminists in the camp of the reformers rather than revolutionaries' (Ibid:207). She suggests that 'for a whole whole range of issues, the experience of women of color and working-class women needs to become the basis for agenda-setting in future [feminist] activism' (Ibid:211).

Similarly, Delia Aguilar, Anne Lacsamana (2004), Torry D. Dickinson and Robert K. Schaeffer (2008), position class analysis and class-based struggles and resistances as central to working-class women's agency, identities, and location within the global patriarchal-racist-capitalist system. These scholars do not privilege class over other forms of oppression, but argue as Eisenstein does, that an analysis of oppression/resistance that does not consider class as central becomes complicit with capitalism. Thus, class struggles, as well as those oriented to undermine other forms of oppression such as racism, patriarchy, the destruction of the environment, heterosexism and other hierarchical relations must be fought simultaneously. However, these scholars do not favor a unified movement of peoples to confront global capitalism. Instead, they suggest working towards collaboration among them. Likewise, Wendy Harcourt and Arturo Escobar (2005) argue for what the have named 'mesh-working', which entails creating new non-hierarchical and self-organizing alliances and networking, as well as deploying multiple strategies to alter current global diverse power relationships.

To be Sure, Marxist-feminism, socialist feminism, feminist political economy, and feminisms developed by women of colour in the global South and North, historically have been in agreement on developing analyses and activism in intersectional terms (as developed by Kate Bezanson, Meg Luxton, Antonella Picchio, Patricia Hill-Collins, Chela Sandoval, Gloria Anzaldúa, Maxine Molyneux, Clara Fraser, Mariarosa Dalla-Costa, Selma James, Maria Mies, Nighat Said-Khan, Heleieth Saffioti and Virginia Vargas, to name just a few). I join these scholars in positioning class at the center of analyses of working-class women's struggles, which simultaneously consider the challenges posed to workers of colour by the racist structures of capitalism, as well as to women by the patriarchal structures of the new economy, and the international division of labour derived from location, nationality, citizenship and other forms of discrimination (i.e., heteronormativity, ableism, ageism). Additionally, the emancipation of racialized working-class women does need to acknowledge and address the reality of the intersections of production and reproduction in women's lives (Molineux, 1979; Bezanson and Luxton, 2006; Sedef

Arat-Koç, 2006). All of these must assume central positions within our writings as we develop encompassing and non-essentialist analyses. As these authors argue, if class and all oppressions are simultaneously considered in mainstream feminism and other writings, they would not only become more inclusive, but could contribute further towards a radical transformative project to confront global capitalism, as opposed to being complicit with it.

Although arguing for simultaneous consideration in our analyses and activisms of diverse struggles and discriminations is by no means a new argument, what is refreshing is that those coalitions have been developed in activist praxis in case such as the CFI resistance movement. Thus, the CFI is an example of coalition building in activist praxis, although in a developing stage, since for example, the racist and gendered aspects of labour practices in the industry remain unchallenged. In spite of this, much in tune with diverse theorists' claims for networking and the deployment of diverse strategies, for decades now, the resistance movements in the CFI have practiced these strategies at local and transnational levels. This diversification of strategies, as well as networking and coalition building has been examined in the previous sections. I summarize this argument in the conclusion.

Conclusion

Women workers in the CFI have organized and become the leaders of many courageous labour movements. They have successfully created independent unions in a number of plantations throughout the decades of CFI's existence. However, collective organizing is not widespread in the CFI and in 2010, independent unionism represented less than 3% of its total workers, lower than the national average of 5%. Organized workers in the CFI, leaders and members of unions have faced many battles–legal, political and even physical violence—in exercising their their basic right to associate as workers.

Women leaders and members of unions have not walked alone in their search for more dignified work in the CFI. They, however, have carried the lion's share of activist work with its positive and negative consequences. These include the rewards of experiencing solidarity and empowerment for collective work, but also the material consequences and anxieties associated with the uncertainties surrounding the loss of their jobs, incomes, unions, and in one instance, enduring the injuries perpetuated by the violence of right-wing forces.

These independent unions and their female and male members are part of a larger community of social movements in Colombia and elsewhere which throughout the decades, has supported the CFI workers' struggles for dignified work. Members of the unions and supporting organizations and communities have been strategic, thoughtful, passionate, inspiring, and imaginative both in their use of traditional forms of political collective action, and in creating new ways to confront Asocolflores and the owners' deceitful tactics to overpower and undermine organized labour. The courageous challenges by organized labour to unjust practices in the CFI constitute important attempts to resist, transform and counterbalance the dislocations and inequalities associated with globalization and the feminization and racialization of labour relations.

The reality in the CFI, as in other spheres of Colombian society, is that extremely authoritarian relations–based on constructed differences of gender, race, nationality, and class–govern the relations between capital and labour. As seen throughout the experiences examined in the previous sections, corporations in the CFI have attempted to hinder workers' and community initiatives by partially co-opting them. If workers establish an independent union, the plantation introduces company-controlled unions or deploys a range of tactics to undermine and destroy the union, including closing the plantation. As a result, many independent unions have been lost in the struggles. When national and international community organizations proposed to the CFI a Code of Conduct to follow international labour standards, Asocolflores seized control of the process and launched a human-management and re-engineering tool (Green Flower), creating much confusion among consumers since flowers are now certified as 'green'. However, this label is totally unaccountable to labour–it neither certifies that labour practices within the industry are sound and free of exploitation, nor that labour unionization is safe and free of oppression. Asocolflores has even tried to create an alternative to the celebration of international flower worker day, to preserve its corporate interests and image. When a broad-based and coordinated Inter-Institutional Commission of Flowers (the Commission) was established to address globally all the different facets of oppression faced by workers and communities that endure this form of production, the violence perpetrated by right-wing forces against unions leaders in the banana enclaves of production, disrupted the organization.

In spite of the efforts by Asocolflores and the industry to undermine workers' organizations, resistance has persisted and workers now have many victories to count: the formation of the industry-wide union *Untraflores*, the new collective agreements successfully negotiated in DOLE's plantations and some national plantations, a range of local and international communities that are aware of their plight and support their work through different strategies, initiatives, and methods. Among the most important organizations have been Corporación Cactus, some representatives of the Christian militancy from the lower levels of the Catholic Church at a municipal level, and other independent unions in Colombia; Christian Aid; FIAN and Terre des Hommes in Germany; War on Want headquartered in the UK; The National Council of Women of Canada (NWCW); and Bread for the World and the International Labour Rights Fund in the USA. Without doubt, unionization and labour struggles continue to be of paramount importance to low-income racialized working-women under capitalism, since their dignified survival depends in part on achieving dignified working conditions. What is particularly interesting about the coalitions and networking of the resistance movement in the CFI, is that due to their locations in diverse parts of the globe, they have successfully globalized the resistance movement and the plight of women workers through transnational campaigns and solidarity. This solidarity has without doubt, given endorsement and leverage to the local labour movement, so it can more effectively confront capital in its struggle for fairer working conditions.

In this way, the resistance movement to the CFI labour practices is an example of first, the convergence of locally- and transnationally-based networks of organizations and individuals who have worked collaboratively, and have supported and thereby transnationalized the plight of women workers in the CFI and other local labour struggles. And second, without dismissing the agency of CFI's organized labour, this transnational networking has diversified the strategies deployed to alter feminized and racialized labour relations through Flower Workers' Day, the International Flower Campaign and Code of Conduct, and the Inter-institutional Flower Commission. However, I want to address the second reason why the Commission failed—its privileging of labour over other communities as the authentic representatives of oppression under capitalism and its disregard for the contributions of other communities and grassroots organizations to the cause. As seen, the case of the CFI demonstrates that the roles and contributions of local and international communities have been very significant for work done at the local level. This is particularly important due to the violent political context in which the struggle takes place. Furthermore, the fact that the great majority of flower workers are racialized women, means that concomitant to class, aspects of both their gender and ethnic identity and their power struggles with patriarchy and racism, need to be considered and addressed. Capitalism cannot be confronted solely as a class issue. Patriarchy and racism maintain it as well. The nature of oppression and discrimination are such that all exploitations and hierarchies are embedded and interlocked in the processes of domination in capitalism and hence require to be contested in intersectional terms. Simultaneous 'mesh-working' and direct action against all of these diverse oppressions is required to effectively alter global, patriarchal, racist capitalism. Furthering intersectional organizing, coalitions, and networking, as well as the creation of new tactics and strategies to erode all these diverse oppressions can only be developed through uninterrupted engagement and actions to confront them simultaneously. These processes will not only illuminate ways to transform oppressive institutions more effectively, but also will provide the opportunity to learn more about how these intersecting oppressions work.

To be sure, the resistance struggles in the CFI thus far are claiming a different form of globalization, one that includes social justice for workers. These movements, however, do not challenge the basic relations between capital and labour in the way that other social movements have done: for instance, the Landless movement in Brazil, the Mau Mau in Kenya, the struggle against water privatization in Bolivia, indigenous movements for land and autonomy in Colombia, among many others. In the context of CFI, however, similar radical resistance movements have not been viable due to the historical context of political violence and the dirty war. The presence of more democratic political conditions in Colombia could permit the development of alternatives to industrial capitalist forms of production. For now, the current struggles reflect the limits imposed by the historical political economic context in which social movements can operate in Colombia.

NOTES

[1] The pioneering work by Colombians Diana Medrano and Rodrigo Villar, María Cristina Salazar, Alicia Eugenia Silva, together with the video 'Love, Women and Flowers' by Martha Rodríguez and Jorge Silva in the 1980s, denounced for the first time the precarious labour conditions in the industry. This work was followed by Verena Meier, Patricia Sierra, Laura Rangel, Gladys Acosta-Vargas and Corporación Cactus in the 1990's, to the current work by Cynthy Mellow, Nora Ferm, Molly Talcott,

Gilma Madrid, Corporación Cactus, and Olga Sanmiguel-Valderrama. In contrast to the previous authors, all of whom are critical of labour conditions in the CFI, Greta Friedemann-Sanchez sees this type of labor as emancipatory to women, in line with neo-liberal discourses uncritical of global capitalism.

2   For a general discussion of the concept of feminization of labour, see Standing (1989; 1999) and Vosko (2000). Bakker (1996) and Armstrong (1996) discuss it with reference to labour relations in Canada. The nature and consequences of the feminization of labour in the cut flower industry in Latin America in general and Ecuador in particular, are discussed respectively by Lara (1995) and Korovkin (2002; 2005). Sanmiguel-Valderrama applies this concept, along with introducing the notion of the racialization of labour, to an analysis of Colombia's flower industry (2004; 2007a; 2007b; forthcoming).

3   I have been engaged with workers and civil society organizations related to the Colombian flower industry since 1999. Interviews cited in this article were conducted in the municipalities surrounding Bogotá, where most of the CFI production takes place at different times between 1999 and 2000; this fieldwork was partially funded by the Social Sciences and Humanities Research Council of Canada (SSHRCC). All interviews were conducted in Spanish and have been translated by the author. Since 2006, I have been to Colombia several times to gather updated printed information.

4   The relations between capital and labour have been closely monitored by the state, which has controlled every aspect of the process of the 'freedom' of association of workers or unionization. Laws include the requirement for unions to petition the government to be legally recognized as such; the prohibition to engage in any money-making activities, accompanied by periodical audits of unions' incomes and expenditures; the prohibition to participate in politics or to belong to a political party, accompanied by the government's authority to intervene and investigate trade union activities and organizations, for most of the 20th century (the new 1991 Colombian Political Constitution, made it legal for organized workers to participate in politics); the prohibitions against federations or confederations calling a strike; the prohibition to strike in industries providing essential services as listed by law; the government's prerogative of imposing mandatory arbitration on a conflict when the strike goes beyond a certain period of time.

5 The latest edition of the International Trade Union Confederation Annual Survey of Trade Union Violations, expected for publication in June 2010, will this year again highlight the situation of trade union rights in Colombia. This year, to date 25 unionists have been murdered, by far the largest number in the world (ITUC, 2010).

6 See the case of La Celestina (currently known as La Belinda) and the case of 'La Vereda', the case of Wesmax in: *Boletín Cactus* 13 and 14. More recently see the case of Sintrasplendor at LAC (2006:10).

7 The case of WEXMAX in 'Un día esta Lucha va a ser un Grato Recuerdo' in *Boletín Cactus* 14, Oct. 2002, 6-8; and *Boletín Cactus 15,* Nov. 2002.

8 See The case of Tuchany S.A. from Síbate, in "Pasajes de una Historia" *Boletín Cactus* 7, Oct. 1997, 6-7.

9 Asocolflores argues that the percentage of unionized workers in the flower industry is 10%, which is double that of the rest of the country. However, Untraflores claims that there are not more than 3,000 unionized workers, or less than 3% of the total workers in the industry. See Asocolflores' webpage, 'social aspects', 2010.

10 By 1998, La Belinda was known as 'La Celestina' and used to contract directly its labor force of around 1,400 workers. Through the past decade, the plantation slowly replaced more than half of its labor force from full-time direct contracts to subcontracts.

11 Blacklisting union leaders is a widespread practice in the CFI and Colombia in general, see LAC (2006) and Mantilla (2009).

12 A major mechanism of capital organization has been the so-called Washington Consensus. 'John Williamson, a British economist, coined the phase "Washington Consensus" to describe a set of policies that the IMF, the World Bank and the governments of various aid-giving countries have been jointly advocating for economic management and growth of developing countries, and for the effective insertion of these countries into the globalizing world economy', that is, the neoliberal economic agenda. See U.N. General Assembly, 'Global Financial Flows and their Impact on Developing Countries: Addressing the Matter of Volatility'. Report of the Secretary-General, A/53/398, September 16, 1998, 2.

13 The participation of scholars from the National University was conceived to contribute to documenting the problematic and to work under Participatory Action Research (PAR) methods, which aim to 'facilitate processes of personal and social transformation

by oppressed people' (Yarmol-Franko, K, "Editorial Introduction" 29 *Convergence* 3, 1996, 4.), based on democratization of knowledge. For an account of the work of Orlando Fals-Borda and Maria Cristina Salazar, two scholars from the National University of Colombia who has worked under PAR and in the CFI. See Pyrch, T., 'The Participatory Action Research Challenge Re-Issued in Colombia' 29 *Convergence* 3, 1996, 5-16, 7. See also 'Algunas Reflexiones y Evaluación del Proyecto sobre la Floricultura en la Sabana de Bogota' Documento No. 9 in: Universidad Nacional de Colombia, Centro de Studios Sociales–CES, *La Floricultura en la Sabana de Bogota: Proyecto Piloto en el Municipio de Madrid, Cundinamarca* (Santafe de Bogota: Mimeo, 1995).

14   For the memoirs of these Forums see 'Foro: Impacto de la Industria de las Flores', October 13-14, 1991 (Bogotá: Mimeo available at 'Fondo de Documentación Mujer y Genero', Universidad Nacional de Colombia, 1991).

15   Ten documents were produced under the title: Universidad Nacional de Colombia, Centro de Studios Sociales–CES, *La Floricultura en la Sabana de Bogotá: Proyecto Piloto en el Municipio de Madrid, Cundinamarca* (Bogotá: Mimeo, 1995).

16   In fact, in 1994, while I was working in a completely unrelated activity a block away from the offices where these unions are housed in Bogotá, I recall that a bomb exploded in their offices.

17   Organizations such as: IUF–International Union of Food, Agricultural, Hotel, Restaurant, Catering, Tobacco and Allied Workers Associations, Geneva; IGBAU–Trade Union for Construction, Agriculture and Environment, Germany; FNV–Trade Union Confederation, Netherlands; OLAA–Organisatie Latijns Amerika Activiteiten, Netherlands; Fair Trade Center, Sweden; Flower Coordination, Switzerland; and Christian Aid, and War on Want, U.K. (see FIAN).

REFERENCES

Acosta-Vargas, G. (1995) 'Flowers That Kill: The Case of the Colombian Flower Workers', in Schuler, Margaret A (ed.) *From Basic Needs to Basic Rights: Women's Claim to Human Rights.* Washington, D.C.: Women, Law & Development International.

Aflonordes and Sena (1996) *Programa Empresarial de Aprendices para el Sector Floricultor.* Santafé de Bogotá: Mimeo Aflonordes.

Aguilar, D.D. and Lacsamana, A.E. (2004) *Women and Globalization.* Amherst, N.Y: Humanity Books.

Arat-Koç, S. (2006) 'Whose Social Reproduction? Transnational Motherhood and Challenges to Feminist Political Economy,' in Meg Luxton, Kate Bezanson (eds.) *Social Reproduction: Feminist Political Economy Challenges Neo-liberalism*. Montreal and Kingston: McGill-Queen's University Press.

Asocolflores (1998) *Flor Verde, Código de Conducta: Auto-regulación Ambiental y Social, Manual de Mejoras Prácticas*, Versión 2.0. Santafé de Bogotá: Asocolflores.

Asocolflores (2009) 'Informe de Actividades 2007.' Accessed on October 2009 from www.asocolfores.org.

Asocolflores (2010) 'Floricultura Colombiana: Información General, Estadisticas'. Accessed on May 2010 from www.asocolfores.org.

Armstrong, P. (1996) 'The Feminization of the Labour Force: Harmonizing Down in a Global Economy', in Bakker, Isabella (ed.) *Rethinking Restructuring: Gender and Change in Canada*. Toronto: University of Toronto Press.

Bakker, I. (ed.) (1996), *Rethinking Restructuring: Gender and Change in Canada* Toronto: University of Toronto Press.

Bakker, I. and Gill, S. (eds.) (2003) *Power, Production, and Social Reproduction: Human In/Security in the Global Political Economy*. Basingstoke, Hampshire, New York: Palgrave Macmillan.

Bezanson, K. and Luxton, M. (eds.) (2006) *Social Reproduction: Feminist Political Economy Challenges Neo-Liberalism*. Montreal: McGill-Queen's University Press.

Bieler, S. Lindberg, I. and Pillay, D. (eds.) (2008) *Labour and the Challenges of Globalization: What Prospects for Transnational Solidarity?* New York: Pluto Press.

Bowe, J. (2007) *Nobodies: Modern American Slave Labor and the Dark Side of the New Global Economy*. New York: Ramdom House.

Brassel, F. and Rangel, C-E. (2001) *International Social Standards for the International Flower Industry*. Bonn: Food First Information and Action Network - FIAN, Mimeo.

Brittain, J.J. (2010) *Revolutionary Social Change in Colombia: The Origin and Direction of the FARC-EP.* New York, Pluto Press.

Calliess, G-P. (2002) 'Reflexive Transnational Law: The Privatisation of Civil Law and the Civilisation of Private Law'. *Zeitschrift Für Rechtssoziologie* 23: 185-216.

Cifuentes-Rueda, R. (2003) *Experiencias de Organización Sindical y Conflictos Colectivos en el Sector Floricultor*. Bogotá: Corporación Cactus.

Colgan, F. and Ledwith, S. (eds.) (2002) *Gender, Diversity and Trade Unions: International Perspectives*. London and New York: Routledge.

Corporación Cactus (1999) *Mujeres y Flores: Flexibilización en Marcha*. Bogotá: Corporación Cactus.
Corporación Cactus (2009) Video 'Situación Belinda'. Available at www.cactus.org.co.
Corporación Cactus (2010) *Informe de la Floricultura Colombiana*. Bogotá, Cactus. Available at www.cactus.org.co.
Corporación Cactus, (1997-2007) *Boletin Cactus*, issues 1 to 23. Bogotá: Corporación Cactus.
Defensoría del Pueblo, Corporación Cactus and Fescol (1996) *Memorias Seminario Taller Sello de Calidad para Flores Colombianas: Condiciones y Criterios*. Bogotá: Corporación Cactus.
Dickinson, T.D. and Schaeffer, R. (2008) *Transformations: Feminist Pathways to Global Change* Boulder, CO: Paradigm Publishers.
Días, M., Salazar, M.C., et. al. (1995) *Trabajo de Niños y Jóvenes en la Floricultura en el Municipio de Madrid, Cundinamarca*. Bogotá: Mimeo Universidad Nacional de Colombia, Centro de Estudios Sociales–CES.
Eisenstein, H. (2010) *Feminism Seduced: How Global Elites Use Women's Labor and Ideas to Exploit the World*. Boulder, CO: Paradigm Publishers.
Ferm, N. (2008) 'Non-traditional agricultural export industries: Conditions for Women Workers in Colombia and Peru'. *Gender & Development* 16(1): 13-26.
Frank, D. (2005) *Bananeras: Women Transforming the Banana Unions of Latin America*. Cambridge, Massachusetts: South End Press.
Harcourt, W. and Escobar, A. (eds.) (2005) *Women and the politics of place*. Bloomfield, CT: Kumarian Press.
Hristov, J. (2009) *Blood and capital: the Paramilitarization of Colombia*. Toronto: Between the Lines.
Hylton, F. (2006) *Evil Hour in Colombia*. New York: Verso.
International Labour Rights Fund (2008) 'Victories in the Flower Industry at Long Last!' Available at www.laborrightsblog.typepad.com.
International Trade Union Confederation (2009) *Annual Survey of Trade Union Violations*. Available at www.ituc-csi.org.
International Trade Union Confederation (2010) *Annual Survey of Trade Union Violations* Available at www.ituc-csi.org.
Korovkin, T. (2003) 'Cut-Flower Exports, Female Labor, and Community Participation in Highland Ecuador'. *Latin American Perspectives* 30(4): 18-42.
Korovkin, T. and Sanmiguel-Valderrama, O. (2007) 'Labour Stan-

dards, Global Markets and Non-State Initiatives: Colombia's and Ecuador's Flower Industries in Comparative Perspective'. *Third World Quarterly* 28(1): 117-135.

Labor Advisory Committee for Trade Negotiations and Trade Policy - LAC (2006) *Report to the President, the Congress and the United States Trade Representative on the U.S.-Colombia Free Trade Agreement.* Washington, Mimeo.

Lara-Flores, S.M. (1995) 'La feminización de trabajo asalariado en los cultivos de exportación no tradicionales', in Lara-Flores, S.M. (ed.) *Jornaleras, temporeras y boias frías: Rostro Femenino del Mercado de Trabajo Rural en América.* Latina, pp. 15-47. Caracas: Editorial Nueva Sociedad.

Mantilla, G. (2008). 'Constructing codes and broadening agendas: the case of Asocolflores, the Colombian Flower Exporters Association', in *Embedding Human Rights in Business Practices II.* New York: United Nations Global Compact and the Office of the High Commissioner for Human Rights, pp. 71-80.

Mellon, C. (2007) 'Roses, Thorns, and Seven dollars a Day: Women's Workers in Colombia's Export Flower Industry', in Cabezas, Emilia, Reese, Ellen and Waller, Marguerite *The Wages of the Empire: Neoliberal Policies, Repression and Women's Poverty.* Boulder: Paradigm Publishers.

Marx, K. (1967) *Capital: A critical Analysis of Capitalist Production, V.1* New York: International Publishers.

Madrid, G. and Wright, C. (2007) 'Contesting Ethical Trade in Colombia's Cut-Flower Industry: A Case of Cultural and Economic Injustice'. *Cultural Sociology* 1(2): 255-275.

Madrid Berroterán, G. (2003) *Working with Flowers: An Analysis of Social, Cultural and Ethical Relations in Colombia and the UK.* Ph.D. Dissertation, University of Warwick.

Medrano, D. and Villar, R. (1983) *Problema de Salud y Trabajo en los Cultivos de Flores de la Sabana de Bogotá: La Vision de las Mujeres Trabajadoras en Torno a su Situación.* Bogotá: Mimeo, Thesis-Antropology, National University of Colombia.

Meier, V. (1999) 'Cut-flower Production in Colombia: A Major Development Success Story for Women?' *Environment & Planning,* 31(2): 273-290.

Molyneux, M. (1979) 'Beyond the Domestic Labour Debate'. *New Left Review* 116: 3-27.

Moody, K. (1997) *Workers in a Lean World: Unions in the International Economy.* New York: Verso Books.

Murray, J. (2001) *Transnational Labour Regulation: The ILO and EC Compared.* Boston: Kluwer Law International.

Novelli, M. and Ferus-Comelo, A. (2010). *Globalization, Knowledge and Labour: Education for Solidarity within Spaces of Resistance.* New York: Routledge.
Picchio, A. (1992). *Social Reproduction: The Political Economy of the Labour Market.* New York: Cambridge University Press.
Pyrch, T. (1996) 'The Participatory Action Research Challenge Re-Issued in Colombia'. *Convergence* 29(3): 5-16.
Salazar, M.C. (1990) *Niños y Jóvenes Trabajadores Buscando un Futuro Mejor* Bogotá: UNICEF and Universidad Nacional de Colombia.
Sanmiguel-Valderrama, O. (2007). 'The Feminization and Racialization of Labour in the Colombian Fresh-cut Flower Industry'. *Journal of Developing Societies* 23(1/2): 71-88.
Sanmiguel-Valderrama, O. (Forthcoming 2011) 'Community Mothers and Flower Workers in Colombia: Transnationalization of Social Reproduction and Production for the Global Market'. *Journal of the Motherhood Initiative* 2(2).
Sanmiguel-Valderrama, O. (2004). *Neoliberalism, International Trade and the Role of Law in Regulating Precarious Labour Relations in the Colombian Flower Industry.* Toronto: Ph.D Dissertation, Osgoode Hall Law School, York University.
Shalla, V. and Clement, W. (eds.) (2007) *Work in Tumultuous Times: Critical Perspectives.* Montreal; Ithaca: McGill-Queen's University Press.
Sierra, C.P. (ed.) (2003) *Floricultura de Exportación en América Latina: Hipótesis y Retos.* Bogotá: Corporación Cactus and Terre des hommes-Alemania.
Silva, A.E. (1982) 'De Mujer Campesina a Obrera Florista', in León, Magdalena (ed.) *La Realidad Colombiana: Debate sobre la Mujer en América Latina y el Caribe.* Bogotá: Asociación Colombiana para el Estudio de la Población.
Standing, G. (1989) 'Global Feminization Through Flexible Labour'. *World Development* 17(7): 1077-1095.
Standing, G. (1999) 'Global Feminization Through Flexible Labour: A Theme Revisited'. *World Development* 27(3): 583-602.
Talcott, M. (2004) 'Gendered Webs of Development and Resistance: Women, Children, and Flowers in Bogotá'. *Signs: Journal of Women in Culture & Society* 29(2): 465-489.
Thrupp, L.A. (1995) *Bittersweet Harvests For Global Supermarkets: Challenges in Latin America's Agricultural Export Boom.* Washington: World Resource Institute.

Union Nacional de Trabajadores de las Flores-Untraflores, *Boletin Florecer* (2001-2010) 1-23. Facatativá: Untraflores.

Universidad Nacional de Colombia, Centro de Studios Sociales–CES (1995) *La Floricultura en la Sabana de Bogotá: Proyecto Piloto en el Municipio de Madrid, Cundinamarca.* Bogotá: Mimeo.

Vosko, L. (2000) *Temporary Work: The Gendered Rise of a Precarious Employment Relationship.* Toronto: University of Toronto Press.

PART 3

Alternative Trade Associations and
Women's Resistance

CHAPTER 6

Free Trade, Alternative Trade and Women in Peru: A First Look

Jane Henrici
Institute for Women's Policy Research

ABSTRACT

Transnational policies affect alternative trade organizations that reinvest their profits in poorer communities. As transnational corporations expand, low-wage workers–particularly the women preferentially hired in this sector–initially find themselves with greater employment opportunities. These then decrease over time as traditional income sources and local businesses decline. Based on earlier ethnographic research in Lima, this article provides the framework for a new study to discern how trade regulations might affect projects that assist low-income women in Peru.

Keywords: free trade agreements, alternative trade, gender, nongovernmental organizations, Peru, handicrafts

Introduction

Free trade agreements among nations and regions are part of a global socioeconomic shift begun roughly 25 years ago that seems to drag women–in different regions and of varied identities–along behind it. Currently, scholarship seems focused on the impact of trade agreements at the national level rather than at the more localized level; while important interdisciplinary and activist research examines intersections between groups or communities and free trade agreements, more work is needed to understand the effects of agreements on women and women's organizations.

This article discusses the relationship between gender and trade with specific concern for the case of nongovernmental alternative trade organizations (ATOs) established to help women in Peru. Following from earlier research in both the United States and Peru on gender, work, development and poverty, I have begun an investigation of responses among ATO members and workers within Lima and the southern highlands to changes in trade regulations. My project involves qualitative ethnographic observations and interviews with those directly affected. In particular, I will learn from their descriptions and experiences the ways in which new policies and laws might affect projects that seek to help low-income women and families in Peru. This article provides the framework for that larger effort.

Trading Commentary

As noted, a number of activist researchers recently have begun to examine this topic. The International Gender and Trade Network (IGTN) is one group that critically examines the differential effects of free trade. The IGTN describes itself as a group of feminists based in the Global South who seek 'to provide technical information on gender and trade issues to women's groups, NGOs, social movements and governments'. IGTN economist Pamela Sparr (2001) observes the relative lack of analyses on gender, trade, and financing in comparison to studies of other aspects of the global economy. According to Sparr, the gap is due in part to the enormous difficulty identifying, with certainty, the causal relationships between trade and other phenomena. Basically, she argues, trade is not a single event or set of events. Contemporary free trade agreements are themselves the expression, rather than the source of, economic and ideological turns taking place within many regions and nations.

As others have noted, the emphasis within transnational processes has become one of fewer shared responsibilities and greater individual burdens. These processes might be relatively recent, yet they certainly seem to exacerbate long-standing gendered and racialized inequities. That is, gaps in salaries, health coverage and care, subsidies and other benefits, and in financing, continue to form along lines of gender, race and ethnicity as well as other constructs of identity and regardless of challenges and criticisms (Lewis, 2000).

Granted, such gaps and even attempts to fill them are not the same in all regions of the world, nor do they affect all individuals and their families to the same extent: contextual differences can occur even between neighborhoods in the same urban center so that someone who is of one ethnicity and socioeconomic class is helped while someone who identifies herself similarly is hurt. More commonly, however, those who are of the same socioeconomic class regardless of nation or region seem to have comparable opportunities and restrictions than those of differing classes, races, ethnicities, and genders within the same place (Giddens, 2000; Held et al., 1999).

Trade agreements alone do not cause feminized poverty or workforces. Nevertheless, general trends regarding the relationship between trade and gender are notable, such as the disproportionate hiring of women in export processing zones (EPZs) for large-scale manufacturing, the displacement of women's homemade or homegrown products by tariff-free imports, and the combination of these pull and push factors leading to rising numbers of women migrants and immigrants (Sassen, 1998).

With respect to a framework for an examination of gendered responses to free trade agreements, I suggest that we use Sonia Alvarez's (1996) concept of 'multilayered entanglements' to acknowledge the simultaneous participation of women of seemingly divergent categories of class, race, and ethnic identity. Further, as Sparr (2001) points out, there needs to be a focus on women with respect to their multiple responsibilities and roles within the household, NGO-ATO, and community. Trade agreements affect all of these, typically challenging how women may spend and view their time, health, and money, particularly if those women are of poorer and minority groups within a region or nation (Carlsen, 2005).

Following from Alvarez (1996) and Chandra Mohanty (2003) among others, I argue that we can think of the relations among the diverse women involved as social networks. Although social networks have the potential for positive mutual support, the efforts of all concerned and their social investment in the process are required, a feature that many social planners fail to acknowledge (Bourdieu, 1990).

Nongovernmental trade organizations, as will be discussed ahead, contain a complex configuration of identities and relations within their activities and memberships (Alvarez, 1998). Given this complexity, it is perhaps problematic to see ATO adaptations and resistances to free trade as anything more than a patch for what is a structural rupture. In other words, local and nonprofit struggles to manipulate the global trade system might be limited in their success, and contribute minimally to long-standing efforts by women and others to protect traditions, create institutions, and survive trade policy shifts.

Trade and Women's Work

Trade policies of any type have an influence on trade organizations, their projects, and their profits, regardless of the identities of those who work in these groups or of those served by them. Although generally representing a small part of a nation's domestic product, the manufacture and sale–particularly through export–of handmade goods is often a large part of household and community economies.

To assist with this form of economic development, local and international intermediaries and producers involved in the making and selling of handicrafts often are incorporated, at least in certain areas of activity, as nongovernmental organizations, or NGOs, and simultaneously as alternative trade organizations, or ATOs. Incorporation allows these groups to benefit from the protections offered to such agencies in the form of support systems, donations, and tax exemptions, and to put their profits into social obligations rather than into business owners' bank accounts (Henrici, 1999, 2002, 2003). These are pragmatic, if seemingly nontraditional arrangements.

In addition to de-romanticizing the nonprofit status of NGOs, we must deromanticize what many of us associate with the production of handicrafts. Most, although not all, of those who make crafts for sale in Peru are not originally artisans, either by inheritance or by a sense of identity. They come from widely diverse backgrounds and make items to sell because money is needed and their typical source of sustenance, whether herding, farming, fishing or working for others, simply is insufficient.

As visitors pass through towns traditionally known for Peruvian ceramics or carpentry, increasingly plastic goods and cement blocks now substitute for local products. Meanwhile, in villages and communities on mountain tops and in densely foliated lowlands, groups of men and women now twist wire by hand or paint tiny beads in order to make rapidly, and in large volume, items that can sell internationally and make at least a marginal profit, in order to substitute for the farming, herding and local barter that generations ago were sufficient.

Regardless of their broader occupational identity, in order to qualify for government exemptions and to be able to compete in local markets and international export, all those who produce handicrafts even part-time must claim themselves as 'artisans' and even register that identity for legal status. That status became associated in the second half of the 20th century with opportunities, both for the individual household to make a profit off the sales of handmade goods and for the Peruvian national government to make a profit through the tourism and relatively low-tariff exportation such goods involved. However, even with any added social and economic gains from their 'artisan' identity, many women producers find that a combination of activities is necessary for their sustenance and that of their families (Henrici, 2002).

The ATOs meanwhile, like the women they serve, also vary in identity and in their involvement with international trade. Some are cooperatives, others are more like charities, and a few are concerned with cultural preservation and the construction of authenticity. Still others help women and their communities by navigating between fostering change among community members and supporting their reinvestment in traditional lifestyles. Many of these ATOs have been in operation for several decades (Henrici, 2003).

In Peru as elsewhere, NGOs form part of the potential network among women of different identities and experiences and can encourage opportunities for all of them. At the same time, NGOs can become part of the neoliberal practice and reinforce existing inequalities particularly for indigenous women in both rural and urban Peru (Alvarez, 1998; Garcia, 2005).

Peruvian NGOs, and the ATOs they create in order to legally export goods, typically are managed by European or African Peruvians from the capital of Lima. In contrast, the majority of those they assist with training, marketing, and business management are lower-income women who have a mixture of ethnic identities including the indigenous, and are from a range of places throughout Peru. Further, all of these Peruvian groups must work with organizations of the Global North, with still other identities, as well as other objectives (Henrici, 2003).

The identities and characteristics of the handicrafts sold also vary, and simultaneously intersect with the differences among those who make and sell such goods. Consider, for example, among items for sale of ancient or modern design, the dolls that bear in their tiny wool construction, the name *cholita*, which is a derogatory and patronizing name for Quechua and Spanish-speaking women of mixed lineage and clothing style in Peru: These dolls are sewn by Quechua-speaking women, packaged by mestiza, European and African-Peruvian women, and ordered through international import sales, perhaps by women of whatever identity, in the Global North.

Handicraft trade is full of contradictions even where importers and funding agencies might be entirely familiar with, sympathetic toward, and accommodating of local customs and standards. This includes disagreement among producers, aid workers, collectors, and scholars about what should and can be sold. The fundamental contradiction is that, for some who are involved, an item that is supposedly pure, sacred, and of the highest price value is inherently not-for-sale so that which is for sale is tainted. 'Real' artists and artisans within this dominant global marketplace often are imagined as extraneous to commerce and without need of profit even as they become noteworthy once their work sells. Ethnicity, gender, labor, and age stereotypically retain dignity or glamour when uncorrupted by sales, but paradoxically are the very characteristics that seem to make items and individuals ready for market (Henrici, 1999). For the middle-person, in this case the NGO-ATO worker mediating between artisans and international agencies and buyers, retaining respect for un-romanticized concerns on the part of the crafts producers while maneuvering within expectations and stereotypes on the part of those with money can be difficult (Henrici, 2003).

So-called fair trade may be additionally problematic within these exchanges because of inconsistencies in payment and expenses in contrast to sales. Fair trade, like free trade, can reinforce false constructs of identity, occupation, and gender and end up failing to send the money earned by, and owed to, the producers of the goods. Opportunities can arise, and so can restrictions (Henrici, 2003).

Hoping for the former, a number of NGOs and ATOs continue to undertake the small-scale and relatively low-cost making and selling of Peruvian women's handicrafts in order to reinvest in profits in poorer communities and/or traditional art forms. At the same time, many international investors, evaluators, and planners also participate in this handicraft sector. They may be incorporated with nonprofit and nongovernmental status, but typically are based in more industrialized nations, while Peruvian NGOs and ATOs are often local in their origins and operations (Henrici, 2002, 2003).

Trade policies and agreements affect these organizations that work to support women in their various economic activities. Elsewhere, I have noted with respect to communication difficulties among NGO-ATO relations that often those who are involved, and those who observe, conflate power discrepancies and differences in identity in what Bourdieu (1990) called 'misrecognition'. Indigenous, African Peruvian, mestiza, and European Peruvian women, as well as those with whom they trade in other nations, have traditionally regarded differences among them as expressions of culture rather than of structural power or money (Henrici, 2003). Such a generous reading of their limited circumstances might help explain why Peruvian women of different class, ethnic and race groups tend to say they value their own participation in all spheres of trade, despite the many difficulties and disparities among them and between them and those with whom they conduct business in the Global North. At the same time that they continue to regard transnational exchanges as opportunities, low-income Peruvian women and the ATOs that work with them have begun to express, along with others in their nation, resistance to entirely Global North-centered free trade.

Peru and Trade Agreements

Peru, meanwhile, has been a signatory of regional free-trade agreements to an increasing level over the last 30 years. Existing agreements include the regional Latin American Integration Association (LAIA/ALADI) since 1980, and multilateral General Agreement on Tariffs and Trade (GATT) since 1987. In addition, Peru has been an established member of the Andean Community, a pact renewed in 1998, and of the World Trade Organization (WTO) since 1996. In recent years, Peru has agreed to a handful of other trade pacts as well.

With respect specifically to Peruvian agreements with the United States, the US government announced in May 2004 that Peru and Ecuador would join Colombia to initiate an Andean Free Trade Agreement (AFTA), later to include Bolivia, which would serve as a critical piece of the long-planned Free Trade Area of the Americas (FTAA). The FTAA has been drafted largely based on NAFTA and WTO negotiations. The FTAA would expand international free trade zones to include every nation in North, Central and South America and the Caribbean except Cuba. At this point, FTAA plans are derailed by protests and counter-negotiations, but Peru continues in AFTA discussions with the other nations of Andean South America and in other talks over possible new agreements with the European Union (Zibechi, 2005).

Meanwhile, as a gesture toward Peru and Ecuador and connected to their cooperation with AFTA, the US federal government and the Overseas Private Investment Corporation (OPIC) in 2004 approved a $54 million loan for microfinancing small businesses, specifically directed at women in those countries. Since Peru reportedly has been key to the formation of these US-initiated trade agreements, an expectation that Peru might fully agree to sign the pacts might have accompanied the loan provision (Ortiz, 2004).

Most trade agreements between Peru and other nations primarily regulate or eliminate tariffs on manufactured and agriculture goods. However, the amounts charged on small-scale products to leave or enter Peru, including the materials needed to make handmade items, and the regulations circumscribing small business shipping and exportation including the transport of handicrafts, are altered. This in turn would seem to have gendered and racialized repercussions: while large-scale enterprises of course are also affected, the small-scale operations of organizations selling low-income women's handmade products are even more vulnerable to shifts in the international trade costs of importing materials with which to make goods for export, and in the fees paid to export in the hope of receiving a profit through sales (Henrici, 2003).

In addition, the legal stipulations of many free trade agreements protect large, transnational corporations as opposed to organizations, regions, or nations, thus reducing further the relative power of small-scale businesses of any type. One of the reasons that feminists are joined by other groups in campaigning against many, if not all, free trade agreements is precisely that aspect of the treaties: the protected (and ensured) rights of corporations to accrue an unlimited profit versus the total lack of guarantee of any rights, human or other, to nations, communities and people (Duina, 2006).

Another gendered feature of all trade agreements made specifically with the US is its 'global gag rule', which is the requirement since 1984 that US aid or financing cannot go to any NGO 'involved in voluntary abortion activities, even if these activities are undertaken with non-US funds'. Marianne Møllmann, the 2004 Americas researcher for the Women's Rights Division at Human Rights Watch in New York, is a legal expert for the women's rights program of the Centro de la Mujer Peruana Flora Tristán in Lima. Møllmann published a paper with the Michigan State University Women and International Development series on what she asserts are the 'criminal consequences' of the global gag rule. According to Møllmann (2004), the regulation came to be known as the 'gag rule' since it labels providing information about certain contraceptives, much less abortions, as abortion activity. Although US President Clinton first repealed the rule, then modified it after the Congress reinstated it, President Bush reinstated it completely.

Abortions are in fact illegal in Peru, so implementing the rule within trade agreements with the US would be redundant. However, while it is not an overt requirement in US-Peru relations, Peruvian government efforts to maintain those relations apparently result in what Møllmann calls 'self-gagging': the zealous over-interpretation of the intent of the rule by local law enforcement and NGOs so that Peruvian women, notably those who are poorer and of color, receive little to no family planning or sexual health guidance (Bant and Motta, 2001; Møllmann, 2004). Thus, trade agreements have gendered repercussions in aspects of daily life beyond tariffs and duty charges on materials and products shipped.

In response to the overall lack of awareness about the relationship between gender and trade in international policy as well as in the popular media, the Women's Edge Coalition (WEC) emphasizes the need for targeted evaluations of trade negotiations. According to the WEC website, an assessment that involves examining both the agreements under discussion and the reactions of the women affected would be the best response to the current imbalance within the process and result:

> The Women's Edge Coalition believes that trade can work for women but the proper procedures need to be put into place. Failure to examine how trade affects the poorest people can cause trade agreements to fail. An in-depth survey, the TIR would examine trade agreements to ensure that women from developing countries–as well as women throughout the United States–would have their voices heard in the negotiating process. (Women's Edge Coalition, 2005)

Activist and researcher Ann E. Kingsolver (2001:209) concluded her study of grassroots-level concern over free trade policy, entitled *NAFTA Stories*, with a suggestion 'to construct multilocal understandings of what is glossed as "globalization" by doing collaborative, activist, social documentation'. While such documentation regarding trade and finance policy is insufficient by itself, the act of acquiring and sharing information through the multilocal participation of many individuals, particularly women of a range of identities, is a step these groups could now undertake.

Conclusion

While it is true that trade brings opportunities for many women to have access to formal training and education as well as nondomestic employment, the opportunities nevertheless often are differentiated between women and men as well as among women, and remain circumscribed by accepted prejudice and practice (Espino, 2003).

Our ultimate goal should be to create a more progressive and enlightened trade policy that assists rather than impedes women, their families and communities. Perhaps the first step to create such policy is to expand the networks that others have begun: first, add to critical feminist scholarship (Molyneux, 2003; Montoya et al., 2002); next, lend judicial support to feminist groups in Peru (Jacquette, 1994; Moser, 2004; Radcliffe and Westwood, 1993; Vargas, 2002); then, selectively assist those ATOs as they in turn seek to help poorer Peruvian women of diverse local identities and requirements. The goal of such transnational collaboration is to rise to the level of engaged evaluation prescribed by Women's Edge and the growing number of feminists in Europe and North America who have mobilized since the creation of the European Union and NAFTA to challenge the current preferential and nonregulated treatment of private corporations within free-trade agreement negotiations and implementations (Duina, 2006:157).

As a part of this engaged evaluation it is important to understand the strategies of small groups of women working on their own behalf, within their households and communities around the world in general and in Peru in particular, as they respond however incompletely, to the larger trends, policies and practices (Barrig, 1996). We need to learn about the realized experiences of ATOs and the women they seek to help in order to produce strong and rigorous support for demands to change existing neoliberal trade agreement practice and policy.

My forthcoming research is intended to add to our knowledge about free-trade agreements and their gendered effects. Analysis of the positive and negative impacts of free-trade agreements on the ATOs from the perspective of the women involved in them, will help to improve future agreements and the implementation of existing pacts.

ACKNOWLEDGEMENTS

Previous versions of this article were presented at the Women and Globalization Conference in August 2005 convened at the Center for Global Justice of San Miguel de Allende, Mexico, and at the 104th Annual Meeting of the American Anthropological Association (AAA) in December 2005 on the organized panel 'Fair Trade/Free Trade: Alternatives and Realities in Cross-Cultural Perspective'. I would like to thank the organizers of the Women and Globalization Conference, the organizer of the AAA panel Sarah Lyon, and the editors of this book, Ligaya Lindio-McGovern and Erica G. Polakoff, as well as the Center for Research on Women and the Department of Anthropology at the University of Memphis for the opportunities to present this research and the helpful comments on revising it. In addition, I would like to thank the Fulbright Scholar Program and the Fulbright Commission for Educational Exchange between the United States and Peru for the funding for the forthcoming development of this investigation. However, none of these individuals or institutions is responsible for the observations and arguments expressed here.

REFERENCES

Alvarez, S.E. (1996) 'Concluding Reflections: "Redrawing" the Parameters of Gender Struggle', in J. Friedmann, R.Abers, and L.Autler (eds.) *Emergences: Women's Struggles for Livelihood in Latin America*, pp. 137-51. Los Angeles: UCLA Latin American Center Publications.

Alvarez, S.E. (1998) 'Latin American Feminisms "Go Global": Trends of the 1990s and Challenges for the New Millennium', in S. Alvarez, E. Dagnino, and A. Escobar (eds.) *Culture of Politics/Politics of Culture: Re-visioning Latin American Social Movements*, pp. 293-324. Boulder: Westview Press.

Bant, A. and Motta, A. (2001) *Género y Salud Reproductiva: Escuchando a las Mujeres de San Martin y Ucayali*. Lima: Movimiento Manuela Ramos.

Barrig, M. (1996) 'Women, Collective Kitchens, and the Crisis of the State in Peru', in J. Friedmann, R.Abers, and L. Autler (eds.) *Emergences:Women's Struggles for Livelihood in Latin America*, pp. 59-77. Los Angeles: UCLA Latin American Center Publications.

Bourdieu, P. (1990). *The Logic of Practice*, translator R. Nice. Stanford: Stanford University Press.

Carlsen, L. (2005) 'Women's Rights Eroding in Latin America'. *Crossborder Updater*, 3(3). Accessed 5 March 2005 http://www.americaspolicy.org.

Duina, F. (2006) *The Social Construction of Free Trade: The European Union, NAFTA, and MERCOSUR*. Princeton: Princeton University Press.

Espino, A. (2003) 'Trade and Female Employment in Some Latin American Countries: "Approaches to the Changes in Gender Relations",' International Gender and Trade Network Latin American Chapter and Centro Interdisciplinario de Estudios sobre el Desarrollo–Uruguay. Accessed 4 April 2005 from http://igtn.org.

Garcia, M.E. (2005) *Making Indigenous Citizens: Identity, Development, and Multicultural Activism in Peru*. Stanford: Stanford University Press.

Giddens, A. (2000) *Runaway World: How Globalization is Reshaping our Lives*. London and New York: Routledge.

Held, D., McGrew, A., Goldblatt, D. and Perraton, J. (1999) *Global Transformations: Politics, Economics, Culture*. Cambridge: Polity.

Henrici, J. (1999) 'Trading Culture: Tourism and Tourist Art in Pisac, Peru', in P. Boniface and M. Robinson (eds.) *Tourism and Cul-*

tural Conflicts, pp. 161-79. London: CABI Publishing.

Henrici, J. (2002) '"Calling to the Money": Gender and Tourism in Peru', in M. Swain and J. Momsen (eds.) *Gender/Tourism/Fun*, pp. 118-33. Elmsford: Cognizant Communication Corporation.

Henrici, J. (2003) 'Non-Governmental Organizations,"Fair Trade", and Craft Producers: Exchanges South and North'. *Visual Anthropology* 16(2/3): 289-313.

Jacquette, J. (ed.) (1994) *The Women's Movement in Latin America: Participation and Democracy*. Boulder: Westview Press. Kingsolver, A.E.(2001) *NAFTA Stories: Fears and Hopes in Mexico and the United States*. Boulder: Lynne Rienner Publishers.

Lewis, G. (2000) *Race, Gender, Social Welfare*. Cambridge: Polity.

Mahler, S.J. and Pessar, P.R. (2001) 'Gendered Geographies of Power:Analyzing Gender Across Transnational Spaces'. *Identities* 7: 411-59.

Møllmann, M. (2004) 'Who Can Be Held Responsible for the Consequences of Aid and Loan Conditionalities? The Global Gag Rule in Peru and its Criminal Consequences', Michigan State University Women and International Development Working Paper #279. Accessed 22 August 2005 from www. isp.msu.edu.

Molyneux, M. (2003) *Doing the Rights Thing: Rights-Based Development and Latin American NGOs*. London: ITDG Publishing.

Mohanty, C.T. (2003) *Feminism Without Borders: Decolonizing Theory, Practicing Solidarity*. Durham: Duke University Press.

Montoya, R., Frazier, L.J. and Hurtig, J. (eds.) (2002) *Gender's Place: Feminist Anthropologies of Latin America*. New York: Palgrave Macmillan.

Moser, A. (2004) 'Happy Heterogeneity? Feminism, Development, and the Grassroots Women's Movement in Peru'. *Feminist Studies* 30(1): 211-37.

Ortiz, M. (2004) 'Negociarán medidas de protección al agro en la sexta ronda del TLC', *La República*, 29 October 2004.

Radcliffe, S. and Westwood, S. (1993) *Viva: Women and Popular Protest in Latin America*. International Studies of Women and Place. London: Routledge Press.

Sassen, S. (1998) 'Notes on the Incorporation of Third World Women into Wage Labor Through Immigration and Offshore Production', in *Globalization and its Discontents: Essays on the New Mobility of People and Money*, pp. 111-31. New York: The New Press.

Sparr, P. (2001) 'Making the Connections between Debt, Trade, and Gender', *Economic Justice News Online* 4(3).

Vargas, V. (2002) 'Struggle by Latin American Feminisms for Rights and Autonomy', in N. Craske and M. Molyneux (eds.) *Gender and the Politics of Rights and Democracy in Latin America.* New York: Palgrave Macmillan.

Women's Edge Coalition (2005).

Zibechi, R. (2005) 'Regional Integration after the Collapse of the FTAA', IRC Ameritas. Accessed 21 November 2005 from www.americaspolicy.org.

CHAPTER 7

Women's Rights and Collective Resistance: The Success Story of Marketplace India

Margaret A. McLaren
Rollins College, Florida

ABSTRACT

The classical liberal theories of rights overemphasize individual autonomy. Feminists from a variety of approaches criticize this individualistic model. Other feminists argue that rights discourse is essential to help end discrimination against women. However, these proponents of international women's rights too often focus on legal and political rights at the expense of economic rights. In a global context it is important to recognize the interconnections between different kinds of rights. A case study of the cooperative organization Marketplace/SHARE illustrates the importance of economic empowerment to the overall goal of advancing the cause of women's rights and equality.

Keywords: human rights, women's rights, cooperatives, globalization

Introduction

In the context of globalization, discussions of rights take on a new urgency. Rights are used as a standard for sanctioning certain countries through economic boycott, and as a criterion for entrance into the European Union. Thus, understanding rights discourse has not only theoretical applications, but also significant political and practical value. This chapter will address the issue of rights in feminist theory with respect to women in the Global South. Feminists seem to take two contradictory views of rights. On the one hand, some feminists criticize the notion of rights as a highly individualistic, abstract Western idea. They argue that rights are a culture-bound construct that does not do justice to more relational understandings of the self, or to communal cultures. Yet other feminists argue that rights are an important tool for securing women's protection from violence, and promoting women's equality. I argue that both of these views inadvertently neglect economic issues, and so long as this is the case, discussions of rights have only limited benefit for poor women in developing countries. I suggest that feminists concerned with global women's issues prioritize economic and social rights, in addition to political and legal rights. I demonstrate that cooperatives provide an important alternative for women in the context of globalization. Cooperatives foster a sense of solidarity and collective empowerment; the structure of shared ownership and resources challenges the competitive individualism of capitalism.

As a feminist philosopher, I adopt two significant features of feminist methodology: First, praxis–the interconnectedness of theory and practice, and second voice/experience. Theory and practice exist in dialectical relationship for feminist praxis, that is, theory informs practice and vice versa. This inquiry resulted from the disconnection between some of the debates within feminist theory and my experiences traveling in and researching the Global South. Like some other feminist theorists, I find it problematic to position third world women simply as passive victims of colonialism, sexism, racism and poverty (Mohanty, 1991a,1991b; Narayan, 1997). Western feminists need to exercise caution about simply imposing a political agenda of rights and equality without attention to the social and historical context. Women's struggles for freedom from oppression invariably intersect with national and cultural struggles, and feminist movements even within nation-states are diverse. Nonetheless, feminist analyses must address structural injustices and oppression; my focus here is on addressing the intersection of gender and class and the grassroots responses aimed at empowering poor women in India.

The second feature of feminist methodology I employ here is letting women speak for themselves, in other words, foregrounding the voices of women about their own experiences, in this case the women who are members of the cooperatives in Marketplace India. Marketplace, a group of 13 cooperatives, exemplifies the power and promise of the cooperative model. The organization seeks to empower women through meaningful employment and social and educational programs. I conducted videotaped interviews with individuals and entire cooperatives. My aim in the interviews was to listen to the women discuss their perspectives on their life situations and possibilities, and about their connection to Marketplace. Since the point of the interviews was to allow the Marketplace women to articulate their own experiences, my methodology was qualitative and my research questions were open-ended. The stories of the women of Marketplace exemplify the courage and commitment of women standing together to make a change not only in their personal lives, but also in their communities. Their stories are not primarily about fighting for rights or gender equality, but simply about surviving, and leading a dignified and sustainable life. Yet in the end, participating in the cooperative provides not only material resources, but also the empowerment to recognize themselves as agents of political and social change.

Feminist Critiques of Rights

Feminist critiques of rights come from several different directions. Here I shall briefly discuss three significant strands: care ethicists, communitarians, and post-colonial feminists. Beginning in the early 1980s, after the publication of Carol Gilligan's influential book, *In A Different Voice*, a spate of literature appeared that developed some of the central ideas of her study of moral development (Gilligan, 1982). Gilligan claims that the privileging of rights in moral discourse reveals a male bias; her research demonstrates that when women's voices are taken into account, the focus of moral reasoning shifts to concerns of care, responsibility, and not hurting others. She contrasts her view that moral considerations arise out of care and responsibility, with the standard view that moral issues fall into the domain of rights and justice. Several other feminists, including Seyla Benhabib, Diana Meyers, Virginia Held, and Marilyn Friedman, have developed and applied Gilligan's insights, arguing that the idea of rights found in the classical liberal political theory of John Locke and John Stuart Mill articulated unrealistic views of autonomy and rights (Benhabib, 1987; Friedman, 1987; Held, 1987; Meyers, 1987). The emphasis on rights and autonomy is characteristic of Enlightenment moral and political theories. The *loci classici* of liberal political theory representing this view are John Locke's *The Second Treatise of Civil Government* in his *Two Treatises of Government*, and John Stuart Mill's *On Liberty* (Locke, 1960; Mill, 1985). The champion of autonomy in ethical theory is Immanuel Kant (Kant, 1994). In fact, Lawrence Kohlberg, the contemporary psychologist whom Gilligan critiques, relies on a Kantian framework for his study of moral development.

Feminists criticize the liberal conception of rights and autonomy as individualistic, and abstracted from social context. One way that this conception is abstracted from social context is that it does not account for those who are dependent or vulnerable (Tronto, 1993, Kittay 1999; Held, 1987). And it does not recognize the role of the family in providing the context for the development and growth of children to adulthood. More specifically, it ignores women's role in nurturing and socializing children. The main issue for care ethicists, then, is the male bias of rights theory, both historically and in practice. This bias manifests itself by ignoring social context, by emphasizing individualism, and by privileging an abstract and rationalistic model for social and political interaction.

Communitarian feminist critiques echo some of these concerns, but focus more on the issues of identity and community and their significance in our lives (Friedman, 1993; McLaren 1996; Mouffe, 1990). The primary claim is that liberal political theory may neglect important aspects of one's identity, such as membership in a cultural group. The abstract individualism of liberalism is at odds with the possibility that one may so strongly identify with a group that one's group identity supercedes one's individual identity. Communitarian feminists claim that shared traditions, history and values play a central role in our political and moral lives. Thus, this criticism of liberalism again questions its assumed abstract individualism, but looks specifically at the role of community and tradition in both constituting the identity of the self and allowing for a notion of a communal or collective self. I shall argue later that the neglect of this idea of collectivity is a fundamental flaw in the liberal approach to rights.

Postcolonial feminism comprises the third strand of feminist critiques of rights. Postcolonial feminist criticisms center around the idea that rights are a fundamentally Western liberal notion and thus the application of rights to other contexts belies a Eurocentric, and biased view (An-Na'im, 1999; Bulbeck, 1998; Mohanty, 1991a, 1991b; Spivak, 2003). One of the features of rights discourse is its claim to universality; and it is precisely this claim that is challenged by postcolonial feminists. By not acknowledging the origin of rights within a particular social and historical context, and thus its specificity as a discourse, theorists who apply rights cross-culturally without attention to context, run the risk of Western cultural imperialism. Interestingly, this criticism of rights itself runs the risk of cultural imperialism by attributing the idea of rights to the European West without regard for indigenous struggles for rights in other contexts. The primary problem here is that the assumption that rights are universal masks the specific origins of rights and suggests that they can be applied without careful attention to social and historical context. Simply applying rights without addressing these concerns can actually serve to undermine feminist and other causes that rely on a different paradigm for political action and social change. However, many feminists claim that rights remain extremely useful in the international context.

Feminist Defenses of Rights

Since 1975 at the first United Nations Conference on Women[1] in Mexico City, women from all over the world have gathered together to discuss how to improve the quality of women's lives in their respective countries, and globally. One of the primary strategies for improving women's lives has been via improving women's status legally and politically (Human Rights Watch, 1995). This strategy can be realized through holding individual countries accountable to international standards, and can be monitored through changes in the law, and women's right to political representation and access to public life. At the international level, women's rights agendas that focus on civil and political rights, such as equal opportunity in education, employment, housing, credit, and health care and protection from rape and domestic violence, have sometimes been viewed as a special interest agenda and hence have been marginalized in favor of mainstream human rights issues (Peters and Wolper, 1995). While the traditional conception of human rights can certainly also serve to protect women from state sanctioned violence and abuse, it does not generally address the private sphere where most violations of women's rights take place:

> Traditional human rights standards categorize violations in ways that exclude women, eliding critical issues. While men may care about reproductive freedom, their lives are not actually threatened by its absence; for women in areas of high maternal mortality, full reproductive freedom may mean the difference between life and death. Likewise, while asylum law protects those with a 'well-founded fear of being persecuted for reasons of race, religion, nationality, membership in a particular social group or political opinion', it rarely protects those persecuted for reasons of gender....And while men may be the victims of private violence, such violence is not part of a pattern of gender-based abuse. (Peters and Wolper, 1995)

Feminists such as Wolper, Peters and Bunch are less interested in critiquing rights than extending them to include women, and broadening them to encompass the private sphere as well as the public sphere (Bunch, 1995). For many years, well-established international human rights organizations, such as Amnesty International and Human Rights Watch have had some success in documenting and bringing to international attention human rights abuses. Often (but not often enough), this publicity, media attention and pressure from the international community, including governmental sanctions against offending countries, have resulted in changes. With evidence of this success in mind, it is no wonder many feminists advocate a strategy that includes women and gender issues in the scope of human rights rather than criticize rights as a framework for change (Friedman, 1995; Saurez Toro, 1995; Singh, 1994; Stamatopoulou, 1995). For example, Kirti Singh argues for legal reform, but claims that the unwillingness of the state and government to abide by India's Constitution inhibits legal reforms that would promote women's equality (Singh, 1994). Working for legal and political reform within countries remains an important aspect of the project of securing women's equality. Internationally, too, women's rights continue to hold an important place in the general struggle for human rights–since 1975, there have been four United Nations Conferences on Women, preceded by a Non-Governmental Organizations Forum on Women (1975, Mexico City; 1980, Copenhagen; 1985 Nairobi; 1995, Beijing). In 1990, the Human Rights Watch established its Women's Rights Project, 12 years after the group was founded in Helsinki. The inclusion of gender issues and women's issues in international politics and policies represents an important achievement of various women's struggles and the international impact of feminism. Yet the emphasis on rights–when the focus is on legal and political reform–often results in neglect of economic issues. Contemporary feminists must acknowledge that the economic status of women is bound not only with their quality of life, but also with their ability to exercise political and legal rights.

Feminism and Economic Issues

The work of feminists fighting for women's rights to be free from violence and gender discrimination of all kinds remains central to the project of realizing equality for all women. But political and legal equality are intimately connected to economic equality. Thus, feminists need to also argue for increased economic opportunities for women. Of the 1.3 billion people in the world who are recognized as the 'absolute poor' (living on less than $1.25 a day), over 900 million are women. Interlocking problems of illiteracy, inequitable wages, and poor health, bolstered by patriarchal systems and social customs make it difficult for women to break free from a life of poverty. The feminization of poverty, where women rank among the poorest members of society, continues to increase in spite of the fact that currently more women perform wage labor. Globalization exacerbates the feminization of poverty as women are hired for low paying and undesirable jobs. Recent research in development links women's status to the improved quality of life not only for individual women, but for their families and communities as well. According to a Population and Development report from the United Nations, 'promoting the status, education, and health of women is an essential human rights goal, and also holds the key to social development in all societies, improving lives and strengthening families and communities' (PCI, 2004).

In the World Economic Forum's 2009 Report on the global gender gap, India ranked 114 out of 134 countries. According to statistics gathered by UNICEF through 2008, 42 percent of the population of India fell below the international poverty line of living on less than $1.25 per day. As a result of this widespread poverty, many people lack access to basic necessities; 48 percent of children under five are underweight and undernourished, 72 percent of Indians do not have access to proper sanitation, and 11 percent lack access to safe water. The immediacy of meeting basic needs often eclipses the importance of education; in India an estimated 34 percent of adults are illiterate, (UNICEF-India-Statistics, 2010). Promoting the status of women and girls is an uphill struggle no matter where one lives, but when resources are scarce, the devaluation of women and girls can result in real harm. One clear example of this is the 'missing women' phenomenon where in some countries boys are desired so much more than girls that sex-selective abortions are common. Poverty and lack of resources obviously affect men and boys as well as women and girls, but societal and cultural gender bias means that poverty disproportionately affects girls and women. Moreover, violence against women in India is on the rise; between 1982 and 1992 crimes against women increased by 104 percent (Singh, 1994).

> The persistence in India of cultural practices that discriminate against girls and women means not only the abuse of but finally, the deaths of countless women...one study showed that 7,997 of 8,000 fetuses aborted were female...If a girl is lucky enough to be born, she experiences discrimination in her infancy. Girl children are fed less and for shorter periods and are not given foods like butter or milk, which are reserved for boys....Access to education, too, is affected by gender discrimination. Only about 50% of girls are enrolled in primary school, compared to 80% of boys. (Jaising, 1995)

While Jaising attributes gender discrimination to 'cultural practices', I argue elsewhere that many discriminatory cultural practices cannot be separated from economic factors (McLaren, 2008a, 2008b). For example, in a place in which there was plenty of milk and butter to go around, (such as the United States) girls would not suffer disproportionately from malnutrition, although gender discrimination might manifest in other ways, such as unequal pay. Singling out cultural factors as the basis for gender discrimination runs the risk of what Uma Narayan calls the 'death by culture' argument; the attribution of deadly gender violence such as sati to cultural practices alone. Narayan argues that this over-simplifies culture, viewing it as static, and divorcing it from history and social context (Narayan, 1999). This type of 'cultural reductionism' obscures other important underlying causes of gender discrimination. For instance, all the examples of culture-based gender discrimination listed above–sex-selective abortion, lack of adequate nutrition for girls, and lack of access to education can be connected to economic factors. In India, boys are more highly valued because they ensure economic security in old age; sons remain part of the family while daughters become part of their husbands' family. Sex-selective abortion has not stopped in spite of the fact that is it illegal, and it is not likely to stop unless girls stop being an economic liability; this would involve changes in economics, and family structures, as well as cultural practices and attitudes.

The issues of legal reform and economic reform cannot be easily separated; Singh mentions that positive changes in dowry laws without corresponding changes in property and inheritance laws do little to improve women's condition: 'All this [these legal changes] makes her financially dependent on her husband and makes it extremely difficult for her to opt out of a violent home' (Singh, 1994). Providing women with opportunities to earn a living wage and contribute to the support of their families can serve to increase their status within the family and allow them to exercise more control over the resources of the family, as well as opt out of a bad family situation. The majority of the women that I interviewed were using part of their earnings to send their daughters to school past the eighth grade, which was the mothers' average level of education. In contrast, the average level of education for boys in this group (poor, and originally rural, but now living in and around Mumbai) was grade 10-12. Supporting girls' education has far-reaching consequences, as higher levels of education for girls and women results in a higher income and correlates with a higher quality of life for their families (PCI, 2004). Marketplace India member, Kavita, affirms, *'It is important for women to get educated, because men will still be seen as superior. Because I was less educated I could never voice my opinions'.*

Women's Cooperatives: Collective Solutions for Economic Empowerment

Cooperatives are owned and controlled by the workers:

> A cooperative is an autonomous association of persons united voluntarily to meet their common economic, social and cultural needs and aspirations through jointly owned and democratically controlled enterprise...cooperative values include self-help, self-responsibility, democracy, equality, equity and solidarity. Cooperatives also believe in social responsibility and include as one of their principles the concern for the community in which they operate. The cooperative movement is significant both in terms of membership and impact. Even by 1994 the United Nations reported that the livelihoods of nearly 3 billion people or half the world's population, were made secure by cooperative enterprises. Nearly 800 million individuals are members of cooperatives. They provide an estimated 100 million jobs. (COPAC, 1999)

Because of their democratic structure, cooperatives provide more than just a job for their members; they also bolster self-confidence and foster solidarity. The three main types of cooperatives are producer cooperatives, service cooperatives, and consumer cooperatives. The positive benefits of collective economic empowerment for women through lending circles and cooperatives are well documented.

A well-known example of the positive impact of providing initial financial support for groups of women is the Grameen Bank started in 1976 in Bangladesh by Nobel Peace prize winner, Muhammad Yunus. The Grameen Bank provides loans to groups of women so that they may start a small business. Lending to groups, rather than to individuals has a proven higher return rate because the members of the group feel responsible to one another in addition to their responsibility to the lender. Additionally, this reinforces the community and kinship ties that already exist among the women. Investing in groups, rather than individuals also makes the group members invested in one another; each person's success depends on everyone else's. The Grameen Bank's tremendous growth is a testament to its success. Currently, it has over 7 million members, ninety-seven percent of whom are women.[2]

A lesser known, but equally important organization is the Self-Employed Women's Association (SEWA) begun in 1972 by Ela Bhatt. SEWA's mission is to organize women workers in the informal sector so that they can have full employment and self-reliance, meaning that worker's basic needs for food, shelter, and health care are met. According to SEWA's 2009 annual report it has over 12 million members in India. Since 2004 it is the largest union in India and the largest women's union in the world. SEWA helps women workers to form cooperatives and unions, recognizing that the most effective gains for workers are made collectively. The Self-Employed Women's Association includes a range of services and benefits for its members, including a cooperative bank, health care and disaster insurance, childcare, literacy and computer training, and video-making classes. SEWA serves as a model for other organizations, in fact, a sister organization, SEWU (Self Employed Women's Union) in South Africa is modeled after it.

Marketplace India is a smaller and newer (30 years old) organization that, like SEWA, promotes cooperatives, and whose membership is almost exclusively women. I first learned about Marketplace India when discussing my research interests in what seemed to me to be a false dichotomy between equal rights for women and cultural traditions. As discussed earlier, some feminist positions advocate a strong defense of universal human rights at the expense of cultural tradition. My experiences at international women's conferences and during my travels provided evidence that some traditions, specifically craft and textile traditions, could be a source for women's empowerment through economic opportunities. Marketplace India exemplifies a successful model of drawing upon traditional textile skills, such as block printing, batik, and embroidery to empower women through dignified and sustainable employment and ongoing educational and enrichment opportunities. The motto printed on every clothing label, 'Dignity, not charity' sums up the mission of Marketplace. The organization promotes principles of equality and power sharing among the women, and simultaneously equips them to challenge their devaluation in society. As a cooperative structure it exemplifies the principles of self-help, self-responsibility, democracy, equality, equity, and solidarity. In addition to SEWA, Marketplace India, and the Grameen Bank there are a number of important organizations whose goal is to promote women's empowerment and to foster economic sustainability. Here I focus on Marketplace India for the following reason: it is a women's cooperative that uses tradition, i.e., traditional clothing and textile techniques, to economically empower women, thus providing a counterexample to the claim that tradition and rights are necessarily contradictory for women.

I discuss the organization at some length because I think that its strategies of economic and social empowerment could provide a model for feminists concerned with global issues. Simply advocating for legal and political rights is not enough when people are dying from malnutrition and poor health care. Furthermore, I think that the cooperative model incorporates not only feminist values, but also may provide an alternative to the unmitigated forces of global capitalism.

Marketplace/SHARE: A Cooperative Organization

Marketplace/SHARE is an umbrella organization for a group of 13 cooperatives providing job training, educational programs, and a centralized structure for marketing goods. I conducted interviews with the women of Marketplace in Mumbai, India, in February and March of 2004. In a two-week period, I conducted 11 individual interviews and three group interviews (with approximately 20 people in each group). Each individual interview lasted an hour and the group interviews lasted between one and two hours. The interviews were arranged by Marketplace, and I also spent a good deal of time talking with the staff and learning about the organization. Most of the staff spoke fluent English; the staff included two social workers, Suchira and Devi, who accompanied me during the interviews and translated for me. The group interviews took place in the workspaces of the cooperatives–tiny spaces filled with sewing machines. Individual interviews took place in the office space of Marketplace. In both the individual interviews and the group interviews participants were remarkably open, not only about their relationship to Marketplace, but also about the circumstances of their lives.

Marketplace/SHARE, a non-profit organization was founded in Mumbai, India, in 1980 by two sisters, Pushpika Freitas and Lalita Monteiro. Originally, they worked with low-income women to make handmade patchwork quilts. They chose to make quilts because the women knew how to sew by hand, but not by machine. Additionally, they could neither afford sewing machines, nor did they have the space in their homes for one. It was also important that they be able to work at home because they all had small children and could not afford child care. During this first year, only three women were involved in the group, in addition to the founders. Producing the quilts was labor intensive, and the sales at venues in Mumbai were disappointing. So, in 1986, Freitas founded Marketplace: Handwork of India to market the artisans' products in the United States.[3]

Since its founding, the organization has grown to include 13 cooperatives that employ over 500 members. They have also expanded their product line to include clothing and household items, and continue to broaden their markets. Five of the 13 cooperatives produce hand-printed fabric, while the other eight cooperatives sew and hand embroider the products. Four of the five fabric-producing cooperatives are located at quite a distance from Mumbai, between 12 to 24 hours away by train. The eight cooperatives that do the sewing and embroidery are all located either in Mumbai or within a two-hour train ride. Every two weeks, representatives from the sewing cooperatives meet to share information and ideas and to discuss any problems with the production work. This collaboration enables the groups to share their experience and wisdom and to collectively problem-solve. This spirit of collaboration runs through every aspect of Marketplace/SHARE. The organization combines gainful employment for marginalized women with social programs that educate and empower them. Marketplace/SHARE provides the structure and resources for each group to participate in workshops about health, parenting, social issues, global issues, and promoting social change. Sunanda states, *'After para-social worker training, I feel able to help others, to respect other opinions'*.

While the organization provides some access to outside programs, most are developed, modified, and managed by the women themselves. According to Sharda, *'The best part of my training is the education and information I am getting: even if I'm not the smartest person in the room, just the feeling of sitting in that chair and learning makes me feel equal and worthy'*.

This involvement at every level serves to empower the women at Marketplace/SHARE. The organization does not seek to control the production and programs of the various cooperatives; instead they facilitate the interaction among the various groups and coordinate the marketing of their products. Because each piece of clothing or household item utilizes hand-printed fabric and incorporates embroidery work, the items are considered wearable or usable art and the producers of items are called artisans. The artisans are involved in decision-making at every level; they help to design the products, and they are trained to check the quality of production at their respective units, as well as do quality control before the products are shipped overseas. The artisans also contribute photographs and stories to the catalog. This involvement in the overall production process allows artisans to understand the entire production process, fosters a sense of empowerment, and leads to a sense of shared responsibility for the welfare of the whole organization.

The products produced by the artisans of Marketplace/ SHARE are developed with attention to the needs and skills of the artisans. Some of the artisans choose to work at home, while tending to children, cooking and dealing with other household responsibilities so each article made includes some handwork, such as embroidery, crochet, or patchwork that can be done at home. Even the artisans involved in machine-sewing the items enjoy somewhat flexible work schedules depending on their personal situation. Some women bring their children to work with them, or leave work to make the big midday meal. Sunanda's son had unexplained seizures and she appreciates being able to bring him to work, *'At first I was scared to leave my sick child at home, but then I was able to bring him to work and he stayed at the crèche'*. The artisans' needs are taken into account in other important ways as well. Although every item includes hand-stitching, care is taken not to choose small designs that can cause eyestrain, or that the older women cannot do because of arthritis. Members of the coops appreciate the fair working conditions and living wage that working with Marketplace/SHARE provides them. But their appreciation for their work goes far beyond that–virtually everyone I interviewed thought of their coop as a supportive community, almost like an extended family. Kavita says, *'The coop is like a family. The first thing that came with the job is self-confidence which I didn't have before because I never left the house, and did not take public transportation'*.

Significantly, many Marketplace India artisans discuss dramatic changes in their levels of self-confidence and in their ability to deal with problems in their personal lives and in the communities to which they belong. Sunanda reports, *'I have been empowered in all the senses, for example, I used to give all my wages to my husband and he would spend it on drink. But now I only give him the money if he's sober'*.

This new-found self-confidence is a result of the combination of the skills and abilities that they have achieved in relation to their work, and the information and skills they have developed as a result of the social programs in which they are involved. Members of the coops not only make fabric, sew garments and do hand sewing, they also run every aspect of the coop, from keeping accounts, to traveling, to picking up supplies. Many women had never traveled alone before, even on a local train or bus. Most of them had never been responsible for large sums of money. Some women knew only their local language and not Hindi, which is widely spoken, and at least one woman had never used a telephone before. Women who were members of all female cooperatives said that one of the benefits of being a member of an all women's group was that tasks were not assigned by gender. Sharda observes, *'If we were a mixed gender group then men would have taken up all the responsibility, but because there are no men the women take on all the jobs even the taxing [physically demanding] ones'*.

The expectation was that women were capable of participating in every aspect of running a cooperative, and each new experience added to the women's sense of themselves as capable in ways that they had not previously realized. The realization that they are capable not only of earning a living, but also of running a business contributed to the women's self-confidence. Kavita exclaims, *'Everything I did increased my confidence, including buying buttons. A woman can do everything. I have proved that there is nothing that women can't do'*. This increased self-confidence, combined with their newfound earning power, allows them to change some of the conditions of their lives.

One clear example of this capacity for social change is the social action program.[4] The social action program involves each individual coop choosing an issue that is important to them and their local community and developing a strategy for change and implementing it. For instance, in 2000, several of the cooperatives focused on the issues of community health and preventive health. The Pushpanjali cooperative was concerned about the fact that there were no covers on the raw sewage ditches in their neighborhood. Not only was this dangerous for children playing in the neighborhood and people walking, but also it contributed to significant health problems, both in terms of hygiene and because disease-carrying mosquitoes were breeding in the sewage water. Pushpanjali decided their social action project would be to get the city government to address this situation that so far had been consistently ignored. They educated city officials about the problem, conducted a door-to-door campaign in their neighborhood to elicit widespread support, and demonstrated at the offices of local politicians. Within a year, the problem had been addressed and the sewage ditches were covered. This change in infrastructure has positive ramifications for everyone in the community, including a lower infant mortality rate, fewer breeding grounds for malarial mosquitoes, and a generally cleaner and safer environment. No small feat for a group of women, many of whom had never left the house or spoken in public before they started working in the coop.

Also in 2000, several coops undertook a social action program to call attention to the corruption in the distribution of government rations of rice and oil. The Government of India provides rations of rice and oil for some of the poorest sectors of society; however, those distributing it were intentionally shorting people on their allotment so that they could sell the extra. In order to curtail this corruption in the distribution of food, the women worked in teams, some going in to claim their food, some observing, and some waiting outside with the police. In spite of this strategy, the practice of shortchanging the needy on their food was so widespread that in May 2000, the women demonstrated in the streets of Mumbai to bring widespread social and political attention to the situation. After the demonstrations, the government intervened and improved the supervisory process of distributing rations.

Another example of a successful social action program is health education. In one coop, all members went through an outside workshop on preventive health, with an emphasis on inexpensive home remedies. After this coop went through the workshop, they put together an educational health program themselves. They created all the material such as posters, flip charts, etc., and they ran peer workshops for the other coops. Through these social action programs the women learn that they have the power to create positive change not only in their own lives, but also in the community. Sharda proclaims, *'All the programs have had effects on my life, especially the social action program because I circulate the information in my mandel [cooperative group], and my neighborhood'*. Because the women in Marketplace share their knowledge and promote change within their communities, the scope of change looks like an inverted funnel, starting with the group of women within the cooperative, but broadening out to include each woman's extended family, neighbors and community. Focusing on particular, local issues helps each group to successfully set and reach their collective goals. With each small success, they are encouraged to tackle larger issues. Asha says, *'If tomorrow I see something happening in my neighborhood, I will fight for change'*. Marketplace/SHARE not only provides each individual with knowledge, skills and a fair wage, but also fosters a sense of solidarity and collective empowerment.

Conclusion

Because of its focus on political and legal rights and its individualism, the liberal model of rights does not always serve feminists well. This is especially true in the context of global issues, particularly in light of the neoliberal strategies of global capital. In order for feminist theory to be relevant it must address economic issues, including the issue of wage labor for women. Cooperatives represent an important alternative to both the exploitative conditions of factory work and the ever-increasing pattern of women's migration of labor overseas to take up low status, low paying jobs such as domestics, agricultural workers, caregivers and sex workers. Cooperatives allow for control over the process of production, and for shared responsibility and benefits among the members of the coop.

During my research I found that the women I talked to were able to make positive changes in their own lives as a result of their economic independence–one woman left her abusive husband and returned only when he promised to stop the abuse; all of the women were sending their daughters to school past the average educational level; and a widow who had contemplated suicide was able to support herself, her children, and her mother. Their role as wage earners gave these women the power to make financial decisions and to exert more control within the family. But more important, their experience as part of a collective in which they were each given responsibility for decision-making and were introduced to tasks and roles that went beyond traditional women's roles, facilitated a sense of empowerment that translated into a new found ability to create change both in their individual lives and collectively. As Sunanda so beautifully put it, 'Work is something that everybody needs and only when you have work do you have human dignity'.

ACKNOWLEDGEMENTS

I would like to thank Erica Polakoff for her careful reading of this chapter and her helpful suggestions on it. Thanks also to Ligaya Lindio-McGovern and the audience at the Women and Globalization conference sponsored by the Center for Global Justice in San Miguel de Allende for feedback on an earlier version of this paper.

NOTES

[1] I have been fortunate enough to attend two of the Non-Governmental Organizations Forums that met concurrently with the United Nations Conferences on Women: Nairobi, Kenya, 1985 and Beijing, China, 1995.

[2] Of course, there are differences between microfinance institutions such as the Grameen Bank and cooperatives such as SEWA and Marketplace India. But because my focus here is on the collective economic empowerment of women, I discuss the similarities among these organizations, rather than the differences.

[3] Information about the history, background, and operation of Marketplace/SHARE was gathered from their website, www.marketplaceindia.org and from discussions with Marketplace members and staff while I was in Mumbai in February and March 2004, and January 2006.

[4] Information about the particular social action programs was obtained from my conversations and interviews with the Marketplace/SHARE staff and members in February-March 2004. General information about these programs can be found on the Marketplace website.

REFERENCES

An-Na'im, A. (1999) 'Promises We Should all Keep in Common Cause', in J. Cohen, M. Howard, and M. Nussbaum (eds.) *Is Multiculturalism Bad for Women?* pp. 59-64. Princeton: Princeton University Press.

Benhabib, S. (1987) 'The Generalized and The Concrete Other: The Kohlberg-Gilligan Controversy and Moral Theory', in E.F. Kittay and D.T. Meyers (eds.) *Women and Moral Theory*, pp. 154-77. Totowa: Rowman and Littlefield.

Bulbeck, C. (1998) *Re-Orienting Western Feminisms: Women's Diversity in a Postcolonial World.* Cambridge: Cambridge University Press.

Bunch, C. (1995) 'Transforming Human Rights from a Feminist Perspective', in J. Peters and A. Wolper (eds.) *Women's Rights, Human Rights: International Feminist Perspectives*, pp. 11-17. New York: Routledge.

Committee for the Promotion and Advancement of Cooperatives (COPAC) (1999) 'The Contribution of Cooperatives to the Implementation of the World Summit for Social Development

Declaration and Programme of Action'. Accessed 30 October 2002 from http://copacgva.org/wssd99.htm.

Friedman, E. (1995) 'Women's Human Rights: The Emergence of a Movement Perspective', in J. Peters and A.Wolper (eds.) *Women's Rights, Human Rights: International Feminist Perspectives*, pp. 18-35. New York: Routledge.

Friedman, M. (1987) 'Care and Context in Moral Reasoning', in E.F. Kittay and D.T. Meyers (eds.) *Women and Moral Theory*, pp. 190-204. Totowa: Rowman and Littlefield.

Friedman, M. (1993) *What Are Friends For? Feminist Perspectives on Personal Relationships and Moral Theory*. Ithaca: Cornell University Press.

Gilligan, C. (1982) *In A Different Voice: Psychological Theory and Women's Development*. Cambridge, MA: Harvard University Press.

Held, V. (1987) 'Feminism and Moral Theory', in E.F. Kittay and D.T. Meyers (eds) *Women and Moral Theory*, pp. 111-28. Totowa: Rowman and Littlefield.

Human Rights Watch (1995) *The Human Rights Watch Global Report on Women's Human Rights*. New York: Human Rights Watch.

Hausmann, R., Tyson, D., and Zahidi, S. (2010)*The Global Gender Gap Report 2009*. World Economic Forum.

International Development Exchange (IDEX) (2005) 'India'. Accessed 4 February 2005 from www.idex.org/country.

Jaising, I. (1995) 'Violence Against Women:The Indian Perspective', in J. Peters and A. Wolper (eds) *Women's Rights, Human Rights: International Feminist Perspectives*, pp. 51-56. New York: Routledge.

Kant, I. ([1785] 1994) 'Grounding for the Metaphysics of Morals', in J.W. Ellington and W.A. Wick (eds.) *Immanuel Kant: Ethical Philosophy*, pp. 1-62. Indianapolis: Hackett.

Kittay, E.F. (1999) *Love's Labor: Essays on Women, Equality and Dependency*. New York: Routledge.

Locke, J. ([1690] 1960) 'The Second Treatise of Government', in P. Laslett (ed.) *John Locke Two Treatises of Government*, pp. 304-477. Cambridge: Cambridge University Press.

McLaren, M. (1996) 'Communitarianism: A New Ethical and Political Agenda', in T. Kent and M.B. Gentry (eds.) *The Theory and Practice of Ethics*, pp. 83-98. Indianapolis: The University of Indianapolis Press.

McLaren, M. (2008a) 'Women's Right's and Economic Empowerment: The Story of the Self-Employed Women's Association of India', in S.K. Masters, J.A. Hayden and K. Vaz (eds.) *Florida Without Borders: Women at the Intersection of the Local and the Global.* Newcastle: Cambridge Scholars Publishing.

McLaren, M. (2008b) 'Gender Equality and the Economic Empowerment of Women'. *Forum on Public Policy*, Spring 2008.

Meyers, D. (1987) 'The Socialized Individual and Individual Autonomy: An Intersection between Philosophy and Psychology', in E.F. Kittay and D.T. Meyers (eds.) *Women and Moral Theory*, pp. 139-53. Totowa: Rowman and Littlefield.

Mill, J.S. ([1859] 1985) *On Liberty.* G. Himmelfarb (ed.). London: Penguin Books.

Mohanty, C.T. (1991a) 'Cartographies of Struggle: Third World Women and the Politics of Feminism', in C. T. Mohanty, A. Russo, L. Torres (eds.) *Third World Women and the Politics of Feminism*, pp. 1-47. Bloomington: Indiana University Press.

Mohanty, C.T. (1991b) 'Under Western Eyes: Feminist Scholarship and Colonial Discourses' in C.T. Mohanty, A. Russo, L.Torres (eds.) *Third World Women and the Politics of Feminism*, pp. 51-80. Bloomington: Indiana University Press.

Mouffe, C. (1990) 'Rawls: Political Philosophy without Politics', in D. Rasmussen (ed.) *Universalism vs. Communitarianism: Contemporary Debates in Ethics*, pp. 217-35. Cambridge: The MIT Press.

PCI. (2004) 'Population and Development in the 21st Century', Report from Population Communications International (PCI). New York: Population Communications International.

Peters, J. and Wolper, A. (1995) *Women's Rights, Human Rights: International Feminist Perspectives.* New York: Routledge.

Saurez Toro, M. (1995) 'Popularizing Women's Human Rights at the Local Level: A Grass-roots Methodology for Setting the International Agenda', in J. Peters and A. Wolper (eds.) *Women's Rights, Human Rights: International Feminist Perspectives*, pp. 189-94. New York: Routledge.

Singh, K. (1994) 'Obstacles to Women's Rights in India', in R.J. Cook (ed.) *Human Rights of Women: National and International Perspectives*, pp. 375-96. Philadelphia: University of Pennsylvania Press.

Spivak, G. (2003) 'Righting Wrongs', in N. Owen (ed.) *Human Rights, Human Wrongs*, pp. 168-227. Oxford: Oxford University Press.

Stamatopoulou, E. (1995) 'Women's Rights and the United Nations', in J. Peters and A. Wolper (eds.) *Women's Rights, Human Rights: International Feminist Perspectives*, pp. 36-48. New York: Routledge.

Tronto, J.C. (1993) *Moral Boundaries: A Political Argument for an Ethic of Care.* New York: Routledge.

UNICEF (2010) India-Statistics. Accessed 22 March 2010 from www.unicef.org/infobycountry/India_statisitcs.html.

PART 4

Responses to Poverty:
Women's and Children's Resistance

CHAPTER 8

Urban Poverty Reborn
A Gender and Generational Analysis

Jeanine Anderson
Catholic University of Peru

ABSTRACT

This chapter draws on a longitudinal study of a poor neighborhood in Lima, Peru, to question received wisdom concerning the intergenerational transmission of poverty. The research follows a sample of 56 families over nearly 30 years. It focuses on the efforts of parents to launch their children on what they hope will be different and superior life courses (compared to their own), despite their limited resources. Members of the second generation are still likely to begin their adult lives in poverty, with notable differences in the positions and trajectories of men and women. The sources of second generation poverty are different from that of the parents, however. The case demonstrates how poverty is a dynamic and contingent process that must be related to the specific historical, political, social and cultural factors contributing to its rebirth in successive generations.

Keywords: urban poverty, urban livelihoods, intergenerational transmission of poverty, gender, Lima, Peru

Introduction

Understanding urban poverty is a critical task for our times. Migration from rural to urban areas is a continuing process in most of the 'Two Thirds' world (see Ferguson, 1999, however, for a vision of reverse migration, not altogether voluntary). Urban squatter settlements and shantytowns are the habitat of millions of human beings. Living conditions here are often worse than those of depressed rural areas. There are high levels of pollution; water tends to be scarce, expensive, and of poor quality; disease propagates rapidly. Even the occasionally well-administered and well-intentioned government programs cannot keep up with the demands for basic services, schools and health posts. Vast tracts become densely inhabited slums before they complete their evolution from squatter invasions to underserviced informal suburbs.

One of the prevalent notions about urban poverty is that it is self-reproducing, at least as concerns a large percentage of the 'hard core' or 'chronic' poor. Under this view, poverty is somehow handed down from parents to children. Different analysts have suggested different mechanisms that might contribute to this pattern: cultural beliefs and practices (Lewis, 1961); enclosure in socially homogeneous ghettos (Wilson, 1987); dense and interdependent social networks (Stack, 1975); lack of bridges to other social sectors (Lomnitz, 1975); prestige hierarchies that reward self-destructive behavior (Bourgois, 1995). In Latin America, low educational aspirations and achievements are a favorite candidate as a mechanism of reproducing poverty (see, for example, Larrañaga, 1997). Recently, the concept of social capital has received attention (Atria and Siles, 2003). According to this view, poor people are deficient in social capital insofar as they have few ties to strategic actors and may not use their ties effectively; often, they cannot represent themselves as trustworthy persons (Roberts, 1973). Here, as in other attempts to explain the 'reproduction' or 'intergenerational transmission' of poverty, a basic question is whether the poor are to be regarded as agents or victims, and in what proportion.

The problem of correctly attributing responsibility and agency is real and important, and it has serious implications for the anti-poverty strategies deployed by governments, international agencies, and the poor themselves. Clearly, neither poverty nor wealth strike at random in the second generation: rich parents tend to have rich children, poor parents tend to have poor children. But exactly how and why does this occurs? At stake is a vision of poverty as static, inexorable, vegetative in its mode of replication, versus a vision of poverty as dynamic, actively created under circumstances that are never a simple copy of anything that happened before.

> By using new theoretical approaches that situate different groups' experiences of poverty in dialectical relation to global, national, state, and local political-economic change and to the interconnected ideologies of race, class, gender, sexuality, and nationhood, the new poverty studies treat poverty not as a static 'moral' *condition* but as a dynamic historically and geographically contingent *process*. (Goode and Maskovsky, 2001:16)

This chapter explores some of the specific mechanisms that help explain the persistence of poverty and inequality in Latin American, specifically Peruvian, cities. In Lima as in most other cities of the region, the 'older' generation of the urban poor consists predominantly of migrants from the countryside. The younger generation is urban born, raised, and educated. Thus, a sociocultural dimension must be added to the list of contingencies that influence poverty.

Some of my central arguments have to do with the ways in which adolescents and young adults in the urban population are deprived of opportunities at critical moments of transition into adult life. I will argue further that this process is different for young women and young men, and that young women are at greater disadvantage in starting their adult lives. In many respects, the gender gap was narrower in their mothers' generation as, in many respects, it continues to be so in rural settings.

Methodology

My empirical base for the analysis that follows is a series of research rounds in an area on the southern edge of Lima, Peru. Called Pamplona Alta, this is part of a dry, hilly area that lies between the Pacific Ocean and Pan-American Highway, on one side, and the wealthy residential districts of Monterrico and La Molina on the other. It began to attract squatters in the 1960s, and informal occupation of the more remote hilltops still goes on today. Pamplona Alta exemplifies the typical pattern of formation of poor neighborhoods in Peruvian cities.[1] Families spot a tract of land in a suitable area and prepare the straw mats and poles they will use as shelters until they gain provisional recognition and security of occupation. Much of the desert surrounding Lima is publicly owned, and the Peruvian government has generally been tolerant of such informal solutions to the country's problem of housing the poor. The earliest such settlements tended to be sudden, overnight invasions by several hundreds of families that had previously formed an association, distributed the lots, and plotted the streets and common areas for the future community. By the 1970s, it was more common for occupation to take place gradually, through a filtering process by which individual families or small groups of relatives pushed out the borders of existing settlements. The particular area of my research began as this second type of community and, in five years' time, by 1975, it had grown to nearly 1,000 households distributed over 42 blocks of housing. Some of the occupants of new squatter settlements arrive directly from the countryside, but most have accumulated a few years of living in rented rooms in squalid inner-city areas or crowded in with relatives. This also was the case for my research area.

Squatter settlements share a history of organizing around community projects to obtain basic services. They undertake a mixture of self-help construction, appeals to *padrinos* (godparents or sponsors), which may include, in recent years, agencies of international cooperation and nongovernmental organizations, and marches and demonstrations outside strategic government offices. Obtaining a school and a health post, installing a potable water and sewer system, getting electricity, and eventually paving streets and sidewalks occupy a cycle of 15 to 20 years. In 1977, when I first went to the community, water was still being purchased from cistern trucks and stored in steel drums or concrete tanks outside the entrance to each house. A contract had been signed with the electric utility, however, and holes were being dug for posts and cables. Many of the households were well advanced towards replacing their straw mats with brick and cement walls: a squatter settlement had become a shantytown. Moving around the community was difficult: plodding feet sank into the sand, and few vehicles would venture so far up the hill for fear of getting stuck.

The initial focus of my research was childcare and infant nutrition.[2] Thus, I began with a sample of 74 households, each of which contained one infant and a second child, under five. This requirement ensured that most of the households were at a similar point in the family life cycle. It also set the stage for expanding the second wave of interviews, in 1992, to include, by that time, the adolescent children of the sample households. In 2001, for a third wave, the adolescents were young adults, and some had partners and children. This round of interviewing sought to develop the fullest possible picture of each household group and its process over time. The original parents and children were interviewed, wherever possible. Some of the original sample members had died, some had abandoned the household, and some refused, with arguments such as 'I already told you everything about my life 10 years ago!' Substitutions were made to replace as many as possible, and new family members were added to the roster: younger siblings, sons- and daughters-in-law, new partners of some members of the older generation.

The 74 original households comprised about 7.5 percent of total households in the community. A few of these, discouraged by the difficult conditions or unable to make a living in the city, left the settlement in the early years. In 1992, 66 of the original households participated in the study. All of these were still living in the community in 2001, and 56 agreed to participate in the third wave of interviewing. Neighborhoods that begin as squatter settlements, once past the initial phase of struggle and privation, tend to have low outward mobility. Persons who occupy such areas (land traffickers and political operatives aside) are playing the only card they possess to get a house and lot, and the high investment they make in community building, in both a physical and a social sense, further ties them to the neighborhood.

The principal means of data collection in the three waves of the study was a semi-structured personal interview. In the 1978 and 1992 waves, a family round table was used as a 'thank-you' and means of closure. This was not feasible in 2001 because there were many more people involved, and many households had accumulated complex histories of conflict and antipathy.

In all three rounds of family interviews, and at various points in between, I collected information on services, felt needs, and community organizations. The household life cycles could thus be set against a cycle of community development to explore hypotheses about the effects of men's and women's community involvement on poverty dynamics. At various points over the almost 30 years that elapsed between 1977 and the present, I was involved in research on specialized topics in the same Pamplona Alta area (for example, surveys of women's skills and interests in forming micro-enterprises), and I have participated in several development projects there (for example, promoting a family daycare system).

High Expectations and the Urban Poor

Rural migrants to the city place great hopes on achieving economic security and improved conditions of life for their children, if not for themselves. The language that surrounds the formation of urban shantytowns emphasizes investment in children, their opportunities and future quality of life. For example,'*ella tiene que ser otra gente* (she has to become a different kind of person)' says a resident of Pamplona Alta about her daughter. '*No va a estar hincando aguja como yo* (She's not going to be plying a needle like me).' The self-help efforts to build, organize and establish services in the community are phrased in terms of transmitting a more favorable base of action than the parents enjoyed.

This includes respect and inclusion. The neighborhood must be 'greened' and, with trees and asphalted streets, made to look progressively more like residential areas in the traditional parts of the city. The migrants adopt urban dress styles and model their houses on a middle class, urban pattern. Those that arrived speaking only

Quechua and Aymara (primarily women) gradually learn Spanish and use it instead of their native languages except for intimate family conversations among peers and elders. Children born in the city recognize a few words in their parents' native tongue, but they have very little motivation for learning it. They know full well how Quechua-accented Spanish is the brunt of jokes at school and on television.

To set this in the proper framework, it must be emphasized that Peru is a country with very limited social provision. Some urban families may have access to programs that distribute subsidized food; others may get help with health emergencies from government programs or NGO projects. Health posts charge fees, albeit small and on a sliding scale, and public schools, while theoretically free, require that families buy uniforms, notebooks, books and supplies. Very few families with children under four years of age use home-based daycare services under the government's 'wawawasi' program. It has been calculated that no more than 5 percent of the total basket of goods and services required by urban poor families is provided by social programs.

Data on urban and rural poverty dynamics are only recently becoming available through household panel studies (Chacaltana, 2005). The data show frequent movements in and out of poverty, especially in urban areas. In the four years between 1998 and 2001, 22 percent of Lima households spent one year below the poverty line; 15 percent spent two years in poverty; 10 percent were poor during three years; and 8 percent were poor throughout the entire period. A total of 55 percent were poor at least one year, whereas 45 percent were never poor. Chacaltana calculates Peru's per capita product at $5,000 per year, or $471 per month. The minimum wage in Lima was around $200 a month whereas a basket of basic goods and services for a family of four was priced at $1,000 or more.

In this chapter, I analyze three aspects of the intergenerational transmission or inheritance of poverty thesis. These three provide some of the strongest evidence from Peru and the Pamplona Alta study against the thesis, but they are far from exhausting the many strands of argument that might be proposed. The first has to do with the socialization of values and aspirations, the second with children and work, and the third with parents' transmission of advice and models.

Inheritance of Poverty? Growing Up in the Shantytown

The transmission of poverty from parents to children is said to involve the transmission of low aspirations, defeatist or conformist attitudes, and perceptions of limited opportunities. As I have already suggested, the founding couples in the Pamplona Alta households, by contrast, had high ambitions when they were first interviewed in the late 1970s. The move to the city was in itself a symbol of upward mobility, and nearly all considered the kin they had left in the countryside to be worse off than they were. Most of these men and women migrated in their teens. The initial period in the city was an intense learning experience for all. Some (far more men than women) came with plans for finishing high school and even enrolling in college or at least a teacher training program. They quickly learned to give priority to acquiring technical skills demanded by the urban labor market. The men, with better-paying jobs and connections to a broader range of institutions and networks, had clear advantages over the women. In the mid-1970s, with Peru's economy still growing and a relatively healthy industrial sector concentrated in Lima, the men were taking courses in typing, accounting, a range of specialties in construction, and even theatrical production and airplane maintenance. None of the women embarked on any similar project. Instead, they were receiving short courses in child care and nutrition, family health, and similar 'women's' topics from NGOs and government agencies that worked in the shantytowns.

As young parents, the men and women had similar dreams for their children of both sexes. They would by all means finish high school. If they showed talent and determination, they would go into technical professions or to the university. The parents identified as 'professions' a wide range of occupations that might presuppose either technical, teachers', or college training. They reflected the usual stereotypes in Peruvian society: sons would become doctors, lawyers and engineers; daughters would become nurses, accountants, and teachers.

In point of fact, most young people in Pamplona Alta did manage to finish high school, though repeating a grade or two is a common experience. The quality of the education students receive, however, in both public and private schools within reach of the poor, is steadily declining. Peru occupies the bottom rungs for Latin America on international comparisons of educational quality. A high school diploma, under these conditions, while seen as an achievement by parents who may have little or no formal education themselves, is no more than a small step on the path to becoming established and independent. With respect to their human capital and opportunities available in the labor market, both the parents and the children are quite realistic about what they can offer and what they can expect. The parents made adjustments downward through most of their working careers. The children started with low expectations. For both generations, the determining factors were the objective conditions of the Peruvian economy in successive periods. What was 'inherited,' then, if anything, was extreme adaptability and the lack of illusions.

Inheritance of Poverty? Children and Work

Child labor is one of the principal suspects in the 'intergenerational transmission of poverty' debates. The argument is that families condemn their children to a truncated future when, by forcing them to work, they deprive them of the chance to go to school and do well academically, even as they interfere with play, exploration, and the construction of their personal identity. Work, supposedly, limits their horizons and their exposure to alternative models of success.

Andean children do indeed participate heavily in their families' economic strategies. From an early age, children are expected to be hardworking and to identify with the serious business of getting the family's income and paying the bills. According to economic demands and the abilities that particular children display, boys and girls, almost interchangeably, are assigned various household and extra-domestic tasks. They help their mothers or fathers to sell produce from a market stall, to run a carpentry workshop, to take care of customers in a home-based *bodega*, to sew the buttons and do the hems of clothes made on consignment. Whether sons or daughters, older children will be given responsibility for overseeing younger siblings and cousins.

During the 1992 summer school vacation, in the second round of interviewing in Pamplona Alta, about half the adolescent sons and daughters were working for pay. Adolescents of both genders had long and complex job histories behind them. A slightly higher percentage of boys were working than girls: 40 out of 59 boys (68 percent) and 27 out of 45 girls (60 percent). The adolescents were working to pay for their school supplies and uniforms, to help with the family budget, to meet their own needs for clothes, bus fares and even food, occasionally to permit themselves indulgences like branded jeans or running shoes, music tapes or a guitar, a radio, beer, cigarettes and evenings out with friends. 'Work' here excludes, of course, the 'other' work that many of the adolescents–especially girls–were doing: helping with housework, preparing meals, taking care of siblings.

One robust finding from the longitudinal study in Pamplona Alta has to do with informal education and the importance of acquiring an understanding of complex systems. The families that came through the various economic crises of the late 1970s, 1980s, and 1990s with a certain stability have, in common, experiences of participating in, or observing closely, complex institutions operating in conflictive social and political environments. One example is the experience of the men who worked for large industries in the early 1970s. They participated in unions with their internal hierarchical structures and political cross-currents, shared in a complicated division of labor and functions in the factory, observed the myriad relations of the firm with suppliers and customers, and analyzed the position of the firm and the industry in a complex urban and national economy.

Persons who had such experiences in their portfolios seemed to transfer a 'logic' of complexity, differentiation, conflict and opposed interests to other arenas of their lives, long after the factory jobs and the unions disappeared. They had grasped the notion of a political economy in which they were forced to operate and which has systemic features. This kind of understanding is patently useful for poor people whose access to information is limited by many vested interests and by prejudices that portray the 'lower classes' as simple people on whom complex ideas would be wasted. In Pamplona Alta, men with this kind of cognitive capital were able to expand small businesses into relatively complicated operations that involved markets outside Lima. Women were able to work in social provision and anti-poverty programs (such as these were), using one as a springboard to another and tailoring their approach to NGOs and government offices in strategic fashion.

If this factor is as important to the urban poor in other cities and countries as it surely is in Lima, we would have to look again at the experiences–work, school, social, cultural, mass media–that children and adolescents are exposed to. In Lima, parents understand that having a job teaches their children useful skills and habits (punctuality, saving money, obedience). It may also be one means of compensating for the deficiencies of the educational system, which is relentlessly reductionist and simplifying.[3]

Inheritance of Poverty? Parents as Models

If poverty were 'inherited', parents, other close relatives, neighbors and friends of parents would have to be models for children. In Pamplona Alta, on the contrary, fathers and mothers did everything they could to make their children different from them. Nonetheless, they clearly did wish to be appreciated, respected, and admired by their families, and they did often deliver themselves of advice and judgments that sought to influence their children's decisions and behavior. Much of this had to do with moral issues: excessive drinking, skipping school, a lack of seriousness, dressing provocatively, questionable friends.

Some of the most surprising results of the 1992 round of interviews dealt with personal and emotional relations within the families. By this time, most of the parents were in their mid-30s, and the strains of Peru's economic roller coaster had taken their toll. Some of the couples had separated; some were living in situations of violence and abuse. Some of the men had taken up with other women and had fathered other children that competed for their earnings. The majority of mothers, found at home with their young children in the first round of interviewing, were now out working, often very long hours. Though necessary from an economic point of view, this caused tensions as other family members (especially daughters) were required to replace the mothers in the households' care economy. Some tasks (for example, caring for severely incapacitated or chronically ill family members) became the source of extreme conflict, and others went undone (for example, buying cooking fuel, boiling drinking water). In some households, the job of midday meal preparation was transferred to the 'community kitchens (*comedores populares*)' that sprang up all over the country and became one of the government's favored channels for poverty relief.

In this context, many of the adolescents spoke with great bitterness and disappointment about their parents as well as their relations with brothers and sisters. Fathers, in particular, were portrayed as distant, authoritarian, even threatening figures. The mother-daughter relation was the one most likely to be experienced as friendly and warm, especially when daughters felt recognized for the support they gave to their mothers.

Sexuality, entertainment, and lifestyle were arenas of great conflict. The adolescents complained that their parents did not trust them and tried to keep them from enjoying teen culture. The parents pushed to have both sons and daughters established in jobs or education before they became involved with partners or there was a pregnancy. Many of the older men and women explained their own frustrations in life by blaming their spouse or saying they had fallen in love at the wrong time, too early. Despite warnings and vigilance, many of the young girls did become pregnant in their late teens.

In a setting such as Pamplona Alta, there are vast areas where misunderstandings and cultural conflicts can arise between generations. Most of the older men and women remember growing up on a small farm in the Andes, and they often got their start in the city through a patron or sponsor in situations that their children would find unthinkable (men in domestic service, for example). An 18-year-old denies his father's ability ever to understand him: '*A veces mi papá piensa que una cosa es así y como yo ya he vivido, yo ya conozco. Como mi papá es pues de provincia no sabe cómo es, pues* (Sometimes my father thinks things should be a certain way and since I have been around, I already know things. Because my father is from the provinces, he just doesn't know how it is)'. Beyond the rural-urban gap, the adolescents were almost violent in rejecting their parents as models for the kind of person they wanted to be and– even more emphatically–the kind of life they wanted to have. A young man answers the question '*¿Qué cosas has aprendido de tu papá?* (What have you learned from your father?)' by saying boldly, 'Not to be like him': '*No ser como él. No ser como él pues. Porque no enseña pues a sus hijos lo que debe ser. Consejos pues* (Not to be like him. Just not to be like him. Because he doesn't teach his children what is right. Advice, you know)'.

We might suspect that the children were going through the 'storms' of adolescence, yet I think the situation is far more complicated. Idealistic adolescents were seeing that their parents had to do things the parents never wished or planned for. During this period, fathers who had worked for years in factories, offices and municipal governments were losing their jobs to the restructuring and liberalizing of the Peruvian economy. A drastic structural adjustment package was applied in 1990, and Peru was a model of toeing the Washington Consensus line throughout the 1990s. As families lost access to social security (privatized and made exhorbitantly costly) and to social services (forced by government reform and loss of subsidies to charge fees), mothers intensified their involvement in degraded forms of work such as cleaning and washing. The young men and women who rejected the models their parents represented were in reality rejecting the possibility that they should ever be forced into retrenchments similar to theirs. Unquestionably, some of the parents reacted violently, became depressed, or attempted to resolve the situation by exploiting their children's labor beyond the bounds of reciprocity and reasonable obligation. All this was, for most of the families, a passing phase in the sense that the children, in the 2001 interviews when they were in their mid to late 20s, took a new tone. They spoke with objectivity, understanding, and even compassion about the heroic efforts their parents had made and the obstacles they faced. They accepted, as well, their own obligations to assist their parents in their old age, and they recognized intense ties of interdependence and cooperation, including shared responsibility for family businesses.

Entering Adulthood

By their early and mid-20s, as reflected in the third round of interviews in Pamplona Alta, the young men had inserted themselves into occupations such as taxidriver (own or rented car), construction worker, gardener, fumigator, solderer, municipal garbage collector, mechanic, office maintenance, ticket collector on buses, house painter, carpenter, and employees in businesses such as Internet outlets, wholesale market stalls, poultry shops, supermarkets, and hardware stores. Some had their own workshops and small businesses, fixing locks, repairing and selling used leather jackets, making fiberglass items and promotional materials such as stamped pens and notepads, electronics repairs. A very few had graduated from college and were working as teachers and engineers; one had embarked on a career as member of a musical group that had toured Bolivia. Many of these young men were employed sporadically, and they fell back on odd jobs to tide them over: street vending, washing cars, helping older male relatives on construction jobs.

The young women had gained entry into the Lima labor force in a similarly varied range of occupations, most of them even more poorly paid than the men's. They worked in market stalls which might be rented, on loan, or ceded by a relative. Many worked in different kinds of household services or home caretaking. Several had moveable carts and stands where they sold juice, hotdogs, fruit and the like. They were employed as sales personnel in drugstores, shoe stores, used goods outlets, as supermarket cashiers, servers in casinos and at food stalls in markets. Some worked freelance as hairdressers and seamstresses; others did sewing for sweatshops, export factories, and factories supplying Lima's up-scale department stores. Like the men, a few young women had completed a technical course or college and were working as teachers, hospital nutritionists, administrators, bank sales representatives pushing small loans to micro-enterprises, or in local government offices. Most of their jobs were also insecure, but, during slack times, their labor was in demand at home, where housekeeping and caretaking roles were seldom filled to satisfaction.

While struggling to find their place in the labor market, most of the young men and women were starting their own families. Over half of those in the sample were in unions and had children. Their initiation into marriage and parenthood differed from that of their parents in many ways. The Andean ideal is for young couples to become economically self-sufficient as early as possible, having been endowed with a certain resource base (land, animals, tools) by parents and god-parents in a process that starts at baptism. After marriage the couple may live with parents (usually, the husband's) for a time, but, especially as children arrive, they will be assisted to build a separate house and establish themselves independently. They may carry on with labor exchanges and other forms of mutual aid–with parents, siblings, other relatives and neighbors–but each nuclear household is on its own.

The expense and scarcity of housing, and the difficulties of organizing a self-sufficient domestic economy, cause dramatic distortions to this pattern in the city. Young couples begin married life in Pamplona Alta under extremely stressful conditions. Many occupy a room in his or her parents' house, but in some cases they shared even that small space with siblings. There are high levels of conflict in very complex households involving several spouses and children, all under the strain of insecure employment and low wages. Money is never enough to cover daily needs (water, electricity, food, transportation, school and health services). In closely-knit and expansive family networks, emergencies are frequent. How much each contributes to resolve a health emergency, to provide food or help pay off a debt, implies keeping several running tabs that are each a source of contention. Under these conditions, some of the young people behaved with astonishing altruism. One young woman, an expert seamstress working for a sweatshop that produces clothes for the Pierre Cardin label, was supporting her father-in-law, two or three of her husband's brothers and a variable number of their dependents (spouses, children). She got little recognition in return and in practice was contracting with her sister-inlaw to do the cooking and housekeeping, which were also understood to be her responsibility.

Sources of the New Poverty

It should be clear how I think poverty of the second generation in the shantytowns of Lima has little to do with a process of 'reproduction' of almost any of the habits, attitudes, models or practices of parents and the older generation. By contrast, it has everything to do with the meager opportunities provided for young people launching out on adult life; with the fact that their parents have been unable to endow them with critical resources as would have been the 'traditional' pattern; with the high demands for mutual aid placed on all family members; and with the obstacles put in the way of independence and self-sufficiency for the younger generation.

Meager Opportunities

Neoliberal projects promoting liberalization, flexible labor and the opening of markets, have taken a direct toll on the possibilities for Peruvians, old and young, urban and rural, to leave poverty. After following the economic and employment histories of the Pamplona Alta families, I can conclude that none has truly 'overcome' poverty in the 30-plus years that I can reconstruct. A crucial factor for the men and women of the younger generation is extremely low wages, below their costs of reproduction. The work histories speak of insecurity, long hours (10 to 12 hours daily is becoming the standard) with frequent overtime, discrimination in hiring on the basis of gender, ethnic background, educational limitations, and address. None belongs to a labor union, and a very small number have benefits such as health insurance or pension plans. Work in the 'new economy', in the conditions of Lima, means devoting further long hours to riding crowded buses to and from neighborhoods where, even now, piped water is not necessarily available every day of the week. Although women's pay is notably lower than men's, some women are the economic mainstay in their young families while at the same time they try to fulfil cultural ideals as devoted and protective mothers.

Young people find it almost impossible to accumulate assets; on the contrary, many are indebted. They may owe a few dollars on the purchase of clothing or they may owe several hundreds as a result of failed business ventures, health emergencies, or attempts to buy into new squatter invasions. By contrast, at the same age, their parents had a plot of land and at least a straw shack with which to start building their house. Without consumer credit available, with no microenterprise loans being offered by NGOs or banks, they might become modestly indebted to family members or local shops that extended credit for food, but their exposure did not go beyond that.

Another of the robust findings of the Pamplona Alta study concerns the importance of the economic subsectors in which poor people operate. There is, in fact, a strong tendency for sons and daughters to remain within the subsector that their fathers and mothers are engaged in, whether this be construction, urban transportation, small-scale retailing, services, low-level government employment (municipal garbage collector, kitchen help or nurse's aide in a hospital), or wage work in a factory or shop. Both generations end up trapped in sectors which are low wage, low productivity, resistant to new technologies, vulnerable to shifting political winds and policy decisions (for example, free-trade agreements), in the line of fire under the neoliberal project. Superficially, their situation is similar yet the processes, meanings, and future significance of their entrapment are different.

It should be mentioned that those who emerged in the best position after three decades were members of the older generation who were able to establish businesses of their own (bakery, dental prosthetics, automobile body shop, furniture manufacture for door-to-door sales, baby strollers and playpens, trucking of produce). Some of the family businesses failed but, in the successful cases, sons and daughters grew up working with their parents, and many continued to do so into adulthood. There are limits, however, on how far these businesses can grow, whether for lack of capital or technology or because they serve a narrow niche of the market. For some of the men and women of the younger generation, they were important as a platform for branching out on their own in a related line of activity.

Insufficient and Inappropriate Endowments

Formal education should have been the ticket out of poverty for the young people of Pamplona Alta. As we have seen, basic education even through secondary level is poor preparation for the challenges they face, and complements must be found in circuits of technical, non-formal and informal education. Like their fathers, many of the young men and–unlike their mothers–many young women are taking specialized postsecondary courses, even starting them while still in school. Unlike their parents, however, they face the competition of thousands of other high school graduates vying for the same jobs in the 'new' economy of informatics, services and sophisticated technologies. Peruvian cities are reputed to have one of the highest ratios of Internet cafés to population in all of Latin America, another reflection of the unceasing search for saleable knowledge and skills.

Although their overall state of health is probably better than their parents' at the same age, several of the young women and men of Pamplona Alta suffer from mental health problems, notably depression and what the Peruvian health system broadly diagnoses as schizophrenia. It is easy to imagine the many factors that contribute to states of stress and anxiety in persons who are struggling daily to maintain a sense of competence, integrity, and hope despite all odds. The mothers and fathers have constructed personal myths that emphasize their heroic efforts and ultimate triumph; at least they have not been forced to go back to the village and give up on the dream of mobility in Peru's exciting capital city. By contrast, the children measure their success and failure against urban standards, and they are aware of belonging to a devalued category of '*cholos* (citified peasants)' and migrants. And some do eventually turn their backs on the system. Marking two extremes, some young men are in prison, while around one-fifth of families in Pamplona Alta have sent migrants outside Peru.[4]

What could it have meant for the young women and men to have received the endowments they needed: appropriate in quantity, quality and timing? Self-esteem is an issue that deserves further attention. Shanty residents and new migrants are made to feel inferior to old-time *limeños* (Lima natives) in innumerable ways. Endowments necessary to exercise citizens' rights are also at stake here. The parents of Pamplona Alta were politically involved because of a strong urban popular movement that existed through the 1970s and into the 1980s. They came up through the ranks of organizations such as health promoter groups, parent-teacher associations, and community electrification campaigns. The children are more savvy about the political system and in theory, better equipped to use it (literate, familiar with the mechanisms of government), but they are extremely cynical. To become actively engaged, they would somehow have to be endowed with faith that the democratic system can actually provide them a better life.

High Demands for Mutual Aid

Members of the younger generation find it impossible to leave poverty as long as they remain involved with a large family network, many of whose members are also poor and none of whom has adequate protection through any form of social insurance. The parents participated in block-level or community-wide mutual aid mechanisms such as collections that were taken up when a neighbor was affected by a serious illness or suffered an accident. These practices disappeared long ago, but no one can entirely avoid requests for contributions–money, time, care, putting in a word somewhere–when family members are concerned. The most important obligations involve health emergencies. Here, the health reform of recent years, forcing public health facilities to generate a major part of their budgets out of user fees, has direct consequences. The Peruvian government, under advice from the World Bank, is belatedly implementing a universal health insurance program for the poor, but neither the quality nor the quantity of services to be covered looks likely to be sufficient.

Here, too, there are differences in the situation of young women and young men. Given their higher earnings, the men's contributions in family emergencies cost them less in relative terms. The major difference, however, concerns labor power, time, and the care economy. Daughters, especially if they are still living in their parents' home, whether married or not, remain involved in housework, childcare and the care of other family members. Even many of daughters-in-law that are living in the house assume as their own, the needs of their mothers- and sisters-in-law. In a pattern familiar worldwide and across social classes, the young women organize their work lives around the demands of the household and its members. They lose opportunities for jobs, training, social contacts that might improve their earning capacity, and,–not least,–they lose time for rest.

Obstacles to Independence

Members of the younger generation face enormous difficulties in their search for independence. Moving out while still single is out of the question, and independent housing even for married couples with several young children is a major challenge. Many young men and women end up repeating one of their parents' actions although it is what they least desired: they look to land invasions farther up the hills of Pamplona Alta or farther out towards the edge of the city as the only way of setting up on their own. In these cases, a similar strategy has different meaning for the two generations. The children participated as children in the self-construction efforts of their parents: weekend work parties, block-level organizing, marches to the water utility and municipal government offices. For their parents this involved claiming citizenship in the city; for the young adults of today it is proof of the limits of their citizenship.[5] They see more privileged citizens living in neighborhoods that already have streets, basic services, and even parks and schools. They see the costs they will have to pay to get them.

Again, young women are at a special disadvantage in the struggle for independence and autonomy. Fertility is prized in Andean rural communities, couples marry young, and certain practices of sexual experimentation and 'trial marriage (*servinakuy*)' are enshrined in custom. In the urban-born generation, there is a radical change in the meaning and consequences of many of these practices. Young women who become pregnant have little ability to command the assistance of their childrens' fathers or of their own natal families. It is easy for young fathers to disappear, and mothers must sue for child support, with very uncertain outcomes.

A recent review of the transition to adulthood in the Global South (Lloyd, 2005) speaks of a gradual normalizing trend in the sequence through which personal and family life cycles proceed: childhood, school, specialized training for entry to the labor market, work, economic independence, marriage, parenthood. Poor Peruvians turn such sequences on their head (Anderson et al., 2001). This puts them out of step with their contemporaries from other, more privileged social sectors; with social programs and their logic; and with desirable images of youth and consumption. The unhappiness of starting a family in a makeshift room on the roof of one's parents' house, distracted by work and worries over money, is intensified when young men and women contrast their situation with representations of age-mates in telenovelas, movies, and advertising: the liquor flowing, fast cars, attractive clothes, take-out food, weekends by a swimming pool.

Conclusions

Comparing parents and children at a similar point of life transition–entering adulthood, establishing families, finding a stable footing in the urban economy, embarking on a life project 'of one's own' (Nussbaum, 1993)–has made it clear, I hope, that the intergenerational transmission or reproduction of poverty are notions of extremely limited value. They mask the real differences that lie behind what may appear to be superficial similarities in the position and behavior of young and old. They exaggerate the autonomy of persons who are the frontline sources of social insurance for close family, in the absence of adequate social protection. They distract us from analyses of the structural and contingent forces that continuously create new forms of poverty. They draw us away from the task of seeking to understand, in all their complexity, the particular circumstances that lie behind poverty and inequality at different historical moments, under different political regimes, produced by the action of particular social and economic policies. If poverty is a 'dynamic historically and geographically contingent process', it must be studied and addressed as such. Since it is also clearly a gendered process, this is a program for gender analysts as well.

NOTES

[1] Such neighborhoods have been given a succession of names, both popular labels and legal categories that define their status in relation to Peruvian municipal government and law. First known by the derogatory term 'barriadas (shabby barrios)', they are now officially termed 'asentamientos humanos (human settlements)'.
[2] The initial study, and first wave of interviewing, was funded by the USAID Office of Nutrition as part of a six-country study commissioned for the International Year of the Child. The research was shared with psychologist Blanca Figueroa and pediatrician Ana Maríñez. The second wave was funded by the gender office of IDRC. The third wave was underwritten by an award from the Global Development Network.
[3] It is significant that a concept of 'complex knowledge' or 'complexity literacy' is completely absent from the debates on poverty in international organizations. In the work of Paolo Freire and others of the Latin American popular education movement, it was present as an intuition, as part of the analysis of their environment that poor people were encouraged to make.
[4] One-tenth of the Peruvian population currently lives overseas.
[5] Goldstein (2004) analyzes analogous situations in urban Bolivia.

REFERENCES

Anderson, J. (2001) *Yauyos. Estudio sobre valores y metas de vida.* Lima: Government of Peru, Ministry of Education.

Atria, R. and Siles, M. (eds.) (2003) Capital social y reducción de la pobreza en América Latina y el Caribe: en busca de un nuevo paradigma. Santiago: CEPAL/Michigan State University.

Bourgois, P. (1995) *In Search of Respect. Selling Crack in El Barrio.* Cambridge: Cambridge University Press.

Chacaltana, J. (2005) '¿Se puede prevenir la pobreza?'. Research report presented to CIES (Consorcio de Investigaciones Económicas y Sociales).

Ferguson, J. (1999) *Expectations of Modernity. Myths and Meanings of Urban Life on the Zambian Copperbelt.* Berkeley: University of California Press.

Goldstein, D.M. (2004) *Violence and Performance in Urban Bolivia.* Durham: Duke University Press.

Goode, J. and Maskovsky, J. (eds). (2001) *The New Poverty Studies. The Ethnography of Power, Politics, and Impoverished People in the United States.* New York: New York University Press.

Larrañaga, O. (1997) 'Educación y superación de la pobreza en América Latina', in J.V. Zevallos (ed.) *Estrategias para reducir la pobreza en América Latina y el Caribe.* Quito: PNUD (United Nations Development Programme).

Lewis, O. (1961) *The Children of Sánchez.* New York: Vintage Books.

Lloyd, C.B. (ed.) (2005) *Growing Up Global. The Changing Transitions to Adulthood in Developing Countries.* Panel on Transitions to Adulthood in Developing Countries. National Research Council/Institute of Medicine of the National Academies. Washington, D.C.: The National Academies Press.

Lomnitz, L.A. (1975) *Cómo sobreviven los marginados.* Mexico: Siglo Veintiuno Editores.

Nussbaum, M. (1993) 'Non-Relative Virtues: An Aristotelian Approach', in M.C. Nussbaum and A. Sen (eds.) *The Quality of Life.* Oxford: Clarendon Press.

Roberts, B. (1973) *Organizing Strangers. Poor Families in Guatemala City.* Austin: University of Texas Press.

Stack, C.B. (1975) *All Our Kin: Strategies for Survival in a Black Community.* New York: Harper Colophon Books.

Wilson, W.J. (1987) *The Truly Disadvantaged: The Inner City, the Underclass, and Public Policy.* Chicago: University of Chicago Press.

ADDITIONAL READING

Anderson, J. (2000) 'Gender and Generations in Shanty Community Development. Lima, Peru.' Paper presented to the Annual Meeting of the Global Development Network, Tokyo, Japan.

Moser, C. (2003) *Urban Longitudinal Research Methodology: Objectives, Contents and Summary of Issues Raised at the Joint DPU-ODI-World Bank-DFID Workshop.* DPU Working Paper No. 124. London: University College London.

CHAPTER 9

Challenging Traditional Female Roles through Social Participation: Tensions in Women's Experiences in Argentina's Picketing Movements

Ada Freytes Frey
University of Buenos Aires, Argentina

Karina Crivelli
University of Buenos Aires, Argentina

ABSTRACT

Based on case study analysis of four picketing organizations in Argentina, this chapter analyzes the impact of women's participation in the picketing movements on the ways in which women think about themselves and the social roles they claim. Women's initial involvement in the picketing movements was tied closely to their performance of the traditional roles of mother and wife. Over time, and as a result of women's social participation, these roles acquired new meaning. Women began to reject certain stereotypes linked to the feminine, and to challenge some aspects of the gendered division of tasks and responsibilities. Redefinition of feminine roles, however, has limitations, which are evident through analysis of the unequal participation of women in the movements' leadership.

Keywords: women's political and social participation, gender roles, social movements, subjectivity, women's leadership

Introduction

The research focuses on the picketing movements that sprang up in Argentina towards the end of the 1990s, and emphasizes the importance of considering gender as a factor for their analysis. These movements, whose members are unemployed workers living in conditions of extreme poverty, seem to debunk sociopolitical theories asserting that it is virtually impossible for the unemployed poor to become collective actors with the capacity to influence public policy (Castel, 1997).

In addition, the noticeable majority of female membership in the movements (women make up about 75 percent of their members)

seems to challenge traditional stereotypes of women that usually exclude them from the public sphere, and relegate them to the domestic realm. This 'division of labor' into the public/political sphere and the domestic/familial sphere contributes to the perpetuation of gender inequalities and was one of the earliest targets of women's movements.

Nevertheless, a review of the studies about Argentina's social movements constituted by women during the 1980s (i.e., the Mothers of Plaza de Mayo or the Housewives' League) establishes that women's participation in the public sphere does not always imply a challenge to traditional gender stereotypes. Sometimes, neither the content of their demands nor the method of their participation generates a redefinition of commonly held beliefs that associate women with the domestic domain (Jelin, 1985).

Also, in Latin America, there are several examples of women's movements in which participation is organized around the struggle to obtain goods and services related to basic needs (Mothers' Clubs in Peru, Bolivia and Brazil; Mothers' Centers in Chile). In those movements, women's involvement in the public arena is legitimated by invoking naturalized 'female responsibilities', such as children's feeding and care or homemaking, which some authors call 'maternalism' (Espinosa, 2009).

That is why our research[1] has focused on the meanings born out of women's involvement in the picketing movements. Its main objective is to analyze the representations of work, political participation, and female and male roles that are held by the movements' leaders and neighborhood representatives,[2] studying in detail how such conceptions were incorporated into the demands and struggles of their social organizations.

This chapter will address the impact of women's involvement in the picketing movements, on the way women think about themselves and the social roles that they claim. Subsequently, we will examine some of the limitations in the redefinition of female roles by analyzing the unequal incorporation of women into the leadership positions of the movements. Finally, we will discuss how women's participation and their redefinition of traditional female roles were affected by the demobilization that characterized the last period of picketing movements.

Methodology

The data on which this work is based come from empirical qualitative research designed to capture the processes of meaning construction.

We have carried out case studies in four picketing organizations. In each one we conducted in-depth interviews with leaders and neighborhood representatives (both male and female); observation (with and without participation) of different spaces of social interaction and collective action situations (mass meetings, picket lines and mobilizations); and lastly, analysis of internal documents. Our analysis consisted of a comparison between the movements themselves as well as between the leaders and representatives of specific movements (taking into account their different social backgrounds and political paths).

In the framework of a research project called 'Gender Issues in the Unemployed Workers' Organizations: A Public or Private Problem?', we developed a systematic field study of these picketing movements during 2004 and 2005. As we will discuss later, these were the early years of a demobilization phase of picketing organizations, affected by a change in Argentina's socio-economic and political scene. During the last few years (2006 to 2009), in the context of new research projects, we and other members of our research team have continued to work with some of these organizations. In addition, other empirical studies have been conducted during this period. We incorporate into this chapter the results of those studies, analyzing the challenges that this period of demobilization poses for women's participation in the picketing movements.

In order to explain this distinction, in the next section, we summarize the phenomenon of the picketing movements, and their characteristics.

The Picketing Movements in Argentina: Historical Development and Case Studies

The picketing movements in Argentina arose towards the end of the 1990s, as one of the most visible expressions of protest against the devastating social consequences of the neoliberal policy of structural adjustment that was implemented by Carlos Menem's administration throughout that decade. Structural adjustment led to the expulsion of a great number of workers from the labor market, creating unprecedented growth of unemployment and expansion of the informal economy. Workers in some of the inland areas of the country–especially those affected by the privatization of public enterprises–began to try out 'innovative' protest methods, such as pickets[3] (*piquetes*, in Spanish) to block the main roads and routes. Hence the term *piqueteros*, or picketers, was coined and later brought into vogue by the media. Initial demonstrations were carried out by ex-employees, workers of the now privatized industries, alongside other members of the local civil society (Cross, 2004; Svampa and Pereyra, 2003).

Towards the end of Menem's administration and with the advent of the new government of President De la Rúa in 1999, the epicenter of the social conflict moved to Buenos Aires province.[4] From that point on, picketing movements began to concentrate themselves in the metropolitan area of Buenos Aires city.[5] These new groups had different features from the ones that had arisen inland: they were more stable, better organized and their social base was composed of unemployed poor people (Svampa and Pereyra, 2003).

The picketing movements attained an even greater public significance during the institutional crisis at the end of 2001, when they were recognized as representative of the poorest unemployed sector and of those most affected by the neoliberal model. By early 2002, these organizations enjoyed significant growth thanks to the implementation of a broad social program (*Plan Jefas y Jefes de Hogar Desocupados*, or Female/Male Unemployed Household Heads Plan), reaching 1,987,875 beneficiaries in April 2003 (CELS, 2003) and destined to mitigate the direst consequences of the economic crisis, as well as to alleviate social conflict. It was practically an unemployment subsidy–albeit low paying–for which recipients were to perform four hours of 'social work' per day, either in a state organization (in the municipalities, for example) or in a nongovernmental organization.

The picketing movements were involved in the implementation and management of these *plans*. In fact, they managed 8 percent of the subsidies. This meant an increase in their resources for neighborhood activities and political organization, and led to the growth and development of existing groups and to the emergence of new ones.

Thus, the public legitimacy of picketing movements was fostered during a particular moment of Argentina's contemporary history, characterized by an acute institutional, economic and social crisis. In this context, these organizations managed (through public demonstrations and pickets) to be recognized as representatives of the poorest unemployed people. This scenario began to change with the election of the new democratic government of Néstor Kirchner in 2003. According to Svampa and Pereyra, 'N. Kirchner's policy was to implement, simultaneously, a range of available strategies to integrate, co-opt, discipline and/or isolate all the picketing organizations, making differences between the different movements and organizations' (2006:357).

Indeed, Kirchner's government proposed a transformation of social policies which represented major challenges for picketing organizations. First, a gradual replacement of the Female/Male Unemployed Heads of Household Plan was addressed: no new *plans* were granted and the beneficiaries of the former *plans* were gradually and selectively directed to different new programs. On the one hand, those considered most likely to be 'employable' (based on their gender and their prior labor history and qualifications), were directed to training programs, in order to facilitate their return to the labor market. On the other hand, women with dependent children were assigned to the 'Families for Social Inclusion' Program (*Familias por la Inclusión Social*), which distributed subsidies of variable amounts, depending on the number of minor children in each family. Unlike its predecessor, the new program does not require its beneficiaries to perform any 'social work' in order to receive subsidies. Women just need to prove that their children attend school and that they have received mandatory vaccinations (Freytes Frey, 2008; Cross and Freytes Frey, 2009).

Second, different policies aiming at fostering productive cooperative micro-projects were developed, following a philosophy of local development and social economy. Among them, the most important for the picketing movements was National Plan '*Manos a la Obra*', which provided training as well as financial and technical assistance to such cooperative projects, giving priority to those projects managed by 'poor, unemployed and/or socially vulnerable individuals, families and groups'. Other examples of this 'productive approach' of social policies are the programs for housing and sanitation in poor neighborhoods, which supported the formation of *ad hoc* cooperatives of unemployed workers in order to carry out the public works.

Changes in the approach of policies caused deep discussions in the picketing movements regarding the convenience to support the new government. Some of these policies (such as the promotion of productive cooperative projects) recovered the practices and the discourse of several social organizations. Their projects of social transformation included as an important element, the exploration of alternative cooperative ways of organizing production relations (Freytes Frey, 2008). However, for many leaders, this was just a strategy to put an end to street protests and pickets. This debate caused important divisions within each movement and between them, leading to fractures and defections (Svampa and Pereyra, 2006; Cross, 2008).

Adherence to the federal government's proposals led some of the picketing organizations to demobilize. However, even for those more militant and opposed to the new policies, demonstrations and pickets were soon revealed as an ineffective strategy, given the increasing illegitimacy of this form of protesting for other sectors of the population (particularly the middle classes) and for the mass media (Cross and Freytes Frey, 2009). Moreover, due to the progressive replacement of the Unemployed Heads of Household Plan, mobilization no longer led to accessing resources (by obtaining new 'social plans' to be implemented as 'social work' in the neighborhoods). That is the reason for a period of gradual demobilization of the picketing movements.[6]

Picketing organizations' social work in poor neighborhoods was also affected by changes in other welfare programs: for example, the reduction in the amount of food delivered to communal soup kitchens managed by them (Cross, 2009).

In this scenario, many picketing movements increased the development of productive micro-projects as a means to access additional resources. However, this proved to be a difficult endeavor. Several complications surfaced regarding the composition of the working group, the productive organization, financing and the commercialization of products (Freytes Frey, 2008). Building a cooperative organization with people characterized by highly diverse social and labor backgrounds presented special difficulties. In addition, due to Argentina's progressive economic recovery, the more educated and experienced participants tended to return to the labor market. Thus, picketing movements had to form their cooperatives with unskilled people who had little work experience or were affected by long-term unemployment. In addition, they had a shortage of technical and managerial skills. Finally, commercialization was affected by territorial segregation and isolation: the lack of adequate transportation and poor social capital restricted market opportunities. As a consequence, cooperatives experienced a high level of unpredictability as did workers' income. To sum up, these productive micro-projects were (and still are) very fragile and they presented the risk to become 'work for poor people', given the problematic working conditions, the low income and the lack of social benefits (Freytes Frey, 2008; Cross and Freytes Frey, 2009). They are increasingly unlinked to picketing movements' projects of social and political change as well as to the public struggles that characterized their initial 'epic phase' (Cross, 2008).

In summary, picketing movements reached a period of major expansion, mobilization and public visibility from 1999 to 2004. Since 2004, in Argentina's new political and economic context, they began a process of demobilization, and they experience internal divisions and downsizing. However, they did not disappear, but continued organizing the residents of poor neighborhoods, meeting their basic needs and offering political education. Furthermore, demobilization was never complete: over recent years there were sporadic demonstrations organized, specially, by organizations opposed to the government. They increased in 2008 and 2009, in the context of the local consequences of the international financial crisis. In addition, in the discussion and implementation of social policies, the government still acknowledges picketing movements (or at least some of them) as representatives of poor unemployed people.

As has just been asserted, the picketing movement is not one monolithic movement, but rather, many different organizations with diverse leadership, ideologies, strategies and structures. Our research focused on four of them, two of which (*Federación de Tierra y Vivienda* [FTV] and *Corriente Clasista y Combativa–Sector desocupados* [CCC]) have a long history of local social work: their leaders and oldest members emerged during the 1980s, due to their participation in the public land occupation processes that took place in the Buenos Aires metropolitan area. Afterwards, during the period of the movements' expansion, they have developed mechanisms to achieve national outreach. In spite of their similar origins and structures, they have different political tendencies: FTV adheres to the national popular tradition that is so strong in Argentina, while CCC has an orientation that members define as 'class-conscious'. Nevertheless, these movements on occasion have sown strategic alliances with one another. This confluence ended in 2004, since FTV is one of the strongest supporters of the federal government, while CCC has become increasingly an opponent to it. The other two organizations we studied (*Frente Popular Darío Santillán* [FPDS] and *Movimiento de Trabajadores Desocupados–Línea Varela* [MTD-LV]) were born out of the local social work performed by rank and file members–many of them of the middle class–who, without belonging to a particular political party, decided to 'go to the *barrios* (neighborhoods) with the goal of organizing them'. These two movements, originally tied by a common goal, broke away from each other in 2004 due to ideological and strategic differences (MTV-LV supported the government, FPDS did not).

The Redefinition of Feminine Roles Through Social Participation

Analyzing picketing movements from a gender perspective involves exploring how they create meanings and practices that help establish the difference between sexes. It also involves the analysis of the power relationships legitimized and reproduced through those symbolic constructions (Lamas, 1999; Scott, 1996). Moreover, we are particularly interested in examining whether or not these movements include challenging gender inequalities in their struggles for social change.

Indeed, gender inequalities are rooted in conceptions, norms, and values that contribute to their legitimization and perpetuation throughout time (Ariza and De Oliveira, 1999). Among the causes for the sexual division of labor, we find certain historically and socially constructed stereotypes that propose 'natural' and separated fields of action for males and females. If the public sphere, in all of its different expressions (work, politics, intellectual creation, etc.) has been the realm of the male during decades since the industrial revolution, the domestic sphere, along with its diverse responsibilities (maternity; care of the children, the sick, and the elderly; home economics and homemaking; affective support of the men in the family), has been the realm of the female (Collier and Yanagisako, 1987; Jelin, 1994).

Most of the women interviewed during our research mentioned having been socialized according to these traditional models of gender roles. This kind of socialization was expressed in what they were always told to do as well as in the habitual routines of family life. For example:

> It's like I always say…we were raised with one idea in mind and my grandma always repeated…'you have to get married, keep your husband, you need to take care of your daughter, do the laundry, you have to cook, you need to take care of him.' (Marcelina,[7] CCC leader, interview of 20 September 2004)

Given this orientation, the questions we wanted to address are: what effect has women's participation in the picketing movements had on these representations of female roles? What is the relationship between women's involvement in these organizations and their own conceptions about what it means to be a woman?

There are no simple answers to these questions. On the one hand, we learned from our interviewees that their involvement in the picketing movement and its social struggles was always closely tied to their performance of traditional roles (maternity and the support of their husbands or 'partners'). As we mentioned in the introduction, this is a common feature in Latin American movements formed by women (Espinosa, 2009). But over time, because of the experience of social participation, these roles acquired a new connotation. On the other hand, participation in the different work settings and mobilizations, led women to reject certain stereotypes linked to the feminine, and to challenge some aspects of the gendered division of tasks and responsibilities.

Let us examine this more closely. The female role mentioned most frequently in the interviews, and the one that was often used to legitimize other roles and activities, was the role of mother. This is most notable among the leaders and representatives who shared the same social background as the other members of the organizations. For these women, the feeding, caring for, and rearing of children appeared to be a primordial concern. And, in the circumstances of extreme economic crisis in which they lived, these responsibilities actually became–for them and for the majority of women who make up the 'foundation' of the movements–the reason that motivated their initial involvement in the communal work and in the struggle for social rights.[8] For example, as one woman stated:

> But we also had to work and do something so we wouldn't have to stay at home, to go out to work…out of need…It's difficult…so we had to come together to figure out what we could do. Because when you have little children you can't just quit. (Graciana, FTV, interview of 15 October 2004)

A second commonly mentioned role, albeit less emphasized than the first, was that of wife or companion of the man: the woman is the one who affectively supports the man during difficult times. At this point of the discussion, it is necessary to point out a significant piece of data: in three of the movements studied (FTV, CCC, and MTD-LV) some of the female leaders with the most important roles are, in fact, the wives of the principal male leaders. The female leaders in the first two organizations also have participated in the creation of 'women's space', designed to allow for discussion of the diverse set of problems that directly affect them (from the 'symbolic' obstacles to their equal participation alongside men, to matters having to do with reproductive health, family planning, domestic and sexual violence, etc.). That said, despite the important role that these women play within the movements, they continued to stress their role as the supporters and 'facilitators' of their male partner's leadership duties and activism.

In other cases but especially those of the neighborhood representatives, the role of companionship acquired a new meaning within the context of unemployment. The loss of their traditional role as the 'breadwinner' led many men to call into question their own sense of self-worth and this often resulted in a series of unsettling consequences including depression, self-blame, alcoholism, and violent attitudes. When faced with these issues, it was the women who stood up and assumed an active role in the search for solutions to the family's needs:

> I think the crisis hit us all very hard, but it affected women even more because the family suffering was twofold...We were the ones that had to be strong and fight so we could raise our husbands up from their depression. After all, a man who has worked his entire life suddenly feels that he's worth nothing, not even to collect recycling, eh? Because it's the male dignity, that macho attitude he carries inside, instead we [women] were able to overcome that and not throw our hands up in the air and say: 'I guess we'll just starve to death here inside these four walls'. (Marcelina, CCC, interview of 20 September 2004)

Here one can appreciate that both roles, mother and 'wife', are intimately connected in the interviewee's speech, and that they are related to the place of the woman in her family. At the same time, however, these roles give meaning to the new activities that women develop within the picketing movements.

In contrast, and as we had pointed out earlier, these new practices led to the questioning of other aspects of the traditional 'female' models, especially those linked to the 'confining' of women to the domestic sphere. In our interviews, the representatives and leaders tended to reject the image of womanhood that they received during their socialization process: an image defined by passivity and obedience to men, an almost exclusive devotion to the care of all family members and the responsibility for 'domestic chores'. There are a number of explanations for this rejection. First, among the leaders we interviewed, there were a few with histories of feminist activism whose work within the organizations was specifically directed towards the struggle against gender stereotypes. However, for most of our interviewees, it was their actual involvement in different spaces and activities within the picketing movements that caused them to question such long-established gender roles.

In the first place, female participation in these organizations made it possible for women to begin to step out of a strictly domestic space. Initially motivated by the need to procure the means of survival for the family–and legitimated, as we have seen, by already existing female roles–women's work in their neighborhoods led to the establishment of networks and relationships based on mutual solidarity and struggle. A shared workspace enabled the emergence of common needs and problems, and eventually allowed for the creation of the previously mentioned 'women's spaces' in three of the groups studied (FTV, CCC, and FPDS).

Furthermore, women's involvement in community labor, mobilizations, and meetings contributed to the emergence of an awareness of their own capabilities (in contrast to the previous devaluation of such): not only the ability to tackle urgent and daily neighborhood matters (clothing, food hand-outs, small productive projects), but also the capacity for organizing and for political participation. In a sense, political involvement created political competence[9] (Bourdieu, 1990): the public realm became 'an issue for women', as a consequence of their feeling 'competent' enough to get involved in these types of activities:

> women had to get involved in the picket lines, yes, but it turned out to be very beneficial for them, having to make such a serious move, right?...she now feels that she is somebody, that she is an important person as well...that she can do things, which is not the same thing as being locked-up inside four walls and believing what one has always been told: 'you're good for nothing!'...'what do you think you're going to talk about in a meeting if you don't even have any teeth?'...'how are you going to talk to the officials if you don't have any shoes?'[10] (Gloria, CCC, interview of 3 October 2004)

Lastly, in those movements that created specific spaces for the discussion of women's issues, all of the exchanges within this context (supported by the implementation of workshops and training classes in which feminist activists frequently participated) contributed to the explicit questioning of 'female' stereotypes. Participation in these spaces led women to reject gender injustices (for example, identifying the inherited division of work and roles as 'chauvinistic' and 'unjust') and to pursue the vindication of women's rights (such as reproductive rights). These activities also contributed to their conviction that they had the political aptitude to engage in a collective struggle for these rights (for instance, they started to address the problems of domestic violence in the neighborhood).

The new transformative roles assumed by women have had strong political content and have included social work in the neighborhood, participation in assemblies and other representative bodies, street demonstrations, and mobilization. However, due to the high unemployment rate that has directly affected the population studied, we identified very few changes in women's labor situation. As we have already indicated, in the period of their greatest expansion, one of the achievements of the picketing movements–directly linked to their development as social organizations–has been the granting of 'social plans' (subsidies) for their members. Such plans required their recipients to engage in certain social activities in return, which in the case of these movements, has allowed the completion of many public works in the neighborhoods, and to solve the basic needs of community members (clothing, dining halls, community vegetable gardens, productive micro-projects). It is in these kinds of activities (what we have called 'communal or social work') that women are in charge.

Nevertheless, the payment from these 'plans' affected the traditional division of roles within the home. Since their main beneficiaries were the women themselves, many of the latter became the principal providers of family income, replacing or complementing the men in this function.[11] Even if this situation was seen by both men and women as a temporary arrangement in order to endure economic crises (the general hope was that men would find employment again in the labor market), the collection of monthly subsidies permitted women to control at least a part–and often a considerable part–of the family income.

As we mentioned before, over the last five years, social policies towards poor unemployed people changed, affecting the political construction of these movements. In the last section, we will address the consequences of these transformations on women's participation, which will give us clues about the permanence and depth of the changes in gender stereotypes.

In the next section, we will examine a sensitive aspect of picketing movements: women's participation in their leadership. This will allow us to evaluate, to a certain degree, the scope of the redefinition of feminine roles that we have explored up to now.

Limits and Tensions Involved in Women's Participation: Access to Positions of Leadership

As already mentioned, women perform a fundamental role in the structure and visibility of the picketing movements, since they constitute approximately 75 percent of their membership. Nevertheless, this majority presence of women is not equally reflected in the constitution of the organizations' leadership. We believe this to be a point that underscores a significant limitation in the redefinition of the feminine roles that we discussed earlier, and for this reason, we will analyze it in depth.

Our own interviews show that there are women fulfilling leadership roles on a regional level and, to a lesser extent, on a national level.[12] But, in general, men are over-represented in such leadership positions. Moreover, the leaders with the greatest presence and recognition according to national public opinion are invariably men.

In contrast, many of the neighborhood representatives are women. In fact, the local space of the neighborhood appears to be a center of women's action, particularly in the completion and organization of the daily activities carried out by each movement (dining halls, lunch rooms, vegetable gardens, supply of clothing for the community). Such organizational endeavors, as well as the presentation of the neighborhood's needs and demands before the district and regional boards, is the work of both male and female neighborhood representatives alike.

Furthermore, we may infer from the interviews that there exists for these neighborhood representatives a whole process of legitimacy and recognition construction. The base of such construction lies precisely in representatives' work within communal spaces and on the establishment of relationships of confidence and proximity between neighbors, which stem from the resolution of concrete problems of diverse natures. In this process, we notice once again the effectiveness of the participation mechanisms that we examined earlier: involvement in specific activities of the movement (including mobilizations and assemblies) contributes to the generation of 'political competence' for many women, who little by little assume responsibilities of leadership at a neighborhood level. Their consciousness of their own abilities is reinforced by discussions and workshops carried out within the framework of the 'women's spaces', in the three organizations where such spaces exist:

> And afterwards we women say that we collaborated a great deal because of the many cases in which we have taken grasp of the situation in the movement of the unemployed, and today the women are the leaders of the neighborhood. It helped, right?...all the process we did...[at the 'women's space']. (Gloria, CCC, interview of 3 October 2004)

It is necessary to take into account that a general characteristic of the leadership of these movements is that it is based on face-to-face relationships between the leaders and the other members of the group. Thus, the neighborhood representatives as well as the leaders are people who 'can always be approached for help' in resolving a variety of problems. Their contributions range from facilitating the meeting of basic needs (food, healthcare for the sick, clothing, access to a social plan) to listening to, and mediating, conflicts between individuals, families and neighbors. As one leader said:

> It is as if I were the mother of the movement...They always find in me a person who they can chat with...I am there to listen to the claims or the needs or the suffering of our people. (Marcelina, CCC, interview of 27 September 2004)

As clearly illustrated here, the capacity for listening is linked to the 'feminine' in traditional models of gender. Thus, it is understandable that these women are able to assume the role of neighborhood representatives with relative ease, particularly with the help of the progressive security and confidence provided by their work in the communal space. Nevertheless, this 'close' and 'personal' style is also present among the leaders of the movements (even among those with principal roles in the national public sphere). But in such cases, there exists an additional quality: the strategic vision required to define the political orientation and the specific positions of the movement as a whole. Therefore it is not strange that there are so few women who make it to these upper leadership positions, for deep within many of them the idea persists that such strategic vision, like other kinds of political competence, is a 'masculine attribute':

> I will say again that it is not a question of gender. I have discussed it a couple of times with other women in other organizations, how...'the visible face is always a man'...That could be, but I say, if you want my opinion, it's not that I don't have the capacity to speak, but if the male leader develops his

> language and his style well...In order to transmit a message to society, when you're on live television, where you know that there are thousands of people watching, you have to know how to transmit what you are protesting about, and the male leader is better prepared to do that. It isn't because it's a man or a woman, I say, it's about who has the capacity to do it. So I prefer that they give those five minutes of press to the male leader so he can make the message as clear as possible...(Norma, MTD-LV, interview of 25 November 2004)

Female leaders and representatives who share a feminist ideal–whether coming from a past of previous feminist activism or influenced by the activities carried out in the 'women's spaces'–criticize the naturalization and legitimization of the gender inequalities that such beliefs imply. In effect, even if these leaders recognize that differences do exist in the political capacity of men and women, they are quick to point out that such differences are the product of unequal training and experience in the field and, therefore, such gendered differences may be eliminated through greater women's involvement in the movements and through adequate preparation.

With this in mind, these female leaders and representatives are permanently demanding greater women's participation in the leadership of the movements, noting that often the activities women perform in the organizations reproduce those accomplished in the domestic sphere (feeding, clothing and care for the children and other neighbors, primary healthcare and prevention, small productive projects designed to satisfy basic necessities). As a result, in their eyes, there exists within the picketing movements a certain logic that perpetuates the very gender stereotypes that such leaders strive to break by means of the struggle to redefine what it means to be a woman.

The persistence of such stereotypes are reflected in the tensions that various interviewees mentioned having experienced in relation to the responsibilities associated with the various roles they fulfil: tasks associated with the domestic sphere (responsibilities as a wife; care for the children, which appears to be the most difficult to delegate; general housekeeping) demand time and attention which conspire to make it difficult for women to assume a larger role within the leadership of the organizations.

> A woman who has a man in her house is already limited because attending meetings takes a lot of time...[participa-

tion] also implies the need for training...beginning to feel the predicament of going to such places, to the spaces where there is an education for the members of the movement. And this requires time, and that implies that if you have a man, the man has to be as involved as you are. But even in this case, many times he doesn't understand that a woman can also delegate the responsibility for the children to him or to another relative, and go out and educate herself. So we say 'more is permitted for men than for us'. (Susana, FPDS, interview of 11 November 2004)

Limitations on the redefinition of feminine roles are clearly evident in this statement. We note the persistence of a cultural imaginary that assigns to the woman the exclusive responsibility for the reproductive labor within the hearth. As a consequence, political participation and community tasks appear as new activities that simply are added on to the traditional female functions, generating among the leaders and representatives an overwhelming feeling of overload and exhaustion. At the same time, in cases in which both husband and wife are dedicated activists, the man's participation in the public sphere is generally prioritized, reinforcing the woman's role of nurturer and 'supporter'.

Assessing the Depth and Persistence of Change: Women's Participation During Picketing Movements' Demobilization

As we mentioned before, after a period of great expansion, mobilization and public visibility, since 2004 picketing movements experienced a process of demobilization, internal divisions and downsizing. The issue we want to address in this last section is how these developments affected women's participation and the redefinition of traditional female roles.

We have already discussed how changes in social policies influenced the daily local activities of picketing movements. In the first place, the development of productive micro-projects–a move that many groups had begun to explore as an alternative to promote employment–became more important, as a means of having access to resources. In the first experiences of such projects, women played an important role, since many of these ventures recovered their previous knowledge to develop almost artisanal productions: bakeries, jam and candy products, textiles, metal work, etc. Several of the neighborhood representatives we interviewed mentioned their participation in these types of projects, or their hope to become involved in such projects, as a way to transform their unequal situation as women, not only in the political sphere, but also in the realm of labor. However, the growing importance of such productive projects, supported by government policies, opened new discussions about female and male roles within these social movements.

As mentioned before, the accomplishment of productive activities by women was seen by many participants as a temporary arrangement in order to endure the unemployment of men, considered the family's principal 'breadwinner'. When these micro-projects were promoted as a long-term strategy, resistance against women taking a leading role in them resurged. And this resistance was evident in the interactions between men and women not only within the picketing movements, but also within each family.

As a result of these tensions, women were displaced from some kinds of productive projects, considered purely 'masculine' (e.g., cooperatives for housing and sanitation), establishing new divisions between 'male activities' and 'female activities'. Another point of conflict emerged regarding male resistance to assume as a general claim of the movement, the need to implement arrangements that allow women to work (e.g., daycare for children). Often this type of problem is referred to as 'a matter of women', which they themselves must resolve. However, women did not passively accept these differentiations, struggling to go beyond extended gender stereotypes (with different results depending on the case). Thus, the implementation of cooperative micro-projects was an opportunity to question the established representations of female participation in labor.

Second, transformations in social policies deeply affected picketing organizations' communal work in poor neighborhoods, mostly carried out by women, as previously discussed. The Female/Male Unemployed Household Heads Plan paid for these tasks (even though the pay was poor). With the new policy approach, the payment is tied to the participation in productive projects. Consequently, projects considered 'non-productive' such as community work in soup kitchens, childcare, supply of clothing, etc., appear underfunded and, at the symbolic level, devalued.

> I mean, if we all of us go to work in the cooperative project, who will take care of the soup kitchen? (Marta, FTV, interview of 15 March 2005)

However, daily community work in the neighborhoods is fundamental to secure the territorial political construction of picketing movements. That is why women often take further efforts, increasing their tasks, in order to maintain, at the same time, community work and new productive enterprises (Cross and Freytes Frey, 2009).

> We, in the neighborhood...we are very...we are always thinking in work and we organize micro-projects and other things that later are difficult to maintain over time. I don't know, today we cooked to eat early and then to go to the bridge [to a public demonstration]. And I started to ensure that cooking, I started to peel the onions...all right...Actually, I don't mind, but you are running all day long! Tuc, tuc, tuc! (Nora, MTD-Línea Varela, interview of 20 March 2005)

Nevertheless–and this is the third point we want to raise–the policy that affected women's participation the most and tested the depth of the discussed redefinition of feminine roles was the 'Families for Social Inclusion' Program. Its beneficiaries were women in charge of minor children. It replaced the *plan* (a subsidy for which beneficiaries were to perform four hours of 'social work' per day–*contraprestación*) for a new subsidy, which did not require this kind of work.

This policy was criticized by many female neighborhood representatives, who pointed out that it implies a reinforcement of gender stereotypes linked to the 'confinement' of women to the domestic sphere and to their traditional roles. Furthermore, it ignores the importance of the territorial activities accomplished by these women during the economic crisis as well as the political, organizational and managerial skills developed by them (Cross and Freytes Frey, 2009).

> The 'Families' [Program] sends you back to your home...I spent 30 years inside my home and now if I have to go back I feel suffocated. I can take care of my son's vaccination and also the soup kitchen...I don't know what they think...I don't worry about myself, because nobody's going to prevent me from continuing to deal with things here, but maybe other *compañeras* are going to leave...Besides, if I wouldn't have been forced to go out of the four walls of my house, I would still be there... and I think that the *contraprestación* was a positive thing to get the woman out of her house, the pots, the husband...And the same regarding the unemployed man, who at least had to dress and comb to go to perform the *contraprestación*, instead of being all day lying in bed...In the end, it seems as if they want

to encourage dullness, laziness... I don't know...(Andrea, FTV, interview of 13 April 2005)

This policy made women's participation in picketing movement activities more difficult, since it affected the legitimacy of such participation within the family. Indeed, the 'exit from the domestic sphere' that we have previously discussed appears in the speech of our interviewees to be extremely difficult, for it requires a true struggle within the family. There are recurring accounts of the conflicts produced by female participation in the movements: domestic violence as well as accusations and arguments that can lead to the eventual dissolution of the couple. For example, one woman told us:

There are women who tell you that they've been beaten up by their partners...and that he said to her: 'you are going to the route [to the picket] to look for a macho!!!' (Norma, MTD-LV, interview of 25 November 2004)

In this context, women's participation in the picketing movements was often legitimated, before their husbands and children, in terms of the contribution that such participation implied for the family survival. The "Families for Social Inclusion" Program undermined this kind of legitimation. Consequently, women faced further difficulties to maintain their communal activities, all the more in a scenario where men could find employment again, in many cases.

In summary, the changes in picketing movements' actions from 2004 generated new tensions regarding women's roles in them and thus tested the redefinition of traditional gender stereotypes. The demobilization affected the political construction of picketing movements, producing a general decline in the participation of both men and women. Nevertheless, these groups continued their territorial work in poor neighborhoods, drawing on the know-how accumulated in the relationship with the State and showing creativity in finding new ways of negotiating with it. In this frame, although many women left the movements, others continued to participate.

Regarding the questioning of gender stereotypes and the construction of new meanings about womanhood and female roles, the continuity of the "women's spaces" in the three groups already mentioned (FTV, CCC and FPDS) is particularly important. In their activities, women keep working to widen the scope of their involvement in the organizations' tasks; to remove symbolic and relational barriers to political participation; and to challenge the differential access to positions of leadership.

But, even more important in regard to the transformation of gender inequalities, the workshops, meetings, and training sessions constitute opportunities for reflecting and questioning deeply rooted and naturalized aspects of the social construction of sexual difference. For example, in the FPDS women's space, they are invited to denaturalize motherhood,[13] by also addressing it in terms of 'will', 'desire' and 'pleasure' and thus confronting inherited mandates (Espinosa, 2009; Partenio, 2010).

Similarly, in all the studied groups, addressing the problem of domestic violence is unavoidable. In a social context where power inequalities are very often staged physically, this issue appears as a central problem. Exchanges in workshops and meetings allow breaking the idea that such violence is a private and individual matter. Instead, it is made visible and public: by sharing their experiences, women can discover that physical violence is a reality that affects many of them and can begin to denaturalize the act of being beaten up by their male partners (Rifkin, 2008; Partenio, 2010). Solidarity networks built this way facilitate facing the problem, which is never easy. 'Women's spaces' offer emotional support as well as medical and legal assistance. They also exert pressure on the 'wifebeaters', which is important in the already discussed context of the moral significance of face-to-face relationships. In the CCC movement, this space (formally organized as an NGO under the name of 'Country's Housewives', has come to build a 'Women's House', financed by national NGOs and educational institutions. This is primarily a shelter for battered women, but it is also used for several activities for adult and adolescent women: workshops on domestic violence, educational programs and health workshops (Rifkin, 2008).

However, as Partenio (2010) states, taking Rita Segato's concepts,[14] the violence suffered by women is not only physical, but also moral: emotional abuse, such as ridicule, coercion, suspicion, daily devaluation of their skills and their activities. Women's spaces actively work to denaturalize this kind of violence in gender relationships, both within families and within the movements.

These different tasks are enriched by the convergence of participants with different social and political histories in 'women's spaces' (and, in general, in picketing organizations): women from poor neighborhoods, with or without previous political or territorial activism, and middle class women with previous social and/or feminist activism. Furthermore, the scope of the work performed in these 'spaces' has grown due to the relationships established with other expressions of the women's movement and the feminist movement.

One occasion that is particularly important to generate these links is participation in the National Women's Meetings (Cross and Partenio, 2005; Rifkin, 2008; Partenio, 2010).[15]

In brief, picketing movements keep developing different practices and discussions that intend to denaturalize the beliefs, perceptions and values which are the basis of the power inequalities between men and women in these poor neighborhoods of the Greater Buenos Aires. In this regard, our interviews show the importance that participation in them has had (and still has) for many women, not only in terms of having the possibility of 'leaving the domestic realm' and the revaluation of their capacities, but also in terms of the development of new referential frames to think about themselves and the social roles that they claim.

Conclusions

At the beginning of this chapter, we asked ourselves to what degree and in what manner women's participation in the picketing movements has generated changes in the social roles that women assume and in the way that they think about themselves. There should be no doubt that such participation has the potential to call into question some of the stereotypes surrounding 'the feminine' in which the majority of our interviewees had been socialized, particularly those that propose 'natural' and separated fields of action for males and females.

Certainly, there is continuity between the tasks associated with the domestic sphere, traditionally designated as 'feminine', and the social work that women in the movements accomplish within the communal space of the neighborhood. Nevertheless, this passage from the private to the public produces a true redefinition of such practices, giving a social dimension to personal or familial problems. The same can be said about the persistence of other features of the traditional female model (the importance assigned to the roles of mother and wife): these roles become the motivation for political participation, acquiring new connotations in the process. Moreover, it is important to note that these continuities have permitted the mass incorporation of women into the picketing movements, for such involvement would have been impossible if it had required an absolute rupture from women's previous experiences.

Furthermore, the opening up of the public sphere for women has been reinforced by their participation in movements of social struggle, a process which contributed to the generation of women's own sense of 'political competence', as manifested in the various leadership positions which our interviewees have assumed in the movements. In three of the organizations studied, women's experiences of political participation have been complemented by those lived in the 'women's spaces', where debates are formulated–often with the involvement of feminist activists–which serve explicitly to call into question gender stereotypes. But we must warn that all of this work is still in process and far from complete.

Thus, our discussion also illustrates the permanence– although on an implicit level, as 'common sense' schemes that orient concrete practices (Schutz and Luckman, 2003)–of certain 'cultural mandates' that designate women as the sole bearers of home labor. As a result, women assume new practices and responsibilities, but these only come in addition to the traditional ones. As a consequence, the gendered elements of the cultural imaginary generate, as we have seen, tensions between different roles that limit women's involvement in the movement, and above all, their participation at on the highest levels of leadership.

The demobilization of picketing movements, in the context of major changes in Argentina's socio-economic scene and in social policies, affected women's participation and, thus, tested the depth of the transformation of traditional gender roles. Even if many of them left the movements, many other continued supporting their political construction and, specially, the consolidation of 'women's spaces', as areas of struggle for gender equality.

NOTES

[1] This project was directed by Osvaldo Battistini from Centro de Estudios Laborales (CEIL-PIETTE), CONICET, Argentina and Alvaro San Sebastián from MOST-UNESCO, Argentina. It was financially and academically supported by the Individual Project 8 (IP8)/Swiss National Centre of Competence in Research North South (NCCR N/S).

[2] These expressions ('leaders' and 'neighborhood representatives') refer to two leadership positions that we found in all of the picketing movements we analyzed (despite differences in other features of their organizational structures). The leaders are those in charge of political orientation and strategic stands vis-à-vis other political actors. The neighborhood representatives are those who are responsible for a small territorial zone (the 'neighborhood' or *barrio*) and who dedicate almost all of their work-

time to the movement, and to solving the daily concerns of its members.
3   Actually, the 'picket line' had been a strategy already used in Argentina during the 1960s and 1970s. The workers organized pickets during strikes as a way to prevent their boycott by the employers (through the recruitment of temporary workers) or by some internal opponents from the trade unions.
4   The Argentina Republic is divided into 24 political districts: 23 provinces and the City of Buenos Aires (the capital of the country). Buenos Aires province is the most important: it is located in the central area of the country and has played a fundamental role in Argentina's political and economic history. Its population of 13,827,203 inhabitants represents the 38.13 percent of the country's total population (Census 2001, National Institute of Statistics and Censuses).
5   This area comprises the City of Buenos Aires and its nearer 19 districts (*partidos*) of Buenos Aires Province. It concentrates the 31.6 percent of Argentina's total population (Census 2001, National Institute of Statistics and Censuses).
6   The demobilization was never complete. Public demonstrations were led from time to time by organizations opposed to the government. But the picket line was virtually abandoned. The mobilization increased in 2008 and 2009, in the context of the local consequences of the international financial crisis.
7   The names of the interviewees are fictitious, to honor our commitment to protect confidentiality.
8   On the contrary, this kind of legitimization of their involvement in the picketing movements is not present in the discourse of female leaders with middle-class origins. Instead, they usually justify their participation as an ideological commitment (feminist activism, fight for the poor and excluded people, or both).
9   We use the concept of 'competence', as intended by Bourdieu (1990). To have competence means 'to have the right and the duty to deal with something'. But for this author, such competence is based on the social recognition of those rights and duties, associated with certain properties of the individuals. The feminine stereotypes that exclude the woman from the public sphere are, precisely, the producers of political 'incompetence', since they legitimize women's exclusion from politics not only in the eyes of the others, but also for themselves.
10 Clearly, many of our interviewees have to fight against two sources of 'political incompetence': the stereotypes linked to

womanhood, and their extreme poverty, which usually implies a lack of social recognition.

[11] Actually, in nuclear families, there was a sort of sexual division of labor regarding the *plans*. They were usually collected by the woman, since the man was preoccupied with looking for opportunities of employment in the informal labor market (Cross, 2008).

[12] Only FTV and CCC, the largest and oldest of the picketing movements studied, have national representatives or leaders. In contrast, FPDS and MTD-LV have a logic of political construction more focused on the local level (even though FPDS has developed coordinating efforts that articulate the experiences of diverse territorial areas).

[13] Drawing on many poststructuralist and feminist authors, we use the verb 'denaturalize' to refer to the questioning of the natural character of social phenomena such as motherhood or gender differences. The incorporation of perception schemes (through socialization) that leads to appreciate certain forms of conduct as 'natural' is one of the most important mechanisms of social reproduction (Bourdieu, 1980). Therefore, a central aspect of social change is this process of "denaturalization" through social critique.

[14] Segato, Rita Laura (2003) *Las estructuras elementales de la Violencia. Ensayos sobre género entre la antropología, el psicoanálisis y los derechos humanos.* Buenos Aires: Universidad Nacional de Quilmes/Prometeo. Quoted by Partenio (2010).

[15] The National Women's Meetings are largely self-convened and autonomous three-day gatherings, which are conducted every year since 1986, alternately in different cities of Argentina. Women from various organizations and movements participate in workshops, demonstrations and other activities.

REFERENCES

Ariza, M. and De Oliveira, O. (1999) 'Inequidades de género y clase, algunas consideraciones analíticas', *Revista Nueva Sociedad* 164: 70-78.

Bourdieu, P. (1990) 'Cultura y política', in *Sociología y Cultura*, pp. 251-64. Mexico: Grijalbo.

Bourdieu, P. (1980) *Le Sens Pratique.* Paris: Les Éditions de Minuit.

Castel, R. (1997). *La metamorfosis de la cuestión social.* Buenos Aires: Editorial Paidós.

CELS (Centro de Estudios Legales y Sociales) (2003) *Plan Jefes y Jefas: Derecho Social o Beneficio sin Derechos. Documento de Trabajo N° 4*. Buenos Aires: CELS.

Collier, J. and Yanagisako, S. (1987) *Gender and Kinship. Essays Toward a Unified Analysis*. Stanford: Stanford University Press.

Cross, M.C. (2004) 'La Federación de Tierra y Vivienda de la CTA: El sindicalismo que busca representar a los desocupados', in O. Battistini (ed.) *El trabajo frente al espejo. Continuidades y rupturas en los procesos de construcción identitaria de los trabajadores*, pp. 291-309. Buenos Aires: Prometeo Libros.

Cross, M.C. (2008) *Luchas, prácticas asociativas y procesos de vinculación política en la zona metropolitana de Buenos Aires: Estudio de casos en cinco organizaciones territoriales vinculadas a la FTV*. PHD Thesis. Buenos Aires: Universidad de Buenos Aires.

Cross, M.C. (2009) 'Análisis de la conformación del campo político a partir de las expresiones de la cuestión social en la Argentina entre 2001 y 2007', *9° Congreso Nacional de Estudios del Trabajo* Buenos Aires: Asociación Argentina de Estudios del Trabajo.

Cross, M.C. and Freytes Frey, A.C. (2009) 'Políticas sociales como límite y como herramienta: Reflexiones a partir de experiencias de gestión de dirigentes y referentes piqueteros/as en el período 2001-2007', *Revista El Príncipe*, 1:75-98.

Cross, M.C. and Partenio, F. (2005) 'The Construction and Meaning of Women's Spaces in Organizations for the Unemployed', *Conference on Women and Globalization,* San Miguel de Allende: Center for Global Justice. Available at http://www.globaljusticecenter.org/ papers2005/cross_partenio_eng.htm.

Espinosa, C. (2009) 'Cuando una mujer avanza, ningún hombre retrocede o, ¿hasta dónde llega la "ideología de la armonía"?', *IX Congreso Argentino de Antropología Social*, Misiones.

Freytes Frey, A.C. (2008) 'Los emprendimientos autogestivos como política frente al desempleo: experiencias, dificultades y desafíos en los movimientos piqueteros del conurbano bonaerense', in A. Soto (ed.) *Flexibilidad laboral y subjetividades. Hacia una comprensión psicosocial del empleo contemporáneo*, pp. 311-335. Santiago: LOM Ediciones/Universidad Alberto Hurtado.

Freytes Frey, A.C. and Cross, M.C. (2007) 'Movimientos piqueteros: alcances de su construcción política'. *Revista Política y Cultura* 27: 121-141.

Jelin, E. (1985) 'Otros silencios, otras voces: el tiempo de la democratización en la Argentina', in F. Calderón G. (ed.) *Los movi-*

mientos sociales ante la crisis. México: UNU-CLACSO-INSU-NAM.
Jelin, E. (1994) 'Familia: crisis y después...', in C. Wainerman (ed.) *Vivir en familia.* Buenos Aires: UNICEF/Losada.
Lamas, M. (1999) 'Usos, dificultades y posibilidades de la categoría género', *Papeles de Población* 21:147-178.
Schutz, A. and Luckman, T. (2003) *Las estructuras del mundo de la vida.* Buenos Aires: Amorrortu.
Partenio, F. (2010) 'Género y participación política: los desafíos de la organización de las mujeres dentro de los movimientos piqueteros en Argentina', in B. Levy y N. Gianatelli (coords.) *Las deudas abiertas de América Latina y el Caribe*, Buenos Aires, Consejo Latinoamericano de Ciencias Sociales (CLACSO). In press.
Rifkin, D. (2008) 'Amas de Casa del País: los sentidos de la reproducción social en el espacio público', *IV Congreso Iberoamericano de Estudios de Género*, Rosario.
Scott, J. (1996) 'El género: una categoría útil para el análisis histórico", in M. Lamas (comp.) *El género: la construcción cultural de la diferencia sexual*, pp. 265-302. México: Miguel Ángel Porrúa/PUEG.
Svampa y Pereyra (2003) *Entre la Ruta y el Barrio: La experiencia de las organizaciones piqueteras.* Buenos Aires: Biblos.
Svampa y Pereyra (2006) 'La política de los movimientos piqueteros', in F. Schuster et al. (comps.) *Tomar la palabra. Estudios sobre la protesta social y acción colectiva en la Argentina contemporánea*, pp. 343-364. Buenos Aires: Prometeo Libros.

CHAPTER 10

The Feminization of Poverty in Post-Apartheid South Africa

A Story Told by the Women of Bayview, Chatsworth

Saranel Benjamin-Lebert
Independent Researcher

ABSTRACT

The adoption of neoliberal economic policies by South Africa as it entered into its democratic era, resulted in thousands, if not millions, of poor South Africans plummeting deeper into poverty. The same people who found themselves poor under apartheid, found themselves caught in a cycle of poverty that seemed to be worsening in democratic South Africa. With the privatization of basic services, many South Africans have found that they have no access to water, electricity, or health care and that they are now being evicted from their homes. This chapter tells the story of an urban community in South Africa which is home to one of the community organizations, the Bayview Flat Residents Association, that gave rise to the first wave of community struggles against evictions in post-apartheid South Africa. These struggles and the Bayview Flat Residents Association, have been led by poor, black, urban women who continue to bear the burden of poverty.

Keywords: South Africa, feminism, activism, social movements, poverty, neoliberalism

Introduction

The day democracy dawned in South Africa, a bright light shone on a country that had spent over 300 years in darkness. At the Southern most tip of the African continent, South Africa was held prisoner to 'the dismal socio-economic legacy of five systemic periods of white political domination and economic exploitation' (Terreblanche, 2002:371) that spanned 350 years. The year 1994 was seen as a turning point away from political and economic oppression to freedom and democracy. After the first democratic elections in 1994, millions of South Africans turned to the first democratic government to fulfil their promises of a better life for all.

The story of post-apartheid South Africa was supposed to be a happy one, filled with anecdotal accounts of how life got better for the majority of people living in the new democracy. However, since the beginning of 2005, poor communities in urban townships all across South Africa have risen in protests.[1] Most of the protestors have been women and youth. The protests were an angry, desperate articulation of their frustration of living in worsening poverty: their pleas were for proper housing, water and electricity. The government wondered why the protesters didn't have the patience to wait for the delivery of basic services.[2] Most had already been waiting their entire lives. As of March 2010, community protests still rage on in response to the lack of services delivery.

These scenarios are prevalent in most of the provinces in South Africa. The situation in the Western Cape is replicated in townships in Gauteng, Eastern Cape, Free State and Kwazulu-Natal. It is no different for the people living in Bayview, an impoverished community of 32,000 people, nestled in the inner recesses of a middle- to upper-income Indian township called Chatsworth. Just 20 minutes from the city centre, a community of people in Bayview live in dilapidated government-owned flats. Most have their electricity and water reconnected illegally after the state disconnected them for non-payment and almost all of them live in fear of being evicted from their homes. The majority of the people living in the flats are unemployed without any possibility of getting another job. Almost all of them say that their economic situation worsened after 1996.

This chapter has six parts: Part I introduces the reader to Chatsworth, the area in which Bayview is located and where this study took place; Part II introduces the phenomenal women who participated in this study and whose stories I am trying to tell with sensitivity and respect; Part III looks at poverty during apartheid and the impact that apartheid measures had on the lives of the women in Bayview; Part IV examines the post-apartheid democratic government's shift in economic policy to embrace neoliberal economic policy and the failure of the state to deliver basic services in post-apartheid South Africa due to the constraints created by that policy; Part V examines the impact these shifts have had on poor women in Bayview and the struggles they engage in to survive; and finally, Part VI examines the organization of poor communities into community movements, which have given strength and courage to people who are being pushed to the outer reaches of humanity.

Methodology

The Bayview Flat Residents Association (BFRA) is a community movement that emerged in 1999 and is located in government-owned flats of Bayview, Chatsworth. This organization has been chosen because in contrast to all other community movements that make up social movements nationally, the executive has a membership of 12, with 11 of these members being women. Faced with the looming prospect of their needs and demands being ignored, the BFRA launched a series of challenges against the local municipality. The struggles in Bayview against evictions, relocations, water and electricity disconnections reached a high point in 2000 when a violent clash erupted between the state machinery and a community protesting the evictions. This sparked off sites of resistance all over the country giving rise to social movements in three different provinces as people organized themselves into the Concerned Citizen's Forum (Kwazulu-Natal), Anti-Eviction Campaign (Western Cape) and the Anti-Privatisation Forum (Gauteng).

Michael Buroway asked a basic question as he addressed the division of labour: Why do workers work?[3] The prescient question, used as the basis of Sharad Chari's (2004:76) work in *Fraternal Capital*, forced Chari to answer this question through the use of ethnography. Applying the same principle to this research project, the question 'Why do women act?' in its simplest and basic form, required me, as the researcher to engage in a style of research that had as its central objective the desire 'to understand the social meanings and activities of people in a given 'field' or setting' (Brewer, 2000:11). At the same time, while trying to understand the experiences of the people under study, it became important 'to tell the stories using the concepts and experiences of the people being researched rather than our own' (Boas quoted in Pelto and Gretel, 1978:69) so that meaning is not imposed externally on them (Brewer, 2000:10). Thus, in this research, women were investigated as 'real, material subjects of their collective histories' (Mohanty, 2003:19).

This chapter is based on an ethnographic study of the community of women who live in the Bayview flats.[4] The stories were collected between 2004 and 2005 with the assistance and participation of the women themselves with whom I met once a week over a six-month period. We alternated the venue each week so that all of the women had the opportunity to host the meeting in their homes. The discussions were focused on broad themes with a few guiding questions that changed each time we met. Though we began with about ten women, it seemed that every week a new woman joined the group to tell her story. For many in the room, being able to give voice to their experiences was very liberating.

They talked about their conditions of life before apartheid was abolished and their feelings of being trapped in a cycle of poverty. They talked about how things spiralled out of control after 1996 when the democratic government introduced its neoliberal macro-economic policy for the nation, and the strategies they employed in order to make sure their families did not go hungry. Thus, they discussed their daily battles against a patriarchal State that increasingly, through its austere neoliberal economic policies, had feminized poverty in post-apartheid South Africa. In addition, they talked about their resistance to victimization by their intimate partners. That is, they discussed how, on an interpersonal level, they also struggled daily against oppression and violence from abusive husbands and partners. In other words, the women of the Bayview Flats have had to confront patriarchy on two levels since the patriarchal structure of the State, which subordinates and impoverishes women, is replicated in their families and experienced within their homes.

In spite of the fact that the burden of day-to-day survival falls on the shoulders of the women in the household, these women have dedicated their time to this research project and have spoken candidly about their struggle to survive. They are not perfect women: they have their moments of racial discrimination, backbiting, and bitterness, but through it all they have remained generous, soul-searching women with dreams of someday living a better life. They are mothers, wives, sisters, and activists. All are unemployed, all are living on state grants, and all are struggling to put food on the table.

I have been very humbled by this experience, to sit in the homes of these women and be a witness to their extraordinary existence. It has made me excruciatingly aware of my position of privilege as a middle-class woman working in the elite space of a university. I am therefore conscious of my place in this group of women and write this chapter with profound respect for how they manage their daily lives.

PART I: *The Poors of Chatsworth*[5]

Chatsworth lies about 40 km outside of the central business district of Durban. It was set up in the 1950s as a township within the apartheid framework of the Group Areas Act. Through this Act '... thousands of Indians from all over Durban were corralled into [this] ten square kilometre precincts south of Durban' (Desai, 2000:13)– just as many Africans were also shepherded out of the city to the peripheries of Durban. This was all in keeping with the racial segregation policies of apartheid.

The townships, like Chatsworth, were where poor, black people were sent to live out their 'sordid existence' (Ginwala, in Desai, 2000:19). The residents of Chatsworth were working-class people, who struggled to cope with the payment of rent, electricity, water and providing food for their families. Their payments far exceeded the monies they earned as wages. This was how life played itself out in Chatsworth under apartheid. The fear of not being able to provide food for their families was further exacerbated by the fear of being evicted from their homes. Many had their water and lights disconnected for non-payment.

Today, 55 years later, Chatsworth looks different. It is no longer the vestige of working-class poor Indian people. In fact, if you drive along the never-ending highway that runs through Chatsworth you would be forgiven for thinking that this is the home of rich, well-to-do Indians. The pockets of poverty are hidden away from the public eye, so much so that the existence of the 'poors' is easily denied. From the 1970s onwards, a concerted effort was made to strategically place the middle-class areas of Chatsworth in ways that would hide the 'poors'. According to Desai, '[t]hese pockets of affluence served as a cover for the socio-economic degeneration' (2000:23) that was becoming pervasive in the hidden recesses of the township.

Inside Chatsworth is an area called Bayview. It has a total population of approximately 32,000. According to the Census 2001 results,[6] most of the households (21.5 percent) in this area had an annual household income between R38 401 and R76 800 (R3200–R6400 per month) making this area a lower to middle-income group. On either side of this indicator lie the rich and the poor: only 21 percent of the households have an income higher than R76 800. However, the majority of households (4,767 households or 58 percent) earn below R38 401 per annum. Over half of the households in Bayview are surviving on less than R3200 per month.

Of the 32,000 people living in Bayview, 40 percent have no employment. The statistics also show that in 2001, there were still over 2,000 households in the area that did not have direct access to water in their homes but were accessing water from a tap in the yard, or from a community stand, spring, rain tank, or the river, or buying water from a water vendor. They also show that there were still 348 households that did not have access to any form of sanitation and 159 households were using pit latrines. The remaining 120 households had flush septic tanks, chemical toilets or a bucket latrine. In addition there were still households that did not have access to electricity–519 households were lit by candles. Since 1996, there has been a 63 percent increase in the number of households using candles.

The Bayview flats, however, is a reflection of the impact of poverty at a very micro level. The Institute for Black Research (IBR) conducted a socio-economic survey of the Bayview flats in June 1999.[7] This study investigated the socio-economic living conditions of 504 households. It found that the vast majority (76 percent) of those living in the flats were living below the poverty line with 62 percent of the households surviving on R800 or less per month. The unemployment rate was 57.9 percent and 41 percent of the households survived off welfare grants.

As a result of these characteristics, the municipality categorizes Bayview as a lower to middle-income community in a fairly well resourced area in terms of access to basic services. But Desai (2000: 4) describes these flats differently:

> At the very bottom of the ridge, where a valley is formed, the semi-detached flats mutate into huge, bulky tenement blocks, containing 6 families a piece. Here the poorest of the people of Chatsworth have been put to live and die. These are the proverbial third class coaches of the apartheid train; cramped, ugly, unsafe and hidden from view.

Within Bayview itself, just by looking at the data, it is evident that there is a large number of families living in abject poverty with neither electricity nor in-house water and struggling to cope with unemployment. These families are most likely to be found living in the flats they rent from the government. They are crammed away on hillsides and in valleys unseen, divorced from the rest of existence.

PART II: The Women on the Bayview Flats

'To stand up and be a very strong woman and be very brave to actually stand up and be counted and to still take care of your family, it's a struggle'.[8]

At the first focus group that was held in 2004, seven women crammed into a one-bedroom flat. The session was called 'Establishing Identities' to ascertain where these women were in terms of how they saw themselves. Their stories were filled with sadness, some with regret and there were also moments of joy and happiness.

Julie was 27 years old. She was unemployed. She moved to Bayview 16 years ago and lived with her mother, brother and sister-in-law. Julie said it has been hard for her to get a decent job. Her mum and dad worked so she had to take care of her siblings. She had taken odd jobs just to work and has worked in a clothing company and in a warehouse. Since she joined the BFRA committee she had been exposed to many training workshops such as HIV workshops, a research training programme or whatever came her way and because of this she was able to qualify for the Centre for Civil Society's research grant. This also gave her exposure to other research work. Also after all of the training, she has come out of her shell and knows that there might just be a better job out there for her. In December 2009, Julie passed away. She was only 32 years old.

Queenie has been living in Bayview for the past 10 years. She has two children and is married. She is currently unemployed although she occasionally gets some work as a cook or a caterer. Her husband is alcohol-dependent and sometimes comes home having spent all the money on alcohol. On those days she has to make do with what they have. Her biggest struggle is putting food on the table and keeping her children in school. Joining the committee has changed her life. For her, the members of the committee are the people she has confided in and talked to about her problems. She also feels that she can get away from her problems by attending the evening seminars.

Sweetie has been living in the Bayview area for the past 17 years since 1987. She has two teenage children. Her son is married and her daughter has turned 21. She also has adopted four children whom she puts through school. Sweetie is currently unemployed. She used to work in a warehouse as a quality controller but she lost her job when the company underwent retrenchments. Since then she has found it difficult to get any kind of formal employment. Instead, she sells odd things from time to time. She has endured an abusive relationship with a husband who was addicted to alcohol and drugs. He used to beat her and her two children. Sweetie is now divorced. She said that she used to be introverted opting to stay by herself and not interact with anyone. She sometimes felt suicidal. But since she joined the committee there is more for her to do. She has gotten to meet other people, talk about the suffering they are going through and to know that their suffering is the same as hers.

At the age of 22, Shantal was the youngest in the committee. She is a bubbly, energetic girl, filled with optimism and hope. Shantal completed her matric (Grade 12) but has not been able to get her results from the school because she had not paid her school fees as there was no money. She cannot get a job without those certificates from her school. She also cannot get into any tertiary institution without proof of completing her matric. It has been her dream to become a nurse. Shantal said she was a 'child' when she joined the committee and it was only afterwards that she realised that people were really suffering and that she wanted to do something about it. She said 'when I think about myself I feel happy because I know other people are feeling happy because of us'. She said that they have been able to give water to those who had their water cut-off and have done the same with electricity. They have also been able to put people back in their homes after evictions.

Sally lost her husband in 1999, five years before we started meeting. She does not work anymore because she broke her leg and has not been able to work again. She has a 21-year-old son who used to work for the municipality until he lost his job a year ago due to retrenchments. He had taken over his father's job working for the department of parks and gardens cutting the trees. Sally was 18 when she married her husband who was 15 years older than she. She married him because her family was so poor and he had money and could take care of her and her family. For Sally, the committee is a place she can talk about her problems. In the committee, the women can get together and sort out problems.

Annie studied to be a nurse. She was married and had two children. She divorced her husband because he was cheating on her. She met another man who turned out to be addicted to drugs. To feed his habit he forced her into prostitution, beating her relentlessly if she did not want to go out on the streets. Annie said her choices were either not having a home for her children or going out onto the streets. She was severely depressed and could hardly get through a sentence without bursting into tears. Annie was knocked over by a taxi and suffered severe injuries. She cannot work and is therefore forced to continue prostituting, as she has no other means to survive.

Shirley is a single mother of four children. She started working when she was 15 years old. Shirley said that she came from a very poor background. She said it has been very difficult to raise her children. She worked in clothing companies until those factories started retrenching. Shirley takes on odd jobs to get by. She was married to 'a very violent man' who was addicted to drugs. His public humiliation of her reduced her to nothing, she says. But after joining the committee, Shirley has been outspoken, provocative and strong. She has represented the committee at a number of national workshops. Her main objective at the moment is raising her four children.

Over the six months that the group met before I wrote the first article about them, we talked about who they were in the society and what factors made their lives easier or made their lives insufferable. We also talked about poverty and the cycle they have found themselves in before and after democracy, and we talked about the strategies they were forced to adopt in order to survive.

PART III: The Logic of Poverty During Apartheid

'I think people were more afraid of the white government'.[9]

Apartheid South Africa was structured socially, politically and economically along racial lines. Through the creation of separate systems of operation, including the structure of the economy, larger and wider income disparities existed and functioned in a way that served to racialize South African society. This economic disparity between the races was further entrenched systemically through political and legislative measures resulting in the black majority of the population being ghettoized, politically, socially and economically. Black townships were increasingly marginalized in terms of infrastructural development, access to basic services, educational opportunities, housing and jobs.[10] In other words, poverty has been institutionalized and as a result South Africa has one of the highest Gini Co-efficients in the world (Saul, 2002). The translation of these measures was the development of a system that served to protect and keep secure the interests of the minority white population at the expense of the black majority who were systematically disposed from their land, resources, wealth and jobs.

In his historical analysis of the South African economy, Terreblanche observes that the structure of the apartheid economy created a situation that served the interest of white capital (Terreblanche, 2002). An elite group of white businesses developed a pact with the Afrikaner governments during the apartheid era that saw the structure and system of the South African economy being twisted and convoluted to serve the interests of this elite group. This system and the structure of the economy have remained unchanged in the post-apartheid era.

The old apartheid structure of the economy had a direct impact on the structure and workings of the labour market. The creation of a steady supply of cheap, unskilled labour into mining, manufacturing and farming assisted white-owned industries to develop and amass large profits. It also allowed for the creation of policies and legislation that developed the architecture for the apartheid landscape. These policies and pieces of legislation were designed to push black people onto the periphery of social, political and economic existence creating a cesspool of poverty and at the same time creating an abundant flow of wealth to a minority group.

The insidious nature of apartheid and its objective of dehumanizing black people has had an enormous impact, holistically, on the lives of black people. Also racial segregation and economic deprivation combined with patriarchy has had a staggering impact on the lives of millions of black women. For many poor black women it meant living on the periphery: economically, politically and also in the labour market. The denial of proper education through apartheid and being wrenched out of school to take care of siblings or to earn more money for their poverty-stricken families resulted in many black women being pushed into unskilled, low-paying jobs as domestic servants or in factories.

Sweetie remembered having to leave school when she was 13 years old. She said that her family had no money and she was taken out of school to earn extra money for the family. Those dark days of poverty under apartheid saw Sweetie, as a 13-year-old girl, washing clothes for middle-class women across the railway tracks that divided the rich from the poor in Chatsworth. She did this for two years until she got a job in a clothing factory. She had no qualifications, no skills, but needed the job even though the pay was bad. Sweetie remembered:

> *When I left school I was too young to get a job in a factory so I had to wash clothes for other people. If you had to wash clothes to make some money then you have to do it. Sometimes the ladies you washed clothes for gave you old clothes, food.* (Focus Group 1, 26 May 2005)

Sally also recalled having to drop out of school at age 12 because her family didn't have money and could not manage. She had no shoes or clothes to wear. She would have to wait until she was 18 years old to taste her first chocolate.

The differential treatment of the white and black races was pervasive in all aspects of life. From the provision of education, where people could live and where they could go, the jobs they were given access to, the kind and amount of welfare they received right through to the provision of basic services, were all calculated and implemented in ways that would secure the interests of the white population at the expense of black communities. However, whilst McDonald (2002) acknowledges that the apartheid state, no matter how schizophrenic it was, did subsidize the delivery of basic services such as water, electricity, houses and education, black people still experienced the harshness of the state in the form of evictions and water cut-offs:[11]

> *There were lots of people who were evicted at that time [during apartheid]. If you were evicted, and like I said we didn't have a committee then, people would have to stay outside until they arranged their monies to pay to get back into their houses. It happened to my neighbour...Remember [the community] gave them a massive tent. The municipality threw all their furniture outside in their yard and they had this big tent with all their furniture under and they used to stay there.* (Sweetie, Focus Group 3)

Julie remembers her family's experience of having their electricity disconnected during the days of apartheid:

> *It happened to us twice and once we made it to pay it the same day. They cut it in the morning and I phoned my mother and somehow she borrowed the money and went straight to the department and paid it...so they came and connected it the same day. But there was another time we couldn't get the money and we couldn't pay and we had to spend the night without lights.* (Julie, Focus Group 3)

The violence of state repression instilled fear in black communities. It divided communities and made people fearful of each other. Organizing people into groups that could act collectively was difficult. The building of trust within communities was not an easy task because the state was all seeing, all knowing, everywhere. Families were torn apart by the persecutory nature of the state: people were hauled out of their homes in the middle of the night, and tortured in prison for information. Some never returned home. Today, the non-delivery of basic services by the democratic state is met with resistance from communities in the form of illegal reconnections of disconnected water and electricity. This is a form of contemporary activism rooted within the new social movements. But back then, during the dark days of apartheid, people were terrified to reconnect their disconnected water or electricity even though it meant just lifting a switch:

> *I remember the guys around here saying to my mum and dad, 'It's just a switch!' And that time they had wooden doors at the meter room and they could just open it. They said, 'It's just a switch', and they'll put it up for us and we'll have lights and the next day we can go pay the lights because by then we would have the money. My mother refused and my dad refused. They said, 'No way! No!' Because if we put it on and someone sees...if the neighbours know that the lights are cut and then someone sees that the lights are on we will get into trouble. And we were so scared. My mother was saying, 'they are going to lock us up'.* (Julie, Focus Group 3)

> *People were very scared of the community then. People never had the freedom to talk.* (Shirley, Focus Group 3)

The apartheid state used the strategy of divide and rule to dislocate black people into their individual identities of Coloured, Indian and African where

> the inequalities of the system were distributed unevenly amongst the black population...Indian and Coloured workers also had greater and easier access to the resources necessary for enhanced mobility within the system, resulting in growing middle classes in both these groups by the 1970s. (McKinley and Veriavia, 2005:13)[12]

However, the social security system that was set up from the 1970s onwards to assist the development of an Indian and Coloured middle class also served as the only life line for impoverished communities. In Bayview, the women talk about life before 1994 and see those years, despite the darkness of apartheid, as golden years: a time in their lives when they could actually afford to pay for their rent, electricity and water and still be able to put food on the table:

> *Majority of [the community] used to pay their rental because they used to collect that big amount of grant...we could make it to pay.* (Julie, Focus Group 3)

It was very hard. The only time I put my lights back on was when my first grant came through. I could manage. (Shirley, Focus Group 3)

That time [during apartheid] people could survive, could pay their rent. People had grants to help them... That time when we had the white government you could pay school fees of up to 50 cents per month. Then you got schoolbooks and stationery. And your children weren't chased out of school because they couldn't pay or if they didn't have school shoes. (Sweetie, Focus Group 3)

Black people living under apartheid suffered enormously, living in fear, humiliation and poverty. They also gave their lives to the struggle to free themselves from the shackles of apartheid. This struggle was not just for political freedom and the chance to vote. It was also a struggle to right the wrongs of the past, to give to all the black people the spoils of the land so that there would not be poverty, that everyone would have a job, a roof over their heads and food on the table. That is what the African National Congress (ANC) promised the millions of oppressed black people on the eve of the very first democratic elections in 1994. And millions believed that they would deliver on the promise and so they voted in their millions securing for the ANC, a majority hold of the government.

PART IV: Neoliberalism in Post-apartheid South Africa

'They [ANC] promised so many things to the poor just to get the vote. We voted for that better life. But now we are still waiting'.[13]

The ANC's 1994 national election campaign was premised on not just delivering democracy and freedom to the citizens of South Africa but it was also rooted strongly in the memory of apartheid's denial of basic resources to black people. The Reconstruction and Development Programme (RDP)[14]–the ANC's proposed economic plan for the post-liberation era–promised to right the wrongs of the past and to give to the people what they had long been denied. Election posters blazing with the black, green and gold colours of the Party screamed out to the poor: 'A better life for all!', 'Free basic services!', 'Jobs for all!' promising to redistribute the wealth accumulated by the apartheid government, white businesses and the white population. The poor believed the rhetoric and millions voted in the ANC as the first democratic government.

Today, the poor, like Julie (quoted above), claim they were duped by the ANC just so they could get into power. As Sweetie puts it: 'The only good thing that the black government (ANC) did was abolish apartheid' (Focus Group 3).

The ANC party's decision to turn away from its former redistributive stance to one that strongly embraced neoliberalism happened early on in the transition period.[15] The negotiated settlement of the transition talks focused more on what the macro-economic policy was going to look like and what stake in the country's economy big business would have. According to Saul (2002:8):

> the relative ease of the political transition was principally guaranteed by the ANC's withdrawal from any form of genuine class struggle in the socioeconomic realm and the abandonment of any economic strategy that might have been expected directly to service the immediate material requirements of the vast mass of desperately impoverished South Africans.

The ANC's capitulation to the charms of a market-driven economy saw the party ditch clauses in the Freedom Charter and the RDP to emerge with a macro-economic policy that was 'a fairly standard neoliberal one' (Habib and Padayachee, 2000:3). The choice of a market-driven policy that would ensure maximum profit accumulation of those already rich was made by the ANC with the full knowledge that in South Africa,

> the poorest 60% of household's share of total expenditure is a mere 14%, while the richest quintile's share is 69% and where, across the decade of the nineties, a certain narrowing of the income gap between black and white (as a growing number of blacks have edged themselves into elite circles) has been paralleled by an even greater widening of the gap between rich and poor. (Saul, 2002:8)

Although the capitulation to big business happened early on in the transition phase, the announcement and implementation of the ANC government's macro-economic policy, the Growth Employment and Redistribution (GEAR) policy was only in 1996. Former president, Nelson Mandela, announced in one of the national newspapers that the new economic policy for the country had 'not a single reference to things like nationalization, and this is not accidental. There is not a single slogan that will connect us with any Marxist ideology' (Marais, 2001:122).

The focus of GEAR was centrally located in the main tenets of neoliberalism as instituted globally with the main objective being to create an environment that enabled maximum private investment. Hence GEAR proposed cuts in government spending to reduce the deficit, tax concessions for big business, reduction of tariff barriers (in the clothing, textile, leather and car manufacturing industries), privatization of government assets (which included the provision of basic services), reduction in state welfare programmes and a more flexible labour market. Adelzadeh (in Marais, 2001:163) and Saul both agree that the ANC had 'come, full circle, back to the late apartheid government's Normative Economic Model. For the central premise of South Africa's economic policy now could scarcely be clearer: ask not what capital can do for South Africa but what South Africa can do for capital...' (Saul, 2002:12).

The ANC government's embracing of neoliberalism and giving capital the run of the economy within the same economic structure as during apartheid did nothing for the poor black person. Instead, it facilitated the same process that had been used by the Afrikaaner Nationalist Party to create an Afrikaaner bourgeoisie. The only difference was that the ANC set out to create a black bourgeoisie. *The Economist* writes:

> Though black incomes are barely a sixth of white ones, a black elite is rising on the back of government jobs and the promotion of black business. It is moving into the leafy suburbs, such as Kelvin and Sandton, and adopting the outward symbols of prestige–the BMW, swimming pool, golf handicap and black maid–that so mesmerize status-conscious whites. (cited in Saul, 2002:15)

The push for GEAR from the ANC's side was that GEAR could achieve economic growth, attract foreign direct investment, boost employment and increase socio-economic equality. The verdict thus far has been resoundingly negative:

> GEAR has been associated with massive deindustrialization and job shedding through reduced tariffs on imports, capital flight as controls over investments are relaxed, attempts to downsize the costs and size of the public sector, and real cuts in education, health and social welfare spending. (Saul, 2002:13)

This neoliberal economic framework adopted by the ANC government precludes the development of any form of social security system for the growing band of unemployed, informal sector workers and the poor. GEAR argues for a decline in state expenditure. An examination of the budget allocation shows that a greater decline took place in social assistance grants (pensions, old-age homes, children's feeding schemes, the child support grant) whilst spending on defence budgets increased (Benjamin, 2001).

PART V: The Lived Experience of the Poor

'Everyday is a struggle...You wake up in the morning and you wonder where that meal is going to come from'.[16]

The harsh effects of the GEAR policy have been felt most by those who came into the era of democracy already poor. Most were black, working-class women, both urban and rural. GEAR has left the poor more vulnerable to increasing poverty and most workers debilitated and unemployed due to deindustrialization.

Unemployment

Despite the fact that GEAR was sold to the public on the basis that it would create jobs and thus assist in the alleviation of poverty, the neoliberal nature of the policy and its saddling up to the market has resulted in a massive haemorrhaging of low skilled and unskilled jobs.

The consequences of the GEAR policy saw formal employment decline by about 12%, between 1993 and mid 1998 (Carter and May, 1999:12) The loss of jobs was highest in those sectors that largely unemployed unskilled labour, with the manufacturing sector suffering a 6% loss in jobs between 1993 to 1998, compared to 21% in construction and 27% in mining (ibid). By 2005, unemployment in South Africa was at its highest with just over 40 % of the population unemployed (Bhorat and Kanbar, 2005:5). Not only were people losing their jobs, but young people and graduates were also finding it difficult to obtain employment. By 2002, unemployment had gone up to 41.8 percent (Kingdon and Knight, 2004:4). These rates include those who have never worked before and who are looking for jobs. Within this context of growing unemployment, the larger proportion of those unemployed are women. In 1999, 56 percent of the unemployed were women (Kehler, 2001:2).

The decimation of industries took place through the reduction of trade tariffs in industries that employed large numbers of poor semiskilled and unskilled black women workers. For example, the clothing, textile and leather industries in which women workers are the majority, shed 17,000 jobs in 2004 with 3,100 being lost since the beginning of 2005.[17] The rate of job losses in this sector has been on an upward projection. The car component manufacturing sector loses on average about 13,000 jobs per year. And the reduction in subsidies for agriculture has caused the deterioration of this sector.

Julie's mother works in a clothing factory. She lives every day with the fear that it may be her last day in the factory. Julie says that the factory goes on short time[18] a lot recently and during those times the family has to *'borrow [money] and then [her mother] has to pay it back and it's just to have a meal for that week that we are at home'* (Julie, Focus Group 1, 26 May 2005). Most of the women in Bayview provided a steady stream of cheap labour to the clothing, textile and leather industries that are located close to Chatsworth. But this soon came to an end. The destruction of the clothing industry happened almost overnight when the GEAR policy allowed for the tariffs in the clothing, textile and leather industries to be reduced faster than the rate expected by the GATT agreement. The result was almost instantaneous:

> *Now that we are open for imports and exports, it has made things so difficult. Factories are closing down, people are losing their jobs left, right and centre. There is no clothing industry anymore. Most of the big companies are closing down.... In our area majority of the people here are working in clothing factories.* (Julie, Focus Group 3, 6 June 2005)

According to Desai, 'the downward spiral of the industry has forced many of the women of Chatsworth into unemployment' (2002:64). It has also rendered this sector unstable and vulnerable to the point that in order for companies to survive and for people to have a semblance of a job, women workers have been forced to be 'flexible' in the way they work. This space has allowed for sweatshops to flourish in the backyards of middle and upper class homes. Unprotected and not unionized, women retrenched from clothing factories take up jobs in these sweatshops. Julie paints a picture of the exploitation of vulnerable women desperate for a job:

> *They [sweatshops] make you work overtime and until late at night. If that order doesn't go out you don't get paid that Friday. And you are set on that Friday because you got things to do with that money...and then the following week he [owner] will pay you but he won't pay you the full two weeks wages, he'll pay you half of the money he owes you and he will say next week he will pay you the rest. You had to work because you needed that money. I used to get paid R30 (less than $5USD) a day but I accepted it because I needed that money...[I worked] from 7 am to 4 or 4:30 pm. Sometimes you will work later if he needs the order to go out. But he's not paying you very good for the overtime. It's just a couple of hours. He'll pay you about R3 or R4 for the hour. You can't do anything with that money.* (Julie, Focus Group 3, 6 June 2005)

Because the burden of maintaining the home falls so squarely on the shoulders of women, many are forced to find jobs that will be able to feed their families. The women in our discussions say they will take whatever jobs they can. Queenie also tried to get a job. She travelled about 20 km to work in a tote office. She says that the male owner of the tote office wanted her to work from 6:30 am until after 9 pm. He was willing to pay her R30 for the day, i.e., 15 hours of work (Focus Group 1). The women agreed that sometimes they are forced to do whatever work comes their way, including washing clothes for other middle-class women because at the end of the day *'if a child is hungry it will go to its mother for food [because the] men can just sit around or walk around here with no care about how food will get onto the table'* (Sweetie, Focus Group 1, 26 May 2005).

The massive unemployment through the destruction of the clothing, textile and leather industries has torn apart the social fabric of many communities across the country. Other industries and sectors also shed millions of jobs further entrenching poverty and ghettoizing 'the poors'.

Basic Services

The adoption of neoliberal policies has meant the privatization of basic services such as water, electricity, housing, education, health care, and transport (formerly public transport). Privatization has led to an escalation of the costs of these services, increasing the level of poverty inherited from the era of apartheid.

By privatizing basic services, GEAR totally contradicted the RDP's promise of free basic services to all. Based on the premise of cost recovery, electricity, water, housing and education have become beyond the reach of millions of poor people. Cost recovery policies in basic services have been defined as:

> [T]he recovery of all, or most, of the cost associated with providing a particular service by a service provider. For publicly owned service providers, this may or may not include a surplus above and beyond the cost of production, whereas, for private sector providers it necessarily includes a surplus (i.e., profit). In either case, the objective is to recoup the full cost of production. (McDonald and Pape, 2002:18)

McDonald (2002) asserts that although the apartheid state discriminated against the black townships in its delivery of services, the provision of these services was subsidized, albeit unevenly. The democratic state has removed most of the state subsidies in the provision of basic services and over and above that has inserted the cost recovery policies in the provision of these services in the quest to maximize profit. It has subsidised the provision of water by providing the first six kilolitres of water free of charge, thereafter the cost-recovery prices are charged. Criticism that six kilolitres is insufficient water supply especially for extended families has been levied on the government's six kilolitres. In poorer areas, like Orange Farm and Phiri in Gauteng[19] and in Mpumalanga in Kwazulu-Natal where the state has installed pre-paid water meters, has ensured that people are entitled to these basic services only if they have the money to pay for them.

Contrary to popular opinion, McDonald (2002:7) concludes that people cannot pay for basic services because they cannot afford to and not because they are lazy or because they embody a culture of non-payment. In addition, many sacrifice basic needs such as food and clothing to be in a position to pay for access to water and energy. However not paying for the exorbitant and unaffordable water and electricity means that they can now have some food to eat (Sweetie, Focus Group 3, 6 June 2005).

The dilemma of either paying for basic services or putting food on the table has precipitated a crisis around food. In a study conducted by the Chronic Poverty Research Centre to assess food security, it was found that:

About 70% of the respondents indicated that their households had experienced a food shortage at some time during the previous 12 months. About a quarter–25.8%–of children exhibited a degree of stunting.[20]

The study by National Labour and Economic Development Institute (NALEDI) into the food security crisis confirms that there has been a steady increase in food prices and this has created a crisis in food security. Just in 2002 alone, the price of a maize meal doubled, having a devastating effect on the working class. It noted that 'workers typically spend more than a third of their income on food. The ultra-poor spend over 50% of their income on food and up to 20% on maize alone'. It further mentioned that 'over two thirds of ultra poor households are located in rural areas and more than half have members who are pensioners and whose main supporters are women' (Watkinson and Makgetla, 2002:1).

In Bayview, despite the fact that all the women in the focus group are unemployed, the responsibility of providing food fell on their shoulders. Some borrowed money from loan sharks and drug dealers to buy something to cook for the day. Others bought on credit from tuck shops in the area.[21] In both instances, the interest rate is so high that they end up merely paying the interest. There are some women who go begging at street corners and shopping malls while others are forced into prostitution to pay off their debts and buy some food:

> *Sometimes…if I owe R300 I have to stand there till I get that money. And maybe just R30–40 for my son and I for the day. But sometimes, it's like a gamble, you make nothing…On the nights that I do this I find myself drinking excessively to forget who I am. I have to do it. I couldn't do this in my normal senses.* (From an in-depth interview with Annie)

Many of 'the poors' found that the inability to pay for the escalating costs of basic services such as water and electricity as well as the rental on the government flats saw them fall into arrears with their payment. Some of the arrears for water are estimated to be over R20,000 per houschold per month (Sweetie, Focus Group3). *'As a community it's the majority that earns a little bit of money. It's not to say that we are not going to pay. If they scrap the arrears then our people will pay'* (Ibid).

However, the ANC government has responded to the inability of 'the poors' to pay for basic services by disconnecting their water or electricity or evicting from their homes. In a report done by the Coalition Against Water Privatisation, it was found that despite the ANC government's claim that it provided an additional seven million people with access to clean running water and connected an additional 3.5 million people with electricity, it had nonetheless disconnected 10 million people's water, 10 million people's electricity and evicted more than two million people from their homes, all because of non-payment (Coalition Against Water Privatisation, Anti-Privatisation Forum and Public Citizen, 2004:7). In an additional study done by the Municipal Services Project it was found that of the people interviewed who could not afford access to basic services, most were unemployed or in flexible, insecure, unprotected, low paying jobs; or had access to a social grant like a pension. Most were black women.

These poor communities, like Bayview, have responded by illegally reconnecting the electricity and water. 'The poors' have turned the household into a site of resistance by refusing to pay for unaffordable water and electricity and by illegally taking what they firmly believe is theirs to take. Shirley points out vehemently: *'It's not for nothing, we fought for something too you know!'* (Focus Group 3). The democratic state has cottoned on to this old form of resistance[22] and has introduced a 'tampering fee':

> *Let's say the first time they cut your lights, we put it on (illegally reconnect). So when they come again and they find your lights are on they say 'tampered meter' and they put R820 on to your bill.* (Julie, Focus Group 3)

The state's answer to people being unable to pay their rental on government flats is to relocate them to low-cost housing in areas far away from where they currently live. When the ANC came to power in 1994 it promised to build two million houses in five years. Eleven years later it has not met its target.[23] Instead of building houses for those living in squatter camps and informal dwellings, the government has built low-cost housing to relocate those who cannot afford to pay for their rentals thus making space for those whom the government assumes can pay. Those in the flats are threatened with relocation to houses that cost less than the flats they are currently living in:

> *That low cost housing is just one room. It's made with hollow bricks. Its not plastered. It's terribly, terribly built...If they are*

going to move us to low cost housing then they are still not going to get their money's worth. (Julie, Focus Group 3)

None of the women in the discussion group want to leave Bayview. They love the community, 'warts' and all. Most of them carry the legacy of forced removals during apartheid. Many of them have already been relocated at least once in their lifetimes. They refuse to be relocated a second time and this time by a government they actually voted for.

Social Grants

Despite the history and intentions behind the apartheid government's plan for social grants, not all Indian and Coloured people rose through the class ranks to become middle-class homeowners. Those who got left behind live in squalor in townships like Bayview. For these people, the social grants are a lifeline, a safety net preventing them for falling into the dark abyss that poverty promises.

In our discussions, it was very clear that all of the women sitting in the room survived on social grants during the days of apartheid. From disability grants to child support grants, these safety nets helped to pay for rent, water and electricity and put food on the table. Falling into arrears was something that happened occasionally to individuals but not to an entire community. But things changed. All of the women pointed to 1996 as the year their lives changed for the worse: their poverty worsened and they attributed it directly to the cut in the social grants they were receiving: *'People fell into arrears because the grant was cut'* (Shirley, Focus Group 3, 6 June 2005).

According to a report published by the Centre for Civil Society on social grants and in particular the Basic Income Grant, the ANC government was intent to restructure the grants' system to eradicate the racial distortion that had taken place during apartheid.[24] However the ANC had made a series of public statements that giving people hand-outs in the form of state support would inevitably lead to a culture of dependency and laziness. Coupled with the ANC's anti-poor attitude was the fact that the neoliberal leanings of its macro-economic policy allowed for only a minimal, if any, social welfare programme. The lack of commitment from government to the development of a basic income grant was evident in the entire policy process leading up to the development of the grant.

Knowing full well that the majority of people surviving on the grants were poor black women, the government still went ahead and decreased not only the amount of the child support grant but also the age of eligibility, thus cutting off a large number of children whose families desperately needed the grant to pay for increasing school fees and the rising cost of living. In addition, some of the other grants were also reduced and some disappeared completely. Sweetie explains that before 1996 she was receiving R700 for the two foster children she had with her. Not long after 1996 the foster child grant was reduced to R180 per child however, by 2010, it had been standardised to R710 per month (Sweetie, focus group 3). Not only were the grants of the poor slashed, the access to these grants was very difficult with some people having to wait over a year or two to obtain their grant. After an advocacy campaign initiated by some civil society organisations in South Africa, like the Black Sash, the state was forced to implement a better distribution mechanism which gave the poor better access to the grants.

PART VI: The Struggle to Survive

'Women go through life with much more struggle'.[25]

The poverty that the women of Bayview face daily is a microcosm of the struggles faced by millions of poor black women in South Africa. For thousands of women living in rural areas the situation is far worse. Most of the women living in rural and urban townships, have been poor before and remain poor today. The burden of survival has fallen squarely on their shoulders with the historical responsibility of taking care of the household being women's. Under the ANC government, the attack on women has filtered from the state into the workplace and into the household: state grants are being cut, industries that hire mostly poor black women are being decimated and the delivery of basic services to the household are in remission.

In South Africa, both during and after apartheid, men have held, and continue to hold power over women and not alongside them. Patriarchal power obtains in both the public and private domains where men have made essential decisions both for the nation, the community and within the family. 'Such power would include the power to define the values and explanatory systems of the society and the power to define and control the sexual behaviour of women' (Lerner, 1986:31). According to Cock (1988:205) the intersection of race, class and gender is how most black women in South Africa experience oppression. Women who are at the lower rungs of the economic ladder find it increasingly difficult to free themselves of the patriarchal nature of society. In fact, the poorer the woman, the more she finds herself trapped by the oppressive nature of patriarchy as she encounters it from the state, in the workplace and within the family.

The women in the focus group have all confronted patriarchy. Julie's experience with an exploitative male boss who held the power over her work, what she earned and her working conditions led to her oppression in her workplace. Sweetie and Shirley both suffered at the hands of violent and abusive husbands. They both married these men because they were struggling financially and these men were working and earning an income. The same holds true for Annie. Unable to get employment after working for years in the clothing industry these women saw their escape from poverty in the job security and steady income that their husbands were earning. But soon their husbands saw that providing for the family financially gave them a degree of power. It wasn't long before this power was used by the husbands to oppress their wives into submission and to create some dependency. The submission was achieved by violent abuse and withholding money for food. For Annie, her oppression went a step further where her husband also doubled-up as her pimp forcing her into prostitution to feed his drug habit.

Molyneux (2003:102), quoting Engels, notes and recognises the family as a site of female oppression in which the 'open or disguised enslavement of the women' was condoned.

South Africa's patriarchal constructs have survived its colonial and apartheid pasts to become embedded in the bedrock of democratic dispensation. It has become South Africa's legacy that has remained for decades. From colonialism through to apartheid, the state used its power to act out the most heinous forms of oppression on the black population. Black women felt much of the repercussions of these acts of oppression from the state. In addition, many were oppressed by the patriarchal nature of their culture and tradition that the apartheid and colonial state embodied in law. Because of this, black women understood inherently that the white state was the immediate enemy and the primary oppressor. They fought to maintain the family unit, regardless of the fact that this unit was also oppressing them. It was important then to maintain that very same oppressive family unit as it was the black family unit that was under attack and disintegrating (Basu, 1995:133).

It was therefore articulated, in many of the mass-based antiapartheid organizations like the ANC and the Black Consciousness Movement, that the most pressing issue facing the nation was the state's attack on black people and that to entertain the 'woman' issue was indulgent. The ferociousness of these attacks meant that the issue of women's oppression and equality could not be dealt with immediacy within the organizations themselves. Despite the fact that black women were severely oppressed by the apartheid and colonial states, they were also subjected to gender discrimination within the anti-apartheid movement. According to Kemp et al. (1995:138-139) adult women in the anti-apartheid movement were confined to 'playing traditional roles of supplying material and psychological support' to the predominantly male leadership:

> Survival dictated that we viewed gender contradictions as non-antagonistic ones, which meant that their existence was acknowledged but for the time being would not be taken to issue....When they said that the liberation of women was 'inextricably linked' with the national liberation of the country, they did not mean that political liberation meant overall freedom for women. It was to imply that at some time in the future...there would be a direct confrontation with patriarchy.

As such, the equality of women was placed in a queuing system behind race and class. This situation still persists in democratic South Africa both in terms of the state's attack on the public and private spaces of poor, black women and in organizational structures that are still the vestiges of male domination.

However, in her book *Women and the Remaking of Politics in Southern Africa*, Gisela Geisler (2004:63), talks about the political achievements of women in post-liberation countries in Southern Africa. She labels the South African experience as exceptional because 'women managed to make substantial gains in the transition to majority rule'. Geisler's work recognizes the entry of women into the South African Parliament, the transformation of institutions to allow the entry of women and the development of institutions such as the Commission on Gender Equality as the key achievements of gender equality. As Giesler (2004:9) points out, South Africa, in 1999, was ranked eighth in the world for representation of women in parliament. This, she describes as an overwhelming success for women in post-apartheid South Africa.

Whilst the entry of women into parliament must be seen as a victory for South Africa's democracy, it has meant little for poor, black women still oppressed by a patriarchal state. Kemp et al. (1995: 155) and others point out that women activists are skeptical and wary of the ability of women ministers to apply a gendered analysis and approach to the general responsibilities their positions demand. The inability of women in parliament to act on behalf of their sisters in communities was evidenced by their collective silence when cuts were made to the Child Support Grant and other social welfare provisions, when the government refused to provide anti-retrovirals to HIV positive people or when the clothing industry (largely dominated by low-skilled poor, black women) was decimated due to tariff reductions. Hence the gains made by women at the level of parliament and legal/constitutional advances, have been made at certain costs. Kemp et al. (1995:157) and others point out that these gains have been made mainly by middle-class women, both black and white, with better access to education and resources whilst the majority of women 'still suffer from the secondary status imposed on women in the community and at home through a patriarchal ideology expressed through religion, culture, customary law and tradition' as well as being caught in an endless cycle of poverty.

In a society structured under the notions of patriarchy, women have been siphoned off into the private sphere of the household. It is therefore their social responsibility to take care of all things related to the home and the welfare of their family. In addition, old forms of patriarchy in capitalist economies ensured that this work that women provided in the home was never valued. However, in some instances, providing free basic services such as education, health care, water, electricity can be perceived as the state giving value to the private household work of women. Under the auspices of capitalist globalization and through neoliberal economic policies, the private sphere of women is under attack.

It becomes impossible to view contemporary society through filters that separate class and gender. Maria Mies (1986) has often argued that seeing patriarchy and capitalism as two separate entities, risks the separation of women's exploitation in the private sphere from the performance of productive labour in the workplace or public sphere. Women are the most obvious targets for exploitation because patriarchal capitalism defines women as performers of unpaid labour, as wives and mothers responsible for the care of the family. The ANC government's attack on this private space of poor black women and the household, is not only indicative of its lack of commitment both on the level of creating class and race equity but also indicative of the lack of interest in relieving the burden of women. It is clear that capitalist patriarchy, once considered to be something that was part of apartheid, has installed itself into the essence of this democratic society in which 'the woman issue' was traded off in the interest of capital accumulation.

However, all across the country, a new phenomenon has entered the South African political landscape. Growing numbers of people frustrated by the non-delivery of basic services from the government have organized themselves into social movements and have waged a war on the attack against poor people. They have garnered the support of thousands of poor black women and have, through their political action raised consciousness around the plight of poor women and the continued attack by the state on the private sphere of the home, in terms of the privatization of basic services.

The BFRA is part of the growing number of communities that have organized themselves and are part of the new social movements. The women in Bayview who are members of the BFRA see the organization as the only light in their lives. Through the committee they feel their voices are being heard. They are at the forefront of the struggle against evictions, disconnections and relocations and they have faced the police during evictions and cut-offs. They have asserted that they not only protect their own families and homes from the police and from security guards but they do the same for any family in the community.

Through the new social movements and their collective participation in the war against the poor, women are occupying new historical spaces. They are producing a new sense of themselves as a collective of women and the movement is providing the space for them to articulate their voices as a collective against the destruction of the lives of the poor by the state. In this way, they are not developing an autonomous definition of 'woman' but are seeing themselves holistically as belonging to the oppressed blacks, or oppressed poors. As Desai points out, the social movements have become a space where identities get rethought in the context of struggle.

Of course, this may be seen as a shortcoming that the new movements must view as a challenge. Most of the membership of the new social movements consists of women who see their experiences centrally rooted in the fact that they are women. If it is true that the movements are spaces where identities are rethought then the push by women and the leadership to rearticulate the struggle in the name of gender, race and class as a holistic struggle (as opposed to a delineated class and race struggle) must be forced to happen.

Conclusion

The situation created by the historical nature of poverty with its roots embedded deeply in colonialism and apartheid begged for a revamping of the economic system when democracy was ushered into the country. But in the transition, the charms of the market appealed more to the ANC government than the pleading eyes of millions of poor people who voted them into power. The tragic 'victims' of the ongoing cycle of poverty have been and continue to be poor black people who have no means of escaping this cycle. The adoption of neoliberalism not only removed all possible means for the poor to survive poverty but it added on to people's poverty.

Neo-liberalism combined with an already established patriarchal society has resulted in a growing number of women becoming poor. This mixed with the legacy of apartheid has created a cocktail of poverty that has debilitated poor black women, urban and rural. Crippled by growing unemployment and lack of adequate social security, the denial of basic services has seen many of these women forced into survival mode that has taken the form of borrowing, cycles of debt, begging or prostitution. Some see marriage as a potential alleviation of their poverty situation only to find that the men they have married turn out to be abusive, violent men wanting to control them.

The women in Bayview have placed on record all of their experiences with poverty. The key point that is being raised is that they were poor once and they are poor again. The ANC government reneged on its promise to the poor to create a better life for all. It delivered this better life to a growing number of black businessmen with a few black women thrown in for good measure. This has now become the measure of success while the poor continue to suffer from the ANC's anti-poor stance.

The other key point that the women in Bayview raised is that they are no longer afraid to stand up and take what they, together with thousands of other poor people, feel is theirs to take. They feel that they have fought just as hard for democracy and to free themselves from poverty and they will no longer be denied the right to live a better life. They have organized themselves into a formidable force that is waging a battle with the government for the basics that will ensure a life worth living: jobs, water, electricity, housing, health care, education. It becomes heart-breaking when people who fought so hard for their freedom look at the government and say: *'How can the President have luxury jets when his people are starving. Can't he see how poor we are?'* (Shirley, Focus Group 3)

NOTES

[1] Protest action for housing, water, electricity, education, and HIV treatment started as early as 2000, just after the second national election.

2   From the 'enews' 10 pm news coverage on the 23 May 2005.
3   Buroway quoted in Chari (2004).
4   I began this study using a focus group format as a way to get to know the women whose stories I wanted to tell. I had known some of them for a few years so it was relatively easy for me to gain their trust. As we went along it became clear that the study was no longer a focus group study, but had instead evolved into an ethnographic study. For the ease of referencing directly quoted statements, however, I have indicated that they were derived from the focus group discussions.
5   Taken from the title of Ashwin Desai's study, *The Poors of Chatsworth,* a detailed account of the history of people's living conditions in Chatsworth prior to apartheid and their struggle to survive in post-apartheid South Africa. This work was one of the most important pieces of empirical research done to articulate the frustrations of poor people living in a democratic state with Chatsworth being the case study. This book was followed by 'We are the Poors', which extended the story into a national one. Desai, through his work, introduced the concept of 'The Poors' as a valid identity for people struggling against poverty.
6   All statistics quoted here are from the Census Survey 2001 conducted by Statistics SA. This institution is a government research institute and these are the official statistics. www.statssa.gov.za/census2001/atlas_ward2/ stats/stats_59200069.html.
7   This study was later updated by a qualitative study done by a young group of researchers from the BFRA. They have generously allowed me to use their research findings here.
8   Julie, Focus Group 1, 26 May 2005.
9   Shantal, Focus Group 3, 6 June 2005.
10   This is not a comprehensive list but rather gives an example of some issues.
11   David McDonald has done extensive work in the area of commodification of basic services in post-apartheid South Africa and the impact these policies have had on the living conditions of the poor. The policies for cost recovery are a new phenomenon and were not a strategy considered or adopted by the apartheid regime. It does therefore account for why people often feel that life was considerably easier (in terms of accessing food, basic services) under apartheid. This will be addressed later on in the article.
12   This was further exacerbated by the establishment of the tricameral parliament which was a three-tiered racialized parliamentary structure. According to McKinley and Veriavia, this structure

was rejected by the liberation movement as a tool that was being used for co-option and a means of dividing oppressed groups.
[13] Julie, Focus Group 3, 6 June 2005.
[14] The RDP focused on redistribution of the wealth and resources of the country. It promised to give land back to the dispossessed. It spoke about free basic services to all. It promised that the state would take back the wealth through nationalizing certain industries and then redistribute it back to all those who had been denied a better life.
[15] Patrick Bond (1996) and Hein Marais (2001) describe the process of elite-pacting that took place between the ANC, the National Party and the business community. Hein Marais starts his discussion from around 1987 when some members of the ANC were in exile where international as well as local business communities were courting them. Patrick Bond starts his discussion from 1990 until 1994 and focuses his attention on the local developments. A lot of their focus is spent on the transitional arrangements that were made to safeguard the economy from any socialist ideas and to steer the economy in the direction of market-driven economics, a similar kind of arrangement that existed with the Nationalist Party.
[16] Julie, Focus Group 2, 1 June 2005.
[17] *Mail and Guardian*, 22–28 April 2005, p. 5.
[18] 'Short time' refers to when a company operates on shorter hours and on skeletal staff because there is not enough work coming into the company. This has a detrimental effect on workers who are paid only for the hours they work.
[19] For more information on this please refer to Coalition Against Water Privatisation, Anti-Privatisation Forum and Public Citizen 2004.
[20] See *Mail and Guardian*, 15–21 April 2005, p. 28 for a summary of the findings. The full report is published by Andries Du Toit at the Centre for Social Science Research, University of Cape Town.
[21] 'Tuck shops' are little stands run by members of the community. These small little shops built on the side of the road inside communities, provide the basic foods like bread, milk and vegetables. These shops are more inclined to provide food on credit.
[22] During apartheid, the anti-apartheid movement engaged in the rent boycott refusing to pay rentals on government-owned flats. This also extended into non-payment of rates.
[23] From www.wsws.org/articles/2005/jun2005/safr-j14.shtml.

[24] See Kumiko Makino's, (2004) report on 'Social Security Policy Reform in Post-apartheid South Africa'.
[25] Julie, Focus Group 1, 26 May 2005.

REFERENCES

Basu, A. (ed.) (1995) *The Challenge of Local Feminisms: Women's Movements in Global Perspective.* San Francisco: Westview Press.

Benjamin, S. (2001) 'The Masculinisation of the State and the Feminisation of Poverty', *Agenda* 48: 68-74.

Bhorat, H. and Kanbar, R. (2005) *'Poverty and Well-being in Post-Apartheid South Africa: An Overview of Data, Outcomes and Policy,'* Development Policy Research Unit Working Paper 05/101.

Bond, P. (1996) *Elite Transition from Apartheid to Neoliberalism.* Pietermaritzburg: University of Kwazulu-Natal Press.

Brewer, J.D. (2000) 'What is Ethnography?' *Ethnography*, Buckingham: Open University Press, pp. 10-26. Census 2001 Survey. Available at http://www.statssa.gov.za/census2001/atlas_ward2/stats/stats_59200069.html.

Carter, M.R. and May, J. (1999) *'One Kind of Freedom: Poverty Dynamics in Post-Apartheid South Africa,'* Staff Paper No. 427, University of Wisconsin.

Chari, S. (2004) *Fraternal Capital: Peasant Workers, Self-made Men and Globalisation in Provincial India.* Delhi: Permanent Black.

Coalition Against Water Privatisation, Anti-privatisation Forum and Public Citizen (2004) 'Nothing for Mahala: The Forced Installation of Prepaid Water Meters in Stretford, Ext.4, Orange Form, Johannesburg, South Africa'. Durban; Centre for Civil Society. Available at www.ukzn.ac.za/ccs.

Cock, J. (1988) 'Trapped Workers: The Case of Domestic Workers in South Africa', in *Patriarchy and Class*, pp. 205-19. Boulder: Westview.

Desai, A. (2000) *The Poors of Chatsworth: Race, Class and Social Movements in Post-apartheid South Africa.* Durban: Institute for Black Research.

Geisler, G. (2004) *Women and the Remaking of Politics in Southern Africa: Negotiating Autonomy, Incorporation and Representation.* The Nordic Africa Institute.

Habib, A. and Padayachee, V. (2000) 'Economic Policy and Power Relations in South Africa's Transition to Democracy', *World Development* 28(2): 245-263.

Kehler, J. (2001) 'Women and Poverty: The South African Experience', *Journal of Inter-nation Women's Studies* 3(1).

Kemp, A., Madlala, N., Moodley, A., and Salo, E. (1995) 'The Dawn of a New Day: Redefining South African Feminism', in Basu, A. (ed.) *The Challenge of Local Feminisms: Women Movements in Global Perspective.* San Francisco: Westview Press.

Kingdon, G. and Knight, J. (2004) 'Unemployment in South Africa: The Nature of the Beast', *World Development* 32(3).

Lerner, G. (1986) *The Creation of Patriarchy.* New York: Oxford University Press.

Makino, K. (2004) 'Social Security Policy Reform in Post-apartheid South Africa: A Focus on the Basic Income Grant', *Centre for Civil Society,* Research Report 11.

Marais, H. (2001) *South Africa: Limits to Change.* Cape Town: University of Cape Town Press.

McDonald, D.A. (2002) 'No Money, No Service', *Alternatives Journal* 28(2). Available at www. alternativesjournal.co.

McDonald, D.A. and Pape, J. (2002), *Cost Recovery and the Crisis of Service Delivery in South Africa.* Cape Town: HSRC Publishers.

McKinley, D. and Veriavia, A. (2005) *Arresting Dissent: Violence and Transition.* Johannesburg: Centre for the Study of Violence and Reconciliation.

Molyneux, M. (2003) *Women's Movements in International Perspective: Latin America and Beyond.* University of London: Institute of Latin American Studies.

Mies, M. (1986) *Patriarchy and the Accumulation on a World Scale: Women in the International Division of Labour.* London: Zed Books.

Mohanty, C.T. (2003) *Feminism without Borders: Decolonizing Theory, Practicing Solidarity.* Durham: Duke University Press.

Pelto, Pertti J. and Gretel, H. (1978) *Anthropological Research: The Structure of Inquiry.* Cambridge: Cambridge University Press.

Saul, J. (2002) '*Cry for the Beloved Country: The Post-apartheid Denouement*', RAU Sociology. Available at www.ukzn.ac.za/ccs.

Terreblanche, S. (2002) *A History of Inequality in South Africa: 1652–2002.* Pietermaritzburg: University of Natal Press.

Watkinson, E. and Makgetla, N. (2002) *South Africa's Food Security Crisis.* NALEDI.

CHAPTER 11

Global Capitalist Penetration, Child Labor and Children's Collective Resistance in Defense of Their Rights

Erica G. Polakoff
Bloomfield College, NJ

ABSTRACT

The impact of global capitalist penetration (aka economic globalization)[1] on low-income families in the global North and South provides the context for this chapter, which focuses on the exploitation of child labor in agriculture, manufacturing, and the commercial sex trade. Young girls and young women are particularly vulnerable and thus increasingly targeted as laborers by global capitalism in these, and other sectors of the economy. The chapter reviews the relationship between global capitalist penetration, poverty and child labor, and highlights the ineffectiveness of domestic laws and international conventions for protecting children's rights and well-being. It also emphasizes the diversity of children's experiences, their resiliency and agency, and their empowerment through participation in collective associations. Solutions to the problems of child labor and the exploitation of children will necessarily have to address the underlying processes of global capitalist penetration that are exacerbating global poverty and, consequently, increasing the need for poor families to depend on the paid labor of their children for survival. Furthermore, in order for real change to take place, children's voices and perspectives must be integrated into decision-making and policymaking processes.

Keywords: child labor, global capitalist penetration, economic globalization, poverty, children's rights, children's collective associations

Introduction: The State of the World's Children

The United Nations estimates that 30% of the world's total population of approximately seven billion consists of children under the age of fifteen (UNICEF, 2009). Nearly ten million children under the age of five die each year, four million from diarrhea, malaria and pneumonia; nearly four million newborns die in the first month of life (Ibid). Approximately two million children under the age of fifteen are living with HIV (Ibid). Twenty-five percent of all children in developing countries live in abject poverty (UNICEF, 2005a), and 25% of children under the age of five in developing countries suffer from malnutrition; 148 million are underweight for their age (UNICEF, 2009). Over 200 million children (about 10% of the world's children) 'suffer from some form of physical or mental disability or developmental delay (low cognitive ability) often the result of food insufficiency' (UNICEF, 2000a). Food insufficiency is present even in wealthy nations like the United States where an estimated 12 million children do not get enough to eat (Schwartz-Nobel, 2002). Poverty, food insufficiency and poor nutrition–all of which have been exacerbated by global capitalism–increase risks to life and health for all, but especially for mothers and their children (Farmer, 2003; FAO, 2002; Stiglitz, 2003; Yong et al., 2000).

In addition, hundreds of millions of children are victims of exploitation, abuse and violence each year, with approximately 275 million children suffering the consequences of domestic violence (UNICEF, 2006). Three hundred thousand children are recruited or abducted into armies and militias to work as child soldiers, laborers and sexual slaves (Becker, 2004); at least 1.2 million are trafficked in the international sex trade (UNICEF, 2000b). There are approximately 250 million hired child laborers (UNICEF, 2005a), 150 million between the ages of 5-14 (UNICEF, 2009). Seventy percent of child laborers work in dangerous, life-threatening environments including mines and factories, or with dangerous substances like pesticides and other chemicals in agricultural production (UNICEF, 2005b).

Children work to survive and to support their families. While historically the contributions made by children to the survival of their families have been important, contemporary neoliberal policies of 'structural adjustment' and 'free trade' which characterize globalization have created unprecedented levels of poverty worldwide (Stiglitz, 2003; Yates, 2004), which in turn, have made children more vulnerable to exploitation, and their contributions to their families increasingly significant. This chapter will examine five issues essential to understanding child labor in the contemporary global capitalist economy: 1) relationships between global capitalist penetration, world poverty and child labor; 2) social and cultural constructions of 'child' and 'childhood'; 3) international conventions protecting the rights of children and domestic laws prohibiting child labor; 4) gendered aspects of the expansion of global capitalism and consequences of the exploitation of child labor in agriculture, manufacturing and the commercial sex trade, for the well-being of children, families and communities; and finally 5) children's active participation in collective associations that serve to defend their rights and challenge the dominant perceptions of children and childhood held by those in positions of power and authority.

Economic Globalization, World Poverty and Child Labor

Joseph Stiglitz, Chief Economist and Senior Vice President of the World Bank from 1997-2000, and Nobel laureate in Economics in 2001, defined economic globalization as, 'the removal of barriers to free trade and the closer integration of national economies' (Stiglitz, 2003: ix). Removal of the barriers to 'free trade' has been accomplished primarily through international trade agreements. Most notably, these include: the North American Free Trade Agreement (NAFTA), which was signed in 1992 by the U.S., Mexico and Canada; and the World Trade Organization (WTO), which was signed by 100 countries and replaced the General Agreement on Tariffs and Trade (GATT). The Central American and Dominican Republic Free Trade Agreement (CAFTA-DR), '*Plan Puebla Panama*' (the previously proposed free trade agreement between the United States and the countries spanning from Puebla, Mexico to Panama), and the Andean region initiative–known as '*Plan Colombia*' (in Colombia) and '*Plan Dignidad*' (Plan Dignity, in Bolivia)–also are relevant to the Americas and considered necessary for the future ratification of the Free Trade Area of the Americas (FTAA). The United States has free trade agreements 'in force' with more than 17 countries (www.ustr.gov/trade-agreements/free-trade-agreements).[2]

Removing barriers to 'free trade' facilitates foreign investment and has been an essential ingredient of structural adjustment programs which detail the conditions under which loans are provided to (or imposed upon) debtor nations seeking financial assistance from the World Bank and the International Monetary Fund (IMF). Structural adjustment effectively restructures the economies of debtor nations to reduce government spending and ensure that loans and interest on the loans are repaid, while opening up access to resources–both natural and human–for mostly foreign (and some domestic) private corporate interests. Structural adjustment policies require governments to cut social spending (on public education, health care, housing, social welfare, social security, for example), reduce the public sector labor force, lower or freeze wages, privatize public and state industries, institutions and resources (e.g., mining, banking, forests, oil and mineral reserves, land and water), devalue or 'dollarize' the currency, increase export production, increase interest rates on domestic loans, and raise domestic food prices to world market levels. Structural adjustment has consistently resulted in an increase in the number of people unemployed and an increase in the number of poor, and it has exacerbated the desperate conditions of life for the majority of people in the countries on which it has been imposed (Chossudovsky, 2003; IFG, 2002; Stiglitz, 2003).

While at the World Bank, Stiglitz (2003:ix) 'saw firsthand the devastating effects that globalization can have on developing countries, especially the poor within those countries'. He noted an increase in both the number of people living in poverty and in the gap between the wealthy and the poor. 'Despite repeated promises of poverty reduction…the actual number of people living in poverty has increased by almost 100 million. This occurred at the same time that total world income increased by an average 2.5% annually' (Stiglitz, 2003:5).

In addition to increasing poverty, structural adjustment has resulted in greater world hunger, 'massive unemployment', the destruction of the environment and 'social dissolution' (Stiglitz, 2003:5-8). Furthermore, 'crises around the world have been more frequent and deeper. By some reckoning, close to 100 countries have faced crises' (Stiglitz, 2003:15). Whole regions, indeed, whole continents have been affected. The African continent

> plunges deeper into misery, as incomes fall and standards of living decline….Crises in Asia and Latin America have threatened the stability of all developing countries…and in Russia and most other countries making the transition from communism to the market…(there has been) unprecedented poverty. (Stiglitz, 2003:5-8)[3]

Globalization has led to the creation of a 'Fourth World,' which, unlike the designations of 'First,' 'Second,' and 'Third' Worlds, is *not* recognizable as a separate geopolitical entity. According to Castells (1998:164): the 'Fourth World':

> comprises large areas of the globe, such as much of Sub-Saharan Africa and the impoverished rural areas of Latin America and Asia, but it is also present in literally every country, and every city in this new geography of social exclusion…it is populated by millions of homeless, incarcerated,

> prostituted, criminalized, brutalized, stigmatized, sick and illiterate persons...(who) are growing in number and increasing in visibility (Castells, 1998:164).

Thus, economic globalization–or what some researchers and scholars have named 'global apartheid'[4] or what I refer to as 'global capitalist penetration'–has produced and reproduced poverty worldwide, on an unprecedented scale, and created greater polarization and social exclusion (Castells, 1998).

One dire consequence of these processes has been the super-exploitation of workers, generally, and of children, specifically. 'Child labor is one of the clearest and worst manifestations of how poverty has a child's face' (UNICEF, 2001:12). Throughout the world as economic conditions have worsened for the majority, that is, as poverty has increased and social services have been dismantled, large numbers of children have been forced to labor–in mines, on farms, in factories, as domestic workers, street vendors and prostitutes–in order to survive and help support their families.

> If poverty is defined not merely in terms of low income but as a state of deprivation of basic capabilities, nothing illustrates that more forcefully than child labor...A child laborer is a child denied the liberating benefit of education, one whose health, growth and development are threatened. (UNICEF, 2001:3)

Furthermore, poverty 'makes children more vulnerable to exploitation, abuse, violence, discrimination and stigmatization...Children experience poverty with their hands, minds and hearts. Material poverty...hinders emotional capacity as well as bodily growth' (UNICEF, 2005c). In other words, poverty and the exploitation of child labor effectively deny children their childhood. In so doing, their future and the future of their nations have been compromised.

Although the relationship between poverty and child labor may seem intuitive, few empirical studies have been undertaken to demonstrate whether economic growth leads to an improved standard of living and a decrease in child labor. In fact, some policymakers have even argued that economic growth, especially through trade 'liberalization' and the expansion of foreign 'investment' in poor and indebted nations–which have been mandated both in trade agreements and structural adjustment programs–could lead to an increase in child labor. However, these claims are misleading. They focus on macro-economic growth indicators that are far removed from how wealth is distributed, and they are not generally concerned with human development or well-being. Studies of poverty and child labor at the household level, however, can provide us with a sense of how poverty is experienced, and what the impact of increasing or decreasing levels of poverty is on families with limited resources.

Edmonds' (2004) study, 'Does child labor decline with improving economic status?' used data from the Vietnam Living Standards Survey (VLSS), and offers some insight into the relationship between poverty reduction and child labor. The VLSS interviewed several thousand rural households at two points in time, first in 1992-93, and then again five years later. Edmonds' study included over 3,000 households with children between the ages of 6 and 15. He compared differences in the economic status of households and the incidence of child labor between 1992-93 and 1997-98. He reported that the incidence of child labor declined as household poverty declined:

> economic status improvements can explain much of the dramatic decline in child labor that occurred in Vietnam during the 1990s...For households that emerge from poverty between 1993 and 1998, per capita expenditure improvements can explain 80% of the observed decline in child labor...In fact, improvements in economic status, even in the face of rising earnings opportunities for child laborers, are associated with a very dramatic decline in child labor. (2004:21)

Furthermore, Edmonds (2004:22) noted that, 'punitive policies such as trade sanctions designed to punish countries with high levels of child labor may actually increase child labor if trade sanctions lower economic status.' Moreover, punishing legitimate businesses for their child labor practices, may in fact serve to push more children into illegal businesses and services where they are likely to experience even graver threats to the health and well-being.

Another recent study tracked the education, labor market and health consequences of child labor for children's development. Beegle, Dehejia and Gatti (2009) also used data from the Vietnam Living Standards Survey, including over 4,000 households in their research. They looked specifically at children 8-13 years old who were in school in 1992-93 and were also 'engaged in income-generating work' (Ibid:877), and also those who were in school but did not work. Then they looked at the educational attainment, labor force participation and health of children who were 13-18 years old in

1997-98. They found that, 'Working as a child ... leads to a significantly lower level of school attendance five years later' (Ibid:881). Working an average of twenty-four hours per week while attending school, 'leads to about a 46% reduction in the proportion of children attending school five years later...a 21% decrease in educational attainment' (Ibid:881-883), and a much greater likelihood of being in the labor market five years later. The researchers also noted that girls spent much more time than boys on domestic tasks at home; this was the case regardless of whether or not the girls worked for wages. Furthermore, with regard to the impact of working on children's health, they noted, 'Child labor significantly increases the probability of illness' (Ibid:886).

These two studies provide us with concrete empirical evidence that first, there is indeed a relationship between poverty and child labor among low-income households such that as household poverty declines, so does the incidence of child labor; and second, that there are significant negative consequences of child labor, even when children are only working on average, 24 hours per week. It is reasonable to assume that the health and education consequences for children who work more than 24 hours per week, are even more severe.

This chapter contends that increased poverty leads to increased exploitation of, and dependence on, child labor. Furthermore, I will demonstrate that regardless of the existence of international conventions and domestic laws prohibiting child labor, children have been consistently targeted as workers, especially within the 'Fourth World' of both the global North and South, and their contributions are often critical to their families' survival. Moreover, global capitalism is both a gendered and racialized process, specifically targeting the labor of girls and young women, particularly those from the most marginalized communities, in a number of different sectors–both formal and informal–including the manufacturing industries, domestic service, and the sex trade. Young women and girls have become increasingly responsible for productive and reproductive labor, working for wages in the global factories, for example, while also caring for younger siblings and carrying out the daily work of surviving at home. However, defining who is a child is not as simple as one might expect.

The Social and Cultural Construction of 'Child' and 'Childhood'

The most basic problem when studying children is defining who should be counted as a child. A person may be considered a child in one culture, but an adult in another, with radically different responsibilities and expectations. Instead of indicating some 'natural' or biological demarcation in the life span of a person–which, presumably, would be universal–the categories of 'child' and 'childhood' are socially and culturally constructed (James and Prout, 1997; Scheper-Hughes and Sargent, 1998; Schwartzman, 2001; Stephens, 1995). Indeed, 'the experience of childhood is deeply embedded in the larger social matrix of the community, tribe and family' (O'Kane, 2003:2). Also, definitions of 'child' and 'childhood' have changed over time, and vary not only from one culture to another but also according to social class and gender.

Furthermore, culturally distinct definitions of childhood cannot be understood in the abstract or isolated from their larger context (Stephens 1995)–namely, the complex, contemporary world of 'globalization' which has produced profound changes in people's lives, transforming nations, communities, families, and identities (Castells, 1998; Giddens, 2000).

Analysis of the impact of global relations of power on the daily experiences of children has revealed, for example, a deterioration in child and maternal health in the Dominican Republic (Whiteford, 1998) and in the Philippines (Lindio-McGovern, this volume), as a direct result of structural adjustment policies imposed by the IMF. An increase in the abandonment of children in Jamaica as a consequence of high unemployment and economic collapse, also has been attributed to IMF policies (Sargent and Harris, 1998). In Brazil, Guatemala, Tanzania, Bangladesh, India, Nepal, and Pakistan, for example, millions of children are forced to forego an education and work to survive as a consequence of worsening economic conditions (UNICEF, 2001). Indeed, every nation that has experienced economic crises (which include over 100 countries), where increased poverty has been accompanied by a decline in the provision of social services, children's health, well-being, growth and development, have been compromised (UNICEF, 2001).

Worldwide, children today benefit from few protections; they face increased exploitation in the labor force; assaults on their health and well-being by worldwide epidemics and by poverty, hunger, and poor sanitation; state-sponsored political violence; and immigration, forced displacement, relocation, and abandonment resulting from war, natural disasters, and economic necessity (Schwartzman, 2001: 9). They also face exclusion from many of the decisions that affect them, which, ironically, is often due to adult perceptions of children as dependent, naïve and inexperienced, or as delinquents and perpetrators of crime, or as victims of crime or abuse. Adults in positions of authority–parents, public officials, NGOs and law enforcement–often treat children as passive, naive recipients of policy, rehabilitation and/or services, rather than as citizens and active participants in social change (Feinstein and O'Kane, 2009; O'Kane, 2003).

National and International Conventions Against Child Labor

Historically speaking, the children of poor families have almost always worked. Children, in fact, are often viewed as a valuable resource necessary to ensure the survival of their families. In Latin America, for example, especially during times of economic crisis, children from poor families have labored in farm work, slaughterhouses, the building and construction trades, domestic service, the production of handicrafts for sale and in the marketing and trading of goods (Green, 1999; Polakoff, 1988). In today's global economy, child labor contributes not only to the survival of families but also to the profit of major corporations. Furthermore, the conditions under which children labor are dangerous to their physical, psychological, and emotional health. And, since they must also sacrifice their education in order to work, their labor serves to compromise the future of their families and their communities.

Child labor has been described as 'a *massive* part of the International Political Economy globally, and especially in poorer states, where children as young as *six or seven* toil in agriculture, factories and sweatshops, in domestic labour and sex work' (Pettman, 2005: 438, emphasis mine). Children often experience exploitation because they are thought to be 'less aware of their rights, less troublesome, more compliant, more trustworthy and less likely to absent themselves from work' (ILO, 1998). Girls, especially, are considered more passive, and more easily manipulated and hence more exploitable. Thus, we find that girls tend to start working at younger ages than boys and to be concentrated in the most precarious occupations (UNICEF, 2007). Perhaps not surprisingly, domestic service–one of the least regulated and most vulnerable of occupations–is female-dominated. In fact, 90% of child laborers in domestic service are girls, the overwhelming majority of them are younger than 16 and many of them experience 'severe abuse at the hands of their employers' (Ibid:25). Furthermore, 'paid domestic service is the main economic activity for girls younger than 16, with more girls employed in this sector than in any other form of work' (Ibid:48). But girls and young women are not only concentrated in domestic service; they are also targeted as laborers in the factories and sweatshops or *maquiladoras* (see: Frederickson in this volume), as well as in the commercial sex trade. Thus, there is a gendered aspect to the exploitation of child labor, with young girls and young women paying the price, since they are often the ones who are involved in production for the market *and* responsible for reproduction of the labor force at home.

Concerns about the state of children's lives have been addressed in the international arena. In 1989, the United Nations General Assembly adopted the Convention on the Rights of the Child, which has been ratified by 193 nations, and is the 'most widely ratified international human rights treaty in history' (UNICEF, 2009:2). Unlike the Declaration of Rights of the Child, which was adopted by the United Nations 30 years earlier, the Convention 'is considered legally binding for ratifying states' (Stephens, 1995:35). According to Article 1 of the Convention, 'a child means every human being below the age of eighteen years unless national laws recognize an earlier age' (UNICEF, 2009:9). The Convention provides for children to be protected from discrimination (Article 2), the right to life, survival and development (Article 6), the right to a name and a nationality (Article 7) and an identity (Article 8), the right to express opinions and views (Article 12), the freedom of thought, conscience and religion (Article 14), the freedom of association (Article 15), protection from abuse and neglect (Article 19), and the right to education (Article 28). Article 32 provides for the right to protection from child labor 'that threatens health or development' (UNICEF, 2009:6). The Convention also provides for the right to protection from sexual exploitation (Article 34) and from sale, trafficking, or abduction (Article 35), or other forms of exploitation (Article 36), the right to protection from torture and deprivation of liberty (Article 37), and protection of children under fifteen from being drafted into the armed forces (Article 38). There are also articles that assert the rights of disabled children, indigenous children and minorities.

In addition to the United Nations Convention on the Rights of the Child, there has been widespread international support for the International Labor Organization's (ILO) Convention Concerning the Prohibition and Immediate Elimination of the Worst Forms of Child Labor, also known as the Worst Forms of Child Labor Convention (adopted in 1999), and for the Optional Protocol to the Convention on the Rights of the Child (adopted by the United Nations in May 2000). Article 32 of the ILO Convention on the Worst Forms of Child Labor states, 'children have the right to be protected from economic exploitation and from performing any work that is likely to be hazardous to or interfere with the child's education, or to be harmful to the child's health or physical, mental, spiritual, moral or social development' (UNICEF, 2005b).[5]

Besides international covenants to protect children from exploitation, many countries have domestic laws prohibiting child labor. For example, 'bonded labor' or 'debt peonage' (i.e., when a child is sold as a laborer to help pay off a parent's or guardian's debt) is an illegal practice in a number of countries.[6]

In Central America, there are explicit laws prohibiting child labor and protecting children's rights. In fact, the constitutions of Costa Rica, El Salvador, Guatemala, Honduras, and Nicaragua recognize the need to protect children's physical, mental, and moral development and to ensure that children complete a minimum education (ILO, 2003). However, even though national laws with 'special protections' for children may exist, governments may be compelled to allow their laws to be violated due to pressure from domestic corporate interests, other nations, international financial institutions such as the World Bank and IMF, or as a result of trade agreements like NAFTA, CAFTA-DR, 'Plan Puebla Panama', the Andean Region Initiative, or trade associations like the WTO. As a result of these pressures, labor rights and working conditions have deteriorated worldwide (Chossudovsky, 2003; Houghton and Bell, 2004; IFG, 2002; Parenti, 2002:86), and the international covenants that have been designed to protect the rights of children, have been ignored.

An analysis of the exploitation of children in agriculture, manufacturing, and the sex trade will demonstrate that the categories 'child' and 'childhood' are not only socially and culturally constructed but also politically manipulated to meet the interests and needs of global capitalism. Children's rights are violated frequently and without apology, in both the global South and the global North. The violation of children's rights is the direct result of policies that continue to support and enrich the system of global capitalism and that seamlessly integrate legitimate and illegitimate economic activities, at the expense of the overwhelming majority of families throughout the world. To address the needs and interests of the world's children and their families, policymakers and development planners will necessarily have to reexamine their assumptions regarding children and childhood, and global capitalism. They will need to exert pressure on the world community to radically change the conditions of life that make child labor necessary for survival, establish enforceable laws and empower children to fight for their rights.

Child Laborers in the Agricultural Sector

According to the ILO, worldwide, 170 million or 70 percent of all child laborers work in agriculture. Even though the number of children who work in agriculture is 10 times that of the number of children working in manufacturing, until very recently, little attention has been focused on the problems confronting child farm workers. A cross-national comparison of child agricultural laborers in Egypt, Ecuador, India, and the United States conducted by Human Rights Watch (HRW) in 2004 reveals that despite country differences, the risks to, and abuses of, children working as hired farm workers are very similar. These include violations of rights to health and education, wage exploitation and lack of protection from hazardous working conditions (HRW, 2004).

The wages children receive are very low in all four of the countries studied. Children are subjected to long hours of exhausting physical labor; they suffer high rates of fatalities and work-related injuries for which they or their families get no compensation. In the United States, for example, it is estimated that 8 percent of child laborers work in agriculture, yet children account for 40 percent of work-related fatalities among youth; another 100,000 children in the US sustain farm work-related injuries per year (HRW, 2004). In all four countries, labor practices violate domestic laws as well as international laws and conventions. The next section focuses specifically on the United States.

Child Farm Workers in the United States

Children who are 14 years old and younger, are not counted in any official national survey of farm workers in the United States. The Government Accountability Office (GAO), collects data only on children 15 years and older. The GAO estimates that 300,000 15-17 year olds work as hired laborers in large-scale commercial agriculture each year. In contrast, the United Farm Workers Union estimates the total number of child farm workers (including children under the age of 15) in the US to be 800,000 per year (HRW, 2000):

> Farm workers aged 17 and under...can be found working all across the country. Virtually no state is without child labor in agriculture. Federal and most state laws permit children as young as 12 to work for hire in agriculture, an age far younger than in other occupations. Even children aged ten

and eleven can work as hired farm laborers...regardless of the damage done to their health, their studies, and their overall well being. (HRW, 2000)

An examination of US labor laws reveals that while children are legally protected in nonagricultural labor, they are not afforded the same protections in agricultural labor. According to a 1997 survey by the Child Labor Coalition, 18 states have no minimum age requirements for farm workers; in the state of Oregon, the minimum age is nine; in the state of Illinois, it is 10; in 14 states, the minimum age is 12; in nine states, it is 14 (HRW, 2000).

With regard to federal law, the Fair Labor Standards Act (FLSA), which was passed by Congress in 1938, set the minimum age for child labor, but excluded farm workers from protection. In 1974, restrictions on hired child laborers in agriculture were added to the law (HRW, 2000). Even so, there were, and still are, significant discrepancies between allowable practices in nonagricultural vs. agricultural labor. These include not only minimum age requirements, but also restrictions on the numbers of hours of work per day and per week. For example, the FLSA prohibits children who are 13 years old or younger from working in nonagricultural occupations, but permits 12 and 13 year olds to work unlimited hours (outside of school hours) on any size farm with parental consent. The FLSA also stipulates that 16 and 17 year olds are allowed to work under hazardous conditions in agricultural labor, whereas in other occupations, the minimum age is 18 (HRW, 2000).

Farm work requires mobility, strength, and endurance. Children endure excessive and inappropriate hours of exhausting work that is performed under unhealthy and often dangerous conditions. One of the major risks is exposure to pesticides on a daily basis. Workers are sprayed with pesticides by crop dusters flying over the fields while they work. Also, both children and adults are often required to mix and apply pesticides without the use of protective clothing or equipment. 'In addition to cancer, pesticide exposure has been repeatedly linked to brain damage, endocrine (hormonal) disruption and birth defects' (HRW, 2000). The Environmental Protection Agency (EPA) reports an average of 300,000 pesticide poisonings per year, but this figure is likely to underestimate the total since only a small percentage of pesticide-related illnesses is reported to the federal government, state authorities or health officials (HRW, 2000). Children are especially susceptible to the toxic effects of pesticides:

> Farm children are like canaries in the coal mine. Canaries were placed inside mine shafts where they would breathe the first whiffs of poisonous gas. More susceptible than humans to these gases (in part because of their small body size and rapid respiratory rate), the birds would suffer health effects before the miners, providing an early warning of dangerous conditions. We are putting farm children in a situation where they receive some of the highest pesticide exposures in our country. Children, like canaries, have greater susceptibility to the health effects than do adults. Yet…many of the expected health effects occur years or even decades after the exposures. (NRDC, 1998)

Pesticide use, especially of the most toxic and carcinogenic chemicals, has been increasing in the United States. However, precise figures are difficult to obtain since the federal government and individual states do not require the reporting of this kind of data.[7]

In addition to pesticide exposure, other hazards of agricultural labor include lack of drinking water, water for hand washing, and toilet facilities, which are the minimum sanitation requirements established by the Occupational Safety and Health Administration. But 'even these minimal requirements are often ignored by growers and by farm labor contractors who bring in workers. Furthermore, Congress prohibits enforcement of these regulations on farms with ten employees or less' (HRW, 2000). Thus, workers frequently suffer from heat exhaustion and other illnesses related to insufficient or contaminated water and lack of sanitation.

Another consequence of agricultural labor for children has to do with the demanding physical nature of the work itself, changes in the growing cycle and the shifting location of work, all of which have an impact on children's education and progress in school. Child farm workers in the state of Arizona reported that 12-hour days, six and seven days per week were routine; during peak harvest times, they worked 18 hours, seven days per week (HRW, 2000). Those who managed to attend school endured interruptions in learning due to the seasonal demands of the work, and many were required to change schools several times during the year. Child farm workers tend to get little sleep, have very long days of hard labor; they frequently fall behind in their studies and may eventually drop out of school altogether. The GAO estimated the dropout rate among child farm workers to be 45 percent compared to 29 percent for children engaged in nonagricultural labor (GAO, 1992:37).

Because farm work pays so little, even when all members of the family work, family incomes are very low and the poverty rate is very high. Families whose children work as hired agricultural laborers often depend on their children's contributions for the family's survival. In addition, many parents cannot afford to buy school supplies, books, shoes, or clothing for their children to attend school. Because of obstacles like these to making progress in school, the difficulties of breaking out of the cycle of poverty are formidable (GAO, 1992).[8] Due to the geographic isolation of farm labor, noncompliance with the minimal federal and state laws that do exist is rampant, and, not surprisingly, there is a great deal of exploitation and abuse of farm workers. Those most vulnerable are non-unionized workers, non-English speakers, those who are unfamiliar with US labor laws, and children. Wages are rarely higher than minimum wage and frequently much lower, especially when wages are paid at piece rates rather than hourly rates. 'Unscrupulous employers' withhold social security, but instead of reporting it to the federal government, pocket the money for themselves. Wage deductions cover fees for housing and electricity that are sometimes provided, or for transporting workers to the work site. Overtime pay, or health, unemployment, or disability benefits are nonexistent (HRW, 2000).

Neither US laws nor enforcement practices protect child laborers in agriculture. The US also fails to comply with international conventions including the ILO Convention Concerning the Prohibition and Immediate Elimination of the Worst Forms of Child Labor, and the United Nations Convention on the Rights of the Child.

Industrial Labor in the Global South

Over the past 25 years or so, massive de-industrialization has taken place in the United States and other nations of the global North, as industries have moved south in search of cheaper labor. The integration of young women into the industrial labor force in the Third World has been one of the outcomes of the corporate colonization of the global South. Twenty years ago, the phenomenon of targeting young women in the Third World as workers for 'light assembly production' or 'offshore' manufacturing for export was concentrated in two major regions of the world–Southeast Asia and Mexico–and was referred to as the 'new international division of labor.'[9] The majority of workers were in their early to mid-20s. Young women were the preferred labor force in the *maquiladoras* or subcontracting manufacturing industries because they were believed to have 'nimble fingers', to be docile and more manageable and less likely to object to conditions of work or employment practices (Fuentes and Ehrenreich, 1984:11).

By moving their production operations to the Third World, corporations maximize their profits by exploiting workers. Wages are very low and workers work long hours without overtime pay, health or disability benefits. The US government provides US corporations with taxpayers' dollars to help finance the cost of relocating (Parenti, 2002:86). In addition, corporations often benefit from a five or 10-year 'tax holiday.' They pay little or no import or export duties. They have access to the best resources, and do not have to abide by national labor laws, or health, safety or environmental regulations (Belle et al., 1995; NLC, 1996).

The global assembly line now extends throughout the world, even in remote and previously isolated regions. Wages have deteriorated in both absolute and relative terms, working conditions are dangerous, contamination of the environment is widespread, and the damages are great to young women–who are no longer the 'new' industrial laborers, but rather the primary laborers. Moreover, in spite of child labor laws prohibiting the exploitation of children's labor, the majority of new workers targeted by the global factory are, in fact, children. In communities where there are few other wage-earning opportunities, children often become the primary or sole wage earners in their families. They are forced to forego education and a chance to lift themselves and their families out of poverty in order to provide a minimum degree of sustenance for their families' survival. This is the result of the imperative on the part of global capital to seek out the cheapest labor force in order to reap the greatest profit. Thus, very young workers are being exploited in increasingly depressed regions of the world in what the National Labor Committee (NLC) refers to as the 'race to the bottom'.

In addition to having little regard for the workers, corporate owners and managers are not accountable to the community in which they 'set up shop'. Communities in the global South, not unlike their northern counterparts, are destabilized whenever industries move elsewhere in search of cheaper and more 'manageable' labor. In other words, the mobility of capital and capital enterprises has an enormous impact on children, families, and communities.

In CIVAC, an industrial 'park' on the outskirts of Cuernavaca, Mexico, factories like 'Phantom,' a Canadian-owned swimsuit factory, are experiencing competition from manufacturers that have moved on to set up shop in China. Phantom has a reputation for treating its workers fairly and paying higher wages than many other global factories. According to Phantom's General Manager, Engineer Gabriel Hidalgo, a day's work at Phantom, is 10 hours long, which includes 30 minutes for lunch and a five-minute break in the afternoon. Workers are allowed two additional five-minute breaks during the day, but their 'efficiency coefficient' suffers if they take those breaks, and their pay may be docked as a result. Because Phantom is having a difficult time 'competing with other companies', Engineer Hidalgo recently 'had to lay off 300 workers'. Hidalgo pointed out that at least one company that paid its workers less than Phantom, has already left Mexico in search of younger, cheaper labor in China (Polakoff, 2003). Corporations are feeling the pressure to leave industrial 'parks' like CIVAC in Cuernavaca, and transfer their manufacturing operations to China, where they can pay young workers as little as US$1 per day.

China is the capitalist's dream territory: it has new, previously untapped resources, new and cheap labor, and new markets to exploit, all of which fuel the expansion of corporate capital (IFG, 2003:19-21). In the transition to a market economy, 'the privatization or forced bankruptcy of thousands of state enterprises' will mean that another 35 million workers will be fired (Chossudovsky, 2003:2). These will be added to the already unemployed in China's rural areas. Again, the overwhelming majority of workers (nearly 90 percent) are young women or girls in their early teens. Many come from rural areas in China where there are an estimated 130 million 'surplus workers' (Chossudovsky, 2003:2). Thus, in the 'race to the bottom', the architects and profiteers of economic globalization have staked out China and other poor nations like Vietnam as the next frontier.

The NLC monitors child labor practices in the manufacturing industries worldwide. In Haiti, for example, workers in the garment industry producing goods for Disney, earn the equivalent of US 28 cents per hour–a wage that forces families to 'survive on credit like indentured servants' (NLC, 1996). Apparently, Disney too, has threatened to leave Haiti and go elsewhere if workers make too many demands. Parenti reports wages as low as US 11 cents per hour in Haiti, and reminds us that child labor is widespread among US-based multinational corporations operating in the Third World, as well as within the United States:

> The United States is one of the few countries that has refused to sign an international convention for the abolition of child labor and forced labor. This position stems from the child

labor practices of U.S. corporations throughout the Third World and in the United States itself, where children as young as twelve suffer high rates of fatalities, and are often paid less than minimum wage. (Parenti, 2002:86)

In Central America, the average age of workers in the *maquila* industry is 15, and the average level of educational attainment is the fifth grade (Belle et al., 1995). Honduran labor leader, Jorge Sierra of The Committee for the Defense of Human Rights in Honduras (CODEH), recognizes the sacrifices made by the children who work in the *maquiladoras*, and the ultimate threat to their communities and their nation as a whole:

> For a 15-year old girl... *to fall into the maquila is to fall into a deep, dark well. She must cease to be a person...*the *maquila* is wringing the Honduran youth dry. Within 10 years we are going to have 25-30 year-old women who are tired of life, sick. This will produce serious social problems for our country. We are going to have people without imagination, people who believe in nothing and who will not be able to function in the development that we want for our country. (Belle et al., 1995)

Jorge Sierra expresses concern for the physical, emotional, moral, and spiritual health of Honduran children, especially the young girls who are targeted as cheap laborers for global capitalism. He pinpoints precisely the nature of the problem confronting children, their families and communities worldwide. We might wonder, what are the future prospects of nations whose young people are kept at a depressed level of education? What are the future prospects of nations whose young people are physically and mentally restricted by the conditions of work and the conditions of life they must face every day? Young people whose very aspirations and desires are so depressed that they cannot even imagine or hope for a better world for themselves? By condemning the youth of nations throughout the world to a life of misery and virtual enslavement, do we not simultaneously destroy the future for us all?

Another deeply disturbing trend has been the extreme physical violence against young women in the rapidly expanding industrialized towns on the Mexico side of the US-Mexico border. Portillo (2001) investigated the circumstances surrounding the disappearances and unsolved murders of young women in Ciudad Juárez, across the border from El Paso, Texas. Though uncertain of the exact numbers, Portillo estimated that over a period of 10 years, from 1992–2002, somewhere between 200 and 400 young women, many of whom worked in the *maquiladoras,* were killed in Ciudad Juárez.

Interviews conducted by Portillo with Francisco Barrio, the Governor of the state of Chihuahua from 1992-1998, and with his Assistant Attorney General, Jorge López, revealed the callous and indifferent attitudes that many public officials have had regarding the murders. For instance, Barrio blamed young women for being in the wrong place and hanging around with the wrong kind of people. Furthermore, López's solution to the problem was to impose a curfew on the residents of the city: 'All the good people should stay at home with their families and let the bad people be out on the street'. When Portillo asked him, 'but what about a city like Ciudad Juárez where we have a huge industry–the *maquiladoras* employing over 185,000 very young people, many young women. Many enter at 5 or 6 a.m. and finish at midnight and have to be out because of the necessity to work'. López responded, 'It's a matter of how you look at things. Clearly, if you need to work–you can't impose this on workers. But let's start with the ones who can. People who work follow a clear path and dress a certain way' (Portillo, 2001).

Though it remains unclear exactly who is responsible for the young women's disappearances and murders, implicated in their disappearances are the managers of the factories, local law enforcement agents, and, possibly, the purveyors of the drug trade and/or the sex and pornography industries:

> To some North Americans it (Ciudad Juárez) is where everything illicit is available…One of the leading businesses is illegal narcotics. It is a multi-billion dollar industry…With NAFTA, multinationals have flooded into the city. Eighty percent are American-owned. The *maquiladoras* generate $16 billion per year…For young women arriving from the rural areas, Juárez is the city of the future. Here they can earn $4 or $5 a day and the hope of their economic independence. (Portillo, 2001)

In spite of investigations into the disappearances and murders, the majority of cases remain unsolved and the murders of young women have continued. In August 2005, Amnesty International (AI) sent a delegation to Chihuahua and Ciudad Juárez, led by its Secretary General, Irene Khan. The delegation discovered that between March and August 2005, more than 20 women were murdered. Consistent with Portillo's findings regarding the attitudes of local public officials on these matters, Irene Khan noted a lack of concrete action on the part of public officials. AI reported that:

> Identification of 130 local officials as possibly responsible for criminal or administrative acts of negligence has led to no prosecutions, and impunity for officials...Chihuahua and Ciudad Juárez are symptoms of an epidemic of violence against women around the world. (AI, 2005)

In Ciudad Juárez, there appear to be links between the formal economy and the criminal economy. Global capitalist penetration has played a part in nearly seamlessly integrating the criminal economy into the formal economy. This has had serious consequences for all, but particularly for young women and children who are exploited both as 'goods and services' in the formal economy as well as in the criminal economy. They are robbed of their humanity in a process that actively annihilates their spirit and that has profound consequences for their futures. This is, perhaps, the most obvious and the most egregious in the global sex industry.

Expansion of the Global Criminal Economy: Young Women and Children in the Global Sex Trade[10]

An important and frequently overlooked consequence of global capitalist penetration is the phenomenon of global crime, or the 'networking of powerful criminal organizations, and their associates, in shared activities throughout the planet...Everything that receives added value precisely from its prohibition'[11] is central to the global criminal economy including the smuggling of goods and the trafficking of human beings (Castells, 1998:166-67).

The trafficking of children has been identified as 'one of the worst forms of child labour' (ILO, 2004). Although no precise figures exist, the ILO (2004) estimates that every year, 1.2 million children are trafficked across national borders to work in agriculture, mining, manufacturing industries, armed conflict, and commercial sex work. Most official statistics do not distinguish between human trafficking for the purposes of sexual exploitation and trafficking for other purposes.[12] However, in 2005, the ILO estimated that of the nearly 2.5 million people who were 'trafficked forced labourers worldwide', almost half were trafficked exclusively for the purpose of commercial sexual exploitation, and 98 percent were girls and women (ILO, 2005). Obstacles to collecting accurate statistics include the fact that the sex trade:

> is secretive, the women are silenced, the traffickers are dangerous, and not many agencies are counting. Also, the word 'trafficking' does not have a universal meaning, resulting in different estimates depending on the definition used. (Hughes, 2001:2)

Hughes suggests using a definition of human trafficking that focuses specifically on sexual exploitation. She also identifies underlying economic and political inequalities between women and men, and between children and adults, that make trafficking possible in the first place:

> Trafficking is any practice that involves moving people within and across local or national borders for the purpose of sexual exploitation. Trafficking may be the result of force, coercion, manipulation, deception, abuse of authority, initial consent, family pressure, past and present family and community violence, economic deprivation, or other conditions of inequality for women and children. This definition accepts that trafficking occurs even if the woman consents, which is consistent with the 1949 United Nations convention prohibiting it. (Hughes, 2001:2)

Regardless of how they end up in the sex trade–voluntarily or 'through means of deceit or coercion'–millions of young women and girls participate in the 'ever-expanding sex industry' worldwide; indeed, 'prostitution has increasingly become a means of sustaining and maintaining vast numbers of third world women and their families' (Sangera, 1997:2). Although prostitution itself is not new, new forms of prostitution have developed in our 'globalized' world and are as prevalent in the first world as in the third.

First, globalization has meant the transnationalization of the sex trade itself, which in addition to being one of the most profitable of global industries, is also:

> one of the most diversified, sophisticated and specialized. It offers a vast array of services, caters to a spectacular range of customer demands, offers specialized venues for sex enter-

tainment in different countries of the world, caters to every need in terms of price range in the consumer market, and has designed a mind-boggling repertoire of market strategies to attract prospective clientele. (Sangera, 1997:7)

A second factor has to do with the ways in which the bodies of young women and children in the Third World are increasingly defined as the 'new raw resources', constituting a 'prime export item for national development and international trade. This human cash crop is unique in that it offers a double-featured advantage: women's bodies are both goods and services at the same time' (Sangera, 1997: 8). In the sex trade, the labor of young women and children, 'is exploited beyond acceptable human rights standards through forced labour and slavery-like practices', and 'is one of the prime tools of capital accumulation under globalization' (Sangera, 1997).

A third factor that has contributed to the transformation of prostitution is the fact that many countries throughout the Third World 'have been encouraged by international bodies such as the World Bank and the IMF to develop their tourism and entertainment industries…Without exception [this has meant focusing] disproportionately on developing (the) sex trade into an industry' (Sangera, 1997). Essentially this means that the formal and criminal economies have become integrated in compliance with externally-managed institutions operating through internally-controlled structures. The integration of criminal activities into the formal economy involves: 'Complex financial schemes and international trade networks [that] link up the criminal economy to the formal economy, thus deeply penetrating financial markets, and constituting a critical, volatile element in a fragile global economy' (Castells, 1998:167).[11]

The collapse of the economies of the states of the former Soviet Union, Eastern Europe, and the Balkans in the 1990s, certainly contributed to an increase in sex trafficking of young women and girls from these areas:

> Countries with large sex industries create the demand for women; countries where traffickers easily recruit women provide the supply. For decades, the primary sending countries were in Asia. But the collapse of the Soviet Union opened up a pool of millions of women from which traffickers can recruit. Former Soviet republics such as Belarus, Latvia, Moldova, Russia, and Ukraine have become major suppliers of women to sex industries all over the world. In the sex indus-

try today, the most popular and valuable women are from Russia and Ukraine. (Hughes, 2001:2)

Regardless of whether they arrive from Eastern Europe or Latin America, many of the young women who are headed to the United States are 'processed' in Mexico due to the 'porousness of the US-Mexico border and the criminal networks that traverse it' (Landesman, 2004:32). Furthermore, 'Mexico is not merely a way station en route to the US for third-country traffickers, like the Eastern European rings. It is also a vast source of even *younger and more cheaply acquired girls* for sexual servitude in the United States' (Landesman, 2004:36, emphasis mine).

As economic survival becomes more of a challenge to families throughout the world, we may expect the violence in the lives of many young women and children to increase. Not surprisingly, this has serious consequences, not only for the individuals themselves, but also for their communities:

> The moneymakers are transnational networks of traffickers and pimps who prey on women seeking employment and opportunities. These illegal activities and related crimes not only harm the women involved; they also undermine the social, political, and economic fabric of the nations where they occur. (Hughes, 2001:2)

In other words, global capitalist penetration has increasingly placed women and children–who are specifically targeted by capitalist entrepreneurs of all kinds–at risk. We might expect the consequences of these practices to reverberate through our communities, on both sides of the border, for years to come. However, contrary to dominant stereotypes of children as weak, passive and easily manipulated, on the one hand, or as juvenile delinquents, on the other, many children throughout the world are caring for other children and actively organizing to defend their rights as citizens and full members of the societies in which they live.

Children's Collective Resistance and Participation in Defense of Their Rights

As the previous sections demonstrated, children in many societies worldwide are vulnerable to super-exploitation and have the least amount of power or access to structures of power. Children's voices are typically absent from decision-making and policymaking processes, even on issues that affect them the most. But the fact that children are vulnerable, does not necessarily mean they are incapable of challenging structures, institutions or ideologies that exploit them. As O'Kane (2003:1) noted, 'children are active participants in the construction and determination of their social lives, other people's lives and the societies in which they live'. And, while there are many more child workers in rural areas, urban street and working children and adolescents, have been the most active in collective associations to challenge the dominant stereotypes about them and the prevailing attitudes towards them, resist exploitative working conditions and fight for their rights at local, national and international levels.

The organization *Niños y Adolescentes Trabajadores (NATS)*, or Child and Adolescent Workers is generally acknowledged as the first contemporary collective association of children. NATS was organized by street children in the mid-1970s in Lima, Peru (Cisneros, 1999). A few years earlier, members of the Christian Workers Youth Movement, adherents to the principles of Liberation Theology, had established street and working children's centers for the most marginalized children living in shantytowns surrounding Lima. In 1976, when the city council threatened to close the centers and sell the land, the NATS mobilized to defend the centers and demand that the city provide them with services like water, electricity, sanitation, education and health care (Ibid). The movement grew into the *Movimiento de Niños, Niñas y Adolescentes Trabajadores Hijos de Obreros Cristianos (MANTHOC)*, or the Movement of Working Boys, Girls and Adolescents of Christian Workers.

Today, 5000 child workers in 10 provinces participate in MANTHOC, which is organized and managed by young people who assert, 'MANTHOC is not an NGO: it is a life choice' (www.shinealight.org/MANTHOC.html). Given the politics of Peru, the general attitudes of those in positions of authority toward street children, and the radical politics that MANTHOC espouses, one would probably not expect the organization to have a positive relationship with the police, but apparently it does. In fact, MANTHOC supported police in their efforts 'to create 'Colibri' (hummingbird), a police division that works exclusively with child workers. The police have learned that organized child labor improves public order and reduces gang activity, so they help MANTHOC to organize children into labor unions' (Ibid).

In Nicaragua, youth were a critical component in the 1979 Sandinista victory over the Somoza dictatorship. Young people at that time, were very much part of the Sandinista base of support in both rural and urban areas. After the Sandinistas came to power, the 'Juventud Sandinista' or Sandinista Youth movement was mobilized in the processes of development, defense and democratic participation (Polakoff and LaRamée, 1997). Young people were key in the literacy, vaccination, oral rehydration and sanitation campaigns. For example, 88,000 high school and college students, mostly from urban areas, volunteered for the literacy campaign, which was launched in 1980, leaving their homes and families for five months to live and work in the rural areas of the country. At the end of five months, adult literacy increased from 50% to over 80% (Williams, 1991).

Beginning in the 1980s, and having been inspired by the organizations of child and youth workers in Latin America, a number of initiatives were created that sought to empower children, acknowledge the diversity of their experiences, listen to their ideas, create spaces for them to organize other children and act on their own behalf. Many of these initiatives use the United Nations Convention on the Rights of the Child to re-value children as citizens of society, which is the first step in making governments and corporations accountable to children's needs (O'Kane, 2003).

The Butterflies Programme, an NGO in Delhi, India, began working with street and working children in 1989, and now serves over 1500 children in Delhi and 6,000 children in villages of the Adaman Nicobar Islands, devastated by the tsunami, and many children in several other regions of India and South Asia (www.butterflieschildrights.org/profile.asp). Participants in the Children's Council of the Butterflies Programme elect their own Chair and Secretary, decide their own agenda, and discuss the issues that most concern them as street and working children including: 'police harassment, non-payment of wages, need for better jobs, wages, education, saving schemes, problems of gambling and drugs' (O'Kane 2003:5). The children have created their own collective associations such as a child workers' union, health cooperative, Children's Alternate Media, the Delhi Children's Rights Club and Children's Development Bank (www.butterflieschildrights.org/profile.asp). In addition, children are active participants in other aspects of Butterflies including the Community Kitchen, which is managed by twelve young people. Butterflies' non-formal education and literacy program reaches more than 1,200 children; its Mobile School reaches another 300 children (Ibid).

Their alternate media (newspaper, radio programs and theatre) provide children with the vehicles through which they can publicly voice and communicate their concerns to the community. They also use their own media to challenge the dominant stereotypes of street children as beggars, thieves or victims (O'Kane, 2003). The Child Rights Club discusses policies, organizes workshops and marches, produces reports about their experiences like their 2003 report, 'Invisible and Footloose: An Analysis of Children and Women Working in the Informal Sector', and drafts bills for legislation like their 2005 draft bill, 'Offences Against Children' (www.butterflieschildrights.org/rightsClub.asp). By engaging with other children to discuss the problems and difficulties they face and by organizing a collective response, children take the lead in embracing the values of participatory democracy. According to O'Kane (2003:11):

> By empowering street and working children to reflect upon their experiences, articulate their views, plan effective programs and advocate for their own rights, these children are challenging the *status quo* regarding children's place and power in society.

In New York City, Girls Educational & Mentoring Service (GEMS) works to support young women who have experienced commercial sexual exploitation. The organization was founded in 1999 by Rachel Lloyd, a young survivor of sexual exploitation (www. gems-girls.org/about/mission-history). GEMS provides educational, mental health and legal counseling, health and housing services, and conducts workshops to raise awareness about the problems faced by youth (www.gems-girls.org/what-we-do). Its Youth Outreach Team is active in the movement against commercial sexual exploitation and trafficking in the United States. On the streets and in youth detention centers, members of the Youth Outreach Team contact young women who have been victimized in the commercial sex trade, and 'advocate for their peers at the local, national and international level including through the NY State Legislature, US Congress and the United Nations' (Sun, 2010).

Another organization dedicated to empowering street and working children, to foster a strong sense of self and collective identity, so that they may work toward changing society and the global community is 'Shine a Light'. According to co-directors, Kurt Shaw and Rita da Silva, 'Street kids and children from shantytowns aren't "poor little things"…They're strong, creative, clever…people we want to know, people we want to succeed' (Shaw and da Silva, 2010). Shine a Light networks with over 200 organizations of street and working children in approximately 17 countries throughout Latin

America. Recognizing the marginalization and exclusion of street children, indigenous children and children of low-income families, the approach Shine a Light has adopted is based on the notion that 'visibility is one of the best weapons against exclusion' of all kinds–whether it is exclusion from the job market, educational opportunities, services or protection (www.shinealight.org). Supported by Shine a Light, children are constructing and disseminating their own video images of themselves that challenge mainstream views of children as weak, naïve victims or dangerous delinquents. Their videos reach out and speak to children around the world and educate adults about the diversity of children's experiences. With cameras in hand, indigenous children from Paraguay to Panama, child soldiers from Colombia, migrant children from Central America to New Mexico, and working children throughout Latin America, write scripts, interview siblings, friends and members of their community, create soap operas, fiction films and documentaries that validate their own experiences and identities and help us to understand not only 'how the dynamics of social change and social agency are catalyzed by the camera' (Shaw and da Silva, 2010:27), but that children working collectively have much to teach adults about what it means to create and participate in democratic societies.

Conclusion

The forms of child labor discussed in this chapter are manifestations of deeper structural problems related to global capitalist penetration itself. The forces of economic globalization have penetrated even the most isolated regions of the world and integrated those regions into the global economy, creating vast regions of poverty, misery, and social exclusion.

The interests and values of global capitalism are protected by governments and the military, and upheld by international financial institutions and trade agreements. The policies and practices of international financial institutions have accelerated the integration of local economies into the global market in ways that are detrimental to poor countries and the marginalized sectors of wealthy countries. Governments have been pressured to open up their borders to foreign investment, allow foreign ownership and exploitation of national resources (land, minerals, water, and human resources), gear local economies toward export production, privatize the public or state sector, dismantle social welfare, and remove barriers to the influx of foreign goods onto the local market. Global corporate bureaucracies have been involved in the creation of these policies and the development of trade agreements that have provided them with the power to ignore and/or violate environmental protections, occupational, safety and health regulations, civil rights, and child labor laws. Greater poverty and the super-exploitation of children–whose economic contributions are vital to their families' survival–have resulted.

On 7 June 2005, UN Secretary General Koffi Annan released the United Nations Millennium Development Goals (MDG) 2005 which underscores improvement in the conditions under which children live as central to meeting development goals: 'If we care about making progress on development, we have to care about children. Not one of the MDGs can be attained if childhood continues to be threatened by extreme poverty' (UNICEF, 2005a). Furthermore, 'Child labour condemns children to a harrowing present and a hopeless future and is a throwback to some of the most shameful aspects of human behaviour. Like slavery, it can and must be consigned to history' (UNICEF, 2001:13).

The State of the World's Children 2010 Special Edition on Children's Rights acknowledged that the economic crisis of 2009 would very likely have a negative impact on children and their rights as outlined in the Convention:

> (2009 was) marked by the worst global financial crisis in 80 years…The risks to child rights from current economic crises and other external challenges (like natural disasters and environment shifts) must not be underestimated. There is a real danger that the repercussions of these shocks will have lifelong consequences that span generations, undermining efforts to advance children's rights for the coming decades. (UNICEF, 2009:6-7)

The exploitation of children will not cease until the global economy is restructured to benefit the most marginalized communities and households, rather than global capitalist interests. This will now require even greater organization and struggle, continued sacrifice, and perseverance on the part of all women, men, and children who strive for a dignified, meaningful life, in the global North as well as the global South. Children, especially, have demonstrated that they can be effective participants in democratic processes, changing dominant perceptions about them, resisting exploitation and challenging the violation of their rights as citizens, in order to shape a more just and humane global society. Clearly, the collective organizations and collective resistances of children throughout the world are actively shaping children's identities and roles as agents of the kind of social change that would indeed, lead to a better world.

NOTES

[1] As I discussed in the introduction to this collection, there are many different terms used to name and describe the global processes that are increasing the gap between the wealthy and the poor, privileging a minority at the expense of the overwhelming majority, and creating masses of people who are homeless, hungry, sick, marginalized and disenfranchised. The broadest and most commonly used term is 'globalization' often accompanied by a descriptor–generally, 'economic' or 'neoliberal' or 'corporate'. In this chapter, I tend to use 'global capitalist penetration' or more simply 'global capitalism' in my own analysis. When referring specifically to the work of other scholars and researchers, I use the term they adopted.

[2] It is telling that the U.S. government uses 'in force' to indicate those trade agreements that are in effect–they have been signed by the Executive Office of both countries and they have been approved by the U.S. Congress.

[3] Although critical of some of the negative consequences of economic globalization, Stiglitz and the World Bank manipulate the definition of poverty, underestimating the number of people affected by structural adjustment policies. For example, the World Bank has defined poverty as living on US$2 per day. This is lower than the previous threshold used in the 1980s, of living on US$4 per day. In some cases, the Bank switches to a threshold of living on US$1 per day, which is defined as 'absolute poverty'. When reporting on the percentage of the population living in poverty in Latin America, the Soviet Union and Sub-Saharan Africa, the Bank uses this latter measure which not only vastly underestimates the percent of the poor in these areas but also tells us little about how people manage to survive on US$2, US$3, US$4 or even US$5 per day. When defining poverty as living on US$1 per day, 16 percent of the population of Latin America is poor (Stiglitz, 2003:259). However, recent household surveys that take into account domestic prices of basic food staples, housing, health, education and clothing reveal that more than 60 percent of the population of Latin America cannot even meet the *minimum calorie and protein requirements*, to say nothing of

meeting other basic needs (Chossudovsky, 2003:29-31). People earning the equivalent of US$3 or US$4 a day are poor and have tremendous difficulty providing sustenance for their families, but they are not included in the World Bank's calculations.

4. Booker and Minter (2001) define global apartheid as, 'an international system of minority rule' characterized by 'differential access to human rights; wealth and power structured by race and place; structural racism embedded in global economic processes, political institutions, and cultural assumptions; and international practice of double standards that assume inferior rights to be appropriate for certain "others" defined by location, origin, race or gender'.

5. Hazardous work is defined as: 'a) Work which exposes children to physical, emotional, or sexual abuse; b) work underground, underwater, at dangerous heights or in confined spaces; c) work with dangerous machinery, equipment or tools, or which involves the manual handling or transporting of heavy loads; d) work in an unhealthy environment which may, for example, expose children to hazardous substances, agents, or processes, or to temperatures, noise levels or vibrations damaging to their health; or e) work under particularly difficult conditions such as work for long hours or during the night or work that does not allow the possibility of returning home each day' (UNICEF, 2005b).

6. UNICEF estimates that there are 5.7 million children working as bonded laborers *worldwide* (UNICEF, 2000b). However, according to a Human Rights Watch report, in India *alone*—a country where 'bonded labor' is an illegal, but widespread practice—there are at least 15 million children working as bonded laborers (HRW, 2000).

7. 'California is the only state in the nation that requires commercial pesticide users to report the time, location, and amount of pesticides applied' (NRDC, 1998).

8. The GAO (1992) reported that 80 percent of all adult migrant farmers had a literacy level equivalent to the fifth grade or lower.

9. Early analyses of this phenomenon included those by Elson and Pearson (1981), Fernandez-Kelly (1983), and Fuentes and Ehrenreich (1984).

10. The issue of human trafficking for sexual exploitation has received considerable recent attention by the media in the United States, in feature films (e.g., 'Taken' directed by Pierre Morel and released in 2008; and 'Trade' directed by Marco Kreuzpaintner and released in 2007), in documentary films (e.g., on Tuesday, 7 February 2006, PBS's Frontline series aired, 'Sex Slaves',

a documentary on the trafficking of women from Eastern Europe which was directed by Bienstock and released in 2006), and in a made-for-TV mini-series ('Human Trafficking' which was directed by Duguay and aired in 2005). In 2004, a feature article for *The New York Times Sunday Magazine*, 'The Girls Next Door: Sex Slaves on Main Street,' investigated sexual slavery– the process by which young women and girls are abducted, sold by their families, deceived, or coerced to participate in the sex trade (Landesman, 2004). Nicholas Kristof has written a number of editorials for the *New York Times* on the subject of sex tourism and child sex slaves; he has also made several powerful short videos, which are available on his web pages (http://topics.nytimes.com.

[11] These include: 'radioactive material, human organs, and illegal immigrants; prostitution; gambling; loan-sharking; kidnapping; racketeering and extortion; counterfeiting of goods, bank notes, financial documents, credit cards, and identity cards; killers for hire; traffic of sensitive information, technology or art objects; international sales of stolen goods; or even dumping garbage illegally from one country into another' (Castells, 1998:166).

[12] See: UNESCO's Trafficking Statistics Project (2003).

REFERENCES

Amnesty International (AI) (2005) 'Mexico: Truth and Justice for the Murdered and Abducted Women of Ciudad Juárez and Chihuahua'. AI Press release, 9 August 2005. Accessed 10 February, 2006 from www.amnesty.org.

Becker, J. (2004) 'Children as Weapons of War'. *Human Rights Watch World Report 2004: Human Rights and Armed Conflict*, pp. 219-43. New Work: Human Rights Watch.

Beegle, K., Dehejia, R. and Gatti, R. (2009) 'Why Should We Care About Child Labor? The Education, Labor Market and Health Consequences of Child Labor'. *Journal of Human Resources* 44(4): 871-889.

Belle, D., Kean, K. and Stern, R. (1995) 'Zoned for Slavery: The Child Behind the Label' (VHS).

Bienstock, R.E. (2006) 'Sex Slaves'. PBS' Frontline series, documentary video.

Booker, S. and Minter, W. (2001) 'Global Apartheid'. *The Nation* (9 July 2001). Accessed 10 February 2006 from www.thenation.com/issue/july-9-2001.

Butterflies Programme (n.d.) Accessed 6 June 2010 from www.butterflieschildrights.org/profile.asp.
Castells, M. (1998) *End of the Millennium*. Oxford, England: Blackwell Publishers.
Chossudovsky, M. (2003) *The Globalization of Poverty and the New World Order*. Ontario: GlobalOutlook.
Duguay, C. (2005) *Human Trafficking*, first released 24 October 2005.
Elson, D. and Pearson, R. (1981) 'Nimble Fingers Make Cheap Workers: An Analysis of Women's Employment in Third World Export Manufacturing'. *Feminist Review* 7(1): 87-107.
Edmonds, E.V. (2005) 'Does Child Labor Decline with Improving Economic Status?' *Journal of Human Resources* 40(1): 77-79.
Farmer, P.E (2003) *Pathologies of Power: Health, Human Rights and the New War on the Poor*. Berkeley: University of California Press.
Feinstein, C. and O'Kane, C. (2009) 'Children's and Adolescents'. Participation and Protection from Sexual Abuse and Exploitation', *Innocenti Working Paper 2009-09*. Florence, Italy: UNICEF Innocenti Research Center. Accessed 28 May 2010 from www.irc.org/publications/pdf/iwp_2009_09.pdf.
Fernandez-Kelly, M.P. (1983) *For We Are Sold, I and My People: Women and Industry in Mexico's Frontier*. Albany: State University of New York Press.
Food and Agriculture Organization (FAO) (2002) 'Reducing Poverty and Hunger: The Critical Role of Financing for Food, Agriculture and Rural Development'. Paper Prepared for The International Conference on Financing for Development, 18-22 March 2002, Monterrey, Mexico. Accessed 10 February, 2006 from www.fao.org-Y6265E.pdf.
Fuentes, A. and Ehrenreich, B. (1984) *Women in the Global Factory*. Boston: South End Press.
Giddens, A. (2000) *Runaway World: How Globalization Is Reshaping Our Lives*. New York: Routledge.
Government Accountability Office (GAO) (1992) 'Hired Farmworkers: Health and Well-Being at Risk', (14 February 1992).Washington D.C.: GAO/HRD092-46. Accessed 20 April 2004 from www.gao.gov-145941.pdf.
Green, D. (1999) 'Child Workers of the Americas'. *NACLA Report on the Americas* 32(4): 21-27.
Houghton, J. and Bell, B. (2004) 'Latin American Indigenous Movements in the Context of Globalization'. *Interhemispheric Resource Center*, reprinted in P.S. Rothenberg (2006) *Beyond Borders:*

Thinking Critically About Global Issues, pp. 498–504. NY: Worth Publishers.
Hughes, D.M. (2001) 'The Natasha Trade: Transnational Sex Trafficking'. *National Institute of Justice Journal* 246 (January, 2001). Accessed 10 February 2006 from natasha_nij.pdf.
Human Rights Watch (HRW) (2000) 'Adolescent Farm Workers in the United States: Endangerment and Exploitation'. Accessed 10 June 2005 from www.hrw.org/reports/2000/frmwrk/frmwrk006-02.htm.
Human Rights Watch (HRW) (2004) 'Backgrounder: Child Labor in Agriculture'. Accessed 13 June 2005 from www.hrw.org/backgrounder/crp/back0610.htm.
International Forum on Globalization (IFG) (2002) *Alternatives to Economic Globalization*. San Francisco, CA: Berrett-Koehler Publishers.
International Labour Organization (ILO) (2003) 'Fundamental Principles and Rights at Work: Costa Rica, El Salvador, Guatemala, Honduras and Nicaragua'. Geneva: Switzerland. Accessed 20 April 2004 from www.ilo.org/public/english/dialogue/download/cafta.pdf.
ILO (1998) 'IPEC: Finding Out About Child Labour'. Geneva: Switzerland. Accessed 10 June 2005 from www.il.org/public/english/standards/ipec/simpoc/stats/child/ stats.htm.
ILO (2004) 'Child Trafficking'. Accessed 10 June, 2005 from www.ilo.org/public/english/standards/ipec/themes/trafficking/index.htm.
ILO (2005) 'A Global Alliance against Forced Labour'. Accessed 28 April 2005 from www.ilo.org/public/english/standards/ipec/themes/traffi cking/index.htm.
James, A. and Prout, A. (eds.) (1997) *Constructing and Reconstructing Childhood*. London and New York: Routledge/Falmer.
Landesman, P. (2004) 'The Girls Next Door: Sex Slaves on Main Street'. *The New York Times Sunday Magazine* (25 January 2004).
National Labor Committee (NLC) (1996) 'Mickey Mouse Goes to Haiti: Walt Disney and the Science of Exploitation'. Crowing Rooster Arts (VHS).
National Resources Defense Council (NRDC) (1998) 'Trouble on the Farm: Growing Up with Pesticides in Agriculture', 21 October 1998. Accessed 10 June 2005 from www.nrdc.org/health/kids/farm/intro.asp.
O'Kane, C. (2003) 'Street and Working Children's Participation in Programming for Their Rights: Conflicts Arising from Diverse

Perspectives and Directions for Convergence'. *Children, Youth and Environments* 13(1): 1-17 Accessed 28 May 2010 from www.colorado.edu/journals/cye/.
Parenti, M. (2002) *Democracy for the Few* (7th edition). Boston: Bedford/St. Martin's Press.
Pettman, J.J. (2005) 'On the Backs of Women and Children', in P.S. Rothenberg, *Beyond Borders: Thinking Critically About Global Issues*, pp. 437-40. New York: Worth Publishers.
Polakoff, E.G. (1988) 'Surviving the Crisis: Bolivia's Children at Work'. *Transaction/Society* 27(3): 82-85.
Polakoff, E.G. (2003) 'Globalization: Up Close and Questionable'. *The Hispanic Outlook in Higher Education* 14(6): 27-29.
Polakoff, E.G. and LaRamée, P.M. (1997) 'Grass-Roots Organizations' in T.W. Walker (ed.) *Nicaragua without Illusions: Regime Transition and Structural Adjustment in the 1990s*, pp. 185-201. Wilmington, DE: Scholarly Resources.
Portillo, L. (2001) 'Señorita Extraviada/'Missing Young Woman' (VHS).
Sangera, J. (1997) 'In the Belly of the Beast: Sex Trade, Prostitution and Globalization'. *Discussion Paper for the Asia-Pacific Regional Consultation on Prostitution*. Bangkok, Thailand, 17-18 February 1997.
Sargent, C. and Harris, M. (1998) 'Bad Boys and Good Girls: The Implications of Gender Ideology for Child Health in Jamaica', in N. Scheper-Hughes and C. Sargent (eds.) *Small Wars: The Cultural Politics of Childhood*, pp. 202-227. Berkeley, CA: The University of California Press.
Scheper-Hughes, N. and Sargent, C. (eds.) (1998) *Small Wars: The Cultural Politics of Childhood*. Berkeley: The University of California Press.
Schwartzman, H.B. (ed.) (2001) *Children and Anthropology: Perspectives for the 21st Century*. Westport: Bergin & Garvey.
Schwartz-Nobel, L. (2002) *Growing Up Empty*. New York: HarperCollins.
Shaw, K. and da Silva, R. (2010) 'Shine a Light Annual Report 2010'. Accessed 6 June 2010 from www.shinealight.org.
Stephens, S. (ed.) (1995) *Children and the Politics of Culture*. Princeton: University of Princeton Press.
Stiglitz, J. (2003) *Globalization and its Discontents*. New Work: WW Norton.
Sun, B.K. (2010) 'Young Survivors of Sex Trafficking Organize in NYC' *Now Public* (June 21, 2010). Accessed 22 June 2010 from www.nowpublic.com/world/young-survivors-sex-trafficking-organize-nyc.

UNESCO (2003) 'Trafficking Statistics Project'. Accessed 10 June 2005 from www. unescobkk.org/index.php?id=1022.
UNICEF (2000a) 'Facts on Children: Early Childhood'. Accessed 10 June 2005 from www.unicef.org/media/media_9475.html.
UNICEF (2000b) 'Facts on Children: Child Protection'. Accessed 10 June 2005 from www.unicef.org/media/media_9482.html.
UNICEF (2001) 'Beyond Child Labour: Affirming Rights'. Accessed 26 April 2006 from www.unicef.org/sowc05/english/poverty.html.
UNICEF (2005a) 'Children Must Be at the Heart of Development Efforts'. Accessed 10 June 2005 from www.unicef.org/media/media_27306.html.
UNICEF (2005b) 'Efforts to End Child Labour Must Focus on Education', 10 June 2005. Accessed 10 June 2000 from www.unicef.org/media/media_27328.html.
UNICEF (2005c) 'State of the World's Children 2005: Childhood Under Threat'. Accessed 26 April 2006 from www.unicef.org/sowc05/english/povertyissue. html.
UNICEF (2006) 'State of the World's Children 2007: Women and Children–The Double Dividend of Gender Equality'. Accessed 3 June 2010 from www.unicef.org/sowc/archive/ENGLISH/The%20State%20of%20the%20World%2027s%20Children%202007.pdf.
UNICEF (2009) 'State of the World's Children 2010: Child Rights'. Accessed 3 June 2010 from www.unicef.org/rightsite/sowc/pdfs/sowc_SpecEd_CRC_ExecutiveSummary_EN_091009.pdf.
Whiteford, L.M. (1998). 'Children's Health as Accumulated Capital: Structural Adjustment in the Dominican Republic and Cuba', in N. Scheper-Hughes and C. Sargent (eds.) *Small Wars: The Cultural Politics of Childhood*, pp. 186-201. Berkeley, C.A.: The University of California Press.
Williams, H. (1997) 'The Social Programs', in T.W. Walker (ed.) *Revolution and Counterrevolution in Nicaragua*, pp. 187-212. Boulder: CO: Westview Press.
Yates, M.D. (2004) 'Poverty and Inequality in the Global Economy'. *Monthly Review* 55(9). New York: Monthly Review Foundation. Accessed 10 February 2006 from www.monthlyreview.org/0204yates.htm.
Yong, J. Millen, J.V., Gershman, J. and Irwin, A. (2000) *Dying for Growth: Global Inequality and the Health of the Poor.* Monroe: Common Courage Press.

Conclusion

Women and Neoliberal Globalization: Inequities, Resistance and Alternatives

Ligaya Lindio-McGovern
Indiana University

Neoliberal globalization has a detrimental impact on most women and their families in the global South or Third World. But while globalization exacerbates the already subordinate position of these women in the global political economy, they are also fighting back. They have devised various ways to resist the negative consequences of neoliberal policies and corporate globalization on their everyday lives and on their nation states. Their politics of resistance offers strategies, insights and practical ideas about how a better, more just world can be achieved. In this concluding chapter I focus attention to the contradictions of neoliberal globalization and how these contradictions create contexts for resistance to it as well as the search for equitable and empowering alternatives. I suggest areas for further research or study, since deeper understanding of how globalization is gendered and its continuing challenges are part of the politics of resistance itself.

Women's Resistance to Neoliberal Globalization

The negative impact of neoliberal globalization on the different spheres of women's lives reflects the gendered and inequitable character of the dynamics of neoliberal globalization. The neoliberal policies promoted by the macro-structures of neoliberal globalization–the International Monetary Fund (IMF), World Bank, World Trade Organization (WTO), and the transnational corporations–have created many inequities and imposed many economic hardships on women in the poorer countries of the Third World.

As transnational corporations globalize the world economy for profit maximization, they have created economic conditions in which women's labor and child labor are being integrated into the global capitalist system in exploitative and dehumanizing ways, which have either created new or reproduced pre-existing gender, racial, and class inequities. Their capitalist penetration of the global economy has created special economic zones, free trade zones, and export processing zones, especially in Third World countries, where women and children are often employed under insufferable conditions of employment. These economic zones–where the workforce often consists largely of young women–have become the main sites where women's and child labor are linked to the global processes of production and capital accumulation (see the chapters by Frederickson, Lindio-McGovern, Polakoff, Sanmiguel-Valderrama, and Shaw in this collection). To make sure women's and child labor are cheap– which appears to be necessary for profitable global production and capital accumulation–'flexible' labor control regimes are instituted and maintained. These regimes make it extremely difficult and often dangerous for labor to struggle for decent wages, improved working conditions, and labor rights. The experience of the female garment workers in Sri Lanka's export processing zones where there is no labor law enforcement (see the chapter by Shaw) provides a good example of this aspect of neoliberal globalization, as do the experiences of Filipino women who suffer the intolerable consequences of labor flexibilization or contractualization in the Philippines (see the chapter by Lindio-McGovern), and women workers in the Colombian flower export industry who are subjected to exploitative and unhealthy working conditions and a hierarchical division of labor based on gender, class and race or ethnicity (see the chapter by Sanmiguel-Valderrama). In transnational capital's relentless search for cheaper labor, women workers and child labor have become increasingly more attractive both in global manufacturing and in agroexport production because women and children are considered more controllable than men. Moreover, the increasing poverty and unemployment among adults caused by forces of neoliberal globalization compel many families to depend on the labor of their children for survival (see the chapter by Polakoff).

Despite the risks, repressive tactics and other constraints, there is increasing collective resistance among the workers in the special economic zones and export sectors. This is exemplified by the flower workers in independent unions. These Colombian flower worker organizations have evolved into a strong workers' movement with transnational networks–despite union busting and the creation of yellow or company-controlled unions. These types of movements demonstrate the tenacity of women's resistance and their persistent demands for labor rights and respect for their human dignity (see the chapter by Sanmiguel-Valderrama).

Historically, women have been involved in unionization as a collective means for contending with forms of labor control that tend to divide and conquer the workforce. Women's collective resistance against labor exploitation spans the world from the United States of

America, Mexico, Central and South America (Frederickson), Asia and Africa. Women are personally empowered as they develop a new critical consciousness, gain leadership skills, and increase their commitment to progressive ideals. These new attributes in turn become important resources for the growing transgender and transnational movements for global economic justice (see chapters by Benjamin-Lebert, McLaren and Sanmiguel-Valderrama).

Although neoliberal globalization often destroys local economies and creates widespread unemployment, the few employment opportunities that are created by the investments of global and local finance capital are often low paying jobs for women and children. Therefore, a contradictory condition is created where simultaneously some segments of women's labor are integrated into the global processes of production and capital accumulation while others are excluded and/or eliminated (see the chapter by Lindio-McGovern). This contradiction is inherent in the logic of capitalism, which invariably creates conditions that foster 'abundant cheap labor' rather than well-paid full employment (Robinson, 1998).

While neoliberal structural adjustment policies have expanded the number of unemployed and increased the economic pressures on women, they have also created the preconditions for collective resistance, which has expanded beyond those who are directly linked to the various forms of global capitalist production. A good example is Argentina's unemployed *piqueteros* (picketers) movement (see the chapter by Freytes Frey and Crivelli). Their protests have provided eloquent resistance to neoliberal structural adjustment policies. Women's participation in such movements has challenged gendered relations in the domestic as well as in the public sphere. When resistance is waged against neoliberal globalization in these two spheres simultaneously, it greatly strengthens the anti-globalization movement, since neoliberal policies seem to thrive best when they have subtly inserted themselves into pre-existing patriarchal structures (see the chapter by Benjamin-Lebert).

Migrant Labor and Transnational Spaces of Resistance

Neoliberal structural adjustment policies have created economic pressures both on governments and civil societies in the South. For example, the IMF's structural adjustment policies have put countries in the periphery/Third World in a debt crisis. Some governments have promoted the export of labor from their countries to encourage remittances from their exported laborers and thereby to raise their dollar reserves for debt servicing, (e.g., the Philippines, Indonesia, and Bangladesh). Ordinary citizens, especially the poor, also have responded to the economic consequences of neoliberal policies by migrating to countries where they can find employment. This phenomenon has contributed to massive global migration–which is increasingly becoming feminized–from the poorer periphery to the richer core countries of the global economy as well as internal migration within the poorer countries from the rural to urban areas. This mobility of labor within the context of neoliberal globalization fits into the logic of global capital accumulation, as it creates a cheap labor force in the core for richer countries as well as the poorer countries. Labor segmentation/stratification based on gender, race/ethnicity and class occurs when migrant women from Third World countries are largely segregated in domestic service work that is unattractive to most local people. This form of segmentation links women's reproductive labor to global capital accumulation which increasingly promotes the privatization of child care and elder care in richer migrant-labor receiving countries (see the chapters by Lindio-McGovern and Cuesta). In the case of internal migration, labor mobility from high-unemployment rural areas, provides a controllable labor force for export-processing zones where female labor predominates, as revealed in the case of Sri Lanka (see the chapter by Shaw).

The mobility of labor on a global scale, however, has created transnational spaces of resistance against the forces of neoliberal globalization–defying the stereotype that migrant workers are docile and subservient to their own exploitation. One example is the Coalition of Immokalee Workers, which has linked the plight of migrant farm workers to the fast-food industry in the United States (see article by Stacey Tessier in the Journal of Developing Societies Special Issue 1-2, Vol. 23, pp. 89-97, January–June 2007, *Women and Globalization*). Their 'repertoire of contention' (Tarrow, 2006: 30) has included a national boycott of Taco Bell, which targeted corporate structures of food production and consumption. This boycott linked migrant farm workers and consumers and broadened the scope of their resistance against corporate globalization. The Taco Bell boycott not only made visible the dehumanized conditions of workers who produce the food consumers eat, it disrupted the normal operations that create corporate profits, thus forcing the corporations involved to capitulate to the workers' demands.

Migrant workers' organizations have also targeted the governments of labor-receiving and labor-sending nation states when their policies are not protective of the interests and rights of these workers. This tactic has brought to light the extent to which these governments are responsible for the abuses and exploitation suffered by migrant workers. Migrante International, which organizes Filipino migrant workers across the globe, provides a good example of a migrant workers organization that uses this tactic (see the chapter by Lindio-McGovern). When diasporic communities, such as the nine million plus Filipino migrant workers who are spread across more than 180 countries, are politically organized they create the potential for forms of resistance that can challenge multiple centers of power across the globe (Tarrow, 2006:186). These migrants advocate notions of citizenship that challenge the traditional view of rights simply tied to citizenship in a single nation-state: that as human beings migrants are entitled to economic rights (such as dignified and decent wages), social rights (such as respect) and political rights (such as equality and the right to organize to struggle for their economic and social rights)–rights that are made available to citizens of labor-receiving countries.

Migrant workers experience imposed identities in their host societies that reinforce their subordinated and marginalized position in the global political economy (see the chapter by Cuesta). This form of identity construction involves the use of prejudiced stereotypes and terms of exclusion that define them in the electronic media and newspapers as undesirable 'others'. Hence, the politics of resistance on the part of migrants often involves creating a more positive identity that promotes their visibility, contribution to the host societies, and their rights. A good example is how the Ecuadorian migrants in Spain have responded to the negative ways they have been portrayed in the Spanish media. They have created their own radio shows and used other forms of communications media to promote a positive image of themselves. These activities have served as an effective means for interaction, networking and solidarity among the migrants (see the chapter by Cuesta). The visibility they created for themselves as migrants and as Ecuadorians with identities linked to their roots and national origins has raised public consciousness of their multiple roles in Spanish society and the context of their transborder existence. This case demonstrates that the self-definition and reconstruction of the identity of migrant communities is an important form of resistance and survival in the host societies where they work and live. Thus, when they succeed in presenting their alternative views, migrant women can contribute to the democratization of their host societies even though the democratization process has been eroded by neoliberal globalization.

The creation of alternative media is also a means of empowering children who are organizing to protect themselves from the exploitation of child labor and the sex trade that prey on children's vulnerability (see Polakoff in this chapter). When children collectively create their own media, they are able to control it in ways that will serve their needs and enhance their collective identity construction as they challenge the social structures that oppress them. As children collectively engage in resistance they redefine themselves and gain a sense of agency–which is important in sustaining resistance. Resistance denotes a rejection of the system as unjust and a notion of the collective self as 'capable of effecting positive changes' in one's conditions (Pangsapa, 2007:17).

Poverty and Community

Neoliberal globalization, rather than reducing global poverty, has instead exacerbated it (SAPRIN, 2004). Third World women are the ones most affected, not only because they are responsible for meeting the basic needs of their families but also because they are increasingly the ones who experience the most pain of family separation and alienation as migrant workers. They also become vulnerable prey to sex trafficking (see the chapters by Lindio-McGovern and Polakoff), which commoditizes young women for the growing global sex trade.

The social construction of poverty is one of the effects of neoliberal globalization. While poverty can be viewed as one of the consequences of neoliberal policies, the condition of poverty itself helps maintain some of these policies. The neoliberal structural adjustment policies of the IMF and the World Bank have 'significantly contributed to the further impoverishment and marginalization of local populations, while increasing economic inequality' (SAPRIN, 2004: 204). This phenomenon is constructed in four ways:

> The first is through the demise of domestic manufacturing sectors and the loss of gainful employment by laid-off workers and small producers due to the nature of [neoliberal] trade and financial sector reforms. The second relates to the contribution that [neoliberal] agricultural, trade and mining reforms have made to the declining viability and incomes of small farms and poor rural communities, as well as to declining food security, particularly in rural areas. Third, the retrenchment of workers through [neoliberal] privatization and budget cuts, in conjunction with labor market flexibilization

measures, has resulted in less secure employment, lower wages, fewer benefits and an erosion of workers' rights and bargaining power. Finally, poverty has been increased through privatization programmers, the application of user fees, budget cuts and other adjustment measures that have reduced the role of the state in providing or guaranteeing affordable access to essential quality services. (SAPRIN, 2004:204)

This phenomenon is clearly evident in the Philippines where the interlocking policies of neoliberal globalization–economic liberalization, deregulation, privatization, finance capital investment, labor flexibilization, and labor export–have been aggressively promoted with a devastating impact on poor women and families (see the chapter by Lindio-McGovern). Similar conditions exist in post-apartheid South Africa where the feminization of poverty has intensified since the government introduced neoliberal policies a decade ago. Poor women have suffered the brunt of the adverse consequences of these policies (Benjamin-Lebert). These women find themselves more deprived than before, of the essentials (adequate food, water, electricity, health care, housing, and education) that are needed for survival and a decent life due to the privatization of these basic goods and services. The government's neoliberal policies have prevented post-apartheid South Africa from eradicating the poverty inherited from the apartheid regime–thus perpetuating the subordinate position of poor black women who embody the inequalities of gender, race, and class in South Africa.

The experience of Peruvian women also further illustrates the many ways in which the lives of women are made even more precarious under neoliberal globalization. Free trade policies protective of transnational capital have resulted in the destruction of subsistence forms of production and small-scale industries where poor women have found some means of livelihood (see the chapter by Henrici). In Peru, the shantytowns in the capital city of Lima have grown as neoliberal policies have helped to push people off the land in the rural areas and into the cities where they have become the urban poor with few opportunities (see the chapter by Anderson).

Poverty, unemployment, migrant labor all interact in the creation of cheap labor, consisting often of women and children. Unemployment and low wages create poverty. Poverty creates the preconditions for migration, and migration creates cheap labor elsewhere. Thus, cheap labor contributes to the perpetuation of global poverty. Neoliberalism has not eradicated this poverty; instead it has produced poverty and increased gender, race, and class global inequalities.

However, many of the women who have been adversely affected by neoliberalism have not been passive victims. As the chapters in this volume reveal, they are forming communities and organizations to meet their needs, to challenge neoliberal policies, the neoliberal state, and gendered ideologies reinforced by neoliberal globalization. A powerful example is the cooperative movement created by women in Mumbai, India. This movement has sustained the cooperatives organized under the umbrella of Marketplace/SHARE (see the chapter by McLaren). Controlled by the women themselves, Marketplace/SHARE has engaged in income-generating projects that have given these women some degree of economic empowerment, but also created a community where the women have experienced some degree of personal empowerment as they have gained more confidence in dealing with problems in spheres outside of their domestic lives. This cooperative movement has had a positive impact on the larger community as well. They have implemented social action programs and mass actions, such as street demonstrations, that have pressured the state to allocate resources to them. They have tackled issues dealing with the environment, health, food and oil rationing, and government corruption. The success of their actions shows how women's collective power can change their communities and obtain resources from the state. This approach has been an effective form of resistance to the neoliberal privatization policies that have reduced state assistance to the social services essential for a dignified existence. Cooperative movements have the potential to create relations of production that are democratic, communal, collective, and controlled at the grassroots level. They offer an alternative to the 'economic dictatorship of neo-liberal globalization' (quoting Isidor Wallimann in one of our conversations while writing this conclusion) that uses labor control regimes to secure the interests of capital at the expense of the interests of labor.

Women's resistance is also directed at neoliberal trade policies. For example, free trade agreements that have negatively affected the local livelihoods of men and women have become focal points of women's resistance. In Peru, women are engaged in alternative trade organizations because the government has entered into so-called free trade agreements that have increased the cleavages between the rich and the poor and destroyed local industries (see the chapter by Henrici). In these collective organizations they have gained critical consciousness of the unfair nature of so-called free trade between the rich countries and the poorer developing nations, promoted by neoliberal globalization. One of the activities of the Peruvian women involved in this organization is making handmade handicrafts, which they export directly to fair trade outlets in the United States and Europe. These alternative social arrangements allow them to invest part of the profits they make back into their communities in order to uplift their living conditions. There is the potential here for the widespread development of relatively self-reliant communities that might otherwise see the development of their communities eroded by the so-called free trade arrangements.

The nation-state as an instrument of neoliberal globalization, i.e. as a local center of power serving the global economic system, also has become a target of women's resistance. For instance, in South Africa, a poor women's movement has emerged that poses a challenge to the neoliberal policies of the state (see the chapter by Benjamin-Lebert). For example, the poor black women of Bayview, Chatsworth, who have been adversely affected by the post-apartheid regime's adoption of neoliberal policies, have formed focus groups where they regularly discuss the issues that affect their everyday lives. They have organized themselves into a strong collective force that has enabled them to oppose the government's attempts to evict them from their homes and to pressure the government to provide basic services essential to their survival: water, electricity, housing, health care, and education. In the Philippines, the progressive women's movement organization, GABRIELA, has formed a Women' Party that serves as a voice for grassroots women in social legislation and has succeeded in passing a bill that illegalizes sex trafficking. GABRIELA has also participated in mass actions demanding state subsidies for water distribution in order to ensure that poor families have access to this resource so essential to survival. Thus, GABRIELA has brought attention to the particular situation of poor women who are most affected by water privatization (see the chapter by Lindio-McGovern). In these situations, the nation-state as a target of resistance is a recurring theme in the politics of women's movements that are opposed to neoliberal globalization. They recognize that the struggle for a more just society requires transforming the state so that it becomes an instrument for liberation, equality, and justice.

A Re-Conceptualization of Rights

The struggle against labor exploitation, unemployment, and poverty begs for a re-conceptualization of human rights to include 'economic rights' (see the chapter by McLaren). This expansion of human rights to include economic rights means that there are economic needs and services that must be guaranteed for all people because they are necessary for human survival and existence. Neoliberal policies that erode these economic rights must be halted and alternatives must be implemented. However, since neoliberal regimes respond with repression to the demands of anti-globalization or national liberation movements, political rights must also be guaranteed. The promotion of political rights means that the right to organize must be recognized as an inalienable right. The exercise of one's political rights becomes even more urgent as the hegemonic forces of neoliberal globalization erode the potential for economic and political democracy.

There is yet little discussion of children's rights in collective resistance to neoliberalism. Therefore a reconceptualization of rights should also embrace the rights of children. The concept of economic and political rights must also be extended to them. Economic rights for children must ensure the right to be free from exploitation of any form. Political rights for children must ensure the right to be heard and the right to collectively participate in policymaking that affects them.

The collective resistance of women at the local, national, and transnational levels is becoming a significant component of the popular response to the erosion of democracy. But their voices must be heard in policy-making circles if the misery neoliberalization has caused is to be reversed. One of the ways their voices can be heard is to reflect on the policy implications of the issues they raised and remedy the detrimental impact of neoliberal globalization on their everyday lives and their families. Institutions must take into account their views, especially in social legislation that can protect and promote the economic and political rights that have been eroded by neoliberal globalization.

A Re-thinking of Neoliberal Globalization amidst the Global Economic Crisis

Women's experiences and their forms of resistance invite a rethinking about the soundness of neoliberal policies or the so-called Washington Consensus. Globalization has hastened and deepened the global economic crisis (Sison, 2009; Stiglitz, 2000). This crisis has been felt more adversely by poor women, men and children, especially in the global South. Globalization is undermining the movement towards global social justice that is the foundation of world peace and economic security.

The global economic crisis is a clarion call to build a new global social order that is just and gears towards dismantling global structures that perpetuate inequalities between and within nations, exploit human beings, and increase poverty, while the transnational capitalist class and elites continue to get richer. This crisis has brought to the core countries what nations of the periphery have been experiencing since their subjection to colonial control and exploitation and contemporary structural adjustment regimes. As well, structural adjustment and neoliberal policies have been imposed on people in the US and Europe. The crisis has induced local and State governments to raise taxes and cut back on social programs–such as education, public transportation, unemployment compensation– impacting more negatively the already marginalized people who need these services the most. In contrast, CEOs of the largest corporations, especially those that received federal bailouts, received bonuses–even gaining from the crisis.

The IMF, World Bank and WTO must cease being instruments of corporate globalism and radically halt their structural adjustment policies that promote imperial and capitalist plunder of the world's resources and destroy local economies. Development loans should not be used as political weapons to serve transnational capital while subordinating the economic sovereignty of Third World nations. We need to think about corporate citizenship–that corporations have a responsibility to safeguard and protect the well-being of the communities where they operate and respect the political, economic, labor and environmental rights of people. We need to think about corporate stewardship–that corporations do not have the absolute power to do whatever they want with the Earth's resources simply for profit. Corporate stewardship must be conceived within the notion of communal stewardship–that other human beings are entitled to a right to demand social accountability of corporations' practices, social transparency, and violations of existing environmental, human rights and labor laws. Corporate citizenship, corporate and communal stewardship must aim at full employment to reverse labor flexibilization and contractualization. Therefore civil society's increasing contentious challenges to the IMF/WB, WTO, and transnational corporations as propellers of capitalist and imperialist globalization will play an important role.

Labor export as a development strategy to deal with the impact of structural adjustments policies that result in debt crisis, destruction of local industries, and increased unemployment must be reversed–through the generation of jobs in the local economies, development of locally controlled industries and implementation of agrarian reforms that will facilitate local community control of agricultural production. This must be coupled with measures to halt the increasing trend of privatization which make equitable access to basic social services and needs impossible.

Militarization in Third World nations supported by imperial powers to contain political activism and resistance towards dismantling structures within their nation states that entrench neoliberal policies must end. Revolutionary movements, national liberation movements, women's movements, youth movements, student movements, labor movements, peasant movements, poor people's and unemployed workers' movements–have alternative views about development and governance–and must be given a voice in policy formation to alter neoliberal policies. Instead of wasting resources in trying to kill their movements through counter-insurgency or militarization, a new state structure where these groups' demands for change could be given representation must be given a chance to take shape. Third World nation states that suffer the devastating impact of neoliberal policies must align with the national interests that are already being articulated by progressive people's movements in their countries which are critical of neoliberal policies.

We can begin to think of a new economic social order where there is the existence of worker-owned and communally-owned production units both in the industrial and agricultural sectors as well as in the service sectors. We can, for example, think of a people's bank– that can be an alternative to corporate banking. My concept of 'people's bank' is different from the Grameen Bank (given its criticisms), in the sense that it would be collectively owned and collectively managed by the people themselves for starting a cooperative movement–cooperative housing, worker-owned industries or peasant-owned agricultural production units–and its terms would be determined by the people themselves. In the Grameen Bank model, the people are the consumers of its loans, while in the 'people's bank' concept the people are its collective owners and creators. The 'people's bank' concept can include also exchange of labor among members–for example in a daycare cooperative a woman or man can borrow time from another member to care for her/his child which s/he will pay back with equivalent time to care for her/his child at a later time or do other tasks that may require her/his skills. So the exchange relationships among members can also include mutual exchange of time, labor, and skills. The money that the 'people's bank' can raise are available for loaning out among members both for starting cooperatives of all sorts and for reproductive purposes, such as for the education of their children with terms of payment to be collectively decided upon by the members, or the setting up of a cooperative daycare for children and elderly. The logic behind the 'people's bank' concept falls within the concept of Solidarity Economy that Ann Ferguson (2009:113) discusses as an 'oppositional economic and political network against neoliberalism'. She traces the origin of the term 'solidarity economy' from a Brazilian professor Luis Roseto who conceptualized what he calls 'Factor C–cooperation, co-responsibility, communication, and community'–as a form of alternative economy to one that is being promoted by the global capitalist penetration of national economies. This process of creating a more equitable and just global social order, requires a new social consciousness that can be a product of formal and informal education, or social movement organizations. A new social consciousness that is critical and lives the values of community instead of individualism, social justice instead of greed, social responsibility and engagement instead of apathy, equality instead of domination and discrimination, and respect for human dignity instead of exploitation–must accompany the process of structural transformation that we envision.

The struggles of resistance in this volume spark the hope that a better and more just world is possible, and envisioning that kind of world is the starting point of that journey.

Gendering Future Research on Globalization and Resistance

This volume has given voice to the experience of Third World women through reporting the research and discourse about women and neoliberal globalization and has contributed to the growing knowledge and literature on the need to reverse the negative course of neoliberalism. It provides insight into how neoliberal globalization is gendered, and also raises important questions that still need to be investigated. One of these questions is how Third World men and women differ in their experience of, and response to, the pauperization associated with neoliberal globalization. Related to this question is the examination of how household and reproductive labor are transformed by the processes of global production and capital accumulation in the context of neoliberal globalization. This question needs to be examined through comparative studies to determine how culture and gender come into play in these processes.

Another question that needs further study is how women organize creatively to oppose neoliberal globalization in situations where their lives are already endangered by state repression and militarization. More specifically, more research is needed on the connection between state violence, political/military repression, and corporate globalization–and how these conditions affect men and women differently. A related question is, Do women organize differently than men, to contend with labor exploitation, and if so, how? Also, how do they forge alliances to strengthen labor movements that address neoliberal policies? Moreover, more research is needed on how these alliances re-frame the issues of gender and neoliberal globalization.

On the global level more research is also needed on how local women's groups in Third World countries establish international solidarity networks as forms of resistance to neoliberal globalization– specifically how they initiate and maintain these networks, the obstacles and difficulties they encounter, and the requirements for their success.

On migrant or diasporic communities resulting from the economic pressures created by structural adjustment regimes, one area for further empirical inquiry is how host societies produce gendered social representation of identities of these migrants in the way they construct notions of citizenship in an increasingly porous transnational borders for labor and forced economic migration. Equally important is to examine the counter-identity construction of migrant communities in response to such politics of othering and exclusion in order to gain insights in reconceptualizing migrants' rights, citizenship, and 'transmigrant identity' construction (finding a place in the host society one migrates into while continuing to be connected to one's homeland) (Espiritu, 1992), and translating these theoretical insights into more humane, just and human dignity-affirming im/migration and labor policies.

Another important area for further study is action research where initiatives on alternative forms of organizing production that follow non-capitalist principles can be tried and evaluated in an ongoing process in order to document and analyze the factors contributing to their success or failures. How can these non-capitalist production units be made to implement practices that promote gender equality in the workplace? What new norms and principles can they put into practice around the notion of communal ownership of the fruits of their labor and communal decision-making, especially regarding how and what they can produce sustainably?

There are many other aspects of neoliberal globalization that need examination. One important aspect of neoliberal globalization this volume and future research should address more adequately concerns women and the natural environment, particularly in indigenous communities whose natural resources are being plundered and polluted by transnational corporations. We need to know what kinds of strategies and tactics of resistance these communities are employing and what can be learned from them. Indeed, there is a lot we can learn from indigenous communities, such as their concepts of communal ownership and working relations, which run counter to the neoliberal privatization schemes and the other means by which corporate capitalism penetrates their spheres of existence to maximize corporate profits.

A recent phenomenon that must be empirically studied is the oil spill in the Gulf of Mexico caused by BP's allegedly lack of environmental corporate responsibility causing tremendous ecological and human costs. What are the long-term impacts of these to the affected communities and how are women, men and children differentially affected by this human-made disaster? How are the different classes of people responding to this social problem, whose interests do they protect, and what are the consequences of their responses to solving the problem, both immediate and long-term? What collective actions have arisen in response to this problem, who are their targets of resistance, and how have they been listened to or ignored? Instead of BP playing victim to the mess that they themselves have created, how can civil society demand corporate accountability to people's right to a healthy environment? What laws could be put in place to regulate offshore drilling of a non-renewable resource, and re-channel resources instead to exploring alternative sources of energy and to creating goods that are not dependent on fossil fuels?

Research on women, gender, and neoliberal globalization raises important questions of epistemology and methodology such as how do we study these subjects in a way that will not perpetuate the unequal structure of knowledge production between the global North and the global South. This is an important issue that some researchers working in these subjects have already raised (Appadurai, 2001; Grewal, 2005; Lindio-McGovern, 1997; Mohanty, 2003; Sen and Grown, 1987). We believe it is important that scholars and students of globalization give prominent attention to the voice and the experience of grassroots women in the global South, which means being sensitive to one's own position in the global structure of knowledge production and diffusion. Particularly, one's class status is likely to affect one's interpretation of the experiences of women at the grassroots level. Benjamin-Lebert, Cuesta and McLaren (in this volume) have alluded to this problem, and Naples (2003) offers insights into how one can engage in studying women's resistance to produce richer and more valid data for theory construction. Equally important is the perspective we employ in viewing neo-liberal globalization. We need to continue examining this phenomenon with critical analytical perspectives that enable us to identify its contradictions, the power structures and interests it serves, whom it hurts and how, and the on-going efforts that are being made to develop and pursue progressive alternatives (see Lindo-McGovern and Wallimman, 2009; Mittelman, 2005; Robinson, 2005; and the chapters by Benjamin-Lebert, Cuesta, Frederickson, Freytes-Frey and Crivelli, Henrici, Lindio-McGovern, McLaren, Polakoff and Sanmiguel-Valderrama in this volume).

REFERENCES

Appadurai, A. (2001) 'Grassroots Globalization and the Research Imagination', in A. Appadurai (ed.) *Globalization*, pp. 1-21. Durham and London: Duke University Press.

Espiritu, Y. (1992) *Asian American Panethnicity: Bridging Institutions and Identities.* Philadelphia: Temple University Press.

Ferguson, A. (2009) 'Alternative Economies–Women Left Behind: Organizing Solidarity Economy in Response', in L. Lindio-McGovern and I. Wallimann (eds.) *Globalization and Third World Women: Exploitation, Coping and Resistance*, pp.107-119. Surrey, England: Ashgate Publishing Co.

Grewal, I. (2005) *Transnational America: Feminisms, Diasporas, Neoliberalisms.* Durham and London: Duke University Press.

Lindio-McGovern, L. (1997) *Filipino Peasant Women: Exploitation and Resistance.* Philadelphia: University of Pennsylvania Press.

Lindio-McGovern, L and Wallimann, I. (2009) Globalization and Third World Women: Exploitation, Coping and Resistance. Surrey, England: Ashgate Publishing Company.

Mittelman, J.H. (2005) 'What is a Critical Globalization Studies?', in R.P. Appelbaum and W. Robinson (eds.) *Critical Globalization Studies*, pp. 19-29. New York and London: Routledge.

Mohanty, C.T. (2003) *Feminism without Borders: Decolonizing Theory, Practicing Solidarity.* Durham and London: Duke University Press.

Naples, N.A. (2003) *Feminism and Method: Ethnography, Discourse Analysis and Activist Research.* New York and London: Routledge.

Pangsapa, P. (2007) *Textures of Struggles: The Emergence of Resistance among Workers in Thailand.* Ithaca and London: Cornell University Press.
Robinson, W.I. (1998) Promoting *Polyarchy: Globalization, US Intervention, and Hegemony.* Cambridge: Cambridge University Press.
Robinson, W.I. (2005) 'What is a Critical Globalization Studies? Intellectual Labor and Global Society', in R.P. Appelbaum and W. Robinson (eds.) *Critical Globalization Studies*, pp. 11–18. New York and London: Routledge.
SAPRIN. (2004) *Structural Adjustment: The Policy Roots of Economic Crisis, Poverty and Inequality.* London: Zed Books, TWIN, Books for Change, IBON.
Sen, G. and Grown, C. (1987) *Development, Crisis and Alternative Visions.* New York: Monthly Review Press.
Sison, J.M. (2007). ILPS Statement on the Global Forum for Migration and Development, July 2007, cited in 'Development through Systematic Commodification of Migrants, not for the Benefit of the Grassroots: A Critique of the Third Global Forum on Migration and Development', Kowloon, Hong Kong: Asia Pacific Mission for Migrants.
Stiglitz, J. (2000) 'What I Learned from the World Economic Crisis'. *The Insider.* Issue date: 04.17.00, Post date: 04.06.00.
Tarrow, S. (2006) *Power in Movement: Social Movements and Contentious Politics.* 2nd ed. Cambridge: Cambridge University Press.
Tessier, S. (2007). 'Rethinking the Food Chain: Farmworkers and the Taco Bell Boycott'. *Journal of Developing Societies* 23(1-2): 207-219.

ADDITIONAL READING

Dunkley, G. (2004) *Free Trade: Myth Reality and Alternatives.* Dhaka, London and New York: University Press.
Oishi, N. (2005) *Women in Motion: Globalization, State Policies, and Labor Migration in Asia.* Stanford, California: Stanford University Press.

Contributors

Jeanine Anderson received her PhD in Anthropology from Cornell University. She is a US-born, long-time Peruvian resident. She teaches anthropology at the Catholic University of Peru. Her areas of specialization include urban studies, gender, and the anthropology of health. She combines research and teaching with active participation in debates on social policy in Peru and other Latin American countries.

Saranel Benjamin-Lebert was formerly a researcher and project manager with the Centre for Civil Society, based at the University of Kwazulu-Natal, South Africa. Today, she is an independent researcher and development consultant for community-based organizations and non-governmental organizations in Southern and East Africa.

Karina Crivelli is a PhD student at University of Buenos Aires, Argentina, and holds a postgraduate scholarship at University of Buenos Aires, Argentina. She also holds a Master 2 en Sciences Sociales degree from *École des Hautes Études en Sciences Sociales*, Paris, France. Her areas of interest are: precarization, subjectivity, low-income families, social policies, unemployment and unemployed workers' movements.

estheR Cuesta is currently Consul of Ecuador in Genoa, collaborating with diasporic Ecuadorians living in the Regions of Liguria and Emilia Romagna, Italy–while writing her dissertation on the documentation and study of diasporic Andean women's narratives in Southern/Mediterranean Europe for the Comparative Literature Program in the Department of Languages, Literatures and Cultures, University of Massachusetts Amherst. Her essay 'Guayaquileña (In)Documentada: One-Way Ticket to My Diaspora(s): A Testimonio', in *Techno-Futuros: Critical Interventions in Latina/o Studies* (2007) addresses her own diasporic experiences in the United States. 'A modo de testimoniar: Gloria Anzaldúa's *Borderlands*, papeles, and academia' in *Bridging: How and Why Gloria Evangelina Anzaldúa's Life and Work Transformed Our Own* (2010), currently in press, centers the work of Anzaldúa in her own ethico-political feminist consciousness.

Mary E. Frederickson is a faculty member in the Department of History at Miami University, Ohio. Her PhD is from the University of North Carolina, Chapel Hill, where she served as Assistant Director of the Southern Oral History Program. Previous positions include Visiting Bye-Fellow, Selwyn College, Cambridge, UK; faculty in History, University of Alabama, Birmingham, where she established and directed the UAB Oral History Program; and post-doctoral research fellow at the Center for Research on Women, Wellesley College. Named Distinguished Educator by the Ohio Academy of History in 2010, Frederickson trains graduate and undergraduate students in women's history, oral history, and the history race and ethnicity. Her research on women's labor history has both academic and activist components. Her next book, forthcoming in 2011, is *Looking South: Race, Gender, and the Transformation of Labor from Reconstruction to Globalization.*

Ada Cora Freytes Frey is a PhD student at University of Buenos Aires, Argentina, and teaches Sociology at El Salvador University, Buenos Aires, Argentina. She holds a PhD Fellowship of the Swiss National Centre of Research North-South. She is an associated researcher at Centro de Estudios Laborales (CEILPIETTE)–Consejo Nacional de Ciencia y Tecnología (CONICET), Buenos Aires, Argentina. Her areas of interest are: subjectivity, social movements, gender, youth and education.

Richard L. Harris is Professor Emeritus at California State University, Monterey Bay. He has a PhD in Political Science and a Masters of Public Administration from the University of California, Los Angeles. He is a lecturer, researcher, consultant, writer, and editor. Professor Harris has taught, carried out research, and directed programs at various universities in the United States and elsewhere, including the University of California, Harvard University, Suffolk University, California State University, the University of San Francisco, the University of the Americas in Mexico, the Universidad Autónoma Metropolitana in Mexico City, the Universidad de Chile (Santiago), the Universidad Nacional de Santiago del Estero in Argentina, La Trobe University in Australia, the University of Zambia, and the University of Ibadan in Nigeria. Richard Harris is currently the managing editor of the international *Journal of Developing Societies* and one of the coordinating editors of the popular journal *Latin American Perspectives.* He has published books, monographs, and journal articles on a wide range of topics, including Latin American history and politics, international affairs, globalization, neoliberalism, African politics, socialism, democracy, revolutionary change, and comparative public administration. He lives in Hawai'i and travels extensively.

Jane Henrici, Ph.D., is a Study Director at IWPR and an anthropologist who studies gender, race, and ethnicity and their relationship to policy and development. She received her doctorate from the University of Texas at Austin in 1996; her doctoral and early postdoctoral research focused on the effects of development tourism and non-profit export projects on gender and ethnicity in Peru. Between 1998-2003, Dr. Henrici was a Postdoctoral Research Fellow and Research Scientist working with an interdisciplinary project on the effects of welfare reform in the US (Welfare, Children, and Families: A Three-City Study). Based on that material, Dr. Henrici co-authored *Poor Families in America's Health Care Crisis: How the Other Half Pays* (Cambridge, 2006) and edited *Doing Without: Women and Work after Welfare Reform* (Arizona, 2006) while she taught anthropology full time at the University of Memphis. In 2006, she returned to research on development and women outside of the US supported by a Fulbright Scholar Award to Peru where she also lectured in anthropology and gender studies at Pontificia Universidad Católica. She has published on women and poverty, health care, job training, tourism development, free trade, fair trade, and non-profits/NGOs. Dr. Henrici has been with IWPR since January 2008, currently directs two of the Institute's projects, and is a researcher and analyst for several others. In addition, she is adjunct professor in anthropology at George Mason University. In 2009, Dr. Henrici was elected to serve in the American Anthropological Association as Councilor to the Society for Latin American and Caribbean Anthropology and as President-Elect of the Association for Feminist Anthropology, for which she'll serve as President 2011-13.

Ligaya Lindio-McGovern, PhD, is a Filipina Associate Professor of Sociology with Full Graduate Faculty Status at Indiana University. A former Director of Women's Studies at Indiana University Kokomo, she is author of *Filipino Peasant Women: Exploitation and Resistance* (University of Pennsylvania Press, 1997), and co-editor of *Globalization and Third World Women: Exploitation, Coping and Resistance* (published by Ashgate Publishing, 2009). She has also published several journal articles and book chapters, spoken in national and international conferences, and conducted numerous research projects. Her current research is on Third World women and globalization, Philippine labor export and resistance, and international migration of healthcare workers and professionals.

Margaret McLaren is Professor of Philosophy and Women's Studies and holds the George D. and Harriet W. Cornell Chair of Philosophy at

Rollins College, Florida. She received her MA and PhD from Northwestern University. Her research interests include: Foucault, feminist theory, gender issues, human rights, social justice, and women's cooperatives. She has published articles on these topics in: *Journal of Developing Societies, Forum on Public Policy, Philosophy Today, Florida Philosophical Review, Social Theory and Practice* and *Hypatia*, as well as several chapters in anthologies. McLaren is author of *Feminism, Foucault and Subjectivity* (SUNY Press, 2002). Currently she is working on a book manuscript addressing globalization and feminist theory. She teaches courses in Ethics, Feminist Theory, Foucault, Women and Globalization, and Social and Political Philosophy.

Erica G. Polakoff is Professor of Sociology and Women's Studies at Bloomfield College, NJ, where she co-founded the Women's Studies, Latino/Latin American and Caribbean Studies, and Honors Programs. She received her PhD in Sociology, Women's Studies and Latin American Studies from Cornell University. Her research has focused on low-income communities and grassroots organizations (women's, labor, and neighborhood associations) in Bolivia, Nicaragua, and Mexico, during times of economic and political crisis. Her research has been published in several journal articles and book chapters. A documentary photographer, Polakoff has also published and exhibited her photographs of these and other studies.

Olga Sanmiguel-Valderrama is Assistant Professor in the Department of Women's, Gender and Sexuality Studies, University of Cincinnati, Ohio. She is a Colombian lawyer and holds a PhD in Law from York University, Canada. Focusing on the case of Colombia and the experiences of Latinos/as in North America, her areas of research and expertise include the contradictions between on the one hand, the promotion of neoliberal economic globalization, and on the other hand, deteriorating human rights enforcement, in particular, of labour rights, and the rights of women and racial minorities. She has published various articles on the working and living conditions of women workers in the Colombian export-oriented flower industry (Third World Quarterly, Journal of Developing Societies, Iconos, and the Journal of the Motherhood Initiative; forthcoming, 2011).

Judith Shaw is a Senior Research Fellow at the Monash Asia Institute, Monash University, Australia. Her main research focus is on household livelihoods in developing countries, and she has published on labour migration, microfinance, microenterprises and rural development.

Author Index

A
Abbott, J. 2
ACFFTU 96, 112, 113, 118
Achbar, M. 2
Acosta-Vargas, G. 166, 169
Acosta, A. 82, 87, 89, 90, 166, 169
Aflonordes 169
Africa, Sony 52
Aguiar Lozano, V.H. 77, 89
Aguilar, D.D. 141, 162, 169
Alcoff, L. 86, 90, 91
Alexander, M.J. 25, 29, 134, 135
Alingod, K. 52
Alvarez, S.E. 26, 179, 181, 187
Amnesty International 195, 309, 321
An-Na'im, A. 194, 207
Anderson, J. 21, 213, 230, 231, 232, 333
Appadurai, A. 82, 90, 341, 342
Aptheker, B. 13, 25
Arango, J. 59, 66, 90
Arat-Koç, S. 163, 170
Armstrong, P. 167, 170
Arriola, E. 122, 135
Asocolflores 141, 142, 152, 156, 157, 158, 159, 160, 164, 168, 170, 172
Associated Press 134, 135
Atria, R. 214, 231
Aturupane, H. 98, 100, 118

B
Bakker, I. 167, 170
Balangue, G.C. 35, 36, 37, 53, 55

Banco Central del Ecuador 77, 90
Bant, A. 184, 187
Barcelona, N. 44, 53, 57, 58, 59, 61, 67, 70, 76, 83, 89
Barrig, M. 186, 187
Bass, N. 25, 28
Basu, A. 282, 289, 290
Becker, J. 292, 321
Beegle, K. 296, 321
Bell, B. 301, 322, 330, 343
Belle, D. 306, 308, 321
Bello, W. 35, 38, 39, 53, 56
Beltran, C. 41, 53
Benhabib, S. 193, 207
Benholdt-Thomsen, V. 3, 8, 14, 25, 27
Benjamin-Lebert, S. 23, 259, 329, 333, 335, 341, 342
Benjamin, S. 23, 259, 274, 289, 329, 333, 335, 341, 342
Bezanson, K. 162, 170
Bhorat, H. 274, 289
Bieler, S. 161, 170
Board of Investment Sri Lanka 118
Bond, P. 288, 289
Booker, S. 2, 3, 11, 25, 26, 28, 320, 321
Borrero Vega, A. 65, 90
Bourdieu, P. 179, 182, 187, 243, 255, 256
Bourgois, P. 214, 231
Bowe, J. 141, 170
Brassel, F. 159, 170
Brewer, J.D. 261, 289
Brittain, J.J. 170
Bruin, J. 42, 53

Bulbeck, C. 194, 207
Bultron, R. 45, 53
Bunch, C. 195, 207
Bureau of Agricultural Statistics 36, 53
Business Week Online 87, 90
Butterflies Programme 315, 322

C
Camacho Zambrano, G. 64, 90
Capulong, R.T. 43, 53
Carlsen, L. 179, 187
Carpio Benalcázar, P. 65, 90
Carter, M.R. 274, 289
Castells, M. 1, 26, 294, 295, 298, 310, 312, 321, 322
Castillo, M. 91
Central Bank of Sri Lanka 118
CENWOR 96, 106, 107, 109, 113, 118
Chacaltana, J. 218, 231
Chan, W.L. 127, 136
Chari, S. 261, 287, 289
Cheng, A. 130, 135
China Labour Bulletin 130, 131, 135
Chomsky, N. 1, 26
Chossudovsky, M. 6, 7, 26, 294, 301, 307, 320, 322
Cifuentes-Rueda, R. 149, 170
Clement, W. 173
Clifford, J. 83, 90
Cloward, R. 1
Coalition Against Water Privatisation, Anti-privatisation Forum and

Public Citizen 279, 288, 289
Cock, J. 281, 289
Colgan, F. 161, 170
Collins, P.H. 62, 90, 162
Committee for the Promotion and Advancement of Cooperatives 207
Corporación Cactus 142, 150, 156, 160, 165, 166, 167, 170, 171, 173
Correa, R. 63, 64, 87, 90
Coward, R. 27
Cravey, A.J. 122, 135
Crenshaw, K.W. 11, 26
Crivelli, K. 22, 23, 233, 329, 342
Cuesta, e. 17, 18, 57, 61, 90, 330, 331, 341, 342

D
Daniel, C. 133, 135
Defensoría del Pueblo 171
Dehejia, R. 296, 321
del Rosario-Malonzo, J. 35, 36, 37, 53, 54
Delfino, S. 124, 135
Dent, K. 106, 118
Department of Census and Statistics, Colombo (DCS) 97, 98, 100, 103, 104, 106, 111, 118, 119
Department of Labor and Employment 35, 42, 54
Desa, A.B. 56
Desai, A. 13, 27, 263, 264, 275, 285, 287, 289
Días, M. 171
Dickinson, T.D. 162, 171
Dizon, A. 45, 54
Duguay, C. 321, 322
Duina, F. 184, 186, 187
Dunham, D. 98, 100, 102, 119
Dunkley, G. 343

E
Eastman-Abaya, R. 51, 55
Edmonds, E.V. 296, 322
Edwards, C. 98, 100, 102, 119
Ehrenreich, B. 306, 320, 322
EILER Inc 54
Eisenstein, H. 161, 162, 171
El Universo 65, 77, 78, 79, 83, 91
Elson, D. 320, 322
Epaarachchi, R. 96, 115, 117, 119
Episcopal Commission for the Pastoral Care of Migrants and Itinerant People 45, 54
Escobar, A. 26, 162, 171, 187
Espino, A. 185, 187
Espiritu, Y. 340, 342
Étienne, M. 8, 26, 29, 30
Eurostat 84, 91
Eviota, E.U. 52, 54

F
Falconí, F. 82, 87, 89, 90
Farmer, P.E. 9, 10, 11, 26, 292, 322
Feinstein, C. 299, 322
Ferguson, J. 213, 232, 339, 342
Ferm, N. 166, 171
Fernandez-Kelly, M.P. 320, 322
Ferus-Comelo, A. 161, 173
Fescol 157, 171
Fink, L. 133, 135
Fleeson, L. 133, 135
Fong, M. 125, 135
Food and Agriculture Organization 322
Foster, A. 52, 54, 192, 199, 201, 281, 316, 329
Franco, J. 14, 26, 30
Frank, D. 161, 171
Frazier, L.J. 188
Frederickson, M.E. 19, 24, 121, 122, 126, 133, 134, 135, 136, 300, 328, 329, 342
Freytes Frey, A. 22, 23, 233, 237, 238, 250, 257, 329, 342
Friedman, E. 193, 194, 196, 208
Fuentes, A. 306, 320, 322

G
Galeano, E. 7, 9, 26, 29
Galtung, J. 8, 10, 26, 29
Gamburd, M.R. 107, 119
Garcia, M.E. 181, 187
García, P. 68, 90
Gateway to the European Union 89, 91
Gatti, R. 296, 321
Geisler, G. 283, 289
Gershman, J. 325
Giddens, A. 178, 187, 298, 322
Gikandi, S. 82, 91
Gill, S. 170
Gillespie, M. 124, 135
Gilligan, C. 193, 207, 208
Gilmore, P. 134, 135
Glenn, J. 134, 135
Go, J. 52, 54
Goldblatt, D. 54, 187
Goldstein, D.M. 231, 232
Goode, J. 214, 232
Goodman, R. 129, 135
Government Accountability Office 302, 322
Government of Sri Lanka 107, 119
Green, D. 299, 322
Greene, F. 26, 28
Gretel, H. 261, 290
Grewal, I. 341, 342
Griffith, B. 133, 135
Grown, C. 25, 28, 202, 215, 252, 333, 341, 343
Gunatilaka, R. 96, 112, 113, 115, 116, 117, 119
Gunesekara, S. 111, 119

Guzman, R.B. 35, 37, 43, 52, 54
H
Haberland, M. 122, 136
Habib, A. 272, 289
Hall, J.D. 123, 124, 136
Haraway, D. 84, 91
Harcourt, W. 162, 171
Harding, S. 61, 84, 86, 91, 92
Harris, M. 298, 324
Hathaway, D. 133, 136
Hausmann, R. 208
Health Alliance for Democracy (HEAD) 38, 52, 54, 74, 75, 98, 100, 101, 127, 230
Held, D. 47, 54, 178, 187
Held, V. 193, 208
Henrici, J. 20, 177, 180, 181, 182, 184, 187, 188, 333, 334, 342
Hernández Basante, K. 64, 90
Herrera, E.F. 46, 54, 65, 91
Hesse-Biber, S. 86, 91, 92
Hettiarachchi, T. 96, 112, 113, 119
Heward, S. 96, 106, 117, 119
Ho, K. 10, 26
Hollander, E. 133, 136
Honey, M. 133, 136
hooks, b. 71, 91
Houghton, J. 301, 322
Hristov, J. 171
Hughes, D.M. 298, 311, 313, 323, 324, 325
Human Rights Watch 129, 184, 195, 196, 208, 302, 320, 321, 323
Huntoon, L. 67, 91
Hurtig, J. 188
Hylton, F. 171
I
IBON 34, 35, 36, 38, 39, 43, 45, 46, 52, 53, 54, 55, 343
Institute of Policy Studies 106, 119
International Development Exchange 208
International Forum on Globalization (IFG) 4, 5, 26, 294, 301, 307, 323
International Labour Organization (ILO) 6, 119, 120, 129, 145, 172, 299, 300-302, 305, 310, 311, 323
International Labour Rights Fund 165, 171
International Textile, Garment and Leather Workers Federation 131, 134, 136
International Trade Union Confederation 147, 168, 171
Irons, J. 133, 136
Irwin, A. 325
J
Jacquette, J. 185, 188
Jaising, I. 197, 198, 208
James, A. 51, 162, 298, 323
Janiewski, J. 123, 136
Jawara, F. 5, 26
Jayasuriya, S. 102, 119
Jelin, E. 234, 240, 257, 258
Jokisch, B. 65, 91
Joseph, S. 27, 28, 293
K
Kanbar, R. 274, 289
Kant, I. 193, 208
Kean, K. 321
Kehler, J. 274, 289
Kelegama, S. 96, 112, 115, 117, 119
Kemp, A. 283, 284, 290
Keshavjee, S. 26
Kingdon, G. 274, 290
Kittay, E.F. 193, 207, 208, 209
Kloby, J. 27, 28
Knight, J. 274, 290
Kornbluh, J. 133, 134, 136
Korovkin, T. 167, 171
Korstad, R. 133, 136
Kwa, A. 5, 26
Kyle, D. 65, 91
L
La Botz, D. 123, 133, 136
Labor Advisory Committee for Trade Negotiations and Trade Policy (LAC) 149, 168, 172
Lacsamana, A.E. 141, 162, 169
Lakshman, W.D. 102, 105, 119
Lamas, M. 240, 258
Landesman, P. 313, 321, 323
Lara-Flores, S.M. 172
Larrañaga, O. 214, 232
Lavie, S. 27, 29
Lawson, V.A. 80, 91
Leacock, E.B. 8, 26, 29, 30
Ledwith, S. 170
Leech, L. 133, 134, 136
Lerner, G. 12, 27, 281, 290
Lewis, G. 178, 188, 214, 232
Liang, Z. 65, 91
Lindberg, I. 161, 170
Lindio-McGovern, L. 16, 17, 33, 38, 52, 55, 83, 133, 186, 206, 298, 327-333, 335, 341, 342
Lloyd, C.B. 230, 232, 316
Locke, J. 193, 208
Lomnitz, L.A. 214, 232
Luckman, T. 254, 258
Luxton, M. 162, 170
M
Madlala, N. 290
Madrid, G. 159, 167, 172

Mahler, S.J. 188
Makgetla, N. 278, 290
Makino, K. 289, 290
Mananzan, M.J. 33, 55
Mantilla, G. 156, 158, 168, 172
Maquiladora Management Services 122, 136
Marais, H. 273, 288, 290
Marx, K. 172
Maskovsky, J. 214, 232
McDonald, D.A. 2, 5, 269, 277, 287, 290
McGrew, A. 54, 187
McKinley, D. 270, 287, 290
McLaren, M.A. 21, 191, 194, 198, 208, 209, 329, 334, 336, 341, 342
Medrano, D. 166, 172
Meier, V. 166, 172
Mellon, C. 172
Memmi, A. 8, 27
Meyers, D. 193, 207- 209
Mies, M. 3, 8, 12, 27, 162, 284, 290
Miles, A. 65, 92
Mill, J.S. 193, 209
Millen, J.V. 325
Ministry of Women's Affairs 104, 107, 120
Minter, W. 2, 3, 11, 25, 26, 28, 320, 321
Mintz, S.W. 27, 29
Mitra, S. 130, 136
Mittelman, J.H. 342
Mitter, S. 14, 28
Mohanty, C.T. 25, 29, 62, 85, 92, 179, 188, 192, 194, 209, 261, 290, 341, 342
Møllmann, M. 184, 188
Molyneux, M. 162, 172, 185, 188, 189, 282, 290
Montoya, R. 185, 188
Moodley, A. 290
Moody, K. 141, 172

Moser, A. 185, 188, 232
Motta, A. 184, 187
Mouffe, C. 194, 209
Murray, J. 145, 172

N
Naples, N.A. 13, 27, 62, 92, 342
Narayan, U. 86, 92, 192, 198
National Labor Committee 129, 306, 323
National Resources Defense Council 323
National Statistics Office 37, 44, 55
Navarro, S.A. 27
Ngai, P. 127, 128, 136
Nizeye, B. 26
Novelli, M. 161, 173
Nussbaum, M. 207, 230, 232

O
O'Kane, C. 298, 299, 314, 315, 316, 322, 323
Oishi, N. 43, 55, 343
Ortiz, M. 183, 188

P
Padayachee, V. 272, 289
Padilla, A. 38, 55
Pangsapa, P. 332, 343
Pape, J. 277, 290
Parella, S. 59, 69, 92
Parenti, M. 301, 306-308, 324
Partenio, F. 252, 253, 256-258
Pearson, R. 320, 322
Pedone, C. 65, 78, 92
Pelto, P.J. 261, 290
Perraton, J. 54, 187
Pessar, P.R. 188
Peters, J. 195, 207-210
Petras, J. 51, 55, 56
Pettman, J.J. 299, 324
Philippine Overseas Employment Agency (POEA) 43, 56

Picchio, A. 162, 173
Pillay, D. 161, 170
Piven, F.F. 1, 27
Polakoff, E.G. 1, 24, 83, 133, 186, 206, 291, 299, 307, 315, 324, 328, 332, 342
Population Communications International (PCI) 197, 198, 209
Porter, T. 40, 56, 91, 133
Portillo, L. 127, 308-310, 324
Potter, E. 86, 90
Pribilsky, J. 65, 91
Prout, A. 298, 323
Pyrch, T. 169, 173

Q
Quijano, A. 72, 92

R
Radcliffe, S. 185, 188
Rama, M. 102, 118, 120
Ramírez Gallegos, F. 64-66, 77, 84, 92
Ramírez, J.P. 64-66, 77, 84, 92
Ramirez, M.M. 56
Rangel, C-E. 159, 166, 170
Riaño, Y. 60, 66, 67, 92
Rifkin, D. 252, 253, 258
Roberts, B. 214, 232
Robertson, B. 133, 134, 137
Robinson, W.I. 34, 37, 51, 56, 187, 329, 342, 343
Roosevelt, E. 132, 137
Roque, L. 38, 42, 43, 46, 56
Rosa, K. 14, 27
Rothenberg, P.S. 3, 12, 25-28, 322, 324
Rowbotham, S. 14, 28

S
Salazar, M.C. 154, 166, 169, 171, 173
Salmond, J.A. 125, 137

Salo, E. 290
Sangera, J. 311, 312, 324
Sanmiguel-Valderrama, O. 19, 20, 139, 141, 167, 171, 173, 328, 329, 342
SAPRIN 332-343
Sargent, C. 298, 324, 325
Sassen, S. 52, 63, 92, 179, 188
Saul, J. 267, 272, 273, 290
Saurez Toro, M. 196, 209
Schaeffer, R. 162, 171
Schutz, A. 254, 258
Schwartz-Nobel, L. 292, 324
Schwartzman, H.B. 298, 324
Scott, A.F. 129, 137, 240, 258
Sen, G. 25, 28, 232, 341, 343
Sena 169
Shalla, V. 173
Shaw, J. 18, 19, 95, 99, 100, 102, 106, 120, 316, 317, 324, 328, 330
Shiva, V. 5, 28
Sierra, C.P. 166, 173, 308
Siles, M. 214, 231
Silva, A.E. 150, 154, 166, 173, 316, 317, 324
Singh, K. 196-198, 209
Sison, J.M. 40, 56, 336, 343
Sivananthiran, A. 116, 120
Sklair, L. 34, 51, 56
Smith, D. 85, 92
Solé, C. 59, 69, 92
Sontag, D. 134, 137
Sparr, P. 178, 179, 188
Spivak, G. 194, 209
Sri Lanka Bureau of Foreign Employment 120
Stack, C.B. 214, 232
Stamatopoulou, E. 196, 210
Standing, G. 167, 173
Stephens, S. 298, 300, 324

Stern, R. 321
Stiglitz, J. 292-294, 319, 324, 336, 343
Stulac, S. 26
Sun, B.K. 316, 324
Svampa y Pereyra 258
Swedenburg, T. 27, 29

T
Talcott, M. 166, 173
Tarrow, S. 330, 331, 343
Terreblanche, S. 259, 267, 290
Tessier, S. 330, 343
Thrupp, L.A. 173
Toro, M.S. 134, 137, 196, 209
Torres, A. 91, 209
Tronto, J.C. 193, 210
Tujan, A., Jr. 43, 56
Tyson, D. 208

U
UNDP 100, 120
UNESCO 254, 321, 325
UNICEF 173, 197, 210, 258, 291, 292, 295, 298-301, 318, 320, 322, 325
Union Nacional de Trabajadores de las Flores 148, 174
Universidad Nacional de Colombia 169, 171, 173, 174
Urquidi, A. 133, 137

V
Vargas, V. 162, 166, 169, 185, 189
Vega Ugalde, S. 65, 90
Veriavia, A. 270, 287, 290
Villar, R. 166, 172
Villegas, E.M. 40, 41, 56
Vistazo 64, 77, 92
Vosko, L. 167, 174

W
Wade, R. 5, 28
Wallimann, I. 33, 55, 334, 342
Watkinson, E. 278, 290

Westwood, S. 185, 188
Whiteford, L.M. 298, 325
Wichterich, C. 1, 4, 14, 28
Williams, H. 315, 325
Wilson, W.J. 214, 232
Wolf, E.R. 8, 28, 29
Wolper, A. 195, 207-210
Women's Edge Coalition 184, 185, 189
World Bank 6, 7, 10, 11, 38, 50, 64, 98-100, 102, 105, 117, 118, 120, 146, 168, 229, 232, 293, 294, 301, 312, 319, 320, 327, 332, 337
World Health Organization 28, 44
World Trade Organisation (WTO) 5-7, 10, 11, 22, 26, 28, 34, 36, 46, 50, 53, 56, 114, 115, 120, 136, 183, 293, 301, 327, 337
Wright, C. 159, 172

Y
Yaisser, M. 84, 86, 91, 92
Yates, M.D. 292, 325
Yong, J. 292, 325
Yoshihara, K. 35, 56

Z
Zahidi, S. 208
Zandy, J. 127, 137
Zibechi, R. 183, 189

Subject Index

A
Abortion 12, 184, 198
Activism 16, 27, 121-123, 127, 131, 132, 147, 161, 162, 187, 241, 242, 247, 252, 255, 259, 269, 338
Adolescent 216, 220, 252, 314, 323
Africa 2, 16, 23, 25, 28, 36, 39, 41, 43, 45, 52, 132, 200, 259, 260, 262, 267, 271-274, 281-283, 287, 289, 290, 294, 319, 329, 333, 335
Agriculture (also Agricultural) 8, 18, 19, 24, 29, 36, 42, 53, 66, 69, 78, 86, 99, 100, 103-107, 147, 153, 155, 169, 171, 173, 183, 206, 275, 291, 292, 299, 301-305, 310, 323, 332, 338
Alliance 30, 34, 46, 49, 53, 54, 135, 323
Alternative Trade Associations (ATOs) 15, 20, 175, 177, 179-182, 185, 186
Amalgamated Clothing Workers of America 125
Amnesty International (AI) 195, 309, 310, 321
Andean Community 183
Andean Free Trade Agreement (AFTA) 183
Anti-Slavery International 129
Anti-Union (also Anti-Unionism) 121, 125, 126, 159
Apartheid 2, 3, 11, 23, 25, 26, 259, 260, 262-264, 267-273, 276-290, 295, 320, 321, 333, 335
Armed Violence 126
Artisan 21, 23, 180
Asocolflores 141, 142, 152, 156-160, 164, 168, 170, 172
Association for Women's Rights in Development (AWID) 129, 131, 134

B
Basic Services 23, 213, 216, 229, 259, 260, 264, 267, 269, 271, 273, 276-279, 281, 284-288, 335
Board of Investment (BOI) 111, 117, 118
Brain Drain 44
Bretton Woods 6, 7
Butterflies Programme 315, 322

C
Capital (see also Capitalism) 1, 3, 4, 9, 12, 17, 19, 20, 33, 34, 37, 38, 40, 42, 44, 46, 51, 56, 60, 63, 65, 73, 79, 86, 87, 96, 116, 145, 146, 152, 154, 158, 161, 164-168, 171, 172, 181, 206, 214, 219, 221, 227, 228, 231, 238, 255, 261, 267, 273, 284, 289, 306, 307, 312, 325, 328-330, 333, 334, 337, 339
Capital Accumulation 40, 87, 284, 312, 328-330, 339
Capital-Labor Relations 9, 20, 154
Capitalism 1-3, 7-9, 11-14, 16, 24, 30, 34, 40-42, 49, 51, 59, 72, 73, 143, 144, 146, 160-163, 165-167, 192, 201, 284, 291, 292, 297, 301, 308, 317, 319, 329, 341
Central America 5, 19, 124, 128, 129, 133, 134, 301, 308, 317
Centro de la Mujer Peruana Flora Tristán 184
Child Labor Coalition 303
Children's Rights (see also Rights) 291, 301, 315, 318, 336
China 19, 91, 114, 122, 123-125, 127, 129, 130, 131, 135, 136, 207, 306, 307
China Labor Watch 129, 130
Chinese 115, 127, 130, 132, 135, 136
Chinese Working Women Network (CWWN) 127, 128
Citizen (also Citizenship) 39, 59, 80, 88, 132, 162, 229, 261, 279, 288, 289, 331, 337, 340
Civil Rights (see also Rights) 74, 122, 126, 136, 318
Clean Clothes Campaign 116, 129
Coalition for Justice in the Maquiladoras 129, 134
Coalition of Labor Union Women (CLUW) 129
Code(s) of Conduct 19, 116, 142, 143, 156,-159, 164, 165
Colectiva Feminista Binacional 129
Collective 1, 3, 8, 9, 14-16, 18, 19, 21, 23, 24,

42, 62, 80, 86, 121, 123, 126, 128, 129, 132, 134, 139, 145, 147-149, 152, 159, 163,-165, 187, 191, 192, 194, 199, 205-207, 233, 235, 244, 261, 284, 285, 291, 293, 313-316, 318, 319, 328, 329, 332, 334-336, 338, 341
Collective Action 19, 121, 126, 147, 164, 235
Collective Agreement 152
Collective Associations 291, 293, 314, 315
Collective Bargaining 42, 149, 159
Collective Organization 121, 123, 126
Collective Resistance 14, 16, 19, 21, 24, 139, 191, 291, 313, 328, 329, 336
Collective Struggle 244
Colombia (see also-Colombian) 5, 16, 78, 140-142, 145-147, 150, 152, 154, 155, 160, 164-174, 183, 293, 317
Colombian 19, 139, 140, 142, 145, 147-160, 164, 167, 169, 172, 173, 328
Colombian Flower Industry (CFI) 19, 20, 139-173
Colombian Union of Flower Workers 148, 151
Colonial (see also Colonialism) 8, 25, 29, 30, 37, 49, 50, 52, 54, 62, 63, 72, 77, 85, 123, 193, 209, 282, 283, 337
Colonization 3, 6, 26, 30, 52, 86, 87, 305
Colonizers 7-9, 29
Comité Fronterizo de Obreros (CFO) 129, 134
Commercial Sex 24, 291, 293, 300, 310, 316

Committee of Women Workers 129, 134
Community Organizations 128, 139, 141, 142, 153, 157, 164, 217, 259
Congress of Industrial Organizations (CIO) 126, 128, 134, 135
Conscientización 3, 14
Consciousness 9, 14, 17, 19, 25, 46, 47, 82, 89, 121, 131, 133, 245, 282, 285, 329, 331, 334, 339
Contractualization 41, 42, 328, 337
Convention on the Rights of the Child 300, 305, 315
Cooperative(s) 21, 67, 146, 151, 181, 191-193, 199-202, 204-207, 237-249, 315, 334, 338, 339
Cooperative Movement 21, 199, 334, 338
Copa Flowers 150, 151
Corporate (see also Corporation) 2, 4-6, 9, 14, 15, 25, 27, 40, 51, 87, 118, 122, 124, 157-159, 161, 164, 293, 301, 305-307, 317, 319, 327, 330, 337, 338, 340, 341
Corporation 2, 4, 37, 75, 183, 188
Cost of Living 17, 64, 132, 281
Cultural (also culture) 2-4, 9, 10, 12, 13, 15, 26, 58, 61, 63, 67, 70, 71, 74, 78, 82, 87, 90, 98, 113, 128, 160, 172, 181, 186, 188, 192, 194, 197-200, 213, 214, 221, 223, 226, 248, 254, 258, 292, 297, 320, 324, 325

D

Daycare 156, 217, 218,

249, 338, 339
De-Industrialization 305
Debt Crisis 49, 329, 337
Developing Countries 5, 25, 28, 34, 97, 101, 116, 168, 185, 192, 232, 292, 294
Development 5, 6, 11, 17, 24, 27, 28, 44, 47, 53, 56, 63, 64, 80, 82, 96, 116, 119, 120, 129, 131, 132, 134, 143, 153, 157-159, 161, 166, 169, 171-173, 177, 180, 184, 186-188, 193, 197, 207-209, 217, 231, 232, 235-238, 244, 248, 253, 267, 270, 271, 274, 278, 280, 283, 289, 290, 295, 296, 298, 300, 301, 308, 312, 315, 318, 322, 325, 335, 337, 338, 343
Discrimination 12, 15, 17, 18, 20, 45, 57, 58, 72, 80, 128, 132, 143, 145, 161, 162, 166, 191, 196-198, 226, 262, 283, 295, 300, 339
Division of Labor 27, 54, 141, 162, 221, 234, 240, 256, 261, 290, 305, 328
Dollarization 17, 64
Domestic 15, 23, 24, 26, 36, 38, 43-45, 48, 55, 58-60, 66, 69-72, 85, 95, 102, 104, 107, 123, 131, 172, 179, 195, 220, 223, 225, 234, 240-244, 247, 250-253, 268, 289, 291-295, 297, 299, 301, 302, 319, 329, 330, 332, 334
Domestic Abuse 15, 26, 123, 131
Domestic Labour 172, 299
Domestic Servant(s) 59, 107, 268

Subject Index

Domestic Service 24, 43, 44, 59, 102, 104, 223, 297, 299, 330
Domestic Sphere 240, 242, 247, 250, 251, 253
Domestic Violence 23, 195, 244, 251, 252, 292
Domestic Worker(s) 44, 48, 55, 58, 60, 69-72, 289, 295

E

Economic Crises (also Crisis) 19, 42, 69, 91, 119, 123, 221, 236, 241, 244, 250, 298, 299, 318, 336, 337, 343
Economic Empowerment 21, 191, 199, 207, 209, 334
Economic Globalization 2, 4, 21, 26, 63, 291, 293, 295, 307, 317, 319, 323
Economic Justice 121, 123, 127, 129, 132, 133, 135, 188, 329
Economic Liberalization 34, 35, 37, 47, 51, 333
Economic Rights (see also Rights) 21, 153, 191, 331, 335, 336
Ecuador 16-18, 57, 60-92, 160, 167, 171, 172, 183, 302
Employees' Councils (ECs) 113
Employment 10, 17, 18, 21, 22, 35, 40-43, 45, 54, 56, 69, 70, 86, 95, 96, 101-109, 115-117, 119, 120, 126, 140, 146, 151, 161, 174, 177, 185, 187, 192, 195, 200, 202, 225, 226, 227, 244, 248, 251, 256, 263, 265, 272-274, 282, 306, 313, 322, 328-330, 332, 333, 337

Empowerment 21, 159, 163, 191-193, 199-203, 205-07, 209, 291, 334
Environmental Protection Agency (EPA) 303
Equity 199, 200, 284
Ethical Trading Initiative 116
Ethnicity 8, 11, 16, 20, 43, 44, 59, 60, 72, 77, 89, 92, 141, 144, 178, 181, 328, 330
European Union (EU) 35, 59, 60, 66, 78, 80, 81, 83-85, 87, 89, 91, 115, 116, 183, 186, 187, 191
Exploitation 1, 4, 6-8, 13-15, 18-20, 24, 25, 41, 43, 44, 54, 55, 78, 81, 86, 123, 131, 164, 259, 275, 284, 291, 292, 295, 297-302, 305, 306, 310, 311, 313, 316-318, 320, 322, 323, 328, 330-332, 335-337, 339, 340, 342
Export 4, 6, 15-19, 34, 35, 42-45, 47-50, 53-56, 93, 95, 102, 111, 115, 120, 140, 147, 153, 160, 171-173, 179-181, 184, 224, 294, 305, 306, 312, 317, 322, 327-330, 333, 335, 337
Export Processing Zones (EPZs) 18, 19, 42, 95, 96, 105, 106, 108, 109-111, 113, 115-117, 120, 179
Export Production 4, 6, 294, 317, 328

F

Factories (also Factory) 19, 70, 95-97, 101, 104-107, 110, 112-116, 119, 121-126, 129-132, 135, 206, 221, 223-268, 275, 292, 295, 297, 299, 300, 306, 307, 309, 322
Factory Girls 96, 114
Factory Workers 97, 123
Fair Trade 116, 157, 159, 169, 182, 186, 188, 335
Family 8, 12, 17, 19, 38, 42, 45, 47, 60, 61, 67, 73, 75-77, 80-82, 84, 85, 88, 95, 101, 102, 108, 109, 118, 123, 136, 140, 158, 184, 193, 198, 203, 205, 206, 216-230, 237, 240-244, 249, 251, 264, 266, 268, 269, 275, 281, 282, 284, 285, 298, 305, 311, 332
Family Income 108, 109, 244
Farm Workers 302-305, 323, 330
Farmers 18, 36, 100, 320
Female-Headed Household(s) 98-100
Feminism 26, 91, 92, 161-163, 171, 188, 194, 196, 208, 209, 259, 290, 342
Feminist 13, 19, 21, 23, 25, 27, 30, 33, 49, 57, 59, 61, 62, 83-86, 90-92, 121, 123, 128, 129, 131, 134, 137, 143, 145, 161, 162, 170, 171, 185, 188, 191-195, 200, 201, 206-210, 242, 243, 247, 252, 254-256, 322
Feminist Activism 242, 247, 252, 255
Feminist Methodology (see also Methodologies) 192
Feminist Praxis 27, 192
Feminization 23, 43, 68, 139, 164, 167, 170, 173, 196, 197, 259, 333
Feminization of Labour 139, 167
Feminization of Poverty

23, 196, 197, 259, 333
Feminized and Racialized Labour 142, 144, 165
Feminized Labour 20, 139, 140, 141
Finance Capital (see also Capitalism) 56
Flower Workers' Association 153
Flowers of Work 154, 155
Food Insecurity 16, 21, 36, 37
Food Security 100, 277, 278, 290, 332
Foreign 6, 18, 22, 34, 37-47, 55, 60, 63, 77, 80, 82, 88, 95, 107, 112, 117, 120, 159, 161, 273, 293, 295, 317
Foreign Debt 43, 55
Foreign Exchange 43, 45, 161
Foreign Investment 6, 22, 63, 112, 117, 293, 317
Fourth World 24, 294, 297
Free the Children 129
Free Trade 2, 5, 6, 15, 18, 20, 27, 34, 114, 118, 119, 172, 177-179, 182-187, 292, 293, 327, 333-335, 343
Free Trade Agreement (FTA) 5, 172, 183, 293
Free Trade Area of the Americas (FTAA) 183, 189, 293
Free Trade Policies 333
Free Trade Zones (FTZs)18, 27, 118, 183, 327
Frente Auténtico Del Trabajo (FAT) 127, 128, 134, 135

G
G-7 34
GABRIELA 17, 33, 34, 46-48, 50, 53-56, 335

Garment 16, 18, 95-97, 101, 104, 105, 109, 111-119, 123, 125, 131, 132, 134-136, 307, 328
Garment Industry 95-97, 114-116, 119, 134, 135, 307
Garment Manufacturing 95, 131
Garment Workers 18, 95-97, 109, 111-114, 116, 119, 134, 136, 328
Gender 3, 8, 11, 12, 16, 20-23, 25, 29, 43-45, 50, 54, 59, 61, 62, 85, 86, 92, 103, 128, 134, 135, 136, 141, 143, 144, 155, 161, 164, 166, 170, 171, 177-179, 181, 182, 184, 187-189, 192, 193, 195-198, 204, 208, 209, 213-215, 226, 231-235, 237, 239, 240, 242-244, 246, 247, 249-252, 254, 256, 257, 281, 283-285, 298, 320, 324, 325, 327, 328, 330, 333, 334, 339-341
Gender Discrimination 196-198, 283
Gender Equality 103, 193, 209, 254, 283, 325, 340
Gender Roles 22, 23, 29, 233, 240, 242, 254
Gender Stereotypes 234, 242, 244, 247, 249, 250, 251, 254
Gender-Based Violence 12
General Agreement on Tariffs and Trade (GATT) 5, 34, 183, 275, 293
Girls Educational & Mentoring Service (GEMS) 316
Global Apartheid 2, 3, 11, 25, 26, 295, 320, 321

Global Capital 17, 161, 206, 306, 330
Global Capitalist Penetration 1-4, 6, 9, 11, 13-16, 23, 24, 291, 292, 295, 310, 313, 317, 319, 339
Global Criminal Economy 310
Global Economic Crisis 119, 336, 337
Global Economy 24, 129, 140, 141, 170, 178, 299, 312, 317, 318, 325, 327, 330
Global Market 17, 115, 116, 124, 140, 141, 173, 317
Global North 24, 141, 144, 160, 181, 182, 291, 297, 301, 305, 318, 341
Global Sex Trade 310, 332
Global South 13, 14, 18-20, 22, 53, 59, 61, 82, 87, 121-125, 127, 129-131, 133, 141, 160, 162, 178, 191, 192, 230, 301, 305, 306, 318, 327, 336, 341
Globalization 1, 2, 4, 6, 14-16, 19, 21, 24-27, 33, 34, 40- 44, 46-56, 62, 63, 90, 91, 98, 119, 121, 132, 133, 140, 142, 160, 161, 164, 166, 169, 170, 173, 185-188, 191, 192, 197, 206, 257, 284, 291-295, 298, 307, 311, 312, 317, 319, 322-324, 327-343
Green Flower 157, 158, 159, 161, 164
Gross Domestic Product (GDP) 36, 87, 95
Growth Employment and Redistribution (GEAR) 272

H

Haiti 19, 131, 132, 134, 135, 137, 307, 323
Handicraft 181, 182
Health (see also Health Care) 4, 6, 7, 9-12, 14, 16, 19, 21-23, 26, 28, 38, 39, 44, 53, 54, 56, 97, 112, 128, 129, 132, 140, 141, 146, 150, 154-156, 158, 178, 179, 184, 195-197, 200-202, 204, 205, 213, 216, 218, 219, 225-229, 241, 252, 259, 273, 276, 284, 286, 292, 293, 295-306, 308, 314-316, 318-325, 333-335
Health Care 10, 12, 16, 22, 23, 38, 39, 54, 56, 195, 200, 201, 259, 276, 284, 286, 293, 314, 333, 335
Highlander Research and Education Center 128, 129, 134
HIV 28, 265, 284, 286, 292
Household 59, 74, 95, 98-102, 106, 108, 117, 119, 179, 180, 202, 203, 216-218, 220, 224, 225, 229, 236-238, 249, 262, 263, 272, 278, 279, 281, 284, 296, 297, 319, 339
Household Income 95, 101, 102, 108, 117, 119, 263
Human 1, 2, 6, 9, 10, 15, 17, 19, 25-27, 40, 43, 44, 53, 63, 64, 67, 81, 82, 86, 91, 116, 119, 120-122, 129, 131, 132, 134, 142, 154, 157-159, 164, 169, 170, 172, 184, 191, 195-197, 200, 206-210, 213, 219, 231, 293, 296, 300, 302, 308, 310-312, 317, 318, 320-323, 328, 331, 335-337, 339-341
Human Capital 17, 44, 116, 219
Human Rights (see also Rights) 2, 6, 9, 10, 15, 26, 27, 43, 53, 116, 119, 129, 131, 132, 134, 142, 159, 169, 172, 184, 191, 195-197, 200, 207,-210, 300, 302, 308, 312, 320-323, 335-337
Human Rights Watch (HRW) 129, 184, 195, 196, 208, 302-305, 320, 321, 323
Human Trafficking 67, 81

I

Identities (also Identity) 3, 8, 9, 15, 16, 18, 20, 23, 26, 27, 29, 63, 89, 117, 127, 143, 144, 162, 166, 177-182, 185, 187, 188, 194, 220, 264, 270, 285, 287, 298, 300, 316, 317, 319, 321-332, 340, 342
Indigenous Communities 18, 29, 341
Indigenous People 60
Inequalities 1, 4, 20, 21, 33, 50, 164, 181, 234, 240, 247, 252, 253, 270, 311, 333, 334, 337
Informal Sector 96, 99, 101-104, 106, 117, 200, 274, 316
Infrastructure 115, 124, 204
Intellectual Property Rights 152
International Code of Conduct (ICC) 156, 157, 159
International Conventions 291, 292, 297, 299, 305
International Financial Institutions 5, 6, 64, 152, 161
International Gender and Trade Network (IGTN) 178, 187
International Labour Organization (IIO) 6, 119, 120, 129, 145, 172, 299-302, 305, 310, 311, 323
International Sex Trade 292
International Textile, Garment and Leather Workers Federation 131, 134, 136
International Trade 11, 26, 120, 131, 147, 152, 168, 171, 173, 180, 183, 293, 312
Intersectional (also Intersectionality) 20, 26, 139, 161, 162, 166

K

Katunayake Working Women's Centre 97

L

La Belinda 139, 140, 150, 151, 168
La Mujer Obrera 129
Labor Activism 127
Labor Force 41-44, 66, 124, 168, 224, 293, 296, 298, 300, 305, 306, 330
Labor Laws 6, 303, 305, 306, 318, 337
Labor Market 44, 219, 225, 230, 235, 237, 238, 244, 256, 296, 297, 321, 332
Labor Movement 121, 122, 128, 135, 136
Labor Relations 9, 143
Labor Rights (see also Rights) 19, 37, 128, 152, 301, 328
Labor Standards 303

Subject Index 359

Laborer 295, 301
Labour Activism 147
Labour Force 103, 104, 116, 118, 140, 146, 170
Labour Market 95, 96, 102, 103, 105, 106, 108, 109, 117, 173, 267, 268, 273
Labour Movement 113, 144, 145, 153, 161, 165
Labour Relations 20, 140, 144, 146, 149, 153, 154, 164, 165, 167, 173
Labour Standards 96, 106, 112, 115, 116, 140, 141, 145, 153, 157, 164, 171
Land Reform 48
Latin America 26, 29, 63, 81, 82, 140, 167, 171, 173, 187-189, 214, 219, 227, 234, 290, 294, 299, 313, 315-317, 319
Latin American Integration Association (LAIA/ALADI) 183
Law 13, 25, 46, 67, 68, 73, 101, 111, 125, 135, 140, 142, 146, 147, 151, 156-159, 167, 169, 170, 172, 173, 184, 195, 216, 225, 229, 231, 265, 282, 284, 299, 303, 309, 328
League of Women Voters (LWV)128, 129
Legal Rights (see also Rights) 19, 21, 192, 196, 206
Liberalization 2, 10, 16, 17, 22, 34, 35, 37, 38, 41, 42, 47, 49, 51, 63, 226, 295, 333
Low-Income 16, 19, 21, 24, 37, 39, 116, 140, 141, 165, 177, 178, 182, 183, 201, 291, 297, 317
Low-Income Families 21, 24, 39, 291, 317

Low-Income Households 297
Low-Income Women 16, 140, 177, 178, 183, 201
Low-Income Workers 19

M
Management-Controlled Unions 149
Manthoc 314
Manufacturing 18, 24, 35, 95, 102-104, 106, 111, 119, 130, 131, 136, 179, 267, 273-275, 291, 293, 297, 301, 302, 305, 307, 310, 322, 328, 332
Maquila (also Maquiladora) 19, 121, 122, 133, 136, 308
Methodologies 21, 23, 57, 61
Mexican (see also Mexico) 83, 122-124, 134, 136
Mexico 5, 16, 19, 50, 122, 123, 125, 129, 132, 133, 135, 136, 160, 186, 188, 195, 196, 232, 256, 293, 305-308, 313, 317, 321, 322, 329, 341
Migrant 15, 18, 19, 33, 34, 43-45, 48, 53-56, 59, 62, 63, 66, 67, 69, 70, 72, 80, 81, 83, 92, 104, 113, 119, 128, 317, 320, 329-333, 340
Migrant Communities 331, 340
Migrant Farmers 18, 320
Migrant Worker 70
Migrante International 17, 33, 34, 48, 50, 53-56, 331
Movimiento de Niños, Niñas y Adolescentes Trabajadores Hijos de Obreros Cristianos (MANTHOC) 314

Multi-Fibre Agreement (MFA) 95, 114, 115
Multinational Corporations (MNCs) 6, 63, 122, 307

N
National Child Labor Committee 129
National Consumer League (NCL) 128
National Women's Trade Union League (NWTUL) 127
Neoliberal (see also Neoliberalism) 2, 6, 7, 10, 11, 15-18, 21-23, 31, 33, 34, 37, 40- 43, 46, 48-52, 57, 63, 66, 102, 140, 142, 144, 146, 153, 158, 161, 168, 172, 181, 186, 206, 226, 227, 235, 236, 259, 260, 262, 272, 274, 276, 280, 284, 292, 319, 327-341
Neoliberal Economic(s) 168, 259, 260, 262, 274, 284
Neoliberal Policies 6, 7, 10, 11, 15, 16, 18, 21, 23, 31, 33, 34, 37, 42, 46, 49, 50, 52, 57, 63, 172, 276, 292, 327, 329-338, 340
Neoliberal Policy 102, 235
Neoliberal Project 227
Neoliberalism 23, 30, 49, 51, 52, 62, 63, 82, 91, 146, 173, 259, 271-273, 286, 289, 333, 334, 336, 339
New Social Movements (NSMs) 20, 139, 144, 145, 153, 161, 269, 285
Niños y Adolescentes Trabajadores (Nats) 314
Non-Governmental

Subject Index

Organization (NGO) 46, 97, 127, 129, 131, 134, 142, 153, 156, 157, 159, 179, 182, 184, 218, 252, 314, 315
North American Free Trade Agreement (NAFTA) 5, 11, 26, 183, 185-188, 293, 301, 309
Nursing 44, 103, 105

O

Occupation 98, 101, 105, 107, 108, 120, 182, 215, 239
Occupational Health 6, 112
Oppression 1, 3, 8-11, 14, 19, 43, 125, 133, 145, 155, 161, 162, 164-166, 192, 259, 262, 281-283
Organized Labor 124, 135
Organized Labour 139, 144-146, 164, 165
Overseas Private Investment Corporation (OPIC) 183
Oxfam 129

P

Patriarchal (also Patriarchy)7, 11-15, 20, 23, 27, 30, 139, 143, 160, 162, 166, 196, 262, 268, 281-284, 286, 289, 290, 329
People's Bank 338, 339
Peru (also Peruvian) 16, 20, 21, 29, 160, 171, 177, 178, 180-188, 213, 215, 218, 219, 220, 222, 223, 228, 231-234, 314, 333-335
Picketing Movement 239, 240, 251
Plantation 29, 139, 140, 142, 143, 147-152, 154, 158, 164, 168
Political Rights (see also Rights) 37, 191, 195, 201, 331, 336
Popular Movement 228
Private Investment 183, 273
Private Sphere 23, 69, 158, 195, 284, 285
Public Sphere 23, 195, 234, 240, 246, 248, 253, 255, 284, 329

R

Race (see also Racial) 2, 3, 8, 11, 16, 20, 25, 43-45, 59, 60, 65, 72, 77, 86, 89, 91, 136, 141, 143, 155, 164, 178, 179, 182, 188, 195, 214, 281, 283-285, 289, 306, 307, 320, 328, 330, 333, 334
Racial 72, 124, 126, 127, 262, 263, 267, 268, 280, 327
Racism 1, 2, 7, 8, 10, 13, 18, 20, 57, 77, 80, 139, 145, 162, 166, 192, 320
Reflexive Law 156-159
Remittances 45, 46, 52,-54, 63, 74, 76, 77, 95, 101, 102, 110, 111, 117, 329
Rights
  Children's 291, 301, 315, 318, 336
  Civil 74, 122, 126, 136, 318
  Economic 21, 153, 191, 331, 335, 336
  Human 2, 6, 9, 10, 15, 26, 27, 43, 53, 116, 119, 129, 131, 132, 134, 142, 159, 169, 172, 184, 191, 195-197, 200, 207-210, 300, 302, 308, 312, 320-337
  Labor 19, 37, 128, 152, 301, 328
  Legal 19, 21, 192, 196, 206
  Political 37, 191, 195, 201, 331, 336
  Reproductive 243
  Women's 21, 129, 131, 134, 184, 187, 191, 195, 196, 207-210, 243

S

Schengen Visa 80
Self-Regulate (also Self-Regulation) 19, 157
Self-Representation 57
Sex 8, 12, 24, 43, 45, 46, 48, 67, 91, 120, 131, 197, 198, 206, 291-293, 297, 299-301, 309-312, 316, 320, 321, 323, 324, 332, 335
Sex Trade 24, 43, 48, 291-293, 297, 300, 301, 310-312, 316, 321, 324, 332
Sex Trafficking 131, 324
Sexual (also Sexuality) 12, 54, 59, 61, 107, 114, 128, 144, 155, 184, 214, 222, 230, 240, 241, 252, 256, 258, 281, 292, 300, 310, 311, 313, 316, 320, 321, 322
Sexual Harassment 114, 155
Sexual Violence 241
Shantytown 216, 218
Shine a Light 316, 317, 324
Sintrabelinda 140, 148-151
Social Change 13, 14, 21, 24, 170, 193, 194, 202, 204, 240, 256, 299, 317, 319
Social Justice 16, 24, 118, 128, 144, 166, 336, 339
Social Networks 179, 214
Social Welfare 7, 64, 188,

Subject Index

273, 280, 284, 293, 317
Socio-Economic Status
   11, 141
Socio-Economic Characteristics 97
Solidarity 5, 12, 21, 23,
   25, 55, 58, 73, 80, 92,
   128, 131, 133, 134, 136,
   141, 142, 144, 145, 151,
   153, 156, 159, 160, 163,
   165, 170, 173, 188, 192,
   199, 200, 205, 243, 252,
   290, 331, 339, 340, 342
Special Economic Zone
   (SPZ) 127
Squatter Settlement 216
Standard of Living 60,
   295
Stereotype 330
STITCH 128, 133, 134
Strike 126, 130, 135-137,
   140, 149-151, 167, 214
Structural Adjustment 6,
   7, 11, 18, 22, 38, 39, 43,
   46, 66, 223, 235, 292-
   295, 298, 319, 324, 325,
   329, 332, 337, 340, 343
Structural Violence 9-11,
   15, 23, 26
Subcontract 116
Subcontracting 41, 42,
   151, 305
Subsistence 8, 14, 25, 27,
   29, 97, 100, 106, 333
Subsistence Activities 106
Subsistence Activity 100
Sustainability 15, 63, 64,
   82, 201
Sustainable 3, 25, 154,
   157, 193, 200
Sweatshop(s) 122, 130,
   224, 225, 275, 276, 299,
   300

T
Textile 16, 19, 35, 42, 52,
   118, 125, 126, 130, 131,
   133, 134, 136, 200, 201,
   273, 275, 276
Third World 1, 28, 33, 34,
   47, 49, 55, 85, 172, 188,
   192, 209, 305-308, 311,
   312, 322, 327, 329, 330,
   332, 337-340, 342
Tourism 180, 187, 188,
   312, 321
Trade Agreement 5, 172,
   183, 186, 293
Trade Liberalization 16,
   17, 22, 38, 49, 63
Trade Policies 179, 182,
   333, 334
Trade Policy 172, 179,
   185
Trade Regulations 20, 177
Trade Union 15, 96, 111,
   117, 127-129, 131, 135,
   147, 167, 168, 169, 171
Transnational 2, 6, 7, 9,
   10, 13, 15, 19, 20, 27,
   33, 34, 37-40, 42, 44,
   46, 50-52, 56, 60, 61,
   67, 68, 71, 74, 76, 77,
   79-81, 83, 84, 87-92,
   128, 129, 133, 134, 139,
   144, 145, 159, 160, 163,
   165, 170, 172, 177, 178,
   182, 184, 185, 188, 313,
   323, 327-330, 333, 336,
   337, 340-342
Transnational Corporations (TNCS) 2, 6, 7, 10,
   15, 34, 37-40, 42, 46,
   50, 51, 87, 177, 184,
   327, 337, 341

U
Unemployment (also
   Underemployment) 11,
   15-18, 21, 22, 35, 36,
   41, 43, 45, 50, 51, 64,
   88, 96, 99, 102-104,
   116, 119, 120, 235, 236,
   238, 242, 244, 249, 264,
   274-286, 290, 294, 298,
   305, 328-330, 333, 335,
   337
UNESCO 254, 321, 325
UNICEF 173, 197, 210,
   258, 291, 292, 295, 298-
   301, 318, 320, 322, 325
Union(s) 15, 20, 22, 54,
   57, 73, 89, 91, 96, 111-
   113, 117, 118, 121, 122,
   125-131, 135, 136, 140,
   142, 144, 146-153, 155,
   156, 159, 161, 163-165,
   167-172, 174, 183, 186,
   187, 191, 200, 221, 225,
   226, 302, 312, 314, 315,
   319, 328
United Electrical Workers
   Union 128
United Nations 6, 12, 120,
   131, 137, 172, 195-197,
   199, 207, 210, 232, 291,
   300, 305, 311, 315, 316,
   318
United Nations Millennium Development
   Goals 318
United States (US) 16, 19,
   24, 29, 34, 35, 40-42,
   45, 48, 49, 51, 55-57,
   59-63, 65, 66, 77-81,
   84, 85, 87, 105, 115,
   122, 128, 130, 131,
   134-136, 172, 177, 183-
   186, 188, 198, 202, 232,
   292, 293, 302-308, 313,
   316, 319, 320, 323, 337,
   328, 330, 335, 343
Untraflores 139, 140, 148,
   150-152, 156, 165, 168,
   174

V
Vietnam 123-125, 131,
   296, 307
Vietnam Living Standards
   Survey 296
Violence (see also
   Gender-Based Violence)
   1, 3, 7-13, 15, 17, 21,

23, 25, 26, 28, 58, 68, 73, 79, 81, 126, 131, 147, 155, 163, 164, 166, 191, 195-198, 208, 222, 232, 241, 244, 251, 252, 262, 269, 290, 292, 295, 298, 308, 310, 311, 313, 340

Violence against Women 12, 26, 28, 73, 197, 208, 310

Violence of Global Capitalist Penetration 1, 9, 13

W

Washington Consensus 168, 223, 336

Women on the Border 129, 134

Women's Activism 16, 27, 121, 123, 131, 132

Women's Edge Coalition (WEC) 184, 185, 189

Women's Leadership 233

Women's Organizations 46, 122, 125, 128, 131, 177

Women's Participation 233-235, 240, 244, 245, 247, 248, 250, 251, 253, 254, 329

Women's Resistance 1, 13-16, 18-20, 31, 46, 93, 121, 133, 175, 327, 328, 334, 335, 342

Women's Rights (see also Rights) 21, 129, 131, 134, 184, 187, 191, 195, 196, 207-210, 243

Women's Rights Project 196

Women's Spaces 23, 243, 245, 247, 251, 252, 254, 257

Women's Trade Union League 127, 129

Working Class 71, 86, 278

Working Conditions 44, 78, 96, 106, 109, 111, 116, 119, 125, 129, 132, 142, 145, 147, 152, 165, 203, 238, 282, 301, 302, 306, 314, 328

World Market 15, 18, 36, 294

World Trade 5, 28, 34-36, 120, 183, 293, 327

World Trade Organization (WTO) 5-7, 10, 11, 22, 26, 28, 34, 36, 46, 50, 53, 56, 114, 115, 120, 136, 183, 293, 301, 327, 337

Worst Forms of Child Labor 300, 305

X

Xenophobia (also Xenophobic) 57, 58, 77, 80

Y

Young People 22, 219, 225-227, 274, 308, 309, 314, 315

Young Women 18, 19, 22, 24, 71, 95, 102, 105, 113, 114, 117, 121-123, 128, 215, 224, 227-230, 291, 297, 299, 300, 305-313, 316, 321, 328, 332

Young Women's Christian Association (YMCA0 128, 129

Youth 22, 42, 79, 85, 119, 154, 230, 260, 302, 308, 314-316, 324, 338

CPSIA information can be obtained at www.ICGtesting.com
Printed in the USA
LVOW06s2337050514

384509LV00015B/278/P